D1034272

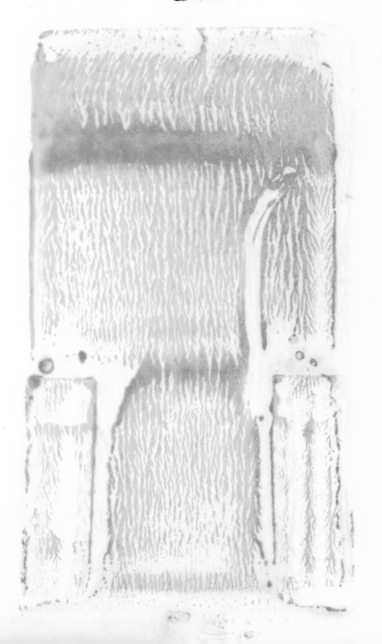

Poetry and Fiction:
Essays

HOWARD NEMEROV

Poetry and Fiction:
Essays

RUTGERS UNIVERSITY PRESS

New Brunswick　　　　　　*New Jersey*

To
KENNETH BURKE
with gratitude and affection

Preface

The writings collected in this book are essays, lectures, and reviews done between 1948 and 1962. I have not arranged them chronologically, however, but according to genre: a first section of essays on general questions of poetry and theory is followed by sections of examples from poetry, fiction, criticism, and translation. Exceptions to this scheme are the essay on the short novel, which though general and theoretical in nature seemed to belong in Part III, and the essay on *The Two Gentlemen of Verona*, which might have seemed somewhat lonely except as pendent to the other Shakespearean considerations.

Many of the pieces in the book are occasional ones, on materials not selected by me but sent me for review by the editors of literary magazines, chiefly the ones now so often lumped together in a tone of modish scorn as "The Quarterlies." The result is naturally not a historical record, but a more or less arbitrary selection of some of the writings of the period, together with some general reflections, usually though not always arising from the consideration of a particular example, upon the art of writing.

It seems to have become fashionable for makers of fictions, whether in poetry or prose, to display a large contempt for criticism, even including their own, which they wearily admit to having done for money, as hackwork, with the left hand, and maybe even by accident. That is a view of the artist having great pathos, as well as considerable support from the circumstance that Shakespeare did not write literary criticism, but it is a view I am unable to share. "Prayer is the study of art," says Blake, as well as "Praise is the practice of art." Poetry and criticism are as a double star, and if we wish to go on in poetry beyond the first ecstatic stirrings of the imagination—which so often turn out to have been derivative, after all—we shall do well to learn all we can of what poetry is, and try to see by means of many examples how the art is constantly redefining itself. Studying one's contemporaries, one gets an idea of what is possible, as well as many ideas of what is not. And that includes doing not only criticism, but also theory—a somewhat lofty word, but it names, as Wallace Stevens said, "one of the great subjects of study."

Many delicate natures in and around the arts these days seem to fear that if they used their wits on the mysteries those mysteries would dry up and blow away. I prefer the relation of art and reflection upon art expressed by Leonardo, who is quoted in Ozenfant's wonderful *Foundations of Modern Art* as saying, "He is a poor master whose achievement surpasses his criticism: he only moves toward the perfection of his art whose criticism surpasses his achievement." Something the same is very bluntly said by Ben Jonson: "Our Poet must beware, that his Studie be not only to learn of himself; for hee that shall affect to doe that, confesseth his ever having a Foole to his master."

Criticism, in whatever fancy dress, however, remains an art of opinion, and though the opinion should be supported by evidence, even that relation is a questionable one. Criticism is not knowledge, but neither ought it to be mystique, even if the sources of our opinions, and the influence of fashion upon these, are mysterious subjects. Whether the writings in this book succeed as criticism is not for me to say, but perhaps it is fair for me to set forth briefly a few of the objects I tried to keep in mind.

Critical method. To try not to have one. Or to have, at the most, two simple precepts: read what is in the poem; do not read what is not in the poem.

To give evidence for assertions, so that the reader may have a way of knowing when his author has gone badly wrong.

To be somewhat temperate, both in praising and damning. That way of putting it brings out the difficulty of the task: you can't really damn anyone temperately, yet no amount of generosity should prevent you from saying a work is bad if you think it is and are prepared to say why you think so. But there are practical solutions, and partial remedies. One of these is to realize from the start that as a critic you are nothing if not critical: the initial set of your mind will be somewhat against, if not all art, at least the piece of art now before you. I don't find anything improper about that; an art unrestrained by criticism— the past fifteen years have made available numerous examples—will be pretty windy stuff. But I have found it best, recognizing this initial set of the mind, to write all the dirty jokes and mean epigrams into the first draft, and then eliminate all but the irresistible ones in the fair copy. Poetry and criticism stand quite properly as antagonists in what Blake calls "mental fight" and the "sports of the intellect," but the giant blows can hurt all the same. And we ought to err toward generosity, even though so many poems and so many novels offer the strongest temptation not to.

Probably I have failed of these objects a hundred times, but they remain.

Finally, it has often been harshly brought to my notice that a critic who is also a practitioner of the art will not necessarily live well. He says to himself at night, "Judge not," though he doesn't add the remaining clausulum because he knows he will be judged anyhow, and often severely. But a failure to judge, as the example of Cordelia seems to show, has the effect of leaving judgment to the mercies of fools and knaves, or stupids and cupids. And because art is too beautiful to be thus abandoned, the critic, stodgiest of martyrs, sins and is damned, over and over again.

HOWARD NEMEROV

Contents

xi

Part III

Part IV

Part V

Poetry and Fiction:
Essays

Part I

The Swaying Form: A Problem in Poetry

The present essay is not an attempt to solve a problem so much as an attempt to make certain that a problem of some sort exists, and, if it does, to put it clearly before you. No matter how many problems really exist—and now, as at all times, there must be plenty of them—the world is always full of people inventing problems simply as make-works for their prefabricated solutions. As a friend of mine wrote in a prize-winning poem at college, "We know the answers, but shall we be asked the questions?" He has since become a novelist.

The problem I want to try to elucidate is most often discussed as one of belief, or of value, which is prior to poetry, and the great instance of Dante's *Comedy* stands at the gate of the discussion. It is usually argued on this basis that an explicit and systematized belief is (a) intrinsically of value to the poet in his composition and (b) a means for improving his communication with the mass of mankind.

Now I shall be taking up this theme by what many people will consider to be the wrong end, and talking from the point of view of the poet. My reflections are very far from being impartial and objective, and positively invite objections, or even cries of protest. I shall be suggesting, roughly, that the poet, if he has not attained to a belief in the existence of God, has at any rate got so far as to believe in the existence of the world; and that this, sadly but truly, puts him, in the art of believing, well out in front of many of his fellow-citizens, who sometimes look as if they believed the existence of the world to be pretty well encompassed in the sensations they experience when they read a copy of *Time*. (These, by the way, are

Reprinted by permission from *Michigan Alumnus Quarterly Review*, Winter 1959. Copyright 1959, by the Regents of the University of Michigan. This essay was presented as the Hopwood Lecture for 1959 at the University of Michigan.

the people who, adapting a metaphor of Aristotle's, think of poetry as a gentle laxative for the emotions.)

So when I hear discussions, or see symptoms, of some *rapprochement* between religion and the arts—A has written a passion play in modern dress, B has composed an atonal oratorio, C has done murals for the little church in the hometown which he left thirty years ago to become a not quite first-rate cubist with a world reputation —my response is not one of unmixed happiness, and I incline to see, in the characteristic imagery of this period, religion and the arts as two great corporations, each composed of many subsidiary companies but both in roughly the same line of business, circling each other warily in the contemplation of a merger, wondering meanwhile where the ultimate advantage will lie, and utterly unable to find out. To unfold a little this metaphor, I should say that in my view the persons seated around the conference table on this occasion are not the inventors of the product—not the prophets, saints, teachers, and great masters of art—but the usual vice-presidents, accountants, and lawyers on either side; the bishops and grand inquisitors, the critics and epimethean pedagogues who arbitrate these matters.

In other words, between ourselves and any clear view of the problematic area lies the Plain of Shinar, where the usual construction work is going forward vigorously, and the serious planners exchange their watchwords: "culture," "responsibility," "values," and "communication." In this Babel, the word "religion" may mean "weekly attendance at the church of your choice," or it may mean the sort of thing that happened to Job—impossible to say. Similarly, the word "art" may be applied equally to the forty-eight preludes and fugues and to advertisements for whisky. That these things are so says nothing against either whisky or church attendance, but may be seriously damaging to art and religion.

Somewhere toward the beginning of things the two have a connection; as our somewhat frequently employed word "creative" will suggest. "Non merita il nome di creatore," said Tasso, "si non Iddio od il poeta." Clear enough: God and the poet alone deserve to be called creative, because they both create things. The recent history of this word is revealing: one reads, e.g., of "creative advertising," "creative packaging," and the possibility of becoming "a creative consumer." A dialect usage may be equally revealing: the mother says of her infant, "he is creating again," meaning either that the child is kicking up an awful fuss, or that he has soiled his diaper.

The relation of religion to more worldly activities is frequently characterized by extreme positions. To show what I hope I am not talking about, I shall give an example of each. Here is the extreme whereby religion, in seeking a connection with the world, becomes worldly itself:

SEES BOOM IN RELIGION, TOO

Atlantic City, June 23 (1957) AP.—President Eisenhower's pastor said tonight that Americans are living in a period of "unprecedented religious activity" caused partially by paid vacations, the eight-hour day, and modern conveniences.

"These fruits of material progress," said the Rev. Edward L. R. Elson of the National Presbyterian Church, Washington, "have provided the leisure, the energy, and the means for a level of human and spiritual values never before reached."

Despite an air of farcical silliness which will accompany any display of *hubris* which is at the same time unheroic, this statement—a kind of cartoonist's exaggeration of what one suspects is the real belief of many right-thinking persons—does fix the attention on a real question: whether it is possible for a religious attitude to exist in the acceptance of prosperity, and with its face set against suffering; a question near the heart of Christianity, and a question asked over and over, always to be answered negatively, in the Old Testament, where any statement that "the land had rest for so and so many years" is certain to be followed by the refrain, "And the children of Israel did evil *again* in the sight of the Lord, and served Baalim and Ashtaroth . . ."

The opposed extreme, wherein religion purifies itself quite out of the world, may likewise be identified by anecdote. At a conference on Elizabethan and seventeenth century poetry, where a number of college students presented papers for discussion, the first three or four essays dealt with the lyrics of such poets as Campion and Herrick; after which a most serious young man arose, frowning, to say that his topic was George Herbert. He completed his impromptu introduction by saying, "We have heard a good deal this morning on the subject of *Love*; well, now we must turn our attention to an entirely different and more serious topic: *Religion*." This inadvertence, I am sorry to say, seemed to me the revelation of something sad and true in attitudes bearing the official institutional name of religious attitudes. We might compare a remark of Yeats, that only two subjects are of interest to a serious intelligence: sex and the dead.

But our problem may be as easily obscured from the other side, the side which professes to be that of art, as from the side of religion. If we look to that great arena of the war of words where there are no poems but only Poetry, no paintings but only Art, we find statements of similar monolithic simplicity, which affect to find nothing problematic in the matter at all.

In that arena, for example, a well-known literary journalist has written (*New York Times* Book Review, May 3, 1959): "What the arts, literature included, need more than anything else just now, is a declaration of faith—faith in man's potentialities, faith in God, however you may conceive Him."

As a citizen, I may incline to accept the vague benevolence of all this. But as a practitioner of the art of writing, I am bored and disturbed by this sort of loose talk; just as I should probably be, were I a member of some religious community, by the pseudo-liberality of that casual rider to the idea of God—"however you may conceive Him." Again we might compare the view of an artist, in the saying of Joseph Conrad that it is the object of art to render the highest kind of justice to the *visible world*: "It is above all, in the first place, to make you see."

By such exclusions I come to some definition of my theme: the elucidation of what things may be called religious in poetical works and in the professional attitude of the artist to the making of such works.

Even in this somewhat narrower definition, the problem is not easy to focus. I shall be trying to say that the artist's relation to spiritual and eternal things is comprised rather in the form of his work than in its message or its content; but that form is itself somewhat elusive, as I have indicated in titling these reflections "The Swaying Form" after the following passage in Florio's translation of Montaigne: "There is no man (if he listen to himselfe) that doth not discover in himselfe a peculiar forme of his, a swaying forme, which wrestleth against the art * and the institution, and against the tempest of passions, which are contrary unto him."

Florio's somewhat dreamlike English duplicates nicely the possi-

* The phrase about "the art" is not included in all editions.

bilities of Montaigne's phrase, "une forme maistresse." The form, that is, is simultaneously ruling and very variable, or fickle; shifting and protean as the form of water in a stream, where it is difficult or impossible to divide what remains from what runs away. The passage, read in this way, speaks of something in us which is double in nature, on both sides of things at once or by turns. And I would identify this "forme" with the impulse to art, the energy or libido which makes works of art. It is no paradox to say that the artistic impulse fights against "the art," for anyone who persists in this business knows that a part of his struggle is precisely against "the art," that is, against the accepted and settled standards of art in his time.

So this "forme" has the following characteristics. It is (1) allied with religion, for it is against "the tempest of passions" and thus in favor of control, discipline, *askesis*, renunciation. But it is (2) opposed to religion, for it is also against "the institution," that is, against church, state, dogma, or any fixed habit of the mind. Finally, it is (3) against something in its own nature, called "the art," against, perhaps, the idea of form itself.

For a curious tension exists between poetry and belief, idea, principle, or reason. That is, while we hear a good deal about poetry's need to be based upon an explicit view of the meaning of existence, we are very often bored and exasperated by the poetry which testifies to such a view, and incline to say that it is bad poetry precisely in the degree that the poet has insisted on referring the natural world to prior religious or philosophic valuations.

Perhaps it will be illuminating now if I try to sum up the swaying form, this complicated condition of the mind, by imagining a poet at his table in the morning. He faces the blank page, the page faces his mind—which, if it is not also a blank, is a palimpsest on which fractions of world, which he receives chiefly through language, are continually being recorded and erased and coming into strange, dissolving relations to one another; these are, for the most part, not the consequential relations of thought, but rather insanely atomic instead.

To be piously in keeping with the values of the age, I imagine this poet as asking himself, "What can I afford this morning?" And going on to consider the possibilities, or impossibilities: A little *saeva indignatio*? Something smart and severe in a toga? A romantic pathos, or pathology, with wild glances *de chez* Hölderlin? The dewy freshness of an early lyricism, say about the period of Skelton and really, after all, noncommittal? And so on, since the alternatives are very numerous.

There is only one, however, which now arises to give him trouble: "How about me? Shall I be me? And who is that?" He looks doubtfully at his tweeds, his grey flannels, stares at his alert (but modern, but rootless) face in the mirror, and tries to view that crew-cut in quick succession as a Franciscan tonsure, an Augustan wig, a Romantic disorder. No good. He would like to be himself, but acknowledges that himself is poetically not what most interests him, nor what is likely to interest others very much. Sighing, he wonders if poetry, if all great effort in the world, does not involve a necessary hypocrisy (even if one calls it, more politely, not hypocrisy but drama or metaphor, a necessary approach by analogy), and now he gratefully recalls having read somewhere (it was in Castiglione, but he likes the elegant indolence of "somewhere") that Julius Caesar wore a laurel crown to disguise the fact that he was bald. Encouraged a little, he jots down a note reducing to iambic pentameter mighty Caesar— "Who hid his baldness in a laurel crown"—and adds, in prose: "Poets do this, too." Comforted, he occupies the rest of the morning contemplating the publication of a small volume of epigrams on this theme. But come lunchtime, his wife having uncanned a can of alphabet soup which seems to him the image of his condition, the problem remains: Hypocrisy. Seeming, Angelo, seeming. The truest poetry is the most feigning. But is it, really? And how shall we edify the common reader this afternoon? By being Plato? Moody and Sankey? The Pope? Alexander Pope? How shall we solve the problems of society? Affirm the eternal verities? Become rich and famous and sought-after for our opinions (the filing cabinet is full of them) on all sorts of important themes?

No, this will never do. Hypocrisy merges with cynicism. Where is that portrait of Keats?

And so the weary circle begins again. Only once in a while it opens, as something comes into his head and he suddenly commits a poem. At that time, curiously, he does not worry in the least about whether this poem faithfully represents himself, his beliefs, values, tensions, or the absence of all these. He simply writes the poem.

By this ordinary anguish, occasionally relieved in action, a great deal of literature, both good and bad, gets itself produced.

The troubles of this hypothetical or generalized poet will perhaps strike some of you as very literary, overeducated, or even positively neurasthenic, and you may be inclined to say impatiently to him, "Fool, look in thy heart and write," not caring to consider that when Sir Philip Sidney made this excellent recommendation, he was speaking, just like our poet, to himself. And, too, such is the confusion over these things, instructions to look in one's heart and write may turn out translated for practical purposes in weird ways, e.g.: "Look in thy heart and be big, free, and sloppy, like Whitman, who is now becoming fashionable again." There is no end, except for that poem once in a while, to the poet's ability at perverting sound doctrine.

If the foregoing description is even partly applicable to the poetic process, it will be plain that the world will wait a long time for "a declaration of faith" in the poems of this poet. It may also be a consequence of his problem with his identity that a good deal of modern poetry is poetry about the problem, poetry that reveals to interpretation one reflexive dimension having to do with the process of composition itself. This development, where the mind curves back upon itself, may be always a limit, not only for poetry but for every kind of thought, for that "speculation" which Shakespeare says "turns not to itself / Till it hath travell'd, and is mirror'd there / Where it may see itself," adding that "This is not strange at all." But perhaps it has become more strange in the present age, that palace of mirrors where, says Valéry, the lonely lamp is multiplied, or where, as Eliot says, we multiply variety in a wilderness of mirrors, and where the "breakthrough," so pathetically and often discussed in relation to all contemporary arts, is most faithfully imagined in Alice's adventure through the looking-glass, the last consequence of narcissism and "incest of spirit" (Allen Tate, "Last Days of Alice") being the explosion into absurdity, very frequently followed by silence.

Silence, alas, may be preferable to the demand of "educators" that the poet should affirm something (anything?) or the often iterated instruction of certain literary persons that he should *communicate* (what?). But silence, for anyone who has set out to be a poet, is an unlovely alternative, containing in itself some religious (that is, some sinful) implication of being too good for this world, so that many poets accept the disabilities of their elected condition by making many small refusals to prevent one great one. The vanities of publication, these seem to say, are better than the silences of pride. And so, for them, the weary round begins again after every poem, as they seek over and over an image of their being: hermit crabs, crawling unprotected from one deserted shell to the next, finding each time a temporary home which, though by no means a perfect fit, is better at any rate than their nakedness.

It is gratuitous, or even impertinent after all this, and surely offers no defense, to say that they sometimes write good poems in their planetary course from house to house. What can we possibly mean, now, by *a good poem*? Let that be another circle, in another hell. While the present purpose is to say something about the process itself, the kind of relation with the world which results in poetic writings and is an attempt to fix for a moment the swaying form.

When people are impatient with a work of art, they assert their feeling in this way: "What does it mean?" Their tone of voice indicates that this is the most natural question in the world, the demand which they have the most immediate and God-given right to make. So their absolute condemnation and dismissal of a work of art is given in this way: "It doesn't mean anything. It doesn't mean anything *to me*." Only in those plaintive last words does there appear a tiny and scarcely acknowledged doubt of the all-sufficiency of this idea of meaning—that there may actually be meanings, which one does not personally possess.

Now we are all forced to believe about large areas of the world's work that this is so: that all around us physicists, financiers, and pharmacists are conducting complex operations which do have meaning though we do not know what it is. While we may occasionally wonder if those emperors are in fact wearing any clothes, we more usually allow that our bewilderment belongs to ourselves and does not say anything destructive about those disciplines in themselves, even where they do not produce any overwhelmingly obvious practical result such as an atomic explosion. But about works of art we continue to ask that question, "What do they mean?" and regard the answer to it as somehow crucial.

In a realm of contemplation, the question about meaning could, though it generally does not, begin a chain reaction involving the whole universe, since the answer can be given only in terms to which the same question is again applicable. But because we are well-mannered people, or because we haven't the time, or really don't care, or because we are in fact reassured and consoled by receiving an answer —any answer—we know where to stop. So that a large part of our intellectual operations takes inevitably the following form:

A. Why is the grass green?
B. Because of the chlorophyll.
A. Oh.*

So, in a realm of contemplation, meaning would itself be inexplicable. The typewriters rattle, the telephones ring, the moving finger keeps writing one triviality after another, the great gabble of the world goes incessantly on as people translate, encipher, decipher, as one set of words is transformed more or less symmetrically into another set of words—whereupon someone says, "O, now I understand. . . ."

But the question about meaning attests, wherever it is asked, the presence of civilization with all its possibilities, all its limitations; attests the presence of *language*, that vast echoing rattle and sibilance buzzing between ourselves and whatever it is we presume we are looking at, experiencing, being in, and which sometimes appears to have an independent value, if any at all, like the machine someone built a few years back, which had thousands of moving parts and no function. The semanticist to the contrary, words are things, though not always the things they say they are. The painter Delacroix expressed it by saying that Nature is a dictionary. Everything is there, but not in the order one needs. The universe itself, so far as we relate ourselves to it by the mind, may be not so much a meaning as a rhythm, a continuous articulation of question and answer, question and answer, a musical dialectic precipitating out moments of meaning which become distinct only as one wave does in a sea of waves. "You think you live under universal principles," said Montaigne, "but in fact they are municipal bylaws."

Language, then, is the marvelous mirror of the human condition, a mirror so miraculous that it can see what is invisible, that is, the relations between things. At the same time, the mirror is a limit, and as such, it is sorrowful; one wants to break it and look beyond. But unless we have the singular talent for mystical experience we do

* That is a made-up example, but here is one from actual play, as Fingarette, writing on "The Ego and Mystic Selflessness" (in *Identity and Anxiety: Survival of the Person in Mass Society*, p. 572), quotes a Chinese mystic as saying: "When neither hatred nor love disturb the mind, / Serene and restful is our sleep," and comments: "While this is surely not meant simply in a literal way, we know from Freud that the literal meaning of the image is perfectly apt. Provided one interprets 'hatred' and 'love' as unsublimated aggressive and libidinal instinctual drives, one hardly needs to change a word to consider the verse as a basic psychological truth."

not really break the mirror, and even the mystic's experience is available to us only as reflected, inadequately, in the mirror. Most often man deals with reality by its reflection. That is the sense of Perseus' victory over the Gorgon by consenting to see her only in the mirror of his shield, and it is the sense of the saying in Corinthians that we see now as through a glass darkly—a phrase rendered by modern translators as "now we see as in a little mirror."

Civilization, mirrored in language, is the garden where relations grow; outside the garden is the wild abyss. Poetry, an art of fictions, illusions, even lies—"Homer," said Aristotle, "first taught us the art of framing lies in the right way"—poetry is the art of contemplating this situation in the mirror of language.

"Only connect . . ." is the civilized and civilizing motto of a book by E. M. Forster, wherein he speaks eloquently of meaning, art, and order in "the world of telegrams and anger," and of what exists outside that world: "panic and emptiness, panic and emptiness." W. H. Auden, also very eloquently, writes of the limiting extremes within which meaning means, between "the ocean flats where no subscription concerts are given" and "the desert plain where there is nothing for lunch."

But meaning, like religion, seeks of its own nature to monopolize experience. For example, in children's playbooks there are numbered dots to be followed in sequence by the pencil; the line so produced finally becomes recognizable as a shape. So the lines produced among stars (which can scarcely all be in the same plane) become the geometrical abstractions of a Bear, a Wagon, Orion the Hunter; and by softening or humanizing the outlines, recognizable images are produced, but in the process the stars themselves have to be omitted. So does meaning at first simplify and afterward supersede the world. Poetry, I would say, is, in its highest ranges, no mere playing with the counters of meaning, but a perpetual re-deriving of the possibility of meaning from matter, of the intelligible world from the brute recalcitrance of things. Poetry differs from thought in this respect, that thought eats up the language in which it thinks. Thought is proud, and always wants to forget its humble origin in things. In doing so, it begins to speak by means of very elevated abstractions, which quickly become emptied and impoverished. The business of poetry is to bring thought back into relation with the five wits, the five senses which Blake calls "the chief inlets of soul in this age," to show how our discontents, as Shakespeare finely says of Timon's, "are unremovably coupled to nature." So the ivory tower must always be cut from the horn of Behemoth.

The relation of poetry to religion is both intimate and antithetical, for poetry exists only by a continuing revelation in a world always incarnate of word and flesh indissolubly, a world simultaneously solid and transpicuous. At the same time, religion can never really dissociate itself from poetry and the continuing revelation; and its attempts to do so turn it into a form of literary criticism, as the scriptures and sacred books of the world, in comparison with their interminable commentaries, will sufficiently show. Poetry and institutionalized religion are in a sense the flowing and the static forms of the same substance, liquid and solid states of the same elemental energy.

This is a simple thing; it has been said many times and forgotten many times plus one. William Blake says it this way:

> The ancient Poets animated all sensible objects with Gods or Geniuses, calling them by the names and adorning them with the properties of woods, rivers, mountains, lakes, cities, nations, and whatever their enlarged and numerous senses could perceive.
> And particularly they studied the Genius of each city and country, placing it under its Mental Deity;
> Till a system was formed, which some took advantage of, and enslav'd the vulgar by attempting to realise or abstract the Mental Deities from their objects—thus began Priesthood;
> Choosing forms of worship from poetic tales.
> And at length they pronounc'd that the Gods had order'd such things.
> Thus men forgot that All Deities reside in the Human Breast.

The poet's business, I would say, is to name as accurately as possible a situation, but a situation which he himself is in. The name he gives ought to be so close a fit with the actuality it summons into being that there remains no room between inside and outside; the thought must be "like a beast moving in its skin" (Dante). If he does his work properly, there won't be any other name for the situation (and for his being in it) than the one he invents, or, rather, his name will swallow up all the others as Aaron's rod swallowed up the rods of Pharaoh's wizards.

Sometimes the name so given is a relatively simple one, as when Alexander Pope gave the Prince of Wales a dog, and had inscribed on its collar:

I am his Highness' dog at Kew.
Pray tell me, sir, whose dog are you?

And sometimes the name so given, the situation thus identified and brought into being, is immensely complex, so that one has to refer to it by a tag, an abbreviation, e.g., "King Lear."

A poem, whether of two lines or ten thousand, is therefore the name of something, and in its ideal realm of fiction or illusion it corresponds to what is said of the Divine Name in several significant respects:

It is unique.
It can never be repeated.
It brings into being the situation it names, and is therefore truly a creation.
It is secret, even while being perfectly open and public, for it defines a thing which could not have been known without it.

As to the poet himself, one might add this. Writing is a species of *askesis*, a persevering devotion to the energy passing between self and world. It is a way of living, a way of being, and, though it does produce results in the form of "works," these may come to seem of secondary importance to the person so engaged.

The young writer is always told (he was, anyhow, when I was young) that writing means first and last "having something to say." I cherish as a souvenir of boyhood that honorable and aged platitude, but would like to modify it by this addition: Writing means trying to find out what the nature of things has to say about what you think you have to say. And the process is reflective or cyclical, a matter of feedback between oneself and "it," an "it" which can gain its identity only in the course of being brought into being, come into being only in the course of finding its identity. This is a matter, as Lu Chi says, of how to hold the axe while you are cutting its handle.

I say that writing is a species of *askesis*. But as it works in an ideal or fictional, rather than in a practical, realm, so it purifies not the character but the style. There is, however, a connection between the two, at least in the hope that a charity of the imagination shall be not quite the same thing as an imaginary charity.

That, then, is what I have tried to characterize as "the swaying form," a process of becoming related to nature and the nature of things (*natura naturata* and *natura naturans*). The view here taken suggests that art has some evident affinities with both religion and science on the very simple basis that all three exist in the presumption that the truth is possible to be told about existence; but these affinities themselves also define differences, distances, and intrinsic antagonisms.

As to art's relation with science. The experimental method was defined, by Galileo, I believe, as putting nature to the question, where "the question" meant the judicial process of torture. The definition seems to imply a faith that nature, so treated, will reveal the secret name for a situation; when once that situation has been isolated, treated as a situation in itself, and considered for a moment apart from the flux of all things, nature will, as it were, confess her presumably guilty secret.

Well, the artist, it seems to me, works on a not so different principle, leading from hypothesis—"what will happen to this noble nature if it can be led to believe Desdemona unfaithful?"—through experiment—the question as put by Iago—to result, to "the tragic loading of this bed." In this sense, and not in the fashionable popular sense, art is "experimental," and its methods to a certain extent resemble those of the laboratory; art, too, produces its process under controlled and limiting conditions, cutting away irrelevancies, speeding up or slowing down the reaction under study, so that the results, whatever they may be, will stand forth with a singular purity and distinction. The instruments of science, of course, have as their aim the creation of an objectivity as nearly as possible universal in character; the poet's aim might be thought of as the same and reversed, a mirror image—to represent in the world the movement of a subjectivity as nearly as possible universal in character.

And art is akin to religion, if we will be nondenominational about it, in that the work (though not, perhaps, the artist, oddly enough) is driven by its own composition to the implication of invisible things inherent in visible ones. The subject, the content, of the art work is sorrowful, because life is sorrowful; but the work itself, by the nature of its form, dances. A beautiful passage from Proust's novel will be relevant here. Marcel is thinking of the writer Bergotte, who died of a stroke while contemplating a detail, a piece of yellow wall, in a painting by Vermeer:

> He was dead. Forever? Who can say? After all, occult experiences demonstrate no more than the dogmas of religion do about the soul's

continuance. But what can be said is this, that we live our life as though we had entered it under the burden of obligations already assumed in another; there is, in the conditions of our life here, no reason which should make us believe ourselves obliged to do good, to be fastidious or even polite, nor which should make the godless painter believe himself obliged to start over twenty times a detail the praise of which will matter very little to his body eaten by worms—a detail such as the section of yellow wall painted with such skill and taste by an artist forever unknown and scarce identified under the name of Vermeer. All such obligations, which have no sanction in our present life, seem to belong to a different world based on goodness, consideration and sacrifice, a world altogether different from this one, and from which we emerge to be born on this earth, before perhaps returning there to live under the rule of those unknown laws which we have obeyed because we carry their teaching within us though unaware who traced it there —those laws to which every profound work of the intelligence tends to reconcile us, and which are invisible only—and forever!—to fools.

So the work of art is religious in nature, not because it beautifies an ugly world or pretends that a naughty world is a nice one—for these things especially art does not do—but because it shows of its own nature that things drawn within the sacred circle of its forms are transfigured, illuminated by an inward radiance which amounts to goodness because it amounts to Being itself. In the life conferred by art, Iago and Desdemona, Edmund and Cordelia, the damned and the blessed, equally achieve immortality by their relation with the creating intelligence which sustains them. The art work is not responsible for saying that things in reality are so, but rather for revealing what this world says to candid vision. It is thus that we delight in tragedies whose actions in life would merely appall us. And it is thus that art, by its illusions, achieves a human analogy to the resolution of that famous question of theodicy—the relation of an Omnipotent Benevolence to evil—which the theologians, bound to the fixed forms of things, have for centuries struggled with, intemperately and in vain. And it is thus that art, by vision and not by dogma, patiently and repeatedly offers the substance of things hoped for, the evidence of things unseen.

The Marriage of Theseus and Hippolyta

Those who believe that the "real meaning" of Shakespeare's Plays consists in the one instruction, "to thine own self be true"—a principle of behavior distinguishing Iago and Edmund not less, certainly, than Polonius—seem to believe also that the poet's thought about the art he practiced is completely revealed in a few lines spoken by Theseus toward the end of A Midsummer-Night's Dream:

> The poet's eye, in a fine frenzy rolling,
> Doth glance from heaven to earth, from earth to heaven;
> And, as imagination bodies forth
> The forms of things unknown, the poet's pen
> Turns them to shapes, and gives to airy nothing
> A local habitation and a name.

From the number of times we read or hear these lines quoted in discussions of poetry we have a kind of habituated impression of their immense significance and finality, though a closer inspection suggests they are neither distinguished nor illuminating.

To know what Shakespeare thought about poetry would be, of course, a matter of great interest to any student of the art; of greater interest than to know the opinion of any number of poets, good and bad, who have been perfectly explicit on this topic. Shakespeare, so far as we know, was not a "literary man" like Matthew Arnold or Mr. Gigadibs, and did not leave (so far as we know) obiter dicta, essays in aesthetics, conversations with Drummond, or even notes for projected work; any statement we have from his hand, on any subject whatever, must be considered in itself as fictive and personative, as having been made not for its own sweet sake but for its place in some larger scheme (nor may remarks made in the Sonnets be ex-

Reprinted by permission from The Kenyon Review, Vol. XVIII, No. 4, Autumn 1956. Copyright 1956 by Kenyon College.

cepted from that condition); so that our assertions on this theme will never be finally confirmed nor—we may be thankful—explicitly denied.

There are places in the Plays at which Shakespeare speculates about the poetic art to greater effect than in Theseus' speech: Achilles and Ulysses, ostensibly discussing reputation (*Troilus and Cressida* III. iii), are really talking, and talking well, about art and life, the thing said and the thing done, poetics and heroics; the relation of art to "great creating Nature" is most subtly resolved, in *The Winter's Tale* IV. iii, along the lines of Hopkins' poem about "Pied Beauty"; and Hamlet's precision in coupling "form and pressure" will bear a good deal of interpretation. But I should like to tease out for a little the sense of Theseus' opinion, in part because this is so frequently offered us as all we know or need to know, and in part because it appears to me that his sentiments are beautifully answered by Hippolyta a moment afterward, in a passage not often remarked.

First, then, as to the context. The night in the dark wood is over, and order has been restored; already the things which have happened "seem small and undistinguishable, / Like far-off mountains turned into clouds," and the lovers themselves "see these things with parted eye, / When everything seems double." Still, they have evidently told their experiences as best they can, and Theseus' speech responds to Hippolyta's opening, " 'Tis strange, my Theseus, that these lovers speak of."

"More strange than true," Theseus replies, and develops his comparison, perhaps remotely based on opinions held by Plato (*Phaedrus*, 245a, *Ion*, 533d) and not necessarily complimentary to poets, among "the lunatic, the lover, and the poet." The immediate point of his criticism is that the events recounted by the four lovers are simply not true and therefore more or less worthless; beyond this, that the predilection for dignifying one's subjective fantasies as objective reality (the infinite capacity, if not for lying, for being deceived about things) is one which lovers share with madmen and poets. The quality he refers to three times as "imagination" has in his description a febrile, unsober, or merely wilful appearance, and though it is not much like what a Romantic poet would call "fancy" it is about as far removed from Coleridge's idea of imagination, and is so called a few lines later by Hippolyta, who says that the lovers' story "More witnesseth than fancy's images." In fact, for all the mysteriousness of his talk about the poet's eye, Theseus seems to mean something extremely simple, as his gloss on his own words will make appear:

> Such tricks hath strong imagination,
> That, if it would but apprehend some joy,
> It comprehends some bringer of that joy;
> Or in the night, imagining some fear,
> How easy is a bush suppos'd a bear!

The lovers, in other words, were deluded, and so are poets; unless we wish to carry this matter one step further, as Proust does somewhere in recounting the anecdote of a man who, entering his own house at night, sees a burglar in the hall and dies of a heart attack, although in reality—?! as the chess critic says—there was no burglar but only a coat on a coat hook; what caused the man's death, asks Proust, the burglar or the coat? Thus also Yeats:

> *Fifteen apparitions have I seen;*
> *The worst a coat upon a coat-hanger.*

Theseus, however, is not interested in such remote speculation, which would, perhaps, in his opinion, be of interest only to poets, lunatics, and lovers, and so far as he is concerned he has said enough when he has said that such people are generally, as well as in the particular instance, mistaken. In effect, Theseus' attitude toward art, as it is brought out by the remainder of this scene, has in it something at least "administrative," probably priggish, and somewhat suggestive of what might be felt by a highly placed civil servant attending a high school performance of *A Midsummer-Night's Dream* in which his son, perhaps, has the part of Theseus. The components of this attitude are these: none of this is real, none of it matters; whether it is well or badly brought off does not matter; the performance of plays, however, is a sign of order in society, it is "done"; what one looks for is not intellectual delight, so much as an assurance of one's own authority in a rationally stabilized commonwealth; not technique, but the appropriately humble intention of giving pleasure.

All these elements are revealed in Theseus' treatment of the coming performance of *Pyramus and Thisbe*—"what masques, what dances shall we have, / To wear away this long age of three hours / Between our after-supper and bed-time? . . . Is there no play / To ease the anguish of a torturing hour?" (It will charitably be remembered that this is his wedding night.) * He decides to hear the play, of all the entertainments offered, against the advice of Philostrate:

> It is not for you; I have heard it over,
> And it is nothing, nothing in the world;
> Unless you can find sport in their intents,
> Extremely stretch'd, and conn'd with cruel pain,
> To do you service.

To which he makes the ducal reply, "I will hear that play; / For never anything can be amiss, / When simpleness and duty tender it." To Hippolyta's embarrassed remonstration that the base mechanicals "can do nothing in this kind," he develops his lofty tolerance to the height of civil power at which the difference between good art and bad quite simply disappears:

> Our sport shall be to take what they mistake:
> And what poor duty cannot do, noble respect
> Takes it in might, not merit.
> Where I have come, great clerks have purposed
> To greet me with premeditated welcomes;
> Where I have seen them shiver and look pale,
> Make periods in the midst of sentences,
> Throttle their practis'd accents in their fears,
> And, in conclusion, dumbly have broke off,
> Not paying me a welcome. Trust me, sweet,
> Out of this silence yet I pick'd a welcome;
> And in the modesty of fearful duty
> I read as much as from the rattling tongue
> Of saucy and audacious eloquence.
> Love, therefore, and tongue-ti'd simplicity
> In least speak most, to my capacity.

Nevertheless, he is as willing as the others to make fun of the tedious brief scene, of which he presently says, with an eloquence which somewhat disguises a certain emptiness and insolence about his sense, "The best in this kind are but shadows; and the worst are no worse, if imagination amend them," leaving no doubt of a quiet confidence that his own "imagination" could "amend" either *Pyramus and Thisbe* or *A Midsummer-Night's Dream*.

---

* Less charitably, that he has been married several times before.

This is of course not all there is to Theseus, who in a certain remote allegory not to be very fully realized in this play is like God (Shakespeare's habit with Dukes) and has a prescriptive right to regard the intention rather than the result ("noble respect / Takes it in might not merit"), being so great in the scheme of things that the greatest human skill not less than the least finds itself incapable in his presence. At the same time he is the secular ruler, uniting in his person and that of his queen mysterious powers of society and nature; in this sense the poet has for his demeanor a proper reverence not altogether free of ironic suspicions. The speeches we have quoted from Act V show Shakespeare in some doubt about the Duke and his attitude, which shifts between a serious wisdom in the allegory—"The best in this kind are but shadows"—and an aristocratic or courtly disdain for art, not bad art only but all art, seriously expressed in the opening speech, more brutally in the speech about the "great clerks," and carried out in his wit at the players' expense. (One suspects, whatever Castiglione's original feeling about "*sprezzatura*," that the attitude must in practice have included a good deal of this rather beefy superiority.) His attitude is not like Hotspur's— "I had rather be a kitten and cry mew / Than one of these same metre ballad-mongers"—but loftier and more indifferent, and, by so much as it is more "tolerant," more contemptuous.

It is, I suppose, perfectly fitting that in a society such as ours these ducal views of the nature of poetry should be vastly admired and identified as coterminous with the views of William Shakespeare. In fact, I can see only two redeeming points about Theseus' opinion: that, being himself a lover, he comes under the aim of his own attack, and that this attack upon poetry is conducted, elegantly enough, in poetry. These two points restore to his character that element of ironic "reduplication" so admired by existentialist philosophers, and in a degree save him from being merely an outsize bore attractively posed with his hunting dogs against a dawn of Tintoretto's blue ("And since we have the vaward of the day, / My love shall hear the music of my hounds").

We have of course no warrant for identifying Hippolyta's reply with the views of William Shakespeare either; her lines, as a matter of fact, do not directly take up Theseus' remarks about poets, nor mention poetry at all, and the reference of the pronoun is to the lovers' minds:

> But all the story of the night told over,
> And all their minds transfigur'd so together,
> More witnesseth than fancy's images,
> And grows to something of great constancy;
> But howsoever, strange, and admirable.

But I feel these words to be one of the poet's fine summarizing moments, at which his action gives him rich rewards; such a moment as occurs also, for example, in *The Merchant of Venice* at just the same place (V. i, at the beginning), where the interlude between Lorenzo and Jessica ("In such a night as this. . . ."), with its music, moonlight, and strange legendary resonance, is wonderfully brought to a close by Portia's entrance:

> That light we see is burning in my hall.
> How far that little candle throws his beams!
> So shines a good deed in a naughty world.

Hippolyta's lines also, for me, have resonance far beyond the play, forming one of those miraculous instances in which poetry can be seen to have for ultimate subject its own self:

> For speculation turns not to itself
> Till it hath travell'd, and is mirror'd there
> Where it may see itself.
> (*Troilus and Cressida* III. iii)

This is not a very complicated or abstruse matter once made visible, and does not call for elaborate interpretations; one either sees it this way or else—like Theseus and other reputable persons, some of them poets—one does not. In the form of propositions, then, as a kind of manifesto of, say, the Amazonian school:

1. The province of the poetic art is "all the story of the night told over," "the night" being a conventional summary expression for all that human beings act and suffer in the world; as Dante calls it near the beginning of his poem, "La notte ch'io passai con tanta pieta." The story is "told over," that is to say, there is one story only.

2. The minds of the participants are "transfigured," and not only so but "together"—the story may be improbable, but they all tell it; their views are changed, but all changed in the same way; the relations among them are transfigured, but harmoniously. This line further refers to the minds of the audience, which also are "transfigured

so together," and ultimately to the minds of all the poets who have told over "the story of the night."

3. The story, therefore, "grows to something of great constancy." It may not at first appear that way, but visibly, while we follow its development, it *grows* to be that way. It is to be judged in the first instance not as true or untrue but simply as composition, placing-together of elements, as approaching the nature of music. It constitutes on its own a world of ordered relation, rhythm, and figure. This world *is*, and, as with the larger world in which it is, our views of its *meaning* are our own responsibility, for which it is only cryptically answerable, yielding to interpretation numerous parables which may contradict but paradoxically do not exclude one another.

4. This world, not less than the material elements of which it is composed, is "strange," both alien and familiar to the one in which we generally believe that we live—"strange, and admirable," the second word having the sense which it is given in *The Tempest*: "Admir'd Miranda! / Indeed, the top of admiration," the sense of the girl's name itself.

I have put the accent all on Hippolyta's part at the expense of Theseus' part, out of inclination and to right a very unbalanced view of this matter. But now, having eased my partisan passion, I must come back to the center and allow that Theseus and Hippolyta do get married; it would be inadvisable for the critic to forget that this marriage is not merely sanctioned but celebrated by William Shakespeare.

Discussions of the nature of poetry, when conducted by the partisans of Theseus (as these days they so often are), are apt to be inadequate for the simple reason that in such a discussion the nature of poetry, like any rational nature, is assumed to be one. The goal of all discussion after that is to arrive at the description of this "one." But as the nature of poetry is not one, but two, or is one only in the way that husband and wife are one flesh (Hamlet says it), or in the way that the Phoenix and Turtle are one but bear single nature's double name, the characteristic consequence of such discussions is that a great deal of poetry gets defined out and thrown away.

This point does not call for more elaborate interpretation than the other, and I shall simply put it out on the page.

The poetry of Theseus is rational, civic-minded, discursive, and tends constantly to approach prose. The poetry of Hippolyta is magical, fabulous, dramatic, and constantly approaches music. The excess of Theseus is to declare that art is entertainment; the excess of Hippolyta, to declare that art is mystery. It is perhaps ironic that Theseus' views should seem allied with those of the mysterious and fable-minded Plato, while in Hippolyta's "great constancy" we hear some echo of the plain-spoken other side ("an action, one and entire, having a certain magnitude," as well as "integritas, consonantia, claritas"), but my intention stops short of those high matters.

Now these two, the London Athenian Theseus and the Stratford Amazon Hippolyta, were joined in marriage by William Shakespeare. Their wedded life, with its vicious quarrels and long intervals of separation (not extending as yet to final divorce), is the history of poetry in the English language; a course of true love of which we might have been forewarned by the same poet, when at the beginning of the ceremony he makes Theseus say:

> Hippolyta, I woo'd thee with my sword,
> And won thy love doing thee injuries,

a piece of analytical and dialectical piety which may fittingly, for the time being, bring these considerations to their close.

The Two Gentlemen of Verona: A Commentary

That this is one of the earliest of the Plays, is an excuse frequently offered for its admittedly odd behavior: an infant, no more house-broken than Launce's dog: " 'Tis a foul thing when a cur cannot keep himself in all companies!" It is not a well-made play, it contains a number of incidental absurdities, its persons certainly do not behave like real, warm, earthy human beings—these are some of the complaints made by critics, who find the chief interest of *The Two Gentlemen of Verona* in its vague foreshadowing of qualities its author does not yet fully possess.

In fact, with the tragedies and last romances in mind—an advantage Shakespeare did not have at the time of composition—we may take considerable interest in watching the poet's first attempts to identify his characteristic materials, in tracing through this play the forms which he would later fill with so rich and individualized a life, and which, still later, he would once again present in abstraction: for if Valentine and Silvia have not in our modern, psychologizing sense got characters—and they haven't—they very much resemble in this Ferdinand and Miranda, who have not got characters either.

Such a tracing ought to have to do not with *ad hoc* resemblances, of which there are a good many, but with revealing certain great structural constants of the Plays, themes of obsession, as they waveringly or plainly appear in this one. For example, the twinned figures of knave and fool, Proteus and Valentine, reappear throughout Shakespeare's *oeuvre*, sometimes as friends, often as brothers. Sometimes the witty and divisive rationalist destroys his faithful, "simple," easily imposed-upon counterpart, as Iago destroys Othello; sometimes, as here, the naïve victim, driven into the wilderness, returns to over-

This essay was written expressly for the Laurel Shakespeare Series published by the Dell Publishing Company, Inc., and is reprinted by permission of the publishers.

come the worldly man (so Edgar at last kills Edmund), or gains the strength to bring about his repentance and the wise charity to forgive him (so Prospero to Antonio); sometimes, too, the struggle between cynical intelligence and idealistic folly or "simplicity" is focused upon the possession of a woman, whose character will reflect that of the winner (so Cressida is faithful with Troilus, fickle when she goes over to Diomed and the Greeks).

A related constant: the good man, if he is to triumph, must first be driven out of city or court. Valentine's exile corresponds to the exiles of Prospero, Duke Senior in *As You Like It*, and the flight of Edgar in *King Lear*. Sometimes, though, this exile is self-moved, like the Duke's in *Measure for Measure*.

Another related constant: this exile is generally to a sort of enchanted realm associated with magical or natural powers which seem antithetical to the civil order but which are really fundamental to it and confer power over it: the magical island of *The Tempest*, the greenwood in *As You Like It*, the heath in *King Lear*, the forests of this play and *A Midsummer-Night's Dream*. Here the exile learns a new identity, often figured by disguise, which enables him to cope with his clever and deceitful opposite. So Valentine becomes king of the outlaws in the forest, and speaks of his new situation much as the other displaced nobility do in other plays:

> How use doth breed a habit in a man!
> This shadowy desert, unfrequented woods,
> I better brook than flourishing peopled towns . . .

Compare Duke Senior in the Forest of Arden:

> Hath not old custom made this life more sweet
> Than that of painted pomp? Are not these woods
> More free from peril than the envious court?

Much more might be said on this subject, but to little purpose. Though it be true that *The Two Gentlemen of Verona* represents the essentials of Shakespeare's most characteristic action, one which he returned to over and over again, every resemblance we point to is also a difference, and one moreover that in the comparison works to the disadvantage of this play. In the action, for instance, Proteus' role is very like that of Edmund, and in its progress shows something of Shakespeare's idea of evil as beginning with reason but proceeding to uncontrollable contagion: thus his initial betrayal of Julia involves him in the attempt to deceive all the others—the Duke, Silvia, Valentine, Thurio—and especially himself; but Proteus is not Edmund, and looks harmlessly inept beside him. Similarly, Valentine's exile and flight into the forest do indeed have the same sense as Edgar's forced flight into the storm of nature and the insane assumptions at the bottom of societies—but those outlaws are pretty silly all the same, aren't they?

Bothers of this sort and others have made the play something of an embarrassment, so that it is not much heard of. Some scholars, those whose theme requires them to discuss all the Plays, or at any rate all the Comedies, have attempted to get round the difficulty in one of two related ways.

The first is to say that what we have here is, after all, apprentice work; that the young Shakespeare has not yet learned to invent a satisfactory plot; that what he has managed to do is marred by inexcusable carelessness; that the characterization, while not much, is at any rate an improvement over that in *The Comedy of Errors* "and gives promise of better things to come." In general, arguing along these lines, "to the student of Shakespeare's development there is much of interest in the story."

The second solution is a specialized development from the first. The play is apprentice work in a particular sense, it shows Shakespeare experimenting with the combination of two genres, Romance and Comedy; he has not yet learned to handle the combination, so that the romantic and the comic parts contradict and corrupt one another, so that the play is, as Valentine says of love, "a folly bought with wit, / Or else a wit by folly vanquished."

Much of all this appears true, or at least probable, to a first look, and the evidence will show an imposing number of faults or seeming faults: for example, that the play's geography is not only internally inconsistent but also absurd to begin with (you don't take a boat from Verona to Milan), that Valentine's character as romantic lover is thoroughly compromised by his extreme stupidity (see II. i, for an instance), that there are two Sir Eglamours, and so on.

Given this mode of the attention, the interest of the play will still reside in its significance for Shakespeare's "development," so that Launce "looks forward to" Launcelot Gobbo in *The Merchant of Venice,* and Julia's going disguised as a boy to Silvia "looks forward to" Viola's going similarly disguised to Olivia in *Twelfth Night.* One may then say something affectionate about Launce and his dog, something judicious about the versification (related to the Sonnets), something appreciative about "Who is Silvia?" ("the pure lyric note"), and have done.

And, given this mode of the attention, these objections to the poet's conduct of his action are serious ones; the play is in some ways arbitrary and irresponsible, it sometimes has an air of plain foolishness.

Now I do not think the scholars were wrong in bringing these matters to attention—somebody had to—nor am I at all certain I can do either other or better. But I do have a difficulty with the mode of attention itself, with a way of regarding works of art which seems peculiarly suited to the study of "development" while somewhat neglecting the specificity of the present example; it tends to see Shakespeare as getting from an earlier play to a later play by means of this one—the hen which is the egg's way of getting to another egg—rather than to see this one as, for the moment, the only object in the world. So I would propose another assumption to begin with, something like this: when a master makes a mistake—let us except the "inexcusable carelessness" (he did write fast, and, as we are told, never blotted)—but when a master makes what looks like a big mistake, look closely and listen, for he may be doing it on purpose, and what you see as incoherence or inconsistency may emerge as his meaning. So it happens, for example, in a greater play than this one, *Troilus & Cressida*, where the way in which things go unpredictably and absurdly wrong with the story turns out to be the story. This view of mine is admittedly based on hero-worship.

The scholarly opinions I have outlined seem to involve some unnecessary and perhaps unwarrantable assumptions as to what plays are, and what poetry is, brought from elsewhere to be applied to this example. If the play is apprentice work, that is surely not because the plot is absurd, for all plots are absurd when considered by themselves; if you don't believe this, say over slowly the plot of *The Tempest*. In fact, the plot of *The Two Gentlemen of Verona* is typically Shakespearean in its outrageously crossing symmetries and improbable manipulations. Were we not so much imposed upon by novelistic ideas of "depth" and "sincerity," we could allow that the apprenticeship of the master poet might show, not a welter of intense emotions and deep thoughts, but just such a brittle and cool charm as this play shows, just such a carelessly brilliant handling of surfaces consistently kept free of the encumbrances of "reality."

Similarly, the idea that the play fails because in it the two separate genres of Romance and Comedy have not been harmonized by the poet seems to substitute a theory for what visibly happens; behind this idea is the old notion, perhaps, of "comic relief." But I do not see that it is necessary to postulate two genres, or that the play fails from any such internal contradiction, or for that matter that the play essentially fails at all—as I shall try to show.

It is perfectly true, and obvious everywhere in the Plays, that Shakespeare believes in romantic love; it is in fact his greatest value, close-allied with a religion of natural sanctions and faithfulness down to the ending doom. But it is impermissible to identify this belief with a Shakespearean belief in the seriousness, moral worth, intelligence, and fascinating individuality of the persons who embody this belief in the value of romantic love; for these qualities they generally do not have, and in this play as in others the young lovers are such nitwits as to make their poet's belief in love exactly what a proper belief has to be: *quia absurdum, quia impossibile,* &c. Here, as in *A Midsummer-Night's Dream,* the characters' belief that they have characters is one of the funniest things in the play, and one of its major points; as Yeats says of the same situation ("boys and girls, pale from the imagined love / Of solitary beds"), "passion could bring character enough." Such character as the lovers have exists only in relation to love, and is in a remarkable degree conferred upon them by their names (a kind of Platonizing evident throughout the play): Valentine, because he is faithful; Proteus, because he changes. The relation of Julia to "jewel" is a little less obvious, but the price of a virtuous woman is "far above rubies" (Proverbs. XXXI.10) and her device is the ring. Silvia's name relates her to the wood where she will find Valentine again.

Now it is the essence of love to spiritualize and idealize not only the beloved but the world as well; and to spiritualize and idealize the world is also in a sense to be silly, even if it is upon that silliness that human life, as distinct from the life of beasts, chiefly depends. Shakespeare does not neglect or attempt to conceal this silliness, inseparable from idealism and romance and all impetuous generosity; on the contrary, he is at some pains to emphasize it throughout by constantly asserting the equation of love with idealism (a world whose charm will be its faithfulness to absurdity), with word, image, symbol, and shadow. The four young lovers sigh in a world of poetry and music, a world of no particular stability but what faith in love can give it, where ecstasy and allicholly may in a moment change places; it is not remarkable, then, but perfectly appropriate, that they should concentrate so much of their attention on symbols: letters, rings, a picture, a song; for this is not the real world, and yet, in the moment of their passion, reality itself becomes to a certain extent malleable, even volatile.

This courtly and Platonic strain is the dominant insistence of the play, wherever we are concerned with the lovers; so ideal is the nature of their worship, whether constant or fickle, that it fixes itself repeatedly on word or image rather than on what they represent, on names rather than on things. Thus Julia, after tearing up a love letter from Proteus, puts his "poor wounded name" in her bosom to be healed, curses her own name for her unkindness, and finally puts both names together:

> Thus will I fold them one upon another:
> Now kiss, embrace, contend, do what you will.

Proteus, denied by Silvia, begs her picture to love instead:

> For since the substance of your perfect self
> Is else devoted, I am but a shadow;
> And to your shadow will I make true love.

It is significant that anyone drawn into the sphere of the lovers, whatever his gravity and consequence, at once assumes their silliness for his own: consider the tale the Duke must invent to make Valentine reveal himself as Silvia's lover:

> There is a lady in Milano here
> Whom I affect; but she is nice and coy
> And naught esteems my aged eloquence.
> Now therefore would I have thee to my tutor—

leading on to a design of climbing up on the lady's roof by rope ladder. True, this tale is a ruse; but the climate of opinion, so to say, in which Valentine could believe it of the Duke and the Duke could believe it capable of imposing on Valentine, has to be one of an exceptionally weightless kind.

The most outrageous example, appropriately, forms the climax of the play. Fifteen lines after trying to rape Silvia, Proteus repents, whereupon in five or six lines more Valentine's forgiveness reaches the point of offering him Silvia:

> And, that my love may appear plain and free,
> All that was mine in Silvia I give thee,

causing Julia to faint—and one scholar to exclaim that by this time there are *no* gentlemen of Verona. But this character of extreme lightness and rapid mobility of feeling is undoubtedly intentional, and has been built up throughout the play with remarkable consistency.

For the world of love is also the world of music and poetry, idealizing and spiritualizing, yet having, like love, a power to transform real experience. The theory of all three in their relations is with an odd propriety entrusted to Proteus, in a speech of grand and subtle brilliance, where truth and deceit, technique and effect, are finely fused, as he tells Thurio how to win Silvia "By wailful sonnets, whose composed rhymes / Should be full-fraught with serviceable vows":

> Say that upon the altar of her beauty
> You sacrifice your tears, your sighs, your heart.
> Write till your ink be dry, and with your tears
> Moist it again; and frame some feeling line
> That may discover such integrity.
> For Orpheus' lute was strung with poets' sinews,
> Whose golden touch could soften steel and stones,
> Make tigers tame, and huge leviathans
> Forsake unsounded deeps to dance on sands.

Now we may be able to see that the comic parts given to the "low people" do not in the least destroy the romance, but act formally as a balancing countersubject, emotionally as the guarantee of a fine, implicit truth of feeling in the play.

To spell out some simple things which the lovers make us for a time forget—what is romance about? It is about getting married, which is both a fulfillment and a comedown for passionate idealism, having to do with the body, with generation, with care for the future, with life in the moderate temperatures of the real world, the sorrowful-funny.

All the servants in the play represent this circumstance to their heedless masters, acting the part of worldliness in relation to spirit, shadowing forth the grotesque countertruths of the flesh to which the last refinements of romantic adoration are nevertheless designed to lead. When Julia decides to dress as a boy, Lucetta's response is typical: "What fashion, madam, shall I make your breeches?" and "You must needs have them with a codpiece, madam."

But it is the wonderful Launce and his marvelous dog, whether visible or invisible, who chiefly develop this carnal wisdom and humility.

Launce is to Proteus his master as body to mind or spirit. The body, being a servant and fool, understands the mind: "I am but a fool, look you; and yet I have the wit to think my master is a kind of knave"—for, as Launce says to Speed, "stand-under and understand is all one." The same relation is duplicated between Launce and his dog, in a brilliantly detailed development of that traditional wisdom which views the body as a beast—Brother Ass, as St. Francis called it.

In the intermission of the lovers' passionate but abstract bewilderments the poet has placed this most marvelous of clowns in his sorrowing humility. And what does Launce talk about? At his first appearance he talks about—and acts out—family life and the pains of parting, the tears shed by all except the dog:

> My mother weeping, my father wailing, my sister crying, our maid howling, our cat wringing her hands, and all our house in a great perplexity —yet did not this cruel-hearted cur shed one tear.

Later on, he parodies the main action by trying to choose a wife from a catalogue which lists her qualities, e.g. "*Item*. She is not to be kiss'd fasting, in respect of her breath." And at his last coming on stage, in a kind of abject sermon addressed to the dog, he tells in a parable how the body embarrasses, disgraces, and punishes the spirit, how the spirit humbly, lovingly, necessarily suffers the body's dumb unruliness, and puts this behavior of the flesh in direct relation with the romantic heroine:

> Nay, I remember the trick you serv'd me when I took my leave of Madam Silvia! Did not I bid thee still mark me and do as I do? When didst thou see me heave up my leg and make water against a gentlewoman's farthingale? Didst thou ever see me do such a trick?

If the worst that has been said of the play were true, the existence in it of Launce would alone make it beautifully worth attending to. But the existence of Launce is not merely a brilliant solo irrelevantly set against a mediocre background; rather, he is integral to the play, and in a certain sense the key to the truth of its youthful and pale but spirited charm.

Poetry and Life: Lord Byron

The Selected Letters of Lord Byron. Edited with an introduction by *Jacques Barzun.* Farrar, Straus and Young, 1953.
Lord Byron: Christian Virtues. By G. *Wilson Knight.* Oxford University Press, 1953.

The argument about the relations between art and life has a long and frequently tedious history; the counterpositions can be arrived at by dialectic alone and the entire debate seen as a particular reflection of the general theme having to do with immanence and transcendence, man as nature and man as spirit opposed to nature. Once the debate is seen in this way it must also be seen as the subject not of solution but of choice, and the choice is always difficult; there is the golden mean, latterly called "honorable mediocrity," but perhaps for that very reason extreme positions become all the more appealing. The volumes here to be considered give us a choice of these choices, and put the general question very keenly in that neither volume is directly concerned with the poetry of Lord Byron, a knowledge and view of which is, however, assumed in one or another degree to illuminate and be illuminated by the life which is the immediate subject.

This approach has not recently been fashionable; neither has Byron's poetry, and I confess to having first gone about this review on some such line as "the return of Lord Byron"—only to discover that he had not, after all, been away: neither as a subject of study—of numerous authors writing on Byron during the past three decades I would particularly mention Harold Nicolson and Peter Quennell—nor as the emblem of an attitude deeply and pervasively influential upon life, nor as the image of a strange heroism in whose generation may be numbered such diverse figures as Stavrogin, Lafcadio, Tom

Reprinted by permission from *The Hudson Review*, Vol. VII, No. 2, Summer 1954. Copyright 1954 by *The Hudson Review, Inc.*

Swift, and Tony Last reading Dickens in Brazil. All that has been forgotten, then, is the poetry, which remained—for me as, I suspect, for many others—as a memory from childhood of "She walks in beauty" and an Assyrian coming down like a wolf, together with a blurred collegiate impression of hundreds of pages of small type in double column, a format which lumped together in one indistinguishable mass many poets of the nineteenth century. So that the preparation for this review took me back to the poetry, and especially to *Don Juan*, and took me not back but for the first time to the plays, especially *Sardanapalus* and *Marino Faliero*; and all this has been an impressive experience and a source of much pleasure. At the same time it becomes clear that the study of this extraordinary life, and the study (which is not the same thing) of "Byronism," ought not to rely to any very great extent on the representations of the poetry, certainly not on the earlier poems. Childe Harold, Manfred, Lara, the Corsair and the Giaour, represent the pure efficiency of an attitude which the life shows as existing in solution with a good deal else, much of it genial and much of it the stuff of very rueful comedy. The other side, characterized by Goethe as the side of *"empeiria* and *mondanité"* (dutifully elaborated by Eckermann: "the presence of a nefarious, empirical spirit"), also appears somewhat detached and purified in the poetry, in *Mazeppa, Beppo*, and *Don Juan*. The last cantos of *Don Juan*, the adventures in England, do seem to represent the fullest poetical expression of Byron's nature, but they do so digressively and at the expense of action, and the best of his poetry shows his mind acting against the institution of form. Yeats put this lucidly in *A Vision*, describing the man of the phase to which he assigned Byron: "He is doomed to attempt the destruction of all that breaks or encumbers personality, but this personality is conceived of as a fragmentary, momentary intensity."

Early ideas of Lord Byron begin with the poetry, which they directly translate into the life; of these ideas Mario Praz (*The Romantic Agony*) gives a summary and, to a surprising degree, an example. Though he demonstrates that the "Byronic hero" is not original with Byron but comes in every detail from *The Mysteries of Udolpho, The Monk*, and *Zeluco*, though he quotes, on the supposed incest of Byron and Augusta, the excellent warning, "on renonce à l'interpréter comme une confidence autobiographique, quand on sait de quelle abondante littérature elle n'est que le reflet littéraire," he nevertheless tends to see Byron as just such a Byronic hero, his necessity "le bonheur dans le crime. To destroy oneself and to destroy others." It is on such a view that the poet's career in England is exaggerated by earlier writers from recklessness into villainy with the aid of hints from the poetry, in order that the death at Missolonghi may be portrayed as a dramatic reversal and moral redemption, somewhat in the style of Sydney Carton.

It might be said that what modern writings on Byron chiefly add to this idea is detail; but that is not the mere addition of quantity, for the spirit of detail is the spirit of comedy, and the portrait that emerges is, without being less dramatic, less conventionalized, broader, more inclusive, and more individual—rather the novelistic than the poetic hero. Pattern, rhythm, are still reflected in this life, but criticized and given indirection no more by circumstances than by the poet's own extreme degree of irony and self-awareness. In modern biographies the *sins* of Lord Byron receive less emphasis, and his end is accordingly seen as an organic result of his character from the beginning; the drama turns on recognition rather than reversal. So Mr. Barzun writes that Byron's life is "the reverse of a tragedy . . . the flaws are not in the end obliterated, they are transcended" (though one must ask if this is not exactly the moral definition of tragedy), while G. Wilson Knight, not content with restoring the balance, goes to the other extreme, forms a counterimage to traditional Byronism, and sees a religious mystery capped by apotheosis.

Jacques Barzun's book makes available for the first time a selection of the Byron letters out of the six volumes of the *Letters and Journals* which form part of Lord Ernle's edition of *The Works of Lord Byron*, and out of the two additional volumes called *Byron's Correspondence*. This selection, which covers the whole of the poet's letter-writing days, beginning in fact with his tenth year, is so made as to give in reflection, indirectly, a continuous and fairly coherent impression of the events of Byron's life, but its chief value consists naturally in the continuous, informal, and detailed indication of personality and character.

Though the two people to whom his letters are most frequently addressed are his publisher John Murray and the poet Thomas Moore, Byron is seldom and only incidentally concerned with poetry—though what he does say makes one wish he had said more—and not much oftener with publication; Murray's fidelity as a correspondent appears to have been characteristically that of a publisher, and he had to be implored several times to "send the red tooth-powder by a *safe hand*

and speedily," as well as checked and rebuked on other scores: "I will have none of your cutting and slashing." Byron's letters are usually topical, anecdotal, descriptive; his descriptive powers, which constituted for him nearly the sole justification of his poems, the one ground on which he ever defended them, show up very well, whether he speaks simply as a traveler, as in the letter to his mother about Turkey, written in his twenty-first year, or as a strategist in military and political matters, as in various letters from Greece, where he also shows himself enormously capable in practical things, humorously discouraged, undeceived without being cynical: "Some of their bankers tried to make me pay interest for *my own money* in my *own possession*, which I came to spend, for their cause, too! . . . But 'I sorted them, I trow,' having the staff for the present in my own hands."

The impression that emerges from these letters is chiefly of courage, intelligence, humor, and generosity; also of loneliness, which makes him respond to bad situations with pride and obstinacy indeed, but always fairly, it seems, and with justification. His love of Italy, often expressed in detail, gives a tone of balance and solidity to his detestation of England and perhaps slightly theatrical feeling for the rôle of exile which is the only thing in the letters suggesting any resemblance in him to Manfred, Childe Harold, and the others. His remarks on poetry, casual as they are, and betraying his active and aristocratic contempt for "scribblers"—"the pen peeping from behind the ear, and the thumbs a little inky, or so"—strike one nevertheless as modest, penetrating, and full of concern for the art. He wrote to Moore of telling Hunt, about *Rimini*, "that I deemed it good poetry at bottom, disfigured only by a strange style. His answer was that his style was a system, or *upon system*, or some such cant; and when a man talks of system, his case is hopeless. . . ." But this was not decisively his view of the matter, and to Murray he expressed his conviction that "*all* of us—Scott, Southey, Wordsworth, Moore, Campbell, I,—are all in the wrong . . . that we are upon a wrong revolutionary poetical system, or systems, not worth a damn in itself . . . and that the present and next generations will finally be of this opinion. . . . I took Moore's poems and my own, and some others, and went over them side by side with Pope's, and I was really astonished (I ought not to have been so) and mortified at the ineffable distance in point of sense, harmony, effect, and even *Imagination*, passion and *Invention*, between the little Queen Anne's

Man, and us of the Lower Empire. Depend upon it, it is all Horace then, and Claudian now, among us; and if I had to begin again, I would model myself accordingly." And his assessment of his own career and quality, in a letter to Shelley in 1822, seems unusually exact as well as exacting:

> As long as I write the exaggerated nonsense which has corrupted the public taste, they applauded to the very echo, and, now that I have really composed, within these three or four years, some things which shd. "not willingly be let die," the whole herd snort and grumble and return to wallow in their mire. However, it is fit I shd. pay the penalty of spoiling them, as no man has contributed more than me in my earlier compositions to produce that exaggerated and false taste. It is a fit retribution that any really classical production shd. be received as these plays have been treated.

Mr. Barzun contributes to his selection of letters an introductory essay which is a model of sense, "Byron and the Byronic in History." Here he speaks of the reductive nature of "Byronism"—"one of the poet's fictional types has engrossed his name"—briefly describes the historical climate into which that fictional type was introduced, reminds us, as we need to be reminded, that Byron's reputation was not made by fools but by "the strongest, ablest minds" of his time, and points out that in the course of the nineteenth century "the figure of the mysterious evil-doer who is also the vindicator of justice draws to itself every important acquisition of psychology and social thought."

I think, myself, that Mr. Barzun is too sanguine in saying that the "psychic wound" of the modern artist "makes Byron's look like a scratch"—for after all there is some evidence that Byron did die of his—and that the Byronic image of freedom "ceased to have meaning . . . when the triumph of political democracy made group action possible and necessary, thereby dwarfing the value of the individual acts and rendering 'the hero' ridiculous." These judgments would strike me as simplistic in spirit even if I did not believe them wrong. But otherwise, in its description of the life, its assessment of the poetry and of certain factors standing between ourselves and the poetry, this essay is admirable.

Mr. Barzun contends that "the spectacle of such a life can only be called edifying—unless, as often happens, one confuses 'edifying' with 'blameless' and a great man with a saint." G. Wilson Knight, however, would not be satisfied to leave the matter at that; for him, Byron is "our greatest poet in the widest sense of the term since Shakespeare," and the greatness of the poetry, even so, is "outdistanced by Byron's importance as a man." Byron was "a living incarnation of a synthesis," "a third term" between "democratic conscience" and "aristocratic valuations"; finally, covering as man and poet "the whole gamut of Shakespearian passion and Shakespearian humour," he is "what might be defined as the next Promethean man in Western history after Christ."

Mr. Knight has already written an essay about Byron's poetry in *The Burning Oracle,* and about his plays in an article in the *Times Literary Supplement* (3 February, 1950). The present book, *Lord Byron: Christian Virtues,* deals directly with the life, and "is conceived as a trilogy on Byron as man and poet." The book is an unusual sort of biography, "less the story of a life than a mosaic of evidence regarding *qualities,* both the art and the argument lying rather in selection and structure than in any explicit deductions." The method, the "technique of 'spatial' analysis," "involves the massed use of materials wrenched boldly from their habitual associations and grouped about various new centres of interest, often with little or no emphasis on the temporal succession from which they have been removed; thereby being loosed from the trammels of false biographical or narrative accretion to be seen afresh *as themselves*; or, to use a famous phrase, they stand *sub specie aeternitatis.*" This method will be recognized as the same that Mr. Knight has applied with such success to the Plays of Shakespeare, and, more recently, to other works.

Now I have always had the greatest admiration for the essays of Wilson Knight, and particularly those about the Plays; his style of interpretation, sensitive and vastly patient, seems to be precisely that which a good artist would hope for, not without trembling, from his reader, and which a bad artist ought to shun like the face of truth. Still, I am puzzled by this essay in biography, so difficult to read chiefly on account of "the massed use of materials" which caused the text to be constantly broken up by notes of reference, but so worth reading, so fascinating in its easy authority over an immense range of detail. So nearly convincing, too, and if finally I must disagree it is not because the position is an extreme one, for extreme or not it is extremely well supported, but rather because I differ with Mr. Knight in some basic assumptions about the connections of art and life, so that I felt constantly and uncomfortably at odds with the book even while acknowledging the skill of the argument.

"There is something non-temporal about his story," writes Mr. Knight, "his end is implicit in his beginning; and *he therefore lends himself uniquely to the spatial approach.*" (Italics mine.) There follows a comparison linking Byron with Hamlet, Macbeth, and Timon. Elsewhere we have the same dramatic, aesthetic emphasis: "He felt his life as a pattern, and tried to adjust himself to that pattern." "Teresa saw Byron as a being having attained 'perfection,' and for that reason removed from earth by a death suited to his virtues. . . . Whether or not we agree, we can see Byron's death as the perfect completion to an interesting pattern of events." That "whether or not we agree" does not appear to leave much room for disagreement.

But if Byron was "a man in whom poetry became incarnate," if he was "Shakespearian drama personified," if he was also "greater than Napoleon," his intellect "Promethean rather than Napoleonic," then I must ask what was Shakespeare as a man? Or what was Napoleon as a poet? I think Mr. Knight has deliberately run together the poetry and the life and argued unjustifiably from one to the other, overpraising the poetry for the poet's "vitality," deifying the life as perfected poem: "he 'repaid' the Promethean flame to heaven not alone by words, by art, but pre-eminently by his life, and death; and the statue he moulded of its fire was, quite simply, himself." I don't find the matter that simple; Byron's life has, indeed, like most, hints of dramatic pattern, poetic order, some of these hints amply dramatized by the poet himself (the prophecy of Mrs. Williams, the Cheltenham fortuneteller, that he was to beware of his thirty-seventh year), and it is to some extent fair to say that at Missolonghi he did "live out and harmonize the most agonizing dualisms of Western civilization," though to the extent that it is fair it is also not unique or even very distinctive; but Mr. Knight ritually exalts this life at great expense to the grotesque and ludicrous side of the matter (of which Byron was acutely conscious), keen attention to which makes Harold Nicolson's *Byron: The Last Journey* so completely convincing. To a more secular view than Mr. Knight is willing to take, there is an overwhelming air of comic fiasco about the Greek venture, and it is this, not tragedy and not martyrdom, which gives it poignancy and pathos, and makes Byron's life a parable to us: the ironic spirit, laden with prophecies and dark valuations, grossly cancelled by accident, confusion, inefficiency, the mere recalcitrance which life always displays against the prospect of becoming literature. Nicolson quotes an indignant speech of Parry's against the doctors who attended on Byron in his last illness; and this, also by no means the whole truth or even a satisfactory half, is a tone constantly affecting the picture, which Mr. Knight somewhat neglects:

> Had he turned them out of doors, and returned to the habit of an English gentleman as to his diet, he would probably have survived many years, to have vindicated with his sword the wrongs of his beloved Greece, and to have heaped contempt on those pretended friends who, since his death, have vilified his glorious nature, because he could or would not believe that a lithographic press, Mr. Bentham's minute legislation, and conning over the alphabet, were the proper and most efficacious means of giving freedom and independence to that suffering and oppressed country.

This somewhat inflated tone, pompous and righteous, like that of a confidence man being straightforward, is as far from Byron's own tone as could be; yet it is constantly heard in his neighborhood, and one wonders if, after all, his presence brought out something exaggerated and false in those around him.

As for Byron's being "our greatest poet in the widest sense of the term since Shakespeare," I think Mr. Knight has confused the issues again, and this should sort out into 'a person so like a Shakespearian hero ought to be, if he writes, a Shakespearian poet.' I would tentatively mention Wordsworth and "the little Queen Anne's man," but Mr. Knight, by the phrase "in the widest sense of the term," has put this matter pretty much beyond the possibility of being argued about.

The Muse's Interest

Talking to fellow union members has its possibly embarrassing side: one doesn't want to go all mouthy before an audience professionally concerned with mouthing. But it also makes possible a certain brevity; we needn't spell everything out.

First, I should like to recall the beginning of our wanting to be poets, when something whether decisively or diffusely happened between the self and a something already existing, called poetry. Of course, I am the principal butt of these perhaps inaccurate recollections, and if I speak as though what happened with me happened in much the same way with you, well, if the glass slipper pinches, you needn't marry the prince.

The myth about our vocation said that the young person, discovering within himself a message of the utmost importance, acknowledged his duty and set about imparting that message to humanity, which badly needed it. He might or might not make the concession of chopping the message up into convenient lengths with like sounds at their latter ends; for the essence was, in a then famous phrase, "having something to say to people." According to the myth, there would then be no question of people's failing or refusing to listen; in fact, the relation worked backwards, in practice, much better than forwards, so that the undoubted fact of people's not listening became a proof of your not having anything to say to people. Instead, as you quite well remember, you were "an intellectual" and "deliberately obscure"; you had immured yourself in "an ivory tower," and for all the world cared you could die there.

I mention this myth only to remind you what it was we already knew better than. The reality was composed of elements both more and less pretty, as well as more problematic in the compound: vanity, opportunism, snobbery, and preciosity; idealism, hero-worship,

This essay was given at the National Poetry Festival at the Library of Congress, October 23, 1962.

love for a few poems and one or two poets, and a feeling which could be vaguely thought of as religious; also the technical side: imitation, technical learning, a beginner's virtuosity, the doing of a thing because you, sort of, could.

The vanity was immense. Your most facile imitative gesture became, only because you had made it, beautiful. In serious discussions late at night you and your friends conceded to one another that the best of your own productions ranked rather high in the eternal hit parade: modestly just below *The Phoenix and the Turtle*, but well above the *Ode to the West Wind*, which I remember your regarding as too sentimental.

But this vanity, though immense, was not quite monstrous, first because it really referred to your shy hopes, to what you would be rather than what you were, and then because it had no particular regard for a real world, for what we call the public. It was, indeed, part of the pride of your novitiate not to care for "the public," and you were able to look somewhat snootily at poets who had degraded themselves by suffering popularity, a danger you correctly believed you would not have to worry about for a while yet. Your approximation to a public at this time consisted of samples from four small classes: girls, friends, teachers, and the great masters living and dead whom you imagined as sneering, not without a certain respectful condescension, over your shoulder as you rimed, maybe, "jade" with "lewd."

Yet your attitude at that time was appropriate; like Job up to a certain point, you sinned not with your mouth. Given the silliness of trying to be a poet in the first place, you kept the silliness close to home. Your behavior did acknowledge the existence of a sort of stuff called poetry, which you would not have had the wit to invent by yourself; and your relation with it held equally in conformity and revolt—when you wrote sonnets because The Sonnet existed, and when you refused to write sonnets, because The Sonnet existed.

And many years passed. Now you are, within the civil meaning of the term, a poet, and you have a, sort of, public. It is not much of a public, and beyond that you don't get to know much about it. Once in a while someone writes a letter to say that he likes your poetry; such a letter will be, rarely, from another poet, but most often from a person whose epistolary behavior suggests he is a pretty odd type in other ways besides his taste in literature; sometimes the two classes overlap. And it may come to seem that the public for poetry might be somewhat ruthlessly defined by two conditions:

1. Almost no one reads poetry who does not also write it.
2. Many people who write poetry evidently do not read it.

These limiting conditions do not absolutely state that the audience for poetry is a very small one; it may be quite large. Years ago I heard it estimated at six million persons in America alone, by an organization which proposed, for a subscription of three dollars a head, to eternize all six million names on a bronze plaque in Washington. What they were going to do with the rest of the money I don't remember; maybe raise a Poetry National Guard.

But whatever the size of this audience, it doesn't seem to have the character of a public, much less of The Public. Except for such moments of definition as a class reading a poem, or an audience listening to a poem, the audience for poetry is counted by one and one and one; if the poem were read by several million people instead of several hundred, nothing of that would change. Nor do I find any great injustice here, for a reckonable part of the charm of lyric poetry has to do with its subversiveness, and this subversiveness depends upon a certain quiet in the surrounding air, as well as in the poem itself.

Not having much of a public, and being of necessity only faintly and by indirection aware of the character of what public he does have, the poet is in no position to say much about what this relation might be, or ideally ought to be. Certainly he is in no position to consider the public when he writes his poems.

So it is fair for people to ask: Are you serious? Is poetry serious? What does it mean to accomplish, or what do you mean to accomplish by doing poetry? Or is it merely a civilized amusement?

My response has several parts. One is rueful. Alas, yes, a vast deal of poetry is merely a civilized amusement. Too bad. Another is defensive. I do not think my own efforts in the art raise such barriers of intellect, learning, subtlety, as would defeat the well-intentioned effort of any ordinarily literate person to read what I produce. And I do have a few readers; I hope they are happy.

A third part of the response needs to be more elaborately put. As a poet, which is to say when I am writing poetry, I am not much aware of anything beyond the demands of the theme; which are demanding enough.

I do not mean you to infer from this any particular greatness of soul in myself; that the poet may in fact be an inferior soul altogether is an occupational hazard. I mean only that when something comes to you to be dealt with according to such skill and energy as you may have to give it, you give it what you have; which may not be much, or nearly enough, but excludes for the time all thought of whether it will be acceptable to "the public"—an entity, I repeat, of which poets have very little opportunity of forming an image.

The poet hopes to articulate a vision concerning human life; he hopes to articulate it truly. He may not be much of a poet, he may not be much of a human being, the vision perhaps is not so special either; but it is what he hopes to do. I stress his *hoping* to do so because much of the available evidence tells us that his effective control in the matter, his conscious will to do all this, may make no difference whatever, or none but a technical and executive difference —which I don't mean to slight, as it is not negligible, but it is not what I am talking about now.

This 'vision' need not be thought of in religious terms, as a dramatic one-shot on the road to Damascus; its articulation may be slow indeed, and spread over many works; the early and late parts of it may elucidate one another, or encipher one another still more deeply.

This is so, according to the belief of poets, because such a vision is itself alone, and really has no other verbal equivalent, so that it cannot be reached by translation from a more abstract and rationally amenable language. A fine description is given by Antony, the vision being disguised as a crocodile:

> It is shaped, sir, like itself; and it is as broad as it hath breadth. It is just so high as it is, and moves with it own organs. It lives by that which nourisheth it; and the elements once out of it, it transmigrates,

&c., ending with the information that it is a strange serpent, and the tears of it are wet.

For the substance of this vision the poet listens, he watches, and when he speaks in his character of poet it is his conviction, possibly his illusion, that something other speaks in him. Even the illusion that such a thing is happening, or might happen, makes of writing poetry a very great privilege; as I need not remind an audience of poets, though I may make a note of it for the many people who at any given time are making the same attempt for just that reason, that poetry is a privileged activity, conferring a view of freedom on whoever tries—even when it doesn't work, perhaps especially when it doesn't work. So if we incline to complain over the want of a large public it might reasonably if rudely be said to us, as it used to be said in the air force, Nobody drafted you, you volunteered.

All this does not in the least mean that poetry relinquishes its large claim on the world, its claim to teach the world, its prophetic claim on the ultimate realization of all possibility. For the whole business of poetry is vision, and the substance of this vision is the articulating possibilities still unknown, the concentrating what is diffuse, the bringing forth what is in darkness.

In one way, the public for poetry is made of multitudes, of generations, incalculably transformed by the stuff, often without having read it. A new inflection of the voice may be the seed of new mind, new character, and many persons still to be born will enact in their lives the poet's word. Ours is a power the more immense for not being directed to a specific or immediate end other than the poem itself.

On this ceremonious occasion I may appropriately choose a most exalted illustration. In bringing forth upon the world the character of Hamlet and his play, Shakespeare had no object we know of other than writing *Hamlet*. Presumably there was something for him diagnostic in his identification of this character; that is, it concentrated a vision of the human somehow implicit in his own life, in the lives he saw around him; from elements in solution the poet precipitated out the solid of a figure strange and new, yet recognizable. But in his poetic act there was also something prophetic and world-transforming, some magnetic claim which far into the future drew (and draws) human character to itself, in such improbable variations and resolutions as Byron, Coleridge, Stendhal, Dostoevski. . . .

This thing that poetry does, this opening of the ways, is visible not alone in the supreme dramatic example, but wherever a poet illuminates human consciousness, or the consciousness of being human, which he does, perhaps, more by his way of speaking than by the morality or general truth of what it is he says.

So poetry does exert a power in the realm of reality, and in this sense does have a public. But its power is, as I have said, subversive, in that it is unpredictable and beyond control or purposive application to the immediate situation; without meaning to, perhaps without especially wanting to, poetry changes the mind of the world.

This power does not belong to the poet personally, and its exercise will most likely do him no worldly good; nor will it achieve for his society that limited, predictable good which is always being asked of poetry by modern society, but which really belongs to the Ministry of Propaganda and Culture.

We may suppose a society in which the poet is fortunate enough, blessed enough, to be rewarded by the serious attention, even the love, of a large number of his fellows; yet there would remain for him the question beyond, of a further opening of the ways:

> Everything he wrote was read,
> After certain years he won
> Sufficient money for his need,
> Friends that have been friends indeed;
> "What then?" sang Plato's ghost. "What then?"

And we may suppose that a serious approximation to such a society has historically existed, in Periclean Athens, Elizabethan England—reminding ourselves that those great flarings of genius not necessarily saved anyone, not Euripedes from exile, Marlowe from early death, any more than the presence of Sophocles, either on the stage as a poet or in the field as a commander, saved Athens from ruinous folly. The Muse's interest is chiefly in matters of life and death, true, but it is not a practical interest. Though our transcription of her will often enough admits such impurities as platitudes, admonitions, and sententious remarks, her interest remains distant and speculative, coldly smiling while full of sorrow. We write, at last, because life is hopeless and beautiful.

The Poet and the Copy-Writer: A Dialogue

OSRIC, a poet
OSWALD, an advertising man

OSRIC: My hair is falling out, and no one reads my poems.

OSWALD: My liver is bad, and everyone reads my ads.

OSRIC: Alas, I am marginal to the economy.

OSWALD: Alas, I am central to the economy.

OSRIC: Of course, you had to sell your soul.

OSWALD: And you were unable to sell yours; perhaps I could write you an ad? Soul, used but in fair condition, one owner, careful treatment, radio and heater. . . .

OSRIC: . . . spine damaged and binding slightly foxed. I know, I know. Lost, one bard. Small reward. Sentimental value. Or else. . . .

OSWALD: I can see you'd enjoy writing ads once you began. And I'd like to write poems, too, if only they had something definite to sell in them, instead of just truth and beauty, beauty and truth.

OSRIC: The idea that poems consist of beauty and truth is a common fallacy which Criticism has dispelled. You are still, perhaps, in the nineteenth century.

OSWALD: You mean that your poems have neither beauty nor truth?

OSRIC: Oh, well, if you want to make it a personal matter . . . I suppose they do, somewhat.

OSWALD: But you can't sell beauty and truth, either because they're free and everyone has all he needs of them, or because no one can afford them any more at all. With soap and gas

Reprinted by permission from *The Nation*, Vol. 183, No. 19, November 10, 1956. Copyright 1956 by The Nation Associates, Inc.

and brassières, though, you know where you are. It concentrates the language.

OSRIC: It does *not* concentrate the language. I think your ads are getting more obscure every day, and if it weren't for the manufacturer's name at the bottom I wouldn't know whether you were discussing soap flakes or democracy.

OSWALD: Well, you know, we do like to put one in terms of the other.

OSRIC: In terms of, in terms of. If I hear that stupid phrase again I'll scream. Everyone uses it now. I heard a fashionable young woman say the other day, "I choose my lipstick in terms of my complexion."

OSWALD: Well, you know, it sounds kind of scientific, and everyone likes that.

OSRIC: It sounds poetical—dirty rotten poetical.

OSWALD: Why do you call yourself a poet if you hate whatever is poetical?

OSRIC: Because whatever is poetical, baby, belongs to you. If you keep telling women that without underarm perspiration they will immediately resemble Venus by Botticelli, then I must give up Venus by Botticelli.

OSWALD: But in exchange you get underarm perspiration.

OSRIC: Yes . . . yes, there's a subject you haven't ruined: sweat, shame, secrecy, hypocrisy. . . .

OSWALD: Go on, you might exude an ode.

OSRIC: Armpits! The smoky armpits of the world.

OSWALD: Yes, I envy you your freedom to deal with the seamy side of life. But it makes you rather coarse in your rhetoric, where we should be delicate.

OSRIC: Yah, your delicacy. Sneaky minginess. But you have hit on a real point there: freedom. Poets may be poor, but they are free. A copy-writer is nothing but a slave.

OSWALD: Ah, yes, that precious freedom. Vergil's freedom to laud Augustus, Tennyson's freedom to admire railroads, Dryden's freedom to adore the smallpox sores on Lord Hastings' chin.

OSRIC: There may have been abuses.

OSWALD: Then never mind the abuses. What about the Great Tradition itself—the centuries of edifying, instructing, bringing virtue out on top, purveying manners and morals to the great unwashed masses? What about "purifying the language of the tribe"? I may be a servile copy-writer, but I think it more honorable to sell people soap than to sell them Cleanliness.

OSRIC: How could you sell them soap if we hadn't sold them cleanliness for all those centuries?

OSWALD: So, you admit we're in the same business!

OSRIC: Nonsense. You deal in Things, material commodities, whereas I deal in spiritual values.

OSWALD: Meaning that you insist on Cleanliness without providing soap?

OSRIC: Yes, dammit, I do. Spiritual cleanliness.

OSWALD: With spiritual soap? Soft soap. As a matter of fact, though, it is the poets who are always talking about Things, and the advertisers who deal in spiritual values. "Roses have thorns, and silver fountains mud." Look at all the Things in one quite ordinary line of poetry. We advertisers, of course, would want to dress the whole proposition up a bit: "You wouldn't dream of having mud in your silver fountain—why have thorns on your roses?"

OSRIC: And there in your other hand, all the while, would be a new, patent rose-depilatory.

OSWALD: Quite likely there would. And what would be wrong with thornless roses?

OSRIC: Everything. The morality of the Western world has depended for centuries on the fact that roses have thorns.

OSWALD: And look at the shape the Western world is in now. No, my friend, I tell you—in confidence—that you poets have had your chance and you're through. The future of poetry, I'm afraid, is with advertising.

OSRIC: That's perhaps the funniest thing I've ever heard said. If it weren't, I'd put my head in the oven.

OSWALD: You'll want to try one of our new, fully automatic, self-regulating ovens. You can leave your head in it while you go out, and when you return. . . . Seriously, though, you're through. Poetry is done for, and advertising is the only hope.

OSRIC: But quite apart from one million other possible objections, your advertisements are so terribly dull.

OSWALD: I agree, I agree—though if it comes to that what about *The Faërie Queene?* But ever so many people seem to disagree. At least, they read advertisements every day and practically never read poetry. That's true even of some poets I know, but never mind that just now. The point is, that in almost any magazine you look at the advertisements take far more space than the stories, poems, articles, editorials—than all the stuff we may broadly call Poetry. Not only that, but the advertisements—dull as they are, and I agree they are dull—are frequently more interesting than the poetry.

OSRIC: Yah, it's because they have pictures.

OSWALD: It is *not* because they have pictures. If you weren't prejudiced, you'd allow that the pictures are, if anything, worse than the prose.

OSRIC: I see you call it prose, not poetry.

OSWALD: A feeble defense. Is poetry like *Moby Dick* and *Urn Burial?* Or is it more like the nearest available sonnet by a lady with three names?

OSRIC: I concede the point.

OSWALD: Then if you'll be quiet for a minute or so, I'll try to explain the present position as we in advertising understand it.

OSRIC: Very well, go ahead.

OSWALD: Now formerly, until not so long ago, buying and selling, and everything we mean by *business*, were considered not to be occupations for a gentleman; they were reprehensible, necessary but suspect, and all the better people pretended that such things didn't happen at all. The reason for this, we find when we go back in the tradition, was that the gentleman's occupations had always been conceived of simply as love and war. Poetry, too, for this reason, and because it was read largely by gentlemen, concerned itself with love and war. And what happened then?

OSRIC: You're telling me, I'm not telling you. Go on.

OSWALD: Buying and selling, because they were necessary, finally became gentlemanly, until now, at the present time, it is believed that these precisely, and especially if conducted on a very grand scale, are fit occupations for a gentleman

—if only because a gentleman must have money, and there is practically no other way of ensuring a steady supply. So buying and selling have become respectable, and, more important than that, they are rapidly becoming total, and soon, if the present trend continues (which it will), they will become absolutely the form of morality.

OSRIC: And what a morality. I spit.

OSWALD: That is a very poetical attitude you take. And I observe that, like a true poet, you say "I spit" but you don't spit; a world of significance there. And poetry, indeed, was the last human discipline to be left standing helplessly on the untenable platform which the gentleman himself had deserted a long time before. Poetry was still dreaming of its magical kings and gentle heroes while the real gentleman, having seen the shape of things to come, was out in the market place buying and selling as fast as he could.

OSRIC: But things have always been that way. You are deluded with the delusion of those *esprits simplistes* who fancy that Elizabeth and Essex, Drake and Hawkins, habitually talked iambic pentameter and sounded like Desdemona and Macbeth. But I'm willing to skip that if you'll only stop your half-baked theorizing about history and come to the point: what about advertising?

OSWALD: For all practical purposes you could put it this way: that the gentleman, who were accustomed to having poets celebrate their doings, simply hired a new lot of poets when they saw that the old poets wouldn't celebrate. The new poets were pretty awful; not only were they untrained and without competence in a difficult art, but also they were set to work inventing a new kind of poetry to suit the age, since the real poets had refused to bother with the age. As to what you say about history, I'll admit, of course, that the thing didn't happen in the way I have described, being a process largely unconscious and a response to more immediate pressures; but in effect, as we can see now, it might as well have happened that way, since there now exists a new class of poets writing a new kind of poetry called advertising. They are doing it on the whole very badly still, I admit that, but getting better, getting better.

OSRIC: Ingenious enough, and interesting. But how can you "get better" at selling, say, cigarettes? Doesn't the product, in its ineffable dreariness, impose a very low ceiling on your lyrical flights?

OSWALD: I may remind you here that you and your critical colleagues have been telling us for years that subject is of no importance, while imagination is everything. Granted imagination enough, a fine poem may be produced upon a trivial or disgusting subject—isn't that how the old critical song has been going? At any rate, your belief about the true nature of advertising is quite as naïve as my belief that poetry has something to do with the true and the beautiful. Do you seriously still believe that advertising is primarily interested in *selling things?*

OSRIC: I had heard it mentioned now and again.

OSWALD: It is a vulgar error of the age. The kind of advertising you must mean still exists, of course, in great quantities—people selling one another souvenir salt shakers, bronzed baby shoes, rupture appliances, holy water in plastic tears, and so on up the line to liqueurs and luggage and limousines. But that is advertising directed at the consumer, and compares with real advertising as limericks do with iliads. Major modern advertising, like your major modern poetry, goes right over the heads of the private consumers to begin with, and straight to the elite. How many readers of a news magazine, for instance, are really listening when the ball-bearing manufacturer spreads over a full page his delicate mating call to the maker of aircraft? Of those who hear, how many understand? Of those who understand, how many are in a position to do anything with what they understand? Or when a utilities company expounds for two whole pages the strong and subtle bond of metaphor that connects utilities with democracy, what has that to do with your private citizen? No, such advertisements are as privileged as private correspondence, as secure as messages in cipher, as haughty in their doings as any poetry.

OSRIC: But still selling things, really, aren't they?

OSWALD: You're still not altogether clear about the vast differences separating major and revolutionary advertising from the rest. You're still thinking about mere material commodities—it doesn't matter whether they are corsets or rocket planes—while I want you to lift up your mind to spiritual things, that is, to the Way of Life, the Truth and Beauty which make buying and selling possible. For example, we used to sell refrigerators; but now we have realized that if we sell the Way of Life, refrigerators will follow in great plenty—and I will go further than that. . . .

OSRIC: I am afraid you will.

OSWALD: Please treat this as a confidence, will you? What I am about to describe has not yet come to pass. Presently, you see, we shall have double-crossed the manufacturers along with everyone else.

OSRIC: We?

OSWALD: We of the advertising world. They thought they were making use of us, did all those small-minded *practical* men, when all the while we were making use of them, trying our wings until we should be ready to fly away. Who will care, then, if they never sell another refrigerator? Advertising, which began as practical magic, now becomes spiritual and contemplative, autonomous magic, having its end in itself, just as poetry, which you will agree began as practical magic, with curses and charms and casting of spells, at last became spiritual and contemplative and by definition impractical, and turned inward upon itself. Advertising has mirrored itself long enough in the material world of commerce and production, and now begins to turn inward to contemplation—

OSRIC: Staring at its own soft center.

OSWALD: Go on, laugh while you yet may. But the thing is clearly happening. I foresee the time—for advertising men, you see, are vaticinators now, just as poets used to be said to be—I foresee the time, not far in the future, when advertisement will have driven all editorial content from magazine and newspaper. As various heavy industries combine, and as all heavy industry combines with government, all human relations will be expressible as buying and selling—

OSRIC: But I thought you said . . . ?

OSWALD: There's no contradiction. When all human relations are expressible in market values, as buying and selling, there will be no need to talk about buying and selling, since that language will look as natural then as the language of traditional morality does now—that is what I meant when I said that buying and selling would become the very form of morality. In the same way, when advertising becomes the total content of human communication, as you will allow it is very near to doing already, there will be no need to use the somewhat pejorative word "advertising," since this activity need no longer be defined against other modes of speech, which simply will have ceased to exist. Moreover, on account of the very complex co-ordination of interests as between industries themselves on the one hand, and industry and political power and armed force and education on the other, the advertising writer will develop a much greater freedom in his point of view, simply because everything will be, to the ordinary reader, so dreadfully mixed up.

OSRIC: Quite as usual, in other words. You claim to be describing the future, but as you speak I keep seeing the present. What about this "ordinary reader," by the way—the people, as distinct from those who are so mighty in the buying and selling which you define as the essence of society to come?

OSWALD: The people? I hate to say it, because I'm as good an American as yourself, but I imagine some condition of light and not very unpleasant servitude will be found for the people. They must, of course, continue to buy and sell, and as they are for the most part already convinced that in buying and selling consists the true meaning of earthly life, I imagine they will have little hardship in adjusting to the last turns of the vise. And their priests, as usual, will assist them in the perception that it is all somehow right and necessary. Their God has been made over in the image of a great businessman; well, now He will become a great advertising man.

OSRIC: In the end will be the Word, is that it?

OSWALD: Very poetically and aptly put.

OSRIC: You make it very clear. As the private interest covers the public interest, as the line between advertising and propaganda becomes indistinct, and both discover ever more *recherché* ways of skinning their cats, advertising will become, for one thing, less imperative and more simply declarative, less urgent and more leisured, less hortatory and more contemplative.

OSWALD: Like poetry.

OSRIC: Yes, and I think I see further than that. There will develop an advertising class, or caste, with hereditary succession, as distinct as the class of scribes in ancient Egypt or China, and this class will have altogether in its hands the composition of odes describing, in a highly specialized way, the mysterious connections on which subsists the mystical body of society: the sinews of metaphor uniting, for example, the university with the debutante with the railroad with contraception with the concrete mixer with high tariffs with race prejudice with universities with debutantes. . . .

OSWALD: Stop, you are being carried away. But yes, that is more or less the way it will work out, though I suppose we shall not live to see it.

OSRIC: Being a vaticinator in my turn, and one, moreover, who is only wise after the event, I will tell you that we are already seeing it. Of course, even when your victory is complete, your stuff will always be deficient as poetry because it will have no real—that is, unsubidized—acknowledgment of evil. But that will not be noticed, because all genuine poetry will by that time have disappeared.

OSWALD: Ah, you *genuine* poets are proud. On that day, your heads will be the first to fall.

OSRIC: Our heads will have shriveled long before that day comes.

OSWALD: If you would abandon your pride and save yourself, I might be able to find an opening for you with us. We can always use a man who has your skill with words. And you could write your poetry on the side, evenings and week ends.

OSRIC: Thank you ever so much. But really, and it's no matter of pride. I can't believe I'd be talented enough for your kind of work.

OSWALD: Oh, we'd start you off in a small way, of course. But after an apprenticeship on frozen foods and sanitary napkins —what we in the trade think of as the hot-point and cold-spot of it—you'd go quickly up the ladder, I'm sure of it, a man of your brillance and sincerity and warmth of feeling. It's only a matter of learning to apply those fine human qualities to new objects. After all, as one of your own poets said at the very beginning of his career, "Words alone are certain good." And at the end of that career he also said, speaking directly to poets, "Sing whatever is well made." Cigarettes these days are very well made.

OSRIC: For a man in your line of work, you seem to know an awful lot of poetry.

OSWALD: Ah, my dear man, that is my little secret. I was one of you once, but that is a long time ago. "Who would not sing for Lycidas? he knew / Himself to sing and build the lofty rhyme." Except I didn't, really, or not very well. But I'm certain you'd like it very well with us, we're not at all the vulgar, uncultivated boors that legend makes us out to be; most of the finest minds in the business belong to men who, like myself, started out to be poets. And, of course, as our work has so much to do with truth and beauty, we keep ourselves in shape by much reading, and visits to art galleries.

OSRIC: Sounds a very gloomy life to me. Art galleries remind me of undertakers' parlors, and I very rarely read books. When I hear the word "culture," I take a drink and the feeling passes.

OSWALD: You know, I still write a little from time to time, though I don't like to mention it around the office. I was wondering if maybe you might look over some of my stuff some day, and tell me if you think it's good enough.

OSRIC: Good enough for what?

OSWALD: To publish, I guess, what else?

OSRIC: But I'm not a publisher.

OSWALD: No, you're a snob, that's what you are. You're sneering at my poems without even reading them.

OSRIC: I don't deny being a snob, even my mother used to tell me I was. It doesn't really matter. But I'm not trying to stop you from writing poems, am I? Whereas all that you were saying a while ago indicated that your activities would presently stop me from writing poems, which you seemed to think a perfectly happy result. I'll tell you what, suppose instead of reading your poems I read your ads? Is that fair enough?

OSWALD: No, it's not. No wonder the world doesn't care for your verse, since you persist in that snide attitude of yours. Suppose just for the sake of argument that my poetry turns out to be absolutely wonderful, that I really have something to say to the world? What then?

OSRIC: I'm supposing as hard as I can. Why don't you say it, in that case? And I'll read your poems, if you care that much.

OSWALD: Don't imagine I'm afraid of any criticism you might make. After all, my poems are only a hobby, and not important, I am well aware of that.

OSRIC: Do you see that bird over there?

OSWALD: Certainly. It's only a robin.

OSRIC: Just so. And do you know that though it has been called a robin in English for so many centuries, that bird is so stupid it still doesn't know it is a robin?

OSWALD: What are you driving at?

OSRIC: That is the meaning of poetry.

OSWALD: You're only trying to puzzle me, you think it's a smart thing to do.

OSRIC: I will make my meaning clearer in a parable about poets and poetry, which I made up a long time ago, at a very bad time in my life when I thought that one ought not to do anything without having a clear idea of what it was for. This parable has sometimes comforted me in some odd manner, and perhaps it may do the same for you.

OSWALD: Come on, then, get to it.

OSRIC: It is a parable about the monkish medieval poet Caedmon. Caedmon, a stupid man by nature, became a poet by divine visitation in sleep; waking, he found he could remember quite well the verses to the glory of the Creator which he had been inspired to sing the night before, and he wrote them down. He spent the rest of his life versifying passages from Scripture, which others had translated for him—the Exodus from Egypt, the Passion of Christ, and so on. Now, concerning all these things, which the present taste does not even find very beautiful, scholars now believe, first, that they were not written by Caedmon; second, that nothing from his hand has come down to us, and third, that no such person, it may be, ever lived. What remains, then? Poets ought to consider it well. There remains only the voice in the night: "Caedmon . . . sing the beginning of created things."

OSWALD: I'll tell you what your trouble is. You not only don't communicate to an ordinary man like me, but you don't even want to communicate, that's your trouble, and so far as I'm concerned you can go die for it.

OSRIC: But there's more truth than poetry in that.

The Dream of Reason

Many people of more or less my age, having done their forty years in the wilderness and grown somewhat at home there, show signs of regret and even, occasionally, resentment about entering the promised land of science, that ambiguous utopia which is acceptable only as each day's tomorrow. We were much influenced in earlier years by Aldous Huxley's *Brave New World*, in which the proposition was (perhaps for the last time) seriously stated that Shakespeare was not merely preferable but also antithetical to planned parenthood; it was somewhere between our matriculation and our enlistment that the mad scientist came from the comic strip bearing his death rays, incendiary bats, and apocalyptic powders, and the world settled for a career in science fiction. I am being unjust to the scientists among us, but never mind; for the existence of people of my age proves only that in the matter of planned obsolescence Nature was ahead even of General Motors. When I hear that "science says" or "scientists tell us," I still see that serious, white-coated individual frowning from the car cards of the IRT and making nasty statements about the condition of my gums (perfectly true, they were in terrible shape) as a means to purveying his now vanished tooth powder.

The world has gone a long way since then, and I don't know if I came along. The technical pronouncements of scientists about their various trades are frequently quite incomprehensible to me, and even resemble mystical revelations or metaphysical poems (all that about anti-matter, for example), while the non-technical pronouncements of scientists upon the more generally human concerns of religion, culture, civilization—the future—have sometimes an air of strange and only half-intentional comedy: Archimago the guileful great enchanter as he might be if *The Faërie Queene* were done by Walt Disney, which God forbid.

Reprinted by permission from *Bennington College Bulletin—Alumnae Issue*, Vol. 28, No. 3, February 1960. This article, in shorter form, first appeared in *The Reporter*, February 14, 1960.

The Darwin Centennial as celebrated at the University of Chicago brought together forty-seven leading biologists and geneticists who, according to William L. Laurence in the *New York Times*, "dealt with all the fundamental questions to which the theory of evolution gave new meaning. How did life begin? What happened before it started? Is the evolution of man completed? Does evolution necessarily mean progress? How did man develop mind? Where did society come from? How does culture shape the future? Is there evolution outside the earth? What is man's fate?"

All these questions, and perhaps especially the last, are of some interest also to the non-scientist, or would be if he were able to understand the answers, and I should like to comment here on "one of the most provocative presentations" of the Centennial, the remarks of Professor Hermann J. Muller, Nobel Prize-winning geneticist. My description of these is drawn from the account given by Mr. Laurence (Science in Review: "A Century After Darwin, a Geneticist Foresees Guided Human Evolution") in the *New York Times* for Sunday, November 29, 1959. It will be sufficiently plain that I am not speaking as a scientist, but perhaps I ought to add that my criticisms have no intention of impugning Professor Muller's scientific work, or his high standing in his own mystery.

Professor Muller's thesis is that evolution has been blind through billions of years, but need no longer be so. "From now on, evolution is what we make it, provided that we choose the true and the good. Otherwise we shall sink back into oblivion."

This is delphic enough to raise doubts: one might think that, given the technical means to transform the biological future, evolution would be what we made it whether we chose the true and the good or the false and the evil. As to sinking back into oblivion, it is unhappily not hard to imagine a clan of sages, with refrigerated genes in either hand, deciding that this was a human condition profoundly to be desired, as against the life of conscience and anxiety, and acting accordingly, so that our descendants would browse on salads in the fields, like Nebuchadnezzar. The power of meddling in the future, as many mythologies will show, is a double and dubious one; the fairy godmother appears at the chistening and says of the child, "He may have one Freudian wish."

Still, all moral action is a means of meddling with the future (though none heretofore, unless possibly the project for the Tower of Babel, has proposed itself on so spectacular a scale), and one cannot argue against this particular sample without arguing against the nature of moral action conceived in it. My own doubts concern some of Professor Muller's assumptions about the desirability of what is possible, and about the simplicity with which man, especially scientific man, is able to interpret the true and the good.

'Any relaxation in genetic selection, Dr. Muller said, results in some genetic deterioration by allowing detrimental mutant genes . . . to accumulate to a higher frequency. At the present time, he maintained, modern culture "is giving rein to biological decadence." ' *

Again, this is a matter of assumptions. We may note that the term "biological decadence" is unabashedly a moral and political one, scarcely even masquerading as a scientific one; its opposite, which might be used to describe Dr. Muller's remedy, might very well be called "biological Republicanism." It involves the supposition that you know not only what farm hands and factory workers are for, but also what man is for; further, that you are now able to back up your knowledge with effective action, so that if your idea of what man is for is not at present diagnostically true it can be made diagnostically true in the future—by making man over in the image of your idea.

'The only remedy consistent with cultural progress whereby this situation can be met, Professor Muller holds, would be the extension of social awareness and motivation to matters of reproduction—that is, "the increasing recognition by individuals of their responsibility not only for the education and living conditions but also for the genetic endowment of the generations succeeding them." '

To achieve the desired end, he goes on, "some long-entrenched attitudes, especially the feelings of proprietary rights and prerogatives about one's own germinal material, supported by misplaced egotism, will have to yield to some extent. This feeling [sic] does not represent a natural instinct, since there are primitive tribes yet alive who do not have even the concept of biological fatherhood. . . ."

I do not wish to oppose Professor Muller on sentimental grounds; if they are bad, those rights and prerogatives, let them vanish. Nor do I want to make him appear as a monster purposefully propagating

* The *Times* account is not invariably clear in distinguishing by quotation marks the boundary between Dr. Muller's words and Mr. Laurence's paraphrase; I shall show the difference as plainly as I can by using double quotation marks for the former, single for the latter.

monstrosities, for the values he wishes to achieve genetically are simply "the same as those already recognized in the bringing up and education of children."

And I do not disbelieve in the power of geneticists to accomplish such miracles; I do have doubts about the propriety of their doing so. The propriety I mean is not simply a moral one, or a delicacy about sexual and reproductive matters, but the propriety of employing so immense a force *as though* its results were predictable if its results are in fact not predictable at all.

Here is the program for the endowment of future generations with "a new morality" made possible by artificial insemination, which, given some little technical improvement, would allow children to be adopted "not merely after birth but even, as it were, before fertilization." ("As it were," so placed in the sentence, is a fine stroke of comedy.) "This will provide the opportunity of bearing a child resulting from the union, under the microscope, of reproductive cells one or both of which may have been derived from persons who exemplified the ideals of the foster parents."

He goes on to say that these reproductive cells would "preferably be derived from persons long deceased" (he doesn't say why; possibly on the Greek theory that one should call no man happy—or wise, or genetically sound—until he is dead), and adds, with a certain dry enthusiasm, that 'this procedure would make the .most precious genetic heritage of all humanity—the genetic endowments of the Einsteins, Beethovens, da Vincis, Shakespeares, Lincolns of each generation—"available for nurturing into childhood and adulthood." '

If this were not enough, 'Even more predictability about the nature of the progeny could be attained . . . by a kind of parthenogenesis —the duplication of a complete individual either from a male or female germ cell alone.' In this way, 'the offspring will obtain his hereditary equipment entirely from one individual, with whom he will be as identical genetically as if he were his identical twin.' You would take all this hereditary equipment from 'the cell of some pre-existing person, chosen on the evidence of the life he or she had led, and his or her tried potentialities.'

'In this manner it would become possible to bring back to life outstanding individuals, long since dead, perpetuating for all future generations large numbers of men and women of genius in all fields of endeavor. This would, in a sense, represent a form of physical immortality.'

And the *Times* article concludes with a solemn augury: 'Experiments along these lines have already succeeded in creating parthenogenetic frogs.'

Let me think first about making available 'the most precious genetic heritage of all humanity—the genetic endowments of the Einsteins, Beethovens, da Vincis, Shakespeares, Lincolns, of each generation.' A noble aim. And yet some questions do come up.

First, I observe that Dr. Muller is reported as speaking about these extraordinary phenomena in the plural, and as occurring in each generation; whereas I should have thought that each of his examples represented something in the last degree singular and unrepeatable, not only in genetic but in historical terms. Even on a less world-shaking scale—if we were to consider making available the genetic endowment not of Shakespeare but of, say, Offenbach—might not the prospect of a few hundred Offenbachs in the next generation seem to us absurd and not a little sinister? So much more a gaggle of Shakespeares. And what becomes of the idea of the individual (one of those obsolete misnomers, like "atom," meaning "what cannot be divided")?

In the same connection, consider the historical implications of this device. Would the genes of Beethoven produce new Beethovens who would write—to take it with the most naïve literalism—the sonatas of Beethoven? But we already have those. Well, then, a little less literally, would they write in the style of Beethoven? Imitation Beethoven sonatas? Worse yet (and we already have some of those, too). Assume finally that 'the proper environment and education' would take care of that; there remains the question what all these Beethovens would do in the world; could their genetic equipment comfortably absorb the influences of Wagner, Debussy, Schoenberg? The object, of course, must be that they would do for music in their time what Beethoven did for music in his time (even so, the idea of a lot of them doing it seems odd)—but, to put the extreme question, could their genetic equipment absorb, whether comfortably or not, the influence of Beethoven? He did, after all, exist; and wrote all that music. It appears that the production of an abundance of Beethovens might be only an embarrassment to the world.

Second, is the matter of genetic endowment so simple as all that? Presumably this endowment inseparably contains *all* and not only some of the traits of the person it produces. Would society then settle for the reproduction of numerous Beethovens congenitally gifted with music and syphilis together? Of so many Leonardos in whom painting and pederasty go together? No doubt it is easy to contemplate irritating the oyster to achieve the pearl: but do you deliberately and with a good conscience condemn your Keatses and Kafkas, Mozarts and Schuberts, to suffering lives and early deaths with the object of benefiting from their anguish? Is it so certain, after all, that these disadvantages, whether genetic as with Beethoven's illness, or environmental, as with Mozart's poverty, have nothing to do with art, so that the one may be skillfully detached from the other under a microscope?

Professor Muller is reported as saying that 'an individual with the genetic endowment of a Lincoln, for example, will overcome any obstacle of an unfavorable environment and lack of educational opportunities.' Now, our history books tell us that Lincoln did overcome such disabilities, and that a part of his greatness consists in his having done so; but must you then, following another well-known 'scientific' generalization about history, that of 'challenge and response,' provide your embryonic Lincolns with an unfavorable environment and an ample want of educational opportunities? Cynics would say that we already do so, but that is not the scientific vision.

A third point under this first heading—how do you make up your mind as to which genetic endowment is the most precious? If the selection committee had been required to choose during the period of Beethoven's early maturity, when his reproductive cells would presumably have been fertile, should we not with near absolute certainty have had a progeny of Rossinis instead? Rossinis are a grand and agreeable commodity, but they are not Beethovens.

Again, Professor Muller or his reporter assumes, with a charming kindliness, according to the examples, that the world's loving admiration is extended with a certain uniformity to those contemporaries who will later be renowned for art, science, and statesmanship so far above politics as to resemble a condition of sanctity. But supposing we agreed that "the persons who exemplified the ideals of the foster parents" would be very often the same as the persons whose pictures hang on their walls, whose names are most often and potently in their newspapers, and after whom they do now in fact name their children;—from the past couple of decades what a crop should we not have had, deliberately produced, of Hitlers, Stalins, Maos—balanced, of course, on the cultural side, by thousands of Bing Crosbys, hundreds of Billy Grahams, and a few dozen Immanuel Velikovskys.

Imagine the danger to foster parents, not to mention the children, who had opted for and received likenesses of Stalin, and then had to cross the periods of Beria, Malenkov, and Khrushchev, with those fatal images growing daily more recognizable beside them.

Of course all this will be done, when it is done, with the greatest circumspection and dispassionate wisdom, by committees of—scientists.

My second subject, following Dr. Muller's argument, is parthenogenesis, the duplication of a complete individual either from a male or a female cell alone. By this means, 'even more predictability about the nature of the progeny could be attained' than by the normal procedure of artificial insemination.

As I have already suggested, the idea of 'duplicating' an 'individual' contains a contradiction; but let us allow that to be a fault, or obsolescence, in the nature of language itself, rather than in Dr. Muller's thought, and pass on to ask, concerning the idea of 'predictability,' whether it is possible and whether it is desirable.

I do not doubt the possibility in a technical sense, that is, that what Dr. Muller is able to do with frogs his geneticist descendants will sooner or later, probably sooner, be able to do with us. But once again the theme of history comes in, and in this connection it might be expressed as follows:

> History does not really repeat itself; and the world is full of the ruined cities of peoples who believed it did.

It does not contradict, but only affirms, this proposition to say with Marx that everything in history happens twice, once seriously and once as a parody of itself. That is exactly the issue. Perhaps no better recipe for the mass-production of human suffering has ever been found than bringing people up to believe that the world is as their fathers saw it and need only be faced in the same way; perhaps no better recipe for human suffering could ever be found than to produce people so endowed by nature as to be incapable of believing anything else.

Historians are accustomed to see everywhere this elemental and calamitous want of imagination blinding an old world to the existence of a new: in what numbers, through the ages, the deceived children of royalty and success go to the block, the guillotine, the doomed campaign, making stoical and witty remarks as they disappear from the stage in St. Petersburg and Paris, Byzantium and Peking; lamenting so often that they have not been faithful to the ancestral ways, when in fact it is as often this fidelity which has betrayed them. The same judgment is rendered by Shakespeare, whose armored giants blunder and fall in a world which changed while they refused to look: Richard the Second, Gloucester and Lear, Antony, destroyed by new, efficient, somewhat cold men who can use the present because they do not love or want or understand the past. That all this is sad is undeniable, but there may be some objections to instituting a genetic program which shall ensure a constant supply of tragic heroes.

In a limited sense, what Professor Muller proposes is possible, or will foreseeably become so: 'In this manner [he is reported as having said] it would become possible to bring back to life outstanding individuals, long since dead, perpetuating for all future generations large numbers of men and women of genius in all fields of endeavor.'

In this manner it would become possible for a man to make sure not only that his son carried on his business after he was gone, but also that he made the same mistakes in it; and though we here approach mysteries of paradox, it seems included in the genetic argument that the son would carry on his father's business even if it had gone bankrupt in the interim between his conception and his coming of age.

It is admittedly difficult to see how literally we are to take all of this, or how literally Professor Muller takes it. But what is Leonardo to do in the world, given that he is once again Leonardo? What is he to be, if not Leonardo? The line of thought, not at the best free of mythological elements, here approaches the popular Sunday supplement question, What Would Jesus Do If He Returned To Earth Today? The accompanying picture always shows Jesus costumed *de chez* Raphael and Lloyd Douglas, with a streetful of people not unnaturally gaping after Him—their curiosity kindly rather than mocking, of course—and thus suggests by antithesis some reasons for His perhaps being a touch hard to recognize if He did in fact appear.

Again, parthenogenesis, which might be described as incest squared, or as fertile masturbation, or as sexual solipsism ("As if a man were author of himself, and knew no other kin." *Coriolanus*, 5.3.36), would selectively breed traits considered to be valuable, intensifying these and weakening, or finally excluding, others, all in the name of predictability.

But, considering once more the historical question, and the passage of 'real' time over the genetic 'immortality'—how predictable would be the behavior resulting from a determinate set of characteristics in a new situation? If predictability in this meaning extends to the particulars of behavior, we should have to say that Marie Antoinette, supposing her to be repeated in this manner, would somehow manage to get herself guillotined in the twenty-first century or so. Absurd. Granted, it is absurd. But it is not less absurd to think of predictability as not having this meaning, for then it has no meaning at all except that the behavior of what is predictable will not be predictable. Under this condition, imagine rapidly in succession the reproduction in modern circumstances of Beau Brummel, Thomas Aquinas, Cato the Censor: they are not to behave as they did in fact behave, but they are to behave as they would behave, given their—what shall we say?—characters, personalities, souls, selves, genes, in a situation incalculably altered; and, moreover, with the example of themselves constantly before their eyes; what is so predictable about that, except disaster? Milton, thou shouldst be living at this hour? But if he were, what? And would he read Milton? And if there were more than one of him? From his point of view the situation would be intolerable; not less so from ours. Milton, go home!

It is not considered seemly these days to joke about science, which invites a respectful silence from the lay person, but I am afraid that a number of these jokes make themselves, or have already been made by Professor Muller, and very sorry jokes they are, too. His conclusion about perpetuating the large numbers of dead geniuses by parthenogenesis is a fit punch-line; he is reported as having said: 'This would, in a sense, represent a form of physical immortality.'

"In a sense" comes in here with what a comedian would call good timing. The 'sense' is commonly consented to belong in the first place to Plato, who thought the perpetuating of oneself in children an inferior form of immortality, and is no doubt as good as it ever was, though showing as usual a surprising indifference to what people want physical immortality for, that is, to be always happy and never to die. Whether the latter condition would include the former is another thing, as Swift shows in his parable of the Struldbrugs; but perhaps the scientists, who offer the cold consolation of this immortality 'in a sense' rather often, should find some other term for the expression of their meaning.

Now, following on with the argument about parthenogenesis, what traits are valuable, how do you determine the value of a trait abstractly, by itself, and who does the valuing?

Dr. Muller is reported as believing that the traits to be striven for by artificial insemination, and thus by parthenogenesis which is a species of it, are the same as those already recognized as the chief aims in the bringing up and education of children. Among these the following are enumerated: 'more robust health; keener, deeper and more creative intelligence; genuine warmth of fellow feeling and cooperative disposition; and richer appreciation of man's intellectual and spiritual values and its [the appreciation's?] more adequate expression.'

Here doubt gives way to bewilderment. Can he mean that all these things ought to go together in any human being? Can he mean that examples of such a human being already exist, so as to guide us as to the probable conduct of future models? Are there not internal contradictions among the specifications, so that the possession of one would prohibit its accompaniment by another? Jesus of Nazareth Himself might possibly be characterized as having genuine warmth of fellow feeling, as revealed in His crucifixion for the sake of mankind, but had He a really cooperative disposition as it was manifested in his dealings with the Sanhedrin, the Roman authority, the spirit in the wilderness (Luke, 4.) or even His own mother?

Alas, in the mechanics of value as elsewhere you reap what you sow, and output is determined by input.

So the meaning of Professor Muller's list must be that, as all these traits are good ones, it is good to produce human beings who have only some of them, even if you cannot produce human beings who have all of them together. But Genghis Khan was characterized by robust health, while Richard Wagner suffered all his life from constipation. El Greco's rich appreciation of man's intellectual and spiritual values did not prevent him from saying "a nice man, but doesn't know how to paint" about Michelangelo, whom other authorities have seen as a horrible man who knew how to paint extremely well. And so on, indefinitely.

All this in the name of "human control," "predictability," an attitude toward reproduction which shall be "more rational and more socially directed."

We have raised some questions about the possibility of a genetically induced predictability in human character. Now we should ask,
assuming the thing to be possible, who wants it? Let us resist the
temptation to say, whether despairingly or with cheerful cynicism,
that They want it.

But we see that predictability is associated, by those who do want
it, with rationality and control; and so far as can be seen from the
account of Dr. Muller's talk, no slightest suspicion of the entire benevolence of this enterprise has ever come into his head.

No doubt it is man's earnest and noble desire to control things,
to make them accessible to reason, to make them predictable, and
thus to change such of them as he finds undesirable. As long as he
has to do with things, this object does not conflict with his other
great object of freedom; rather, the one increases the other, and that
is an excellent reason for valuing very highly indeed the methods and
achievements of science. But you cannot long have to do with things,
without also having to do with people, and here the matter is less
settled. Supposing it to be magically within my power to make you
a nicer fellow. Ought not I to do so at once? But of course. On the
other hand, what do I mean by a nicer fellow? It is extremely probable that I mean a fellow who will concur in anything I say or do,
or at least won't get in my way when he can't. This is not the whole
dream of power, but only its first and most moderate form; the gas
chambers come later, when the simple existence of other, not so nice
fellows, even when not directly in the way, becomes an intolerable
itch.

Calmly, please. I am not associating Professor Muller with tyranny
in any form; I am only inquiring what happens to the products of
the laboratory when once they come out of that austere and pure
environment and get into other hands, Tamburlaine's, or Napoleon's,
or yours, or mine.

A few years ago, the grand, supranational unity of science was
badly ruffled by the discoveries, or the pretensions, depending which
side you were on, of the Russian geneticist Lysenko concerning the
possibility of modifying mankind by the hereditary transmission of
acquired characteristics, so that, for example, a Stakhanovite father
might easily be made to conceive a Stakhanovite son, to whom over-
work would be natural and instinctual.

The Lysenko crisis is quiet at present (though not necessarily settled; see for example "The Third Stage in Genetics" by Donald

Michie, in *A Century of Darwin*, ed. S. A. Barnett, London, 1958), but not the least of its effects while it lasted was the widely disputed question whether there could be not one but two biologies, a Soviet one identified with Stalin and Lysenko fundamentally opposed to a bourgeois or capitalist one identified with Mendel and Weismann (at least not with the head of a state, to be thankful for small mercies). According to the former, you might soon be able to change human beings at will in the space of a generation or so; according to the latter, you would never be able to do any such thing, the germ cells being inaccessible, immortal, a direct heritage from Adam playing no part in the life of their individual bearer, and, in effect, an entity as near being the soul itself as you could have without effectively having it. Which of these theories was correct, assuming that either was, bothered some people less than the frightful suggestion behind it, that science itself, pure and rational though it might seem, was in fact socially conditioned and much given to mythologizing, fulfilling wishes, rationalizing phantasies; it did not make matters any better, from our side, that Marx had already said as much. Shakespeare too had observed that reason panders will, but his observation had not achieved scientific status.

Now, although Professor Muller has not raised the Lysenko heresy —and it is odd how that word *heresy* creeps from field to field, and from one authority to another—has he not by some accident propounded a sinister bourgeois equivalent to the Soviet nightmare? In each vision, *Someone* is to decide upon a biological future for man, and do his (doubtless very effective) best to insure that it shall come to pass. The children of the day after tomorrow, and theirs into remote ages, are to live not merely among the ruined cathedrals and nonsensical superstitions of their progenitors, which is what people do already, but also under a genetical compulsion to repeat indefinitely the shallow virtues, moderate intelligences, and doom-ridden phantasies of the same.

Why is this necessary?

Because, says Professor Muller, any relaxation in genetic selection results in some genetic deterioration by allowing detrimental mutant genes to accumulate to a higher frequency. At the present time, modern culture is "giving rein to biological decadence."

The sense in which he employs this term "biological decadence" is probably, in the first place, our failure to embark on a long-range program of breeding with conscious intention as to the results, a failure, in his terms, "to choose the true and the good."

Behind this, however, he passingly recommends his remedy as a 'response to the challenge arising from the modern uses of radiation.'

It is a remedy as staunchly conservative in its human object as it is wildly radical in its scientific means.

But with all good will, I cannot see that the scientist, who has made available 'the modern uses of radiation' which he admittedly is unable to control and does not accept responsibility for, can claim in advance that on account of his responsibility and control the consciously organized breeding of human beings for particular purposes, even if these are thought to be virtuous ones, will not in the same way come into the hands of the possessors of political power.

Let us conclude our discussion with a couple of mottoes to guide all right-thinking persons in their consideration of these great matters. The first is from *The Tempest*:

PROSPERO: I have us'd thee
      (Filth as thou art) with humane care, and lodg'd thee
      In mine own cell till thou didst seek to violate
      The honour of my child.
CALIBAN: O ho, O ho! Would't had been done!
      Thou didst prevent me; I had peopled else
      This isle with Calibans.

The second is that one of Goya's *Caprichos* showing a man asleep with his head on a desk; a huge cat raises its head nearby, and from behind him arise many owl-faced, bat-winged creatures who stare at him and ourselves; on the side of the desk the painter has written: *El sueño de la razon produce monstruos*, The dream of reason begets monsters.

Part II

The Poetry of Wallace Stevens

I begin with a not very precise sense of difference: that the poetry of Wallace Stevens is essentially different from almost everything else in English. If I take at random three or four poets not usually thought of for their similarities one to the other—Donne, Pope, Tennyson, and Frost, say—and consider what poetry seems to mean to them and what poetry seems to mean to Stevens, I find a family likeness among those four and something like a generic difference in Stevens; not only what he does, but what he wants to do, is different. Only sometimes in Wordsworth do I catch some usually tenuous hint of kinship:

> . . . to range the faculties
> In scale and order, class the cabinet
> Of their sensations, and in voluble phrase
> Run through the history and birth of each
> As of a single independent thing.

The resemblance is perhaps neither very close nor identifiable by particulars; if Wordsworth's "voluble phrase" sounds a trifle like a combination by Stevens ("the most prolific narrative," "life's voluble utterance"), we feel nevertheless that the former is being earnest in a way that the latter is not; it is merely that the exact tone of the word "voluble" has changed, for us, from what it was for Wordsworth. Still, compare this of Stevens:

> If the rejected things, the things denied,
> Slid over the western cataract, yet one,
> One only, one thing that was firm, even
> No greater than a cricket's horn, no more
> Than a thought to be rehearsed all day, a speech

First published in *The Sewanee Review*, Vol. 65, No. 1, Winter 1957. Copyright ©
November 8, 1957, by The University of the South.

>   Of the self that must sustain itself on speech,
>   One thing remaining, infallible, would be
>   Enough.

What likeness there is also defines the difference; in Stevens, proportions like the above can take a more abrupt form, and often do: "The deer and the dachshund are one." If Wordsworth is a "philosophical" poet, Stevens is a poet whose favorite disguise (there are several others) is the philosopher, robe, gesture, and speech—the "scholar," the "metaphysician," "Weisheit, the rabbi." And the poems are frequently sermons, lectures, meditations: "Extracts From Addresses to the Academy of Fine Ideas."

All this, though personative certainly, seems far from being otherwise dramatic; and from the idea of drama, of "action," we get these days our greatest pathos as readers of poetry; from the development of particular human fate as the tragic poets and the modern novelists alike teach us to regard it. Yet ideas, like books, have also fates, and Dryden finely says, "Every alteration of the design, every new-sprung passion or turn of it, is a part of the action, and much the noblest, except we conceive nothing to be action till they come to blows." Every alteration of the design—it describes, I think, the "action" in Stevens' poems. This too, of Paul Valéry, is relevant:

> Within the mind, there is a drama. Drama, adventure, agitation, all words of this category can be employed on condition that several are used, and are corrected one by the other. Such dramas are usually lost, like the plays of Menander.

That defines something of Stevens' nearly unique preoccupation in poetry: the recording of that subtle drama of inductions of which we lose or throw away a thousand examples daily, so that we have formed the prudent habit of calling it trivial, just as though all that we regard as decisive in the world did not depend precisely on this triviality: "The poem of the act of the mind."

As such considerations begin to define the distinction, so they do the difficulty of these poems, which have about them an "impenetrable lucidity," a brilliance of surface that defeats sometimes the kind of explication that works tolerably well on a good deal of English poetry. That is, we are sometimes compelled to wish a little wistfully for a moment requiring esoteric knowledge, as with Eliot, or the sorting-out of syntax or complex metaphor, as with Donne, Yeats, and a number of others; but Stevens is most difficult at precisely the moments of greatest simplicity, where the world, so far as meaning is concerned, is summed up and destroyed in a phrase usually balanced upon the point of the verb "to be": "The law of chaos is the law of ideas," "Ideas are men," "Building and dream are one," "Life is a bitter aspic," "The point of vision and desire are one," "The mind is the great poem of winter," etc. Moments of this kind seem to stand, in his poetry, for the arbitrary in all thought; they catch the mind in its fantastic act of deciding; and the same element is present in his argumentative, dialectical habit of phrase: "Suppose . . . ," "Say that . . . ," "For example. . . ." In a way, it is quite true to say that a poetry of this sort cannot be dramatic, because it begins just where thought has arrived at "the ratio of all things," and has only two developments open to it: the closing of the circle, or the transcending leap into something other, which will be something arbitrary—the leap, for instance, from generality to particulars—and either mystical or absurd, if we still care to distinguish those two terms. So metaphor also becomes arbitrary, mystical, or absurd, since particulars may be said to resemble generalities as it were helplessly, whether or not the mind can trace the details of the resemblance:

> The dress of a woman of Lhassa,
> In its place,
> Is an invisible element of that place
> Made visible.

To which we can only sigh assent. Sometimes it works, and sometimes it doesn't; but Stevens had a gift for making it work a great deal of the time.

This principle of composition, which revokes at once all other principles and makes something uniquely recognizable of Stevens' figures, is given us more or less diagrammatically at the beginning of a poem called "Connoisseur of Chaos":

> A. A violent order is disorder; and
> B. A great disorder is an order. These
> Two things are one. (Pages of illustrations.)

The subsequent illustrations—"If all the green of spring was blue, and it is"—play at developing the theme of "a law of inherent opposites, / Of essential unity," which is "as pleasant as port, / As pleasant as the brushstrokes of a bough, / An upper, particular bough in, say, Marchand." The tone is that of philosophic conversation or meditation, but the sense is, with a touch of gentle contempt for philosophic simplicities, that philosophy is over and done with, and of no interest *except* as the poetic act of the philosopher, the poem of the act of the mind:

> After all, the pretty contrast of life and death
> Proves that these opposite things partake of one,
> At least that was the theory, when bishops' books
> Resolved the world. We cannot go back to that.
> The squirming facts exceed the squamous mind,
> If one may say so. And yet relation appears,
> A small relation expanding like the shade
> Of a cloud on sand, a shape on the side of a hill.

The poem continues to debate these contrasts, which dissolve and re-form themselves in being debated—"Just one more truth, one more / Element in the immense disorder of truths,"—and concludes on a figure which for once is rigorously traditional in its combination:

> The pensive man. . . . He sees that eagle float
> For which the intricate Alps are a single nest.

That the poet's view of metaphor, or analogy as he more usually calls it, is such as I have said, is demonstrated not only in the poems but at many places in his very beautiful essays on poetics (*The Necessary Angel*, 1951), from one of which I will draw a somewhat extended passage as evidence:

First, then, as to the resemblance between things in nature, it should be observed that resemblance constitutes a relation between them since, in some sense, all things resemble each other. Take, for example, a beach extending as far as the eye can reach, bordered, on the one hand, by trees and, on the other, by the sea. The sky is cloudless and the sun is red. In what sense do the objects in this scene resemble each other? There is enough green in the sea to relate it to the palms. There is enough of the sky reflected in the water to create a resemblance, in some sense, between them. The sand is yellow between the green and the blue. In short, the light alone creates a unity not only in the recedings of distance, where differences become invisible, but also in the contacts of closer sight. So, too, sufficiently generalized, each man resembles all other men, each woman resembles all other women, this year resembles last year. The beginning of time will, no doubt, resemble the end of time. One world is said to resemble another.

To talk this way is to treat metaphor very largely—handsomely, but largely. Through my bewilderment about a gesture so sweeping I feel that all the *things* mentioned in the passage have in reality but one element common, and that their being *things thought*; they all participate the climate of the mind, and it is that which gives them such resemblance to one another as they may have. On this, I begin to think of, or hear some echo of, Plato—"First, then, as to the resemblance between things in nature"—and I reflect that the philosopher whose robes this poet wears is none other: "the ultimate Plato," "a large-sculptured, platonic person free from time," and so on. There are things, and there are ideas of things; the cross-relations between these are manifold and mysterious, enough to poetize upon perhaps endlessly:

> Poet, patting more nonsense foamed
> From the sea, conceive for the courts
> Of these academies, the diviner health
> Disclosed in common forms. Set up
> The rugged black, the image. Design
> The touch. Fix quiet. Take the place
> Of parents, lewdest of ancestors.
> We are conceived in your conceits.

That is suggestive. But it is not enough. Plato is in the poet's mind, but cannot be there without being modified any more than the theories of "bishops' books" can be there without being modified. One further comparison may be attempted, anyhow.

I have no firsthand acquaintance with the school of existential thought known as phenomenology, but a description of some of its elements by Albert Camus (*The Myth of Sisyphus*, 1955) struck me as immediately relevant to this exposition. Again I must quote at length:

Originally Husserl's method negates the classic procedure of the reason. . . . Thinking is not unifying or making the appearance familiar under the guise of a great principle. Thinking is learning all over again how to see, directing one's consciousness, making of every image a privileged place. In other words, phenomenology declines to explain the world, it wants to be merely a description of actual experience. It confirms absurd thought in its initial assertion that there is no truth, but

merely truths. . . . Consciousness does not form the object of its understanding, it merely focuses, it is the act of attention, and, to borrow
a Bergsonian image, it resembles the projector that suddenly focuses on
an image. The difference is that there is no scenario, but a successive
and incoherent illustration.

(Compare Stevens' "Just one more truth, one more / Element in the
immense disorder of truths.") Camus goes on to develop the phe-
nomenological leap from the above position back once again into a
world of significances:

> For Husserl speaks likewise of "extra-temporal essences" brought to
> light by the intention, and he sounds like Plato. All things are not ex-
> plained by one thing but by all things. I see no difference. . . . There
> is no longer a single idea explaining everything, but an infinite number
> of essences giving a meaning to an infinite number of objects. The
> world comes to a stop, but also lights up.

And a few pages later he enforces the relation of phenomenology to
Neoplatonism by suggesting that the whole attitude already exists in
Plotinus' contention that there is not only an idea of man but also
an idea of Socrates. With this, I think, we are again in Stevens'
realm, where the compositions of analogy touch upon the absurd
because particulars and generalities are really in a certain sense incompatible, and our pages of illustration therefore more or less arbitrary.

To see that this is so is not to accomplish anything essential; there
is about the perception a reassurance largely academical. We are left
still with the nature of the poetry, the nature of the world it com-
poses; and in a way we have always known that the arbitrary is the
beginning of poetry, and suspected it of being the beginning of
worlds. Nevertheless, this may now be said about the figurative center of Stevens' poetry: that every object, in the poet's mind, becomes
the idea of itself, and thereby produces the final illumination which
in the Platonic philosophy would have been produced by the view
of the archetypes themselves; save that this illumination, final as it
is, is meaningless, repetitious as prayer, yet "responsive as a mirror
with a voice"—the epiphany not of what is real, but of the self poetizing. This is our reality, that "we believe without belief, beyond
belief," that "Life consists / Of propositions about life," and that
"The poem must resist the intelligence / Almost successfully."

Yet to speak of the whole world as metaphor
Is still to stick to the contents of the mind
And the desire to believe in a metaphor.
It is to stick to the nicer knowledge of
Belief, that what it believes in is not true.

What follows from the principle of poetics which I have attrib-
uted to Wallace Stevens is this, that the poet's art constitutes the
world. This contention is also, I think, the chief subject of his poems,
which meditate the ambiguity, old as Genesis, whether this poetic
act is a creation *ex nihilo* or the ordering and making perceptible in
language the immense possibilities of chaos, the establishment of
what Joyce called "the ineluctable modality of the visible." The dominance of this subject, which makes the freedom and particular
strangeness of Stevens' poetry—since all objects may be exalted into
poems, the act of looking at them being what is at issue—also sets
their limits and is responsible for their repetitive and sometimes bemused character—since the meditation is endless, or ends only with
death (an end but no solution):

Or if the music sticks, if the anecdote
Is false, if Crispin is a profitless
Philosopher, beginning with green brag,
Concluding fadedly, if as a man
Prone to distemper he abates in taste,
Fickle and fumbling, variable, obscure,
Glozing his life with after-shining flicks,
Illuminating, from a fancy gorged
By apparition, plain and common things,
Sequestering the fluster from the year,
Making gulped potions from obstreperous drops,
And so distorting, proving what he proves
Is nothing, what can all this matter, since
The relation comes, benignly, to its end?

So may the relation of each man be clipped.

It remains to characterize by illustrations the recurring elements
and continuing preoccupations of the poetry. First, as to the ambiguity just spoken of, the poet does not usually think of a creation
out of nothing, but sometimes nevertheless comes close to suggesting it; so that even in thinking of "the Idea of *Order* at Key West"
he views the singing girl as making the world by her song, and not

merely as arranging it; the sea, here, is primordial chaos, the deep, just as in Genesis, "The water never formed to mind or voice," and it becomes something other than itself in her song:

> She was the single artificer of the world
> In which she sang. And when she sang, the sea,
> Whatever self it had, became the self
> That was her song, for she was the maker.

Generally, however, the poem creates by organizing the chaos of experience, "the storm," "the dreadful sundry of this world," producing from it "the mute, the final sculpture," the center, the focusing image which, remaining itself, orders the world about it:

> I placed a jar in Tennessee
> And round it was, upon a hill.
> It made the slovenly wilderness
> Surround that hill.

Yet it is not the establishment of such an image, in Platonic domination, that is the theme; it is, rather, the act of establishing, considered in itself, "the blessed rage for order," the act of seeing the lights which "Mastered the night and portioned out the sea," the act of seeing such things in silence and stasis, "as in the powerful mirror of my wish and will." This act, or spell cast upon chaos, is never final and must always be repeated, since "It can never be satisfied, the mind, never." The tension between mind and world may be harmonized in innumerable ways, on the "harmonium," the "clavier," "the blue guitar," and these precipitated harmonies are poems:

> I know my lazy, leaden twang
> Is like the reason in a storm;
>
> And yet it brings the storm to bear.
> I twang it out and leave it there.

But the resolution so produced, while in its way final, is meaningless and not allegorical, it tells us nothing beyond itself. It brings the storm to bear, but the storm continues, and the use of poetry is, by repeated charms, to create perpetually resolving, dissolving equations between composition and the storm. Thus in "Valley Candle":

> My candle burned alone in an immense valley.
> Beams of the huge night converged upon it,
> Until the wind blew.

> Then beams of the huge night
> Converged upon its image,
> Until the wind blew.

The principle of composition, whereby—to put it very roughly—all particulars may "represent" all general statements, makes for an immense variety of apparently individual subjects and images; yet I have been able to make out some strains of iterative and thematic imagery whereby the central tension is composed many times, and I will indicate briefly the most important of these.

The chaos of the actual is represented, as I have said, in sea, storm, wind, darkness; also in the figure of the jungle: Venezuela, Africa, Brazil, Yucatan, "Florida, Venereal Soil," the Everglades, and (epitomizing its qualities) "that alien, point-blank, green and actual Guatemala," whose antithesis, in a sadly satiric poem, is the Waldorf,

> Where the wild poem is a substitute
> For the woman one loves or ought to love,
> One wild rhapsody a fake for another.

Most often, though, the jungle of immediate experience is placed over against the image of the statue, which may appear in very various forms: the snow man, the Founder of the State, allegorical emblems of Fides, Justitia, Patientia, Fortitudo, "those sovereigns of the soul / And savings banks," Belshazzar, Stalin, Xenophon, etc. We may note that in an essay, "The Noble Rider and the Sound of Words," the poet's image for the meeting-place of imagination and reality is Verocchio's *Condottiere*.

Now this image has many resources central to Stevens' purpose. It is often treated satirically, as "gross effigy and simulacrum," but the satire itself runs into reverence for something too large for human purpose: "The well-composed in his burnished solitude, / The tower, the ancient accent, the wintry size." The statue, like the jar in Tennessee or the valley candle, orders the wilderness (usually a park) in which it is set, providing a center and focus for all that green; but beyond that it alludes to all that is dominating and heroic, all that is too big for man, until, in its remotest ranges, it becomes indistinguishable, with Platonic piety, from the One, and is identified with soldier, giant, hero, captain—"outer captain, inner saint," "a large-sculptured, platonic person, free from time," "the soldier of time grown deathless in great size."

It is between these extremes of the jungle and the monumental hero that the poet produces—with a wistful, hankering eye on the One—his transformations, "As of a general being or human universe," whereby the most random experiences are to be reflected mythically in "the central man," "the impossible possible philosophers' man,"

> our oldest parent, peer
> Of the populace of the heart, the reddest lord,
> Who has gone before us in experience,

with the foredoomed, ruefully Platonic object of "The essential poem at the centre of things."

It is part of this poetical bargain with the world, of course, that one does not bring forth the essential poem at the center of things. The poet, as musician and clown, as Crispin, Peter Quince, Man with the Blue Guitar, must daily renew the contest with chaos which he cannot win; the tenacity with which Stevens held himself at this frontier between the actual and the mind characterizes both the successes and the failures of his genius. Beginning where he began, development was impossible except as abstraction, progressive refinement, development to a stripped simplicity; it is as though what he developed was primarily the sense of what he was about, the simplifying consciousness of his poetry as an assault upon conventions of meaning, conventions of language, upon those people who, as Valéry once wrote, are so little aware of the pains and pleasures of vision that they have invented *beautiful views*.

It is the tragedy of poetry so conceived that, in a certain sense, it produces beautiful views despite itself; and a greater tragedy that all success is briefly sustained upon failure. I must make allowances for the fact that my affection to the poems of Stevens' early and middle periods owes something extra to my having grown up on *Harmonium, Ideas of Order, The Man with the Blue Guitar,* and certain poems from *Parts of a World* which appeared before that volume. And two major works after that, *Esthétique du Mal* and *Notes Toward a Supreme Fiction,* kept still their majesty and power as summaries of an argument of which, however, one had already heard a great deal. Nevertheless, the works of the poet's last few years seem to me most often to represent a falling-off and a repetition at a diminished pitch—for two reasons chiefly. First, a conscious endeavor to purify the terms of the parable: the pages of illustration, in those final volumes, seem more perfunctory than before. Second, a corresponding loss of tension, since the *particulars* of experience, with their resistance to the mind, formed one element in his process, and these particulars were now being treated as though, so to say, they were already dissolved in generality.

I should be sorry to have my reader take this opinion as pontifical, for in a certain, generally undervalued sense poetry is what you like. If there was a failure, it followed many noble poems, and followed them not merely in time but as their consciously accepted consequence in the difficult art of a man who, so far as thought is concerned, may prove to have been the only truly *modern* poet of his time. In considering the sense of his own parable, "How the honey of heaven may or may not come, / But that of earth both comes and goes at once," he rejected all easy solutions, and may be said to have found his artistic life still where he found his profession, in the investigation of surety claims.

> There was no fury in transcendent forms.
> But his actual candle blazed with artifice.

The Bread of Faithful Speech— Wallace Stevens and The Voices of Imagination

In books left by the old magician we find many things, things ill-assorted and not particularly well catalogued according to any scheme we are familiar with. It is as though a supreme identity were turning out the contents of its wallet, going through the desk, the filing cabinets, the closets, preparatory to moving elsewhere, or being other. Here are the licenses and registrations of the self, its snapshots of single raindrops in distant towns, its myths of creation, spells which worked on one occasion only, receipted bills from Guatemala and the Waldorf, inventories, formulae, annotations on unidentifiable texts; one sarcophagus containing one owl, statues of clowns, rabbis, soldiers, invocations of an uncertain someone variously called the outer captain, the inner saint, Don John, John Zeller, St. John, The Backache, turbulent Schlemihl, and so forth. A quiet and final remark, "Wisdom asks nothing more," is followed by a recipe for Parfait Martinique: "coffee mousse, rum on top, a little cream on top of that." Sometimes it seems as though toward the end he gave up doing magic in favor of meditating on its procedures, and he said: "As a man becomes familiar with his own poetry, it becomes as obsolete for himself as for anyone else." Or perhaps everything by this time had been transmuted into magical substance, so that he could say: "Life consists of propositions about life." Or a doubt would arise, so that he said: "Life is an affair of people not places. But for me life is an affair of places and that is the trouble."

Now he is gone the inheritors rummage through what is left, tak-

This essay was presented at the meeting of the Modern Language Association in December 1962.

6

ing various views of their legacy. Some see only a cabinet of curiosities got together by a traveled uncle. Others, understanding they have come into the possession of a gold mine, nevertheless resent his not having had the ore refined so as to be turned in at the treasury for honest paper money that anyone can understand and use immediately. A few young nephews and nieces are upset because when they say the spells nothing happens. And the earnest amateurs of theology search the remains for the single phrase that will transform the world. He would perhaps have said to them:

> It is to stick to the nicer knowledge of
> Belief, that what it believes in is not true.

The true inheritance, if we are able to see it, is a world already transformed, the lucid realization of one among infinite possibilities of transformation, of projection from the shadowy presence at the center. Concerning this he quoted from Whitehead these rather cryptic words: "In a certain sense, everything is everywhere at all times, for every location involves an aspect of itself in every other location. Thus every spatio-temporal standpoint mirrors the world." His comment on this consists of a translation of Whitehead's observation so that it becomes recognizably characteristic of himself and the elegantly slapdash chiaroscuro notation which identifies his voice, his style, and with these the world they alone express: "These words [he says] are pretty obviously words from a level where everything is poetic, as if the statement that every location involves an aspect of itself in every other location produced in the imagination a universal iridescence, a dithering of presences and, say, a complex of differences."

The voice of his poetry is that of a man thinking, a man studying how I may compare this prison where I live unto the world. But it is not philosophical poetry, though it may often adopt the air and gesture of some myth about a philosopher philosophizing. And if it is the poetry of a man thinking, it is nevertheless not "intellectual poetry," not the poetry of "a beau language without a drop of blood," for what the man thinks about is, at last, expressiveness itself, the mystery of the phrase in its relation to the world. There is a difference, which he described, for himself, as the change from a young man to an older one:

> Like a dark rabbi, I
> Observed, when young, the nature of mankind,

> In lordly study. Every day, I found
> Man proved a gobbet in my mincing world.
> Like a rose rabbi, later, I pursued,
> And still pursue, the origin and course
> Of love, but until now I never knew
> That fluttering things have so distinct a shade.

The fluttering things, which in that poem make such a dithering of presences, were pigeons, and he returned to them for an image at the close of another poem, where they have the same expressive function of relating the light and the dark, somewhere between things and the ambience of things, things and the thought of things:

> in the isolation of the sky,
> At evening, casual flocks of pigeons make
> Ambiguous undulations as they sink
> Downward to darkness, on extended wings.

In this poem, which meditates the mysteries of incarnation, of how things come to be and cease to be, the pigeons are as thoughts, or as the manner of our perceiving thoughts between the bright emptiness above and the generative dark beneath, mediators which without solving resolve. In some way, such a poem cannot end, it can only stop at the finish of a cadence, satisfactory for the moment but recognizably inconclusive. A dithering of presences, a complex of differences. All is to do again.

The voice of his poems is the voice of the poet. Even in the poem I have just been quoting from, which begins as though in prospect of a dramatic monologue, it is the poet and not the lady who carries the burden of meditation; she says something once in a while, and he develops the thoughts which she might appropriately have.

This voice has a great consistency over the whole range of the poetry: it is learned, for "poetry is the scholar's art"; it is humorously eccentric, given to French phrases (for in poetry "English and French constitute a single language"), sorrowful and somewhat fatigued, its tone and feeling much affected by the weather and changes of season; it has a balanced gravity owing something to many repetitions; it is a considerate voice, its altitudes of grandeur and nobility are achieved perceptibly in despite of weariness and a leaning toward resignation. It is a poet's voice; or, you might say, it is the voice of wisdom as this might be heard by a poet.

Nor is this so unusual. For whatever our view of the personative, or dramatic, element in lyric poetry, it very often happens that the poet, a middle-aged or an old man thinking of his life and the approaching end of it, of its poetry and whatever all that may mean, projects these thoughts upon the more or less mythified figure of a middle-aged or an old man thinking of his life, and so on. He not so much, that is, bespeaks for himself on the occasion a fictitious character, as he generalizes out the character he has, or thinks he has, or wants to have; often enough he will make this voice of his poem—"as of a general being or a human universe," our poet says —older than himself. For among the poet's ambitions is this unseemly one, to become wise by sounding wise, to be a hermit scholar in a tower first, and only after that find something to study. How odd that it should ever even seem to work.

In this process, the amount of distancing and dignifying that almost necessarily goes on may make it seem that the daily self and the self in the poem are absolutely unlike; thus Yeats and his famous theory of the creation of character from the opposite: "It is perhaps because nature made me a gregarious man, going hither and thither looking for conversation, and ready to deny from fear or favour his dearest conviction, that I love proud and lonely things."

In Yeats's poetry the equivalent thought demonstrates this process of dignifying and distancing by its loftier arrogance of phrase, and by the poet's assigning to Dante what he wished to believe about himself:

> I think he fashioned from his opposite
> An image that might have been a stony face . . .

relating the austere pilgrim of the poem directly with a worldly life of lechery and cynicism.

For some poets, then, the writing of poetry may become an elucidation of character, a spiritual exercise having for its chief object the discovery or invention of one's character: Myself must I remake, Du musst dein Leben ändern, &c. Something of this sort appears in our poet also, and he said about it: "It is the explanations of things that we make to ourselves that disclose our character; the subjects of one's poems are the symbols of one's self or of one of one's selves."

We have said so far, a little foolishly, that the poet's voice is the voice of the poet; and added that the poet hears this voice as that in which the wise might speak, the old and wise and a little foolish, an aged eagle, an old philosopher in Rome, the man in the golden breastplate under the old stone Cross, the magician opening his folio by candlelight in the lonely tower.

To view the poet as a magician is fair, if we remember that magicians do not really solve the hero's problems, but only help him to confront these; as Merlin may be said to have helped Arthur, not so much by doing magic as by being for him a presence and a voice, a way of saying which indicated a way of being. Of this relation our poet said that the soldier is poor without the poet's lines, adding this in explanation:

> How simply the fictive hero becomes the real;
> How gladly with proper words the soldier dies,
> If he must, or lives on the bread of faithful speech.

We observe here, in an aside, that some poets, ours not among them, believe, or pretend to believe, in a magic that more directly affects the world. These poets are like the Friar in the ballad, where the girl fears she will go to hell if she lets him seduce her:

> Tush, quoth the Fryer, and do not doubt,
> If you were in hell I could sing you out.

This has often been the poet's false pride about his magic; but he resembles the Friar in another way, for he too will end up in the well, without the girl.

Our proper magic is the magic of language, where the refrain of the riddling verse, "Sing ninety-nine and ninety," is simply not the same thing as singing a hundred and eighty-nine. It is also the magic of impersonation, and not without its sinister aspect, the being possessed by spirits, or by the spirit. Combining the two, it is being possessed by the word, and about this there is a certain mystery, which we are able to describe, though not to solve, as follows.

We are fond of saying that poetry is personative, hence dramatic. To say this is probably true enough, if not conspicuously helpful, for it does give at any rate our sense that the I of the poem is not quite the poet, even if we have the lingering sense also that this I is not quite not the poet either. It is a problem in style, the beginning of a problem in identities. Browning gives us an idea of Bishop Blougram, but it is an idea we cannot hold without holding at the same time an idea that the Bishop is Browningesque along with Andrea del Sarto and others. Prufrock is distinct from Tiresias, but both recognizably belong to Mr. Eliot, just as Michael Robartes and Crazy

Jane sound like themselves and like Yeats; as all the dead of Spoon River sound like Masters, and so on. In the drama itself, the problem is aggravated, or dismissed: either they all sound like Shakespeare, or none of them does. Proust puts it this way, that all the sitters to one painter have a family likeness in their portraits, greater than the likeness they share with members of their own families.

So the poet's sounding like others may be his way of sounding like himself. And there is a range of possibilities here, between the impossible extremes of sounding exactly like oneself and entirely other than oneself. The limits of this range are given by Keats: the "chameleon poet," on one side, who has no character because he is constantly impersonating someone else; and on the other side the Wordsworthian, or Egotistical Sublime.

Through the other, the poet impersonates the self, his own self or one of his selves, and there are two "voices of poetry." But it doesn't stop there, for we read the poem, and then it speaks in our voice as well; this too is mysterious. When I say over some lines,

> Every thread of summer is at last unwoven.
> By one caterpillar is great Africa devoured
> And Gibraltar is dissolved like spit in the wind.

And when I go on, saying these lines that follow,

> Over all these the mighty imagination triumphs
> Like a trumpet and says, in this season of memory,
> When the leaves fall like things mournful of the past,
>
> Keep quiet in the heart, O wild bitch. O mind
> Gone wild, be what he tells you to be . . .

When I say over these things, I say them as myself and not myself, as a possibility of certain grandeurs and contempts in the self which the poet alone has been able to release, and I ask whether the voice that speaks at this moment is more his or mine, or whether poetry is not in this respect the most satisfactory of many unsatisfactory ways we have of expressing our sense that we are members of one another. That voice, which I add by reading, or which the poet adds to me when I read, a voice which in some way belongs to neither of us personally, is a third voice of poetry. Our poet, who thought of these things, said of this: "The poet seems to confer his identity on the reader. It is easiest to recognize this when listening to music—I mean this sort of thing: the transference."

And there is still one further voice of poetry to be considered, though we can say little enough about it except that at certain times it is there. That is the voice of an eternally other, the resonance that in our repetition of the poet's words seems to come from the outside, when "the shadow of an external world draws near"; as when our poet, calling himself for the occasion Ariel, and speaking in the voice of this Ariel, says of Ariel's poems:

> It was not important that they survive.
> What mattered was that they should bear
> Some lineament or character,
>
> Some affluence, if only half perceived,
> In the poverty of their words,
> Of the planet of which they were part.

Our poet thought also and often about this last voice, of which he said: "When the mind is like a hall in which thought is like a voice speaking, the voice is always that of someone else."

His magic, ever more insistently, was a magic to open this world and not another, but this world as an imagination of this world, a transformation where "what is possible replaces what is not"; for that impossible which was replaced, for "man's mind grown venerable in the unreal," he had at most a half-friendly, half-mocking nostalgia; and of that other, the last voice of all, and the one all poetry seeks to hear, he said: "The mind that in heaven created the earth and the mind that on earth created heaven were, as it happened, one."

We say it over and we feel, as it happens, better.

Summer's Flare and Winter's Flaw

To my mind the most immediately striking thing about John Crowe Ransom's poems is their elegance. I don't know if, in this century of the common man, that word is still allowed to signify praise; a good deal even of fairly good contemporary verse suggests that it is not—that elegance is, in fact, an undesirable quality or at least a trivial one, to nothing so much suited as to the flowered waistcoats of another and outmoded time. If this is so, it is, if nothing more, a sad comedown for the word and the quality; and since my use intends a compliment to the poet I had better begin by illustrating the place of elegance in Mr. Ransom's work.

Elegance, in this connection, is a means to precision of statement, more especially a means to the control of tone: it implies manners, or style—the general code, that is, by which particular choices are made, by which objects are arranged in one order rather than another. At a deeper level the quality insists even abstractly and generally that order and choice always matter, whether the world is reasonable or not. Mr. Ransom has said many lucid things on this theme in his prose writings, and a fairly extensive quotation from one essay will show, I think, how nearly his practice and his preachment are one:

> When a consensus of taste lays down the ordinance that the artist shall express himself formally, the purpose is evidently to deter him from expressing himself immediately. Or, the formal tradition intends to preserve the artist from the direct approach to his object. Behind the tradition is probably the sense that the direct approach is perilous to the artist, and may be fatal. It is feared that the artist who disregards the instruction may discover at length that he has only been artless; or, what is worse, that he will not make this important discovery, which will have to be made for him by the horrid way of autopsy. I

First published in *The Sewanee Review*, Vol. 56, No. 3, Summer 1948. Copyright July 12, 1948, by The University of the South.

suggest, therefore, that an art is usually, and probably of necessity, a kind of obliquity; that its fixed form proposes to guarantee the round-about of the artistic process, and the "aesthetic distance."

A code of manners also is capable of being taken in this fashion; it confers the same benefit, or the same handicap, if we prefer, upon its adherent. . . .*

A little further on Mr. Ransom generalizes the position as follows:

The natural man . . . is a predatory creature to whom every object is an object of prey and the real or individual object cannot occur; while the social man, who submits to the restraint of convention, comes to respect the object and to see it unfold at last its individuality; which, if we must define it, is its capacity to furnish us with an infinite variety of innocent experience; that is, it is a source, from which so many charming experiences have already flowed, and a promise, a possibility of future experiences beyond all prediction. . . . The function of a code of manners is to make us capable of something better than the stupidity of an appetitive or economic life. High comedy, for example, is technically art, but substantially it is manners, and it has the agreeable function of displaying our familiar life relieved of its fundamental animality, filled, and dignified, through a technique which has in it nothing more esoteric than ceremonious intercourse.

As another and in this sense most elegant poet has written, "How but in custom and in ceremony / Are innocence and beauty born? / Ceremony's a name for the rich horn, / And custom for the spreading laurel tree."

The attitude I seek to distinguish has much to do with irony, it is at least a means to the expression of an ironical stance with regard to the affairs of this world and the next as well; it is an adjunct to, in Dante's sense, the "comic" style which strives for exactitude rather than heroism in feeling; and it is most readily remarkable in Mr. Ransom's rigorous and singular choice of epithet. Consider the example of the poem "Blue Girls." The theme is traditional, even worn—it is in part that of the "neiges d'antan." The speaker appeals to the girls to neglect the things of the mind, to think no more of what will come to pass than bluebirds do; and cites the instance of a lady "with a terrible tongue, / Blear eyes fallen from blue, / All her perfections tarnished." "Yet it is not long," he concludes, "Since she

* "Forms & Citizens," *The World's Body*, pp. 32-33, 34.

was lovelier than any of you." But it is the third of the four stanzas that redefines this material and fully secures the right pathos:

> Practise your beauty, blue girls, before it fail;
> And I will cry with my loud lips and publish
> Beauty which all our power shall never establish,
> It is so frail.

In particular the word "practise" seems to be the one on which the effect depends; it characterizes the beauty of the girls as an effort, a discipline, a rigorous act of the will, whose failure is the more pathetic as its history will have been maintained, as a struggle, against nature and time.

The general effect which I describe has only in part to do with the particular precision of the word or phrase involved in a given instance; much is gained also by the sense one gets of the poet's intense interest in distinction and choice, his preference at point after point for the surprising, the esoteric, the highly particularized: autumn days, for example, have "no more color nor predilection / Than cornstalks too wet for the fire. . . ." Here "predilection" contrasts sharply (and not alone by its more remote Latinity) with "color," revises the aspect under which the days are seen, and by its abruptness suggests epigrammatically a description of life itself in terms of these two qualities.

This distinction of voice serves to shade and refine, in Mr. Ransom's poetry, a major duality that is, in its extremes, as unequivocal as the act by which light was divided from dark; even so the ironic manipulation of the world's two hemispheres secures a good deal of dusk, and the condition of the observer is most firmly one of equilibrium, of a poised judgment. Of the extremes first: they are remarkable not only as defining the theme of a poem (love and honor in "The Equilibrists") or as dictating the choice of the *dramatis personae* (Christ and Antichrist in "Armageddon") but also as they appear aphoristically in the detail work: "six little spaces of chill, and six of burning," "the summer's flare and winter's flaw," "hot as fever / And cold as any icicle" and, in the most general way, "All the here and all the there," and, of the Pure Idea, "Both external and internal / And supernal and infernal."

The method of irony is to force attention to the paradox of the human situation by reference to extremes which are essentially and

intellectually but not in existence incompatible. Of the ironic voice
the triumphs are often sad and the defeats funny. "The Equilibrists"
will serve as a fairly full and explicit illustration. The two lovers are
drawn together by "fierce love" and kept apart by "Honor." The poet
considers their predicament in two ways, in anger and in resignation:

> Ah, the strict lovers, they are ruined now!
> I cried in anger. But with puddled brow
> Devising for those gibbeted and brave
> Came I descanting: Man, what would you have?

Developing this theme he shows that for the extreme mind the
lovers have not the possibility of any other situation for they exist in
this dilemma: "Would you ascend to Heaven and bodiless dwell? /
Or take your bodies honorless to Hell?" He details the antithesis
through two opposed stanzas on Heaven and Hell; but the lovers,
when he has done, are still locked in their system of attraction and re-
pulsion, still "rigid as two painful stars, and twirled / About the clus-
tered night their prison world"; and the poet, before he makes for the
lovers a tomb and an epitaph, recognizes that "Their flames were not
more radiant than their ice." As in *The Phoenix and the Turtle*, the
lovers have a tragic triumph; not of the increasing company of those
who would "solve the problems of the world," they have maintained
the original tension of their dilemma and, close but untouching even
in death, they lie "perilous and beautiful."

The dilemma may be otherwise presented, as in "Two in August,"
another poem about lovers, about "Two that could not have lived
their single lives / As can some husbands and wives." Here the tension is the given, and the poem develops the painful stress of its
maintenance:

> How sleepers groan, twitch, wake to such a mood
> Is not well understood,
> Nor why two entities grown almost one
> Should rend and murder trying to get undone . . .

But the middle way is not always or easily acceptable and may take a
sardonic turn. In "Old Man Playing with Children" the grandsire
says to the "discreet householder":

> "May God forgive me, I know your middling ways,
> Having taken care and performed ignominies unreckoned

Between the first brief childhood and the brief second,
But I will be more honorable in these days."

What imparts to Mr. Ransom's poems such firmness and unobtrusive strength is, I think, the fact that they seldom, whatever their lightness or seriousness, leave for long or stray far from this fundamental distinction of the human predicament or paradox: whatever the poems may say about it, they are almost always concerned with it. Variety of effect is secured by other means, but here also great economy is observed. We may roughly distinguish several kinds of poem, with respect at least to the kind of subject involved, though it will be well to remember that any categories we set up do not, strictly, involve theme but only and more superficially method.

Elegies, first, such as "Dead Boy," "Emily Hardcastle, Spinster," "Bells for John Whiteside's Daughter," "Blue Girls," "Here Lies a Lady," and even, perhaps, "Conrad in Twilight" and "Miriam Tazewell." The character of the paradox in these pieces may perhaps have become partially apparent from what has gone before; and in general the poems involve the areas where death is seen in the midst of life, the particular death which is the "subject" of the poem being rather its occasion than its cause. Death is subtly intrinsicate with disinheritance, the separation of the will from the past and the branch from the tree; death is a marriage not hoped for in life ("Emily Hardcastle"); the death of a little girl is depicted as a meditation, a "brown study," which the energies of life had left no time for ("Bells for John Whiteside's Daughter"); while the last stanza of "Here Lies a Lady" sets out the dilemma most explicitly:

Sweet ladies, long may ye bloom, and toughly I hope ye may thole,
But was she not lucky? In flowers and lace and mourning,
In love and great honor we bade God rest her soul
After six little spaces of chill, and six of burning.

Here life is summed up with casual mockery as the meaningless alternation of chills and fever; the poet modestly hopes for the sweet ladies still living that they may bloom long and suffer "toughly." But death is a piece of luck, it involves ritual, meaning, "love and great honor."

Bestiaries, then, fables about animals and birds: "Janet Waking," "Spiel of the Three Mountebanks," "What Ducks Require," "Somewhere Is Such a Kingdom," "Lady Lost," "Dog." The tone here is necessarily light for the most part, as it must be in adumbrating the human by means of the animal kingdom. Only occasionally, as in the instance of the mountebanks, the swarthy, the thick, the pale, and the beasts they advertise, does the increasing seriousness of the poem's demeanor suggest insistence more than the figure will bear—the reader is required, rather against the poem, to remember that the sponsor of Agnus is, equally with the sponsors of Fides and Humphrey, a mountebank. I think the difficulty I have with this in many ways admirable work is that its arrangement prohibits any summation or full composition of its elements: it indicates three Ways with great brilliance and humor, but its artifice may demand too strongly that we consider each Way exclusive of the others; and surely that of Agnus, both by its position and its tone, is as though automatically awarded the victory, so that to my mind we are left with more of a competition than a composition.

My third category is more difficult of description. It consists of fables about people, but I should like to limit it further and call it Dichotomies of the Church Militant and Triumphant: "Armageddon," "Our Two Worthies," "Captain Carpenter," "Necrological," "Judith of Bethulia." The group will include under this head, without more than the least stretching, such poems as "Puncture" and "Antique Harvesters" whose concern with the subject is less apparent on the surface, it may be, but there nevertheless.

The emphasis of these poems is for the most part clearly on intellect and brilliance; the vocabulary is more than usually exotic, the rhymes are witty and boldly slanted, the poet's attitude and stance are in the main remote, often amused. When, in "Armageddon," Christ and Antichrist arm for battle, "The prospect charms the soul of the lean jackal." In the sequel, "the Wolf said Brother to the Lamb," the two antagonists become indistinguishable one from the other so that the patriarch speaks his complaint to the wrong one; ultimately in renewed activity they demonstrate the dilemma:

> Christ and his myrmidons, Christ at the head,
> Chanted of death and glory and no complaisance;
> Antichrist and the armies of malfeasance
> Made songs of innocence and no bloodshed.

In the legend "Judith of Bethulia" the destruction of Holofernes is used, like the deaths which occasion the elegies, as an entry to a more sinister area in which victory and defeat are mixed. The virginal beauty of Judith is described as a weapon, a sword, bright and unrusted; and the ironic, rather ominous ritual by which each stanza ends with a question and answer allows a deepening intensity of tone and a new seriousness just at the end:

> Yet a madness fevers our young men, and not the clergy
> Nor the elders have turned them unto modesty since.
> Inflamed by the thought of her naked beauty with desire?
> Yes, and chilled with fear and despair.

The fourth category consists of poems about lovers. They are not love poems, for they mostly depend on a description of the lovers' situation by a third person; and in any event they are, like the lovers in one of them, "one part love and nine parts bitter thought." Among the poems to be included in this group are "Eclogue," "The Equilibrists," "Two in August," "Spectral Lovers," "Parting at Dawn," "Good Ships," "Vaunting Oak," "Parting, Without a Sequel," and, I should think, "Winter Remembered" and "Prelude to an Evening." In many of these poems Mr. Ransom operates with unusual intensity and seriousness of tone—aptly, because the lovers in whatever vicissitudes represent the perfect and unforced metaphor, susceptible of the highest personal emphasis, for his major dualism; they are the phoenix and the turtle whose miracle has not fully worked, and they are unable to be one or two; they can neither keep separate nor completely agree to their identity. In "Eclogue" the dilemma is poised against the innocence of childhood, when "Our infant selves played happily with our others," and "The cunning me and mine came not between." It is, the lovers say, "the dream of Death" which is the origin of fear and separateness. More closely they cannot characterize it; Jane Sneed says:

> Something, John Black, came flapping out of hell
> And wrought between us, and the chasm is
> Digged, and it digged it well.

And John Black concludes: "We lovers mournfully / Exchange our bleak despairs." Again in "Spectral Lovers" the ghosts of the too-scrupulous pair haunt the April night reconsidering vainly the temptations resisted, and in a line the crucial point is put: "Yet of evasions even she made a snare."

My last group is composed of meditative poems about art and knowledge, more specifically history, and includes: "Philomela," "Old Mansion," "Painted Head," "Survey of Literature," and "Address to the Scholars of New England." The major distinction turns up here in other disguises, other metaphors: body and head, consonants and vowels as against belly and bowels, and most clearly in a wonderful stanza of the Phi Beta Kappa poem:

> But they reared heads into the always clouds
> And stooped to the event of war or bread,
> The secular perforces and short speech
> Being labors surlily done with the left hand,
> The chief strength giddying with transcendent clouds.

The poet has, unsystematically as poets should, created a scale between his major extremes, where his attitudes sweetly may roam.

The classifications above are not, obviously, all-inclusive (they do seem, I hope without forcing, to include thirty-five of forty-two poems); nor do they pretend to be critically conclusive. Even as analytic conveniences both their validity and their relevance may be held subjects of great doubt, especially at a time when "counting things" etc. is deemed the contemptible activity of even more contemptible scholars. Evidently such distinctions do not tell us "all about" any poem, and undoubtedly the particular insights they suggest involve particular blindnesses also. But without bringing up questions of general aesthetic, as of theories of communication against theories of exploration, we may remind ourselves that any theory in the least worth discussing is bound to cover, to have a terminology for, a good number of the phenomena in the field—a good number, and by no means all.

I began by discussing "elegance" as a means to "order," implying that the person particular in vocabulary may very well be found particular in other areas as well. My analytic distinctions of the kinds of Mr. Ransom's poetry (measured in terms of subject) in counterpoint to what, in terms of theme, he is uniquely "talking about" show clearly, I think, the high order of this poet's technical accomplishment and, further, the ordered responsibility of his creation—: as there is little in these poems which is technically slipshod or crude, so there is little in their evaluations which is random or irrelevant.

The Current of the Frozen Stream

My occasion is the publication of Allen Tate's collection, *Poems 1922-1947* (Scribner's, 1948); my purpose the elucidation of a major duality in his poetry, which I would regard as in some sense its generating or operative principle. In some sense . . . those beautiful precautionary and beforehand words which serve the critic so well through all life's appointments and will make him a satisfactory epitaph; but used here with particular intent to deny that the results of this (or any such) study are conceived as historically applicable, as suggesting the origin of the poetry. I am concerned to show the design that exists in the poetry; this does not extend to saying that the design has "caused" the poetry, though it may extend, if the distinction is permissible, to showing that the design could have caused the poetry to be what it is, that the design is a sufficient reason of the poetry though not its specific occasion, and may therefore be taken as really a "generating" principle. The design is a formal, though not a proximate, cause.

It will be objected by some, I think, that any method which commits itself to the discovery of a "major duality" in any body of work offends against right practice by reducing the text to that point of abstraction at which, as the design becomes clear, the poetry vanishes. I do not see that this need be so, not more so at least than is general with analytic criticism. All will depend, naturally, on the success of demonstration from the text, on the right election of essences, on showing that the figuration of the poet's thought in a pair of abstract terms may legitimately be drawn from particular antagonisms or juxtapositions in the poetry:—the distinction of light from darkness does not exclude any shadings of civil, solar or sidereal twilight, and the local weather will also have much to do with the color of the sky.

First published in *Furioso*, Fall 1948. Reprinted in *The Sewanee Review*, Vol. 67, No. 4, Autumn 1959. Copyright © October 19, 1959, by The University of the South. Copyright 1948 by Reed Whittemore.

Now there is, I conceive, one duality that underlies a great deal of poetry, especially the kind of poetry that is called (aptly, as I think) "metaphysical": it is, in largest terms, the duality of the One and the Many. Metaphysical poetry is a poetry of the dilemma, and the dilemma which paradoxes and antitheses continually seek to display is the famous one at which all philosophies falter, the relation of the One with the Many, the leap by which infinity becomes finite, essence becomes existence; the commingling of the spirit with matter, the working of God in the world. This is not precisely my theme, and I cannot give space here to supporting it (but it is a fairly well-known position and the objections to it are also sufficiently current), yet it seemed proper to notice it at the beginning, since my considerations will indirectly refer back to it.

The central concern of Allen Tate's poems is with time and history, their major theme man's attachment to the past, the allegiance of his blood, the queer liaisons of his mind. But to put this statement in a right relation with Tate's text it is necessary to add that it does not mean the entertainment known as "world history" in which scholars seek to demonstrate the ultimate likeness of the world to an Automat. The past for Tate is seen as always, in times not necessarily less confused or angry than the present, first-rate poets have seen it—as the composition of the human will with the unknown and implacable justice or injustice. History, in Tate's poems, is history in the same kind as Judges, Samuel, Chronicles, Kings, where the existence of idea and theme is known through the violence of individuals, and especially in the same kind as *The Divine Comedy*, where people named Ulysses and Boniface and Frederick have exactly the importance of people named Lano and Jacomo da Sant' Andrea and Pier delle Vigne; and in the same kind as the histories of Shakespeare, whose heroes and antagonists are demonstrated actually to have fought for what, the sociologist tells us, would have "inevitably" happened anyhow. For Tate history is primarily a matter of generation and choice, that is of myth, not of pattern and system; the situations of history are family or at least local situations, not paradigms composed of least common denominators called wars, truces, migrations, and laws. As Yeats wrote, "A father, mother, child (a daughter or a son), / That's how all natural or supernatural stories run." And the following passage from Paul Valéry (with whose thought Tate's is at many points in accord) gives the matter the clarity of definition:

Le caractère réel de l'histoire est de prendre part à l'histoire même. L'idée du passé ne prend un sens et ne constitue une valeur que pour l'homme qui se trouve en soi-même une passion de l'avenir. L'avenir, par définition, n'a point d'image. L'histoire lui donne les moyens d'être pensé. Elle forme pour l'imagination une table de situations et de ca- tastrophes, une galerie d'ancêtres, un formulaire d'actes, d'expressions, d'attitudes, de décisions offerts à notre instabilité et à notre incertitude, pour nous aider *à devenir*. . . . L'histoire alimente l'histoire.
—Regards sur le Monde Actuel

This sort of history will perhaps always be a scandal and an offense to those pragmatical positivists who are reassured to see the creation programmatically "working itself out" in terms of "trends," "forces," "cycles," and "designs," because these terms in excluding the will ex- clude also man's responsibility, and because the mind that is satisfied with such terms finds it unlikely that the local, the named, the limited, should assume mythic and universal importance, since after all (they might protest) the world is so full of a number of things. To this view it is unfriendly of the Word to put on flesh, and tends to give a particular a depth of meaning disproportionate to its statisti- cal value. But it is the theme of Tate's poetry, and the theme of tragedy, that man chooses the accident of his fate and by his choice creates necessity, which is his sole dignity. Against this choice the poet places our society, which with its abstract and statistical regard for the past provides a context in which choices are said not to matter, in which we are violent without idea and condemned to self-violence, suicide, "self-inflicted woe." The only possible prayer is not for good- ness but for a situation in which good and evil have some reference:

> O God of our flesh, return us to Your wrath,
> Let us be evil could we enter in
> Your grace, and falter on the stony path!
> —"Last Days of Alice"

Mr. Tate has said in a note to *Poems 1928-1931* that all the books of a poet should ultimately be regarded as one book; at any rate that it was to this end that he worked. This statement, though it evi- dently does not license us to disregard the individuality of particular poems, suggests the poet's responsibility towards his themes, atti- tudes, evaluations, and implies our permission to use on one poem what we have found more fully or more clearly elucidated in another, to expect throughout the work certain recurrent elements not only of theme but of manner and imagery as well. Having just now discussed theme as much as possible in isolation and abstractedly, I wish at this point to begin afresh by considering more particular matters and to be led back to the theme by way of illustration and example.

The composition of the poems may be divided into two general sorts, roughly correspondent to a fundamental distinction of the thought: "there is that / Which is the commentary; there's that other, / Which may be called the immaculate / Conception of its essence in itself." The first sort is reflective, meditative, rhetorical in manner, executed often in a considerably distorted blank verse, and given over to the explicit discussion of theme: such poems as "Causerie," "Fragment of a Meditation," and "Retroduction to American History" are of this kind. The other manner is characterized by brevity, concision, great formality of rime and meter, and (for the reader) those difficulties which must go with subtle thought of which the connections are allowed to remain implicit by a kind of lyrical absolutism: "Ode to Fear," "The Traveller," "The Paradigm," "The Cross."

The two modes are not always to be found in isolation; often both hold place in a single poem, as in "To the Lacedemonians," for example, which begins as public speech and ends with a lyric of six quatrains; or less obviously in "The Meaning of Life," whose explicit discussion of its material issues at last in a splendid and inexhaustibly allusive figure; or in the "Ode to the Confederate Dead," where the rhetoric is controlled by rime and by the dramatic situation.

In these two modes of composition, as I have suggested, we may see the attenuated and *formal* replica of a duality, a basic division —mentioned above as Essence and Commentary—which is central to Tate's poetry and creates his myth, giving rise to the kind of recurrent figure which is this poet's "representative anecdote" about the world. The crucial antithesis is most clearly and explicitly presented in two coupled poems, "The Meaning of Life" and "The Meaning of Death," the first "a monologue," the second "an after-dinner speech." The first begins:

> Think about it at will: there is that
> Which is the commentary; there's that other,
> Which may be called the immaculate

Conception of its essence in itself.
It is necessary to distinguish the weights
Of the two methods lest the first smother
The second, the second be speechless (without the first).

And immediately afterward the poet shows his awareness of the two modes of composition, and of their implications ("I was saying this more briefly the other day / But one must be explicit as well as brief.").

It is the speechless conception which is life, which bears its "meaning" in itself or (no matter) has no meaning, and needs none. This is demonstrated by anecdote: as a boy the speaker wished not to be like the old men in Kentucky who "shot at one another for luck"; at twelve he decided he would shoot only for honor, at twenty he thought he would not shoot at all; but at thirty-three, that age of crucifixion, "one must shoot / As often as one gets the rare chance — / In killing there is more than commentary."

There is a history here, in brief, of rationale, or the explication of motive, of commentary: the old men who shoot at one another for luck live in a universe of possibly placable demons whose will is unknown; they are offensive to secular codes of behavior (honor) and the rational principles of ethical religion (there is no God but if there had been He would have wished us not to shoot at all), but their behavior is not superficially distinguishable from a mystical insistence on mortal and all-committing action.

Before dealing with the concluding figure of "The Meaning of Life" I will consider the antithetical poem. In "an after-dinner speech" the meaning of death is ironically presented as the meaning of life:

Time, fall no more.
Let that be life—time falls no more. The threat
Of time we in our own courage have forsworn.
Let light fall, there shall be eternal light
And all the light shall on our heads be worn . . .

It is, is it not, the earthly paradise currently called the World of Tomorrow? It is to depend on the denial of time, the legislation of eternal light and on "our own courage," on that modern combination of virtues and vices which Dostoevsky called "enlightened greed" and "titanic pride." A program for further action is outlined towards the end of the poem:

> Gentlemen, let's
> Forget the past, its related errors, coarseness
> Of parents, laxities, unrealities of principle.
>
> Think of tomorrow. Make a firm postulate
> Of simplicity in desire and act
> Founded on the best hypotheses;
> Desire to eat secretly, alone, lest
> Ritual corrupt our charity . . .

The antithesis between the two poems is wonderfully clear at this point simply as a matter of argument and exposition; the speaker in the second poem, taking the attitude of protestant scientism, rejects the past because "what happens is therefore imperfect," rejects ritual because ritual rejoices in the repetition of the past and stresses "useless" elements in "useful" charity: he proposes an action based on "the best hypotheses." This attitude, then, would rid itself of the world; it is the attitude of the successful revolutionary who cannot bear, in his triumph, that common things should be called by their ancient names and so invents a new calendar.

But in their concluding imagery the two poems ironically develop the opposition by metaphors that have the same scene. "The Meaning of Life":

> One's sense of the proper decoration alters
> But there's a kind of lust feeds on itself
> Unspoken to, unspeaking; subterranean
> As a black river full of eyeless fish
> Heavy with spawn; with a passion for time
> Longer than the arteries of a cave.

And "The Meaning of Death":

> Lest darkness fall and time fall
> In a long night when learned arteries
> Mounting the ice and sum of barbarous time
> Shall yield, without essence, perfect accident.
>
> We are the eyelids of defeated caves.

Life exists speechlessly but essentially in the fish heavy with spawn, who are not blind, not defective, but simply "eyeless," sight being not an "essential" quality (compare, in "To the Lacedemonians": "The white face / Eyeless with eyesight only, the modern power—"). In the revulsion from time and all continuance, in the election of science, which leads to "perfect accident," is death, and the after-dinner speaker by a superb turn of irony and drama is permitted to know it and to say it, to realize where his program is taking him. The fish are eyeless, but the speaker and his audience in the cold sleep of science close the eyes of the world.

Mr. Cleanth Brooks, in his admirable analysis of these two poems (*Modern Poetry and the Tradition*), has this to say of the closing figure of the first: "The symbol of the concrete, irrational essence of life, the blood, receives an amazing amplification by its association with the cave. The two symbols are united on the basis of their possession of 'arteries.' The blood is associated with 'lust,' is 'subterranean' (buried within the body), is the source of 'passion.' But the added metaphor of the cave extends the associations from those appropriate to an individual body to something general and eternal."

Precisely. And I think this insight may be carried further, and that the division it offers is, in various guises, at work throughout Tate's poetry, of which it is the radical judgment and generative principle. I will try to demonstrate this.

The blood, and the cave: liquid and solid, the hot and the cold, that which is fluid and that which is rigid. The combination occurs over and over in the poems, though it need not take the form invariably of blood and cave; it is the relation that is so insistent. It is used to characterize the relation of becoming to become, of life to death, of process to result; in its more general form it suggests the common metaphor whereby forms "harden" or "freeze" into lifeless conventions, and means that civilization is achieved by "hardening of the arteries," that all effort produces monuments. In "Aeneas at Washington" the hero stands by the Potomac and confesses in these terms: "The city my blood had built I knew no more." In "To the Lacedemonians" the old soldier says, "I was a boy, I never knew cessation / Of the bright course of blood along the vein." And later, "Life grown sullen and immense / Lusts after immunity to pain." And the abstract statement completes the figure: "There is no civilization without death." Likewise the "Romantic Traditionists" are accused of neglecting the essence for the commentary: "Immaculate race! to yield / Us final knowledge set / In a cold frieze, a field / Of war but no blood let."

Sometimes the symbol for generation is water instead of blood, and it is set against "ice," as in the beautiful line from the "Ode to Fear," which I have used as the title of this paper, where Fear is addressed: "You are the current of the frozen stream, / Shadow invisible, ambushed and vigilant flame." (Often flame is equated with generative force, as in "Sonnets of the Blood" II and VI.) And again in "Winter Mask," where the poisoned rat, "driven to cold water, / Dies of the water of life"; by this inversion the figure is seen also as Cocytus, the lowest hell where the traitor is "damned in eternal ice." There is more than a hint of the metaphor in "The Oath," when the speaker decides "what it is in time that gnaws / The ageing fury of a mountain stream" (where "gnaws" carries over to suggest the action of the stream on its bed, which confines it) and thinks he hears "the dark pounding its head / On a rock, crying: *Who are the dead?*" And in the ninth of "Sonnets of the Blood" the sestet employs the relation. The octave has warned the "captains of industry" against their "aimless power" which will lead to the plundering of "the inner mansion of the blood":

> Yet the prime secret whose simplicity
> Your towering engine hammers to reduce,
> Though driven, holds that bulwark of the sea
> Which breached will turn unspeaking fury loose
> To drown out him who swears to rectify
> Infinity, that has nor ear nor eye.

The prime secret (he has already mentioned prime numbers) is the secret of that which is indivisible and thus closed to analysis and commentary; were this not so, and could the towering engine reduce the bulwark, which is regarded as, generally, form, structure, the continence of life, the sea (which is in the terms of the sonnets the blood) would "turn unspeaking fury loose," life would turn destructive once its form had been violated, and would stain the earth, as in Yeats' poem, "The Gyres," with "irrational streams of blood."

As the blood may be conceived as water, as ocean or stream or pond, so the other term, the cave, has thematic extensions, as a well ("Seasons of the Soul"), as the depth of the Inferno, the "vast concluding shell," as womb and tomb (Christ's tomb especially) and Plato's cave; all of these seem to work into one fine passage:

> It [light] burns us each alone
> Whose burning arrogance
> Burns up the rolling stone,
> This earth—Platonic cave
> Of vertiginous chance!

Come, tired Sisyphus,
Cover the cave's egress
Where light reveals the slave,
Who rests when sleeps with us
The mother of silences.
                              —"Seasons of the Soul" IV

This relation, some form of which seems to pervade the work, is in my opinion the central irony of Tate's poetry and fully involves his judgment of the world and of the human situation. In "The Meaning of Life" essence and commentary were described as antithetical elements, both of which in composition form the life of man: the problem is of a certain proportion that must be maintained, and in modern society is not maintained (see "The Meaning of Death" and the ninth "Sonnet of the Blood"). The Freudians employ a somewhat similar trope in their division of the ego and the id; life is of the id, dark, irrational (what Blake called Energy?), and the ego draws on this stuff for the creation of order, but if the ego rejects, out of pride, its rude and raw basis, it rejects its roots and must wither (John Crowe Ransom has a poem, "A Painted Head," which deals with this division). But again I find in Valéry a lucid and beautiful description. In a piece called "Man and the Shell," translated by Lionel Abel and printed in the second number of *The Tiger's Eye*, a periodical, he says:

I note first of all that "living nature" is unable to fashion solid bodies directly. In this state, stone and metal are useless to it. Suppose the problem is to produce a lasting object of invariant shape—a prop, a lever, a rod, a buckler; to produce a tree-trunk, a femur, a tooth or a shield, a skull or a shell, nature always makes the same detour: it uses the liquid or fluid state of which every living substance is constituted, and strains off the solid elements of its construction. All that lives or lived results from the properties and changes of certain liquids. Besides, every solid has passed through a liquid phase, melted or in solution. But "living nature" does not take to the high temperatures which enable us to work "pure bodies," and give to glass, bronze or iron in liquid or plastic states the forms desired, and which cooling will make permanent. Life, to model its solid organs, is limited to the use of solutions, suspensions or emulsions.

Certain kinds of perfection, then, do not belong to life but to death. In various thematic combinations this distinction of the poet's thought is developed, applied, enriched. The blood and the cave are extreme terms for extreme kinds of life, of man, of society. Character-istically, in the War between the States, the South is regarded as the way of life most representative of essence, of blood, and so of ritual and tradition, while the North is conceived as protestant, scientific, and without history; speaking of the present, the old soldier in "To the Lacedemonians" says, "All are born Yankees of the race of men / And this, too, now the country of the damned." Again,

> And in that Blue renown
> The Gray went down,
> Down like a rat,
> And even the rats cheered.

The tragedy, for Tate, is the loss of the possibility of value through the suggestions of positivism, "social science," and all modes of merely statistical consideration, that man is without sin, is ultimately and progressively perfectible, is through with the past. This is the philosophy of the cave, of the commentary. Against this there is the myth of the blood, the "unspeaking fury," the "lust" that feeds on itself, which insists that the past is undeniable, insists on the neces-sity of finding and seizing one's tradition with (and not despite) all the many imperfections that are the simple result of existence, and on the impossibility of a life cut off from its roots in the personal and deeply familiar earth of time.

I hope I have not too much simplified this matter; probably I have, but necessarily when one is exercising oneself to make the theme clear there will be other matters to which one is not (not verbally, anyhow) attending. It seemed an important subject, to consider as closely as possible what is the myth of this poetry, the assumption by which it operates and about which its meanings are organized. The matter of the duality seemed especially worth noticing in some detail, if only because of what reviewers are still likely to call the "obscurity" of these poems.

The poems are, I think, hard, but the complaint about obscurity does not seem just, and may deserve some suspicion of being a rather easy disguise for a very hard moral complaint: some may find it more comforting not to know what the poet is doing than to be forced into a coherent attitude towards his work, and in this sense Mr. Tate's poems still suffer at the hands of critics whose idea of what a poem is has not the splendid certainty to be found in their idea of what Mr. Tate ought to be. Thus, recently, a professor of English: "It is no longer possible to dismiss Mr. Tate's poetry with such adjectives as cultivated, fastidious, and morose." Ah, would it were still possible, meanwhile remarks his tone, those were the halcyon days—something we would perhaps not be entitled to say had we not found later in his review what we expected to find: "It is much easier to discover what Tate is against than what he is for." And, at last, a poet like Tate is "recusant to the wholeness of humanity and it is unlikely that he will attain a higher status than that of poets' poet."

Strong words, and on the whole remarkably without meaning: if one does not know what the poet is "for" one does not know that he is "recusant to the wholeness of humanity," whatever all that may mean. And the question, what a poet is for, with its delicately swaddled ambiguity (What does he like? How can we use him?) may not be, after all, the right kind of question to ask. What, after all, is Shakespeare for? Or what is Yeats for?—the poet whose themes Tate's perhaps most closely resemble, and who wrote:

> Even the wisest man grows tense
> With some sort of violence
> Before he can accomplish fate . . .

But the antitheses are present always, the ranges in which value roams: what happens and history; violence and idea; accident and necessity. You have, the tragic poets say, your choice.

The Poetry of Robert Graves

Collected Poems, 1955. By Robert Graves. Doubleday, 1955.

The dominant criticism of the day is a criticism which explains things; it seems to have appeared as a response to a few difficult poems, and to have proceeded on the presumption that poems were very difficult matters, or that they would be from now on, or that, if they were not, they could be made so by judicious explanations. The habit of such criticism has produced some odd effects both good and bad, of which the good have perhaps been often enough surveyed. As to the bad: certain sorts of difficulty are taken as signs of excellence, and the explanation of them as pre-eminently the business of criticism; poetic illiteracy has mightily increased not for one reason alone, no doubt, but this species of criticism has done its share, with the best intentions in the world, toward producing the situation as we have it. The habit of reading poetry seems largely lost, replaced by the school room habit of "analyzing" it; students seem unwilling, and probably unable, to undertake the reading of, say, "The Ecstasy" or the "Nocturnall on S. Lucies Day" without the help of a professional exegete, while at the same time they look with some contempt on "MacFlecknoe" and "The Medal" as productions which no member of the interpreting priesthood can make difficult enough to be worth a close attention. As "Prufrock," by the course of time and repeated interpretation, begins to look more like a monologue of Browning than it formerly did, the readers of "Prufrock" find themselves incapable of the sustained literate attention demanded by "Bishop Blougram's Apology."

Again, it is odd that the furor of the main attack upon "modern" poetry, upon "obscurity," appears to have dissolved and been left to scattered guerrilla forces more or less in the moment of its victory —for a great deal of good poetry at present is surely easy enough for

Reprinted by permission from *The Kenyon Review*, Vol. XVIII, No. 1, Winter 1956. Copyright 1956 by Kenyon College.

even moderately literate persons, if there are any—and one must conclude that many warriors of the simplistic party wanted poetry to be simple only in order that they might despise it without discomfort, and that since winning this victory they have sensibly gone home to read some more novels.

Another oddity is this, that under the present exegetical conventions much good poetry begins to smell of "literature" before it has had a chance to be contemporary at all; it becomes "immortal," and we may say of it with respectful Roman piety "migravit ad plures" before it has had any worldly career to speak of—

> Renowned Spenser, lye a thought more nye
> To learned Chaucer, and rare Beaumont lye
> A little neerer Spenser, to make roome
> For Shakespeare. . . .

That same tomb is becoming overcrowded also with contemporaries, but I refrain from revising Basse's lines for the demonstration.

A final oddity, not unconnected with this unseemly lust for the Hit Parade and the Hall of Fame: part of the explanations habitually performed by critics is the explanation that the explanations do not matter, that the poet's views of the world are scaffoldings taken away when the poem is done, that such views expressed in his poems have a merely formal and compositional interest and are never addressed to human beings; that in any case the reader, instructed by a criticism largely rationalist, liberal, and secular, will easily free the poem from those notions of the poet which embarrass everyone by being aristocratic, conservative, and magical or superstitious (all those Visions and White Goddesses, etc.); whereupon the beautiful residue will be pure poetry, purely appreciated. ("How does one catch the lions in the desert?" "Strain off the sand, the remainder will be lions.")

An argument on this theme would be amusing and, in my opinion, useful; the other side would have a good deal to say, which I have purposely omitted here. Just now, hurrying to reach my subject, I would suggest only that poetry cannot matter much while all the devotion of its best readers is expended on the proof that it does not matter; and that though the object of poetry is indeed contemplative, that need not imply any indifference to the substance of what is contemplated.

By this roundabout means I finally arrive at the *Collected Poems* of

Robert Graves, who shows, even in the announced intention, very little disposition to elbow his way unceremoniously into a mausoleum:

> Personally, I have little regard for posterity or, at least, make no attempt to anticipate their literary tastes. Whatever view they may take of my work, say a hundred years hence, must necessarily be a mistaken one, because this is my age, not theirs, and even with my help they will never fully understand it. Can I imagine myself sympathizing with their reasons for selecting this or that poem of mine to print in their anthologies? They may even choose to revive verses which, because I know that they are in some way defective, I have done my best to suppress. I write for my contemporaries.
>
> *Poems & Satires*, 1951

The problem was, perhaps, to find the contemporaries. Graves has been a good poet for a long time, but it has only recently become fashionable to say so aloud; like so many of our poetical fashions, this one shows a strongly competitive element, exalting the meek and hurling down the mighty from their seats (not that Graves is especially meek), so that it sometimes seems as though Graves is not being "discovered" so much as invented on the spot, to satisfy a want of one party in that war of words which never speaks of a poem but always and only of "poetry." No doubt his poems will survive this kind of interest.

My object, then, in speaking of these poems is somewhat remote from what is presently called criticism. I am not to explain difficulties, since the poems are not difficult (except as one might use the word of "a difficult child," they are sometimes stubborn and cantankerous), I am not to "analyze"; my object is appreciation, which is something like advertisement; benign descriptions and free samples. How undignified! How embarrassing it has become to have to say, "I like these poems," and, to the reader, "I hope you will give yourself the pleasure of inspecting them." I hope that the following, for example, is not in need of detailed exegesis:

> Down, wanton, down! Have you no shame
> That at the whisper of Love's name,
> Or Beauty's, presto! up you raise
> Your angry head and stand at gaze?
>
> Poor bombard-captain, sworn to reach
> The ravelin and effect a breach—

Indifferent what you storm or why,
So be that in the breach you die!

Love may be blind, but Love at least
Knows what is man and what mere beast;
Or Beauty wayward, but requires
More delicacy from her squires.

Tell me, my witless, whose one boast
Could be your staunchness at the post,
When were you made a man of parts
To think fine and profess the arts?

Will many-gifted Beauty come
Bowing to your bald rule of thumb,
Or Love swear loyalty to your crown?
Be gone, have done! Down, wanton, down!

(My fellow critic Professor Limpkin wishes me to say that a ravelin
is the salient outwork of a fortress, and that "Down, wantons, down,"
is what the cockney cried to the eels, in *King Lear*, when she put
'em i' the paste alive; but there, I think, the interpreter may conclude his labors.)

I will give another sample:

THIEF

To the galleys, thief, and sweat your soul out
With strong tugging under the curled whips,
That there your thievishness may find full play.
Whereas, before, you stole rings, flowers and watches,
Oaths, jests and proverbs,
Yet paid for bed and board like an honest man,
This shall be entire thiefdom: you shall steal
Sleep from chain-galling, diet from sour crusts,
Comradeship from the damned, the ten-year chained—
And, more than this, the excuse for life itself
From a boat steered toward battles not your own.

I take it "analysis" is not what's wanted; what else ought the critic
do, before blessing the poet and passing him quickly through the
customs? Resolutely refusing to discuss theme, imagery, symbolism,
form, and all such high matters, I may yet say briefly something about
the tradition and the principles of Graves's poetry.

Though his measures are generally speaking "traditional"—the word will cover, happily, a multitude of virtues—Graves's handling of the line has about it something pleasantly eccentric, rough, and not easily digestible into English literature; not because it is not literary, but more likely because his masters are not so much the conventional "great" or "major" poets of drama, epic, and narrative, as the lyric masters who are so much neglected nowadays, with one or two exceptions, probably because they are insufficiently *important* (meaning, perhaps, that what you get from them in the first place is more like pleasure than like culture); Graves himself finds his ancestry in Skelton, and gives us the "sepulchral continuity" of "Skel-(e)ton—Church yarde—Graves" (*Poetic Unreason*, 1925); I think also, for these qualities of roughness, irony, humor, and a certain air of being homemade ("handmade, individual craftsmanship quality," says Graves), of Dunbar, Wyatt, Blake, and Hardy.

He is a believer in the Muse, whom he calls the Goddess, as Blake was a believer in the angel, and would probably contend that a certain amateurish awkwardness is an advantage in that service; thus he writes of a certain gardener whose garden flourished although he himself "had not eye enough / To wheel a barrow between the broadest gates / Without a clumsy scraping," that the man's success came "by angelic favour," and ends by assessing the human contribution thus:

> Well, he had something, though he called it nothing—
> An ass's wit, a hair-belly shrewdness
> That would appraise the intentions of the angel
> By the very difference of his own confusion,
> And bring the most to pass.

We may compare and contrast, as the exams say, the attitude of Holofernes: "This is a gift that I have, simple, simple; a foolish extravagant spirit, full of forms, figures, shapes, objects, ideas, apprehensions, motions, revolutions: these are begot in the ventricle of memory, nourished in the womb of *pia mater*, and delivered upon the mellowing of occasion. But the gift is good in those in whom it is acute, and I am thankful for it."

As to the principles of this poetry, doubtless a very complicated discussion could be made on that theme, which I should not have brought up, however, except for my belief that they are essentially simple, only two in number, and simply expressed by the poet in the first and last lines of his celebrated didactic poem "To Juan at the Winter Solstice":

1. There is one story and one story only. . . .

2. But nothing promised that is not performed.

1. About the one story I shall be exegetical after all, for a moment, and pedantic as well: it is the story of the relation between two sorts of time, one seasonal, in which everything returns, and the other linear, in which nothing returns. Its simplest emblem is the tree, which each year suffers death and is born again until, one year, it dies in root and branch forever; a more complex emblem is the life of men and women. 2. About the second principle, nothing promised that is not performed, I would say only that it expresses the technical condition of beautiful works at all times.

And there I may as well leave it, not without a word of reassurance for those who open their newspapers each morning with the sad yet obscurely comfortable reflection that poetry is a dying art. Like all the other arts (not to mention baseball, canasta, and criticism), poetry is always a dying art and can never really be saved; from Linus, Memnon and Orpheus to ourselves reaches an unbroken succession of last words, testaments, and deathbed repentances. The good poems of good poets do not save the world, or keep tomorrow from being more dreadful than today; they are merely good poems, and when they die they become Literature. To spell it out once more: Robert Graves is a good poet. Go read his book.

MacLeish and Viereck

Collected Poems 1917-1952. By Archibald MacLeish. Houghton Mifflin, 1952.
The First Morning. By Peter Viereck. Scribner's, 1952.

The poet's responsibility to society—a matter much debated. In the phrase itself there is implicit some prospective metaphor of the poet as criminal, vainly trying to *discharge his debt* by means of his poems while all the time, really, it is something else that "society" wants. What? This has not been made clear, but seems to have confusedly to do with, on the one hand, messages of life and hope; with, on the other, moral earnestness and a severe, traditional look at current events. Archibald MacLeish takes in many places a severe view—with virtue, with this Republic, with poetry itself, things were formerly different, are now much degenerated, but the poet by his images may redeem the time, "Turn round into the actual air" and "Invent the age! Invent the metaphor!" Peter Viereck brings, so it is held by some, messages of life and hope; "perhaps . . . the promised man who is going to lead modern poetry out of the wasteland" (statement by Van Wyck Brooks, but what wasteland?), he wears his rue with a difference.

Both these poets, the one long established and latterly neglected, the other young and spectacularly successful almost from his first appearance a few years ago, are much given to debating, in poems and elsewhere, the theme of the poet's responsibility to society, and both have been quite downright on this subject; there is some temptation, which I hope I shall avoid, to treat them as the same poet Before and After. This temptation would lead conveniently away from the poetry and into a discussion on the implicit premise that the poetry didn't in fact matter and with the implicit conclusion that poet Before and poet After were of the same caliber, something I do not believe. What would matter, in such a discussion? Attitude (positive), ease and rapidity of "communication," political awareness, the quality of being *contemporary* (as today's newspaper is more contemporary than yesterday's newspaper). Above all, perhaps, the ability to take a revolutionary tone while moving steadily backward, the triumph of strategic withdrawal. Both these poets, perhaps in the largest part of their production, seem deliberately to invite a discourse in those terms, a discourse which, except for a feeble protest at one point, I do not feel drawn to give, preferring for the most part instead simply to record something of my impression of the poetry.

Archibald MacLeish, for a very few poems, is one of the finest lyric poets now writing. That after these few poems, a long way after, there follow many which strike one as forced, incomplete, not thoroughly considered, and some which seem to betray an impatience, an exasperation with the mere idea of poetry as an art, is something that does not affect the position. We do not much like to speak of "immortality" in this connection any more, nor even of future times (for who knows what altogether dreadful nonsense people will admire day after tomorrow?), but if I may pretend the old usage still to apply, as though we looked forward to an Oxford Book compiled by archangels, it is to say that the author of the simple and noble "You, Andrew Marvell" will have a place there, where room will be denied to many whose flabby complexities now pass for muscle. This poem reads, surely, as though it were imperishable; it has no false note, and neither hesitation nor haste in its grave, steady rhythms, the exact timing of its rimes. Though in my opinion Mr. MacLeish nowhere fully equals it in any other poem, this one is yet characteristic of his design, its intention of remote voyages is uniquely his intention (and responsible elsewhere for his bad poems as well as for his good ones); its subject is such that his distantly seen and, so to say, *generalized* details give the greatest intensity with the greatest controlling calm. I am reminded, reading it, of a passage of Dante with a similar subject: the great lyric at the close of Paradiso XXII where the poet at Beatrice's hest turns to look back through the seven spheres at the earth which he has left behind, below; looking through the orbits of the planets, seeing them vary their relations one with another, he sees "from ridge to river mouth" "the little threshing-floor which makes us so fierce" ("L'aiuola che ci fa tanto feroci"). I think the MacLeish poem is of that kind, and of that quality so far as the complete lyric can be compared with the fragment of a greater design.

Of the poems published through 1933 a number of others keep their tension and their strength: "The Silent Slain," "Yacht for Sale," "Grazing Locomotives," "Pony Rock," "The Night Dream"; of the satirical pieces, "Corporate Entity" and, perhaps, the Museum Attendant's speech from "Empire Builders." Two poems, "Nat Bacon's Bones" and "Galán," seem to me to approach, in a different way, the excellence and finish of "You, Andrew Marvell," and as these are brief I will quote the first of them here:

> Nat Bacon's bones
> They never found,
> Nat Bacon's grave
> Is wilderground:
> Nat Bacon's tongue
> Doth sound! Doth sound!
>
> The rich and proud
> Deny his name,
> The rich and proud
> Defile his fame:
> The proud and free
> Cry shame! Cry shame!
>
> The planter's wife
> She boasts so grand
> Sir William's blood
> Makes white her hand:
> Nat Bacon's blood
> Makes sweet this land.

Of the hortatory and political poems, the "Speeches" reprinted from *Public Speech* and *Actfive*, not much remains to be said; they do not seem to be good poems, and if they were ever good speeches that does not now appear about them either. The poet as poet knew what the poet sacrificed as citizen, he had spoken about it boldly enough in "Invocation to the Social Muse":

> We are
> Whores, Fräulein: poets, Fräulein, are persons of
>
> Known vocation following troops: they must sleep with
> Stragglers from either prince and of both views.
> The rules permit them to further the business of neither.

It is also strictly forbidden to mix in maneuvers.
Those that infringe are inflated with praise on the plazas—
Their bones are resultantly afterwards found under newspapers.

In the long poems the poet's characteristic figure becomes his obsession; these works are voyages, their protagonists sailors, explorers over the sea, into the mind, among the dead. In "The Pot of Earth" the dying god sails out on his journey; in "The Hamlet of A. MacLeish" the hero, after passing the night of terror in the Perilous Chapel, goes forth and fails to found his city; "Einstein" explores the universe in the mind and at last invades the earth in search of "reality." There is Bernal Díaz, there is Elpenor, "America Was Promises" has the figure of the voyage west. The cadences of this poetry are in general long, often formed in double-harness or placed in parallel series cataloguing details which are themselves characteristic, a generalized nature, a generalized mythology, with a consequent remoteness of tone even at moments that should be dramatically urgent, a tone that seems distantly to reflect and echo a long swell of the sea—

> Here where the walls end and the ruinous tower
> Leans with its uninhabitable black
> Long builded stones above the ultimate sea . . .

and

> We were the first that found that famous country:
> We marched by a king's name: we crossed the sierras:
> Unknown hardships we suffered: hunger:
>
> Death by the stone knife: thirst: we fared by the
> Bitter streams: we came at last to that water:
> Towers were steep upon the fluttering air . . .

The first of these passages comes from "The Hamlet," the second from "Conquistador." Both these poems are ambitious, well-conceived and in places very moving, yet at last the singleness of tone (in "The Hamlet" there is also some imitation Shakespeare, though) fails in or even defeats its purpose; all becomes too distant, dreamy, too much abstracted and generalized.

I have not yet spoken of the recent poems, first collected here, nor of the new play, "The Trojan Horse." Of the play I cannot say much: its language is more spare and active than much that precedes it; as poetry it reads not very well, perhaps, but one has learned that such language may be extremely well suited to declamation, and that given a competent performance it is likely to surprise by a vigor and tension not always easily seen on the printed page.

Nor will I say more than a few words of the latest poetry. There is an implicit assumption, when poems are "Collected," that the returns are now in, that all is over and the vote may safely be counted. In this instance I doubt it is so. The new poems seem to return to the privacy and seriousness of the earlier ones, but with a more energetic rhythm, a stripped ferocity reminiscent in places of late poems by Yeats. Some brief poems here are fine, though not always fully so—in "Out of Sleep Awakened," for example, the moralizing last couplet seems to spoil—and those pages in this book suggest the hope that this poet has turned from empty and angry public declamation to reach again "The real encounter kept at night / Alone where none will praise our art."

The poetry of Peter Viereck is often both pleasant and accomplished; light in tone, you might say, but never lacking in that suggestion of more serious stuff beneath the surface, a suggestion which no poet these days will do well to do without; there are also mythology and quotations from literature in foreign languages. Here is an example.

HOME, JAMES

Time's tumbling curtain means: "Finita è —".
Hell's jolly beavers gnaw at every sprout.
Mankind's last headline calls it doomsday-day.
The sun stands still and wilts in every way;
Sometimes a comet tries to run away
("Snuffed trying to escape," the Agents gloat);
Sometimes a planet seems to try to pray.
    Now . . . postponed . . . dreams . . . shout.
The hot and disappointed lipsticks pout.
Apocalyptic apoplexies fray
The nerves of Cronos like a Gaffer's gout.
Not ants but grasshoppers have won the bout
Because there is no piper left to pay.
 Who disconnected breath from clay?
                       Hey,
    Who . . . pulled the . . . socket . . . out?

It is difficult, in our excitement, to know what we admire most, or first, about this poem—the skillful regularity of the meter? the way in which the syntactical and metrical units exactly coincide, one phrase to one line, to produce the lilting effect so characteristic of this poet's work? the alliterations and assonances (line 10)? the highly compressed allusions to literature and mythology (lines 1, 11, and 12)? the irony (title)? the nature imagery (lines 2, 4, 5, etc.)? the awareness of the contemporary scene (lines 3, 6, 9, 15)? or perhaps it is the morality (*passim*)? Anyhow, all these features work together to produce, in their intricate weavings and delicate tonal combinations, this poem. This poem is by no means the best in *The First Morning*, any more than it is the worst; probably the worst—allowing for the fact that I can't read German and have had to omit the consideration of three poems in that tongue—is one called "Love Song of Prufrock Junior," the first in a series called "1912-1952, Full Cycle."

> Must all successful rebels grow
> From toreador to Sacred Cow?
> What cults he slew, his cult begot.
> "In my beginning," said his Scot,
> "My end"; and aging eagles know
> That 1912 was long ago.
> Today the women come and go
> Talking of T. S. Eliot.

The word goes round the English Departments that this is the equal of "The Lost Leader," and perhaps it is—though Professor Limpkin has acutely suggested that its allusive qualities (it is almost entirely built of cryptic references to Western Culture) may make it somewhat tiresome to the average undergraduate.

The best poems in this volume—including, on one opinion, "To be Sung," "Again, Again," "The Planted Skull," "Homecoming," and "Saga"—are quite good poems, perhaps a little light in weight. That they are *great* poems, that they constitute in any sense a revolution in the art (a return to this or revival of that), that they are particularly new or original or fresh, I submit that I doubt.

Now it is doubtless *not nice* to speak slightingly of a volume containing, say, half a dozen witty and ingenious poems which have given me pleasure, and I do not so speak merely because this volume contains also a relatively large amount of mediocre verse, fallen epigrams and jotted-down opinions, as well as a relatively staggering amount of simple blank space. But I feel (and feel I may as well express the feeling) a resistance to the pretension involved in the terms on which this verse is supposed to be taken—as "the present hope of poetry" (Robert Frost), "real magic" (Van Wyck Brooks), "conscientious skill . . . that makes much contemporary poetry look like the shabbiest free association" (David Daiches), "a break with the Eliot-dominated past" (Selden Rodman), "The modernist revolt has ended . . ." (Anthony Harrigan). These citations are from the dust-jacket of *The First Morning*, and though I have not quoted them in full the distinctive thing about them, as about so many favorable opinions of this poet, is visibly that it seems nearly impossible to praise Mr. Viereck except by way of taking a swipe at someone else; the ax-grinders seem to find him handy; uplifting Mr. Viereck seems to be the equal and opposite reaction generated by people standing on Mr. Eliot's head and jumping up and down. This suggests a certain expedient quality to the exaltation. When Mr. Harrigan, whom I quoted above, describes Peter Viereck as "the principal standard-bearer of the tradition of humanistic democracy in this country," the battle-lines are drawn; one may or may not shudder for humanistic democracy, but in any event the poetry has been left to one side—as perhaps it should be, for I do not believe it will stand the strain of the program that is being erected for it. It is probably not good for the poet to become the standard-bearer of any party, the thing gets out of control—from being standard-bearer he becomes standard, and people wave him about wildly. I think the results begin to show in *The First Morning*, particularly in the number of pages given over to small versified remarks, parodies (even one of the poet himself, which does not appear to show any great self-knowledge), and pompously humorless jokes about poetry and criticism—the more or less affable informalities, the inflated marginalia, of the arbiter-elect. It is probably not good for the poet to become a myth, any myth but his own, surely; there is the danger of becoming at last, as Mr. Viereck in another connection points out, merely "a *Maerchen* dreamed by the deep, cool clams." Let the clams keep cool, they're not out of this wasteland yet.

A Wild Civility

Collected Poems. By Stephen Spender. Random House, 1955.
Selected Poems. By Randall Jarrell. Knopf, 1955.
The Shield of Achilles. By W. H. Auden. Random House, 1955.

In taking Herrick's phrase for my title I go against his immediate sense. None of these three poets practices an art which is "too precise in every part," and it is on the side of civility, rather than wildness, that I want to put such weight as these remarks may have; keeping finally, I hope, the sense of Herrick's poem, that sweet disorder is a delightful matter, of which the freedom (the "wantonnesse") depends precisely on being, in the first place, dressed—fully clothed and in one's right mind. There are implicit in this theme some notions about the poet's ultimate delight in a civilization which he may indeed have to attack most bitterly, but which he had better attack with the most civilized means at his disposal, becoming thus the lover of what he hates, and becoming—at his own risk, the risk most often of being pompous and a bore—ecumenical. Therefore to Spender's Shelleyan intensities, simplicities, and occasional absurdities, to the erudite nostalgia of Randall Jarrell, I prefer, even in a collection by no means constantly of a high order, Auden's pastoral urbanities. If there is paradox in that last phrase it has an ancient sanction—what could all those shepherds sing about but Town and Court?

Stephen Spender is chiefly celebrated, I think, for some early poems composed in the 'Thirties, under the influence of aesthetic fashions, or principles, different from those of the present. To say this is not to say that those ideas are inferior to these, since if we have learned anything from the past twenty-odd years, it is that the "enduring principles of art" (or of anything else) may depreciate even faster than the works by which we judge them; but there are differ-

Reprinted by permission from The Kenyon Review, Vol. XVII, No. 3, Summer 1955.
Copyright 1955 by Kenyon College.

ences, and we may remind ourselves of two in particular: the interest of that earlier poetry in technology, industry, in making such things as aircraft and power lines subjects for song; and its related interest in politics and society, an interest frequently called Communist but appearing at present more like an ideal and refined utopianism. On the second point, the immediate political passions of some of Spender's early poems, their explicit program for actions, may be condemned unjustly by an age not exactly notable for moral passion of any sort whatever, but may be justly seen as weaknesses because they issue so largely in exhortation, in oratory, and had whatever value they had simply as incitements to belief and future action. As for the first point, the introduction into poetry of "motor-cycles wires aeroplanes cars trains" appears now as both less daring and less urgent than perhaps it did; while the objects themselves have been improved upon and made familiar to such an extent that the mere mention of their names is no longer numinous; nor have they sufficiently receded into the past to gain the quaint pathos of Proust's first view of a flying machine.

Nevertheless, some of these early poems still seem fine in places, in passages, or in single lines, and one or two have kept their shape. "The Landscape Near an Aerodrome" is a good poem, spoiled, I think, only at the last lines, where the note of social protest rises somewhat shrilly to a prosopopoeia, as "Religion stands, the Church blocking the sun." And "The Express" is still a beautiful poem, in which the patient accumulation of details is not obliterated by oratory and opens out as if naturally, with a final strangeness and power:

> Ah, like a comet through flame, she moves entranced,
> Wrapt in her music no bird song, no, nor bough
> Breaking with honey buds, shall ever equal.

But even the most famous of these early works, such as "I Think Continually of Those Who Were Truly Great," and "Not Palaces, an Era's Crown," support with difficulty, or fail to support, some characteristic faults, a kind of windiness at the extreme of earnest passion, an overwrought tone collapsing flatly in abstraction, an occasional bathetic crossing of levels within the figure—"Drink from here energy and only energy, / As from the electric charge of a battery." In going over these poems for the present collection Spender has made certain revisions, "a discreet and almost unnoticeable minimum of technical tidyings up," a thing I do not debate his right to do, and do not care to make a subject of discussion, pausing only to say that the revisions, in such instances as I have noticed, tend to leave untouched the difficulties mentioned above: "Like prompting Hamlet on the castle stair" has become "Like Hamlet prompted on the castle stair"; at its weakest line, "The Express" "plunges new eras of white happiness" instead of, as formerly, "wild happiness," leaving out of question the somewhat blank effect of the eras of happiness themselves.

In his later poems I do not see any very considerable development. There is usually a greater calm, there is technical command which can make a very attractive poem in a subdued mode, such as "The Barn," and there are brief flashes of intensity finely handled in "Elegy for Margaret." But Spender remains a very uneven poet, either wildly soaring or noncommittally flat, and it is as though there goes with this division a division of vocabulary. On the one hand he is the most explicitly detailed of poets, often presenting simply the details, with little or no progression, and this in his flat mood:

> Delicate aluminum girders
> Project phantom aerial masts
> Swaying crane and derrick
> Above the seas' just lifting deck.

But passion or exaltation, on the other hand, turn him into the most abstract of poets, and in this mood he will play contentedly on detached metaphorical relations like darkness and light, circumference and center, will and weakness, or else on a number of words which seem to have talismanic value for him: time, space, history, death, universe, world, etc.

He is a splendid phrase-maker, master of the noble gesture, of which examples will easily occur to his readers. His dramatic stance and sweeping motions imitate poetically his ideal heroes, "Beholders of the promised dawn of truth, / The explorers of immense and simple lines." And I have felt that poetry, for Spender, consists not so much in composition as in what is liberated (the sublime) from composition, and that, accordingly, he is the least interested in technique, and the least accomplished, of these three poets. His subjects frequently are as screens, behind which he awaits the moment for breaking rhapsodically out, and this moment is not always opportune, so that the great phrase gets little or no authority from the poem, referring rather away from the poem and to "the world." He very easily

leaves drama for exhortation, or making sure you get the point, and
he seems to believe in this program quite explicitly: "Holy is lucidity
/ And the mind that dare explain." And sometimes, I will add, explain and explain:

> Within our nakedness, nakedness still
> Is the naked mind. Past and stars show
> Through the columned bones. Tomorrow
> Will blow away the temple of each will.
> The Universe, by inches, minutes, fills
> Our hollowed tongues. Name and image glow
> In word, in form. Star and history know
> That they exist, in life existence kills.

The ironical pathos of Randall Jarrell's poetry, or, sometimes, its
pathetic irony, takes most frequently the form of a dramatic monologue, occasionally a dialogue; inhabited, in either case, by ghostly
presences, aphoristic reminiscences, generalities, profundities—"I find
no fault in this just man," "Man is born in chains and everywhere
we see him dead," "One touch of insight makes the ages kin." Now
and then it looks as though these profundities alone are the object,
as they stand out, free and memorable, from passages which do not
very fully engage the poet's energies. Even so, it is clear that Jarrell
is an intelligent poet, usually interesting to read even when one cannot at last give a clear assent to what has happened, and that our
interest is sustained not alone by witty phrases but by some deep and
constant theme with which he is preoccupied. The concise view of
his development afforded by the *Selected Poems* may allow a fairly
detailed description of this theme.

In his early poems, which were almost exclusively about the war,
I think I can see now that the central concern was not with war or
soldiers as such, but rather with what in these subjects corresponds
with the situation of "the prisoner." It was not simply that there
were several poems about prisoners (now grouped together under that
head) but that this poet's characteristic image of human beings saw
them, with a fair consistency, as prisoners in all their situations—not
only in jails, but in barracks, camps, ships, aircraft, hospital beds,
dreams, and, at last, graves—and that what all these prisoners sym-
bolized for him was some paradoxical intuition of helplessness and
freedom inextricably combined: "Who fights for his own life / Loses,

loses: I have killed for my world, and am free"—this of a dead soldier, a Negro.

It is possible to see a little further than this. Behind the prisoners, who but duplicate in various ways the primal situation which generates helplessness and freedom together, are the children, whose pathos, essential emblem of Jarrell's world, consists in the fact that their sufferings are real while the meanings they assign these sufferings have the quality of dream. Already in the early poems the whole of this deep-rooted complex of metaphor occasionally concentrates—childhood, imprisonment, war, dream—as in "The Death of the Ball Turret Gunner":

> From my mother's sleep I fell into the State,
> And I hunched in its belly till my wet fur froze.
> Six miles from earth, loosed from its dream of life. . . .

This intuition of a center, this cluster, metaphor, theme, expands in Jarrell's later poems in a number of ways, and once appreciated can be felt as a constant current. The primal emblematic figure of the child, his terror and absurdity, his helplessness and freedom—qualities which characterize, with Freudian piety, the rest of life—finds a wide range of reflection, in the world of the *Märchen*, the world of Grimm and Hans Andersen, in the terror and absurdity of dreams, and at last in the terror and absurdity of history, from whose deep imprisonment the dead inform us of our own (as in, e.g., "An English Garden in Austria"). Somewhere close to the heart of all this is, in particular, the tale of Sleeping Beauty, seen however as the tale of the Prince; and the Prince, in a poem which isolates him from the story, is seen in turn as a child.

The fable that most often informs this characteristic material is, so far as I can see, that of the child (or the young boy or girl, or the adult viewed as a child) in unwilling quest and compelled discovery of a reality which the poet resolutely sees as grim and disillusioning; and for this discovery the child, the Prince, and all of us, are very ill-prepared: "We learn from [books] to understand, but not to change." The terrible reality of life is worse than the terrible reality of legend, because it excludes all hopes, even the terrifying ones:

> I start to weep because—because there are no ghosts;
> A man dies like a rabbit, for a use.
> What will they pay me, when I die, to die?

Thus in a fable by Kafka ("Diaries," 1916) the condemned man is to be put to death all alone in his cell by an executioner who responds to his shrieks of protest with: "You are probably thinking of those fairy tales in which a servant is commanded to expose a child but does not do so and instead binds him over as apprentice to a shoemaker. Those are fairy tales; this, though, is not a fairy tale.—" But Jarrell inclines to elaborate on the horror and pity of it somewhat more than Kafka, as also on the irony of it. To secure this last effect, in his later poems, he supplies often, over against the figure of the child, as a dramatic and antithetical reinforcement, the figure of the Good European, or the Old European at any rate, or (at least once) the Old One Himself, who seems maybe the Best European Of All.

Now all this is very interesting, and—if I happen to be right in my descriptions—there is something very appealing, a kind of metaphysical pathos, in the idea that many of these poems perceptibly relate to a center, a constatation of figurative speech which partly yields to the reason. And Jarrell is, as I said, intelligent, and the intelligence characterizes his poetry in such a way that it is usually, not always, interesting even when not altogether convincing. But I am still unable to take seriously, for example, "The Night before the Night before Christmas," which seems to me also thoroughly uninteresting even though, or because, it remorselessly and at great length illustrates those thematic preoccupations I have tried to expound. More usually, as in "A Girl in a Library," a poem I mostly liked once and mostly don't now, there are moments and passages of considerable charm, though the whole leaves me feeling rather blank. So often, with Jarrell, the situation of the poem, and its action, if it has any, are set up and merely exploited for his identifiable pathos and irony, to such an extent that the development of the situation is careless and ill-written, and all the energies of the author concentrate on what can be said *about* it, usually very beautiful and very sad and very deep things that have, we often feel, a general relevance to "life" rather than a particular one to the poems in which they occur: "And yet, the ways we miss our life are life," "This is what happens to everyone," "Behind everything there is always / The unknown unwanted life." Granted that these poems are "dramatic," or at least, lest that should imply any wealth of action, that they are "personative," it still seems that Jarrell's characters are placed there very largely for the purpose of saying all those fine things.

W. H. Auden's new collection, *The Shield of Achilles*, is arranged in three parts. A middle section of more or less miscellaneous pieces, most of them fairly light in nature, is bracketed between the title poem and an "Ode to Gaea," which are both more serious and more massive than the rest; while the opening group of seven "Bucolics" is balanced by the seven sections of "Horae Canonicae," a meditation on Good Friday, at the close.

My first and lasting impression, with this book, is of dealing with a master, a poet of such technical authority that he is always touching accomplishment and doing it, moreover, without much struggle. To his intensities he rises without perceptible strain, showing rather the result than whatever violence of feeling and labor of will the result may have cost, while in his relaxed and even trivial moments (of which there are, as always in his work, a good many) he plays, jokes, parodies, with great brilliance, giving an exhibition which may not be memorable but is always in the fullest sense genial, putting on his wig and becoming Pope—"Nor thought the lightning-kindled bush to tame / But, flabbergasted, fled the useful flame"—and taking it off a few moments after to be Edgar Guest: "The trees encountered on a country stroll / Reveal a lot about that country's soul."

His work in the seven "Bucolics" is mostly of this relaxed kind, some of it perfunctory enough, as though having started with "Winds" he felt in duty bound to carry on through "Woods," "Mountains," "Lakes," and so forth, to the number of seven. The talk throughout is witty and elegant, characterized morally by a cheerful seriousness, but the degree of his engagement with these subjects seems fairly slight: "Just reeling off their names is ever so comfy." I have somewhat the same sense about much of the middle section, where however there are several beautiful pieces, notably a song, "The Willow-Wren and the Stare," a fine set of ironic couplets on the theme, "The Truest Poetry Is the Most Feigning," and the "Ode to Gaea."

"Horae Canonicae" relives and meditates on the events of Christ's Passion as these events are obliquely viewed by Auden's standard "character," his nameless, faceless *homme moyen sensuel*, citizen, member of the SPQR, the lynch-mob and the church—raised to a higher power in this poem, however, by including in himself, as it were, much more of the poet. The poem is, therefore, a dramatized prayer, a rite, not merely a sermon whose acceptance depends upon our prior belief in its themes, e.g., "Can poets (can men in television) / Be saved?" and "*libera / Me, libera* C (dear C) / And all poor s-o-b's who never / Do anything properly." Even in the present age, when masterpieces are produced almost daily, this poem "grows to something of great constancy," where irony and intensity are one and the result, indeed, "strange and admirable." In witness, one passage:

> Soon cool tramontana will stir the leaves,
> The shops will re-open at four,
> The empty blue bus in the empty pink square
> Fill up and depart: we have time
> To misrepresent, excuse, deny,
> Mythify, use this event
> While, under a hotel bed, in prison,
> Down wrong turnings, its meaning
> Waits for our lives: sooner than we would choose,
> Bread will melt, water will burn,
> And the great quell begin, Abaddon
> Set up his triple gallows
> At our seven gates, fat Belial make
> Our wives waltz naked; meanwhile
> It would be best to go home, if we have a home,
> In any case good to rest.

I quote this stanza not so much in order that everyone should be persuaded to like it. I like it a good deal, but "liking" is not really the question; one might be irritated by it (as I am by a number of Auden's poems) and still feel compelled to acknowledge in admiration the solidity, the measured force, the control, to see how fully *made* it is, how grown-up and artful. With Spender and Jarrell, even in some of their best work, I am aware of the nagging presence of something extraneous and impure: call it "the real world," to which they so often appeal as a means of solving the difficulties of art; for them, the poem is not the statement of itself, so much as a means of arriving at statements they wish to make, such as "Death to the killers, bringing light to life" (Spender) or "It is terrible to be alive" (Jarrell). Any single instance, in either poet, can of course be justified; the poem is personative, the "sincerity" belongs not to the poet but to his protagonist of the moment, from whose own lips, presumably, is wrung the slogan that belongs to his experience. But this justification, which in any case has become a justification to be misused in schools, will not cover so constant a modulation from poetic to rhetoric as that by which these poets, neglecting or throwing aside the wholeness of the work, seek to involve us in their anger or pity over a world which, real and terrible as it may indeed be, is not the world created in the poem. This objection is not always true of either Spender or Jarrell, but it is often enough true, in my opinion, to make them to some extent rhetoricians and "men of action."

I would hold that there is, in addition to the emotions dealt with by poetry, an emotion *of* poetry and alone proper to it, a rhythmic or patterned exaltation which takes up and transforms its complex material of feelings and objects, making them dance in a different and noneditorial world, of which, despite the seriousness and sadness of its themes, the dominating traits are gaiety, energy, and control. The wild civility of that other world it is the distinction of poetic art to discover or invent, skill at making metaphors (Aristotle) and melodiousness (Coleridge) being but means to this invention or discovery, or particular signs by which its presence may be known. For this reason Auden seems to me a better poet than either of the others, his world no less serious than theirs but much more of a piece, and his poems the talk *of* that world, not simply talk about it.

On Shapiro, Roethke, Winters

The Waking. Poems: 1933-1953. By Theodore Roethke. Doubleday, 1954.
Poems 1940-1953. By Karl Shapiro. Random House, 1953.
Collected Poems. By Yvor Winters. Alan Swallow, Denver, Colo., 1952.

Three collections, the work of thirteen, twenty, and thirty years, come together more or less accidentally to be reviewed. It won't do to say that all poetry is divided into three parts and these are the parts; yet that is, of course, exactly the reviewer's temptation—a kind of miniature scale-model of the dilemma about form generally—which it may be useful to set out briefly for inspection.

The three are here, quite obstinately separate one from the others; that they are here all at once, for consideration in the one essay, has to be thought of as overwhelmingly produced by accidents; even to think of this circumstance as a product of purpose makes one feel, not far in the background, the uneasy pressures of paranoia. The sensible thing, to write three separate reviews, often has to be accepted, but only as a way out, not quite respectable and which still somewhat pinches the conscience—because there remains, after all, that little matter of form, which may be nothing more than a ridiculous punctiliousness, survival of past ages, about producing purpose from a collection of accidents cryptically presented by the universe. Admittedly it is laughable. Even if the artistic problem is most critically posed here, few would care to maintain that a review need be artful; there is something presumptuous in the idea. Nevertheless, the idea persists, perhaps only as pride in a difficulty and artificiality which shall be clearly set over against what is natural and easy. And by this route one arrives at the realm of suspicion and the problematical, the question of the general position of an art perceptible only in particular reflections, as it is triply reflected, for example, in the volumes to hand; and thus one arrives at the arbitrary.

It is widely accepted that there was a revolution in poetry; Eliot and Pound are thought to have had something to do with it. What is less certain, what has become a good deal less certain during the past ten or fifteen years, is whether this revolution accomplished anything recognizable and definitive, whether it has suffered a Napoleonic reversal and a Bourbon restoration, whether it has reached the characteristic liberal position of being at last able to offer people a freedom they no longer want. The old and the new aristocracies look at one another and tend to sneer; a powerful middle class meanwhile makes its fortune. This is not exactly a parable about Winters, Roethke, and Shapiro, for all poets, I hope, have a more complex relation to their art than that; it is a sufficiently arbitrary beginning.

Karl Shapiro is a poet mostly of the city, of metropolitan scenes and concerns: Hollywood, Washington, Melbourne, Sydney, Baltimore; hospitals, waxworks, railroad terminals, huge cemeteries: "I was born downtown on a wintry day." The War—his major subject, also perhaps informing with its tone his descriptions of the Peace— took him to far and incivil places such as Virginia and the Pacific islands, but still the conscription camp is "The clapboard city like a weak mirage / Of order," and almost everywhere the Army, a portable metropolis, goes with him. A fairly long list of epithets would go to describing the complex and distinctive character of this metropolitan consciousness; he is explicitly—not all of them at the same time—intellectual, political, world-historical, surrealist, Freudian, Marxist, Jewish; he reflects, in personal transformations, a complex body of fashionable opinion about motives; sees *eros* and *polis* each in the light of the other; finds, like Proust, the poet's dispossession imaged in the Jew's. The ideas, though seldom the manner, remind of Auden; the tone more closely suggests that of Delmore Schwartz; but Shapiro is probably a more accomplished as well as a more various poet than Schwartz. And at last there is, less happily, the reverent, grave, somewhat mawkish simplicity which results when, for some occasion having to do with *love*, all this equipment is jettisoned.

Shapiro's is one kind of poetry, shrewd, aware, acquainted with a vast world of objects, most of them of human manufacture: hair tonics, postcards, clocks, guns, liqueurs, telephones, billboards, magazines, and so on. If this were, as some have supposed, the only or the most desirable kind of poetry—it was at one time thought that "the problem for modern poetry" was "to absorb the machine"— Theodore Roethke, our second poet, would be in a bad way; against this imposing collection of artifacts he could offer, at most, one or two trains and a frigidaire and "the inexorable sadness of pencils."

But with Theodore Roethke's poems we enter on something quite different, where neither art nor politics is ever explicit; where almost nothing is done more artificial than raising flowers in a greenhouse; where green theories slowly grow in mud; where the world is not so much left behind as scarcely yet begun. This poetry is "archaic" in its choice of objects, of which a fairly representative sampling is given in the following lines from a poem called "Flower-Dump":

> Cannas shiny as slag,
> Slug-soft stems,
> Whole beds of bloom pitched on a pile,
> Carnations, verbenas, cosmos,
> Moulds, weeds, dead leaves,
> Turned-over roots
> With bleached veins
> Twined like fine hair.

A poetry of organic beginnings, rigorous in its exclusion of the latinate and abstract, the intellectual; but not, for all that, a primitive poetry. On the contrary, its avoidance of metaphor, which is replaced by insistently literal transformations having a magical, incantatory air, its distortion of grammatical relations, displacement of grammatical forms, suggest a great verbal sophistication; in whatever sense, this is no first childhood but a second one; and in its vegetable-animal-infantile preoccupations it is, for all its seeming naïveté, a poetry more securely a result of the Freudian discoveries than Shapiro's is.

Roethke recognizes his own territory quite early, in his first volume, as "My narrow vegetable realm," but does not take it over fully until the second and third, where, through a disorganization and formlessness which are in some sense superficial, a precondition and a clearing-away, the narrow vegetable realm is seen to be quite inclusive after all, and not without adept arrangement in its riotousness—"this elegant ordination of vegetables," as Sir Thomas Browne

called the quincunx, has its mystical and social as well as its purely
natural connections:

> Scurry of warm over small plants.
> Ordnung! Ordnung!
> Papa is coming.

It is no slur on Yvor Winters to say that in this comparison his
is a much more ordinary poetry; this is not to say, at once, Good,
or Bad, but only that it is a kind of thing, I think, which many people would find recognizably a continuation of a considerable part of
the poetry of the past. There seems to be a kind of lyric poetry that
is relatively timeless and for long periods unaffected by fashion, taking place at some distance, so to say, from the poetry that forms and
from the poetry that follows the fashion. At present, such poets as
Walter de la Mare, Arthur Waley, Edwin Muir, and Yvor Winters
are among its practitioners; this poetry runs as though the rhetoric
of the self's colloquy with the self were reluctant to show very much
change after only a few hundred years, or to be in any way flashy,
"modern," or overtly "technical"—even to the degree that such poets
will frequently prefer, probably as a matter of arduous choice, the
easy, worn word with the smoothness of much time on it, to the word
which, accurate though it may be, has too much the air of being
shrewdly selected. This ancient and continuing art, moralizing and
even didactic without being, in its better works, in the least imperceptive of particulars, belongs to life, serves it, and is in the most de-
voted sense *occasional*, finding its subjects in the slightest as in the
greatest events. The "revolution," doubtless out of its own necessities,
did this poetry injustice by confusing it, quite simply, with a large
part of the poetry of the late 19th and early 20th centuries, which
was bad poetry not because it moralized, but because its morality
was gross, abstract, and imperceptive of particulars. But in the present
lax posture of revolutionary affairs, this lyric strain can be seen as
continuous, a heartening connection with a long past which has
more to do with much "modern" poetry than it is usually thought to
do, and which ought also to be allowed as a dominating motive in the
poetry of Graves, Frost, and, at the highest reach, Yeats.

I have been able to make beginning descriptions of Shapiro's poetry
and Roethke's by speaking of their subjects; with Winters this probably won't work, for his distinction is a style, traditional and conven-

tional in its larger lines, which treats a wide range of subjects with equal and controlling temper. Here are meditations on *things*, dogs, the moon, the sea, aircraft, the manzanita; occasional pieces, of which the occasions include both war and the dedication of a reading-room; addresses to various persons; poems on mythological subjects, Theseus, Chiron, Gawain and the Green Knight. All these subjects become transformed in a tone, a way of talking, which has a dry and literate intensity, reminding me of Stendhal's fine saying that "one must write with equal application at all times." There is in all this what many persons nowadays, and many dreary persons indeed among them, would call "academic." Very well. What is impressive in so many of these poems is that discourse is absorbed in illustration and illustration in discourse; a very supple prosody balances against a civil and learned syntax to make results full of pleasing surprises; and this technical skill subordinates the objects in the poem to something else, to the poem as a new existence. Here is a passage, representative rather than outstanding, and chosen from the middle of a poem, not from its finest moment; the poet is speaking of his father and the house his father built:

> Too firmly gentle to displace the great,
> He crystallized this vision somewhat late;
> Forbidden now to climb the garden stair,
> He views the terrace from a window chair.
> His friends, hard shaken by some twenty years,
> Tremble with palsy and with senile fears,
> In their late middle age gone cold and gray.
> Fine men, now broken. That the vision stay,
> They spend astutely their depleted breath,
> With tired ironic faces wait for death.

What is good here, what is nearly always so in this poet, is the colliteration, the stitching of vowels and consonants, not so overt as to become the center of attention but continually exalting the discourse. This is in no way "original" or "modern," but it is fine, one of the things it ought always to be possible for poetry to be, and has about its movement that "cold certitude— / Laurel, archaic, rude," which Winters calls, indeed, "The poet's only bliss."

It does not seem to be the only one; or at least the means of reaching it are very different in the other two poets. A stanza from Shapiro's "Hospital," chosen also to be representative rather than outstanding:

This is the Oxford of all sicknesses.
Kings have lain here and fabulous small Jews
And actresses whose legs were always news.
In this black room the painter lost his sight,
The crippled dancer here put down her shoes,
And the scholar's memory broke, like an old clock.

This moves by examples, is brilliant but at the expense of discourse, the examples even become rather too desperately sought-for by the end. Shapiro's best poems, for me, are those in which a certain elected craziness of tone allows the objects to form a weird kind of order together, an order dependent upon rather calm syntactical relations among things really yoked by associational violence, by great energy; among the new poems, "The Figurehead" and "Going to School" have this impressive strangeness, but the poem I like best is still "Scyros," of which the second and third stanzas go like this:

High over where the storm
Stood steadfast cruciform
The golden eagle sank in wounded wheels
White negroes laughing still
Crept fiercely on Brazil
Turning the navies upward on their keels

Now one by one the trees
Stripped to their naked knees
To dance upon the heaps of shrunken dead
The roof of England fell
Great Paris tolled her bell
And China staunched her milk and wept for bread

And, rarely, these huge constellations of imagery come together with a seriousness and consecution of tone to form metaphor, and you get something of such majestic and equal tension as these lines, from "The Potomac":

Yet he shall speak though sentries walk
And columns with their cold Corinthian stalk
Shed gold-dust pollen on Brazil
To turn the world to Roman chalk.

Frequently, however, the multiplicity of objects defeats the line, which breaks up and loses sinuosity; the excitement, the "something happening every minute," is gained at some expense to qualities of language that seem to me indispensable: flexibility, fluency. Shapiro's sounds seem placed together with a too insistent angularity and jaggedness.

In these matters also, Roethke is as different as can be; his verse, which seems to be free, perhaps, only because the unit is the strophe not the line, has the air of incantatory, apocalyptic mumblings from underground, Diotima doing nursery rimes:

> When I took off my clothes
> To find a nose,
> There was only one shoe
> For the waltz of To,
> The pinch of Where.

There's no use, here, for the word "discourse," for that is not how these poems go; they are moved instead by processions, transformations of imagery, and through brief, abrupt explosions of energy, often in sequences of four-line stanzas; they are impulsive in every sense, exclamatory, and run to a kind of desperate happiness which is already implicit in the equivocations of such a title as "Praise to the End!":

> Such owly pleasures! Fish come first, sweet bird.
> Skin's the least of me. Kiss this.
> Is the eternal near, fondling?
> I hear the sound of hands.

> Can the bones breathe? This grave has an ear.
> It's still enough for the knock of a worm.
> I feel more than a fish.
> Ghost, come closer.

It is a little disturbing to find this poet, in some of his new poems, such as the "Four for Sir John Davies," returning to "the world," to a conventional stanza and syntax, a more conventional kind of statement. There are good things in these works, there are even places where his unique qualities combine well with traditional ones; in a way these would be distinguished poems had he not done the other (a wretched sort of judgment!) and it is a little as though he has emerged leaving his odd Eurydice behind. But these poems are doubtless only the earliest expressions of the Next Phase, which will perhaps define itself more clearly in time.

And now, what of the problematic, the question of the general position, and all that? Not much, I'm afraid. Since after all the three poets are not one poet, since the art of poetry is not exhausted with reference to the three poets, the little matter of form, with its pre-disposed relations and possibilities, will take me no further. It will not do to say, nor am I tempted to say, that poets A, B, and C, taken together and purged of their faults, would make the Great American Poet whom such a number of people have been looking for, chiefly under stones, for a long time; nor to say that the thesis of A and the antithesis of B have met in the glorious synthesis of C. I mention these possibilities, or impossibilities, only because they represent a kind of activity which Literary Criticism frequently hankers after, under the general head of Getting Things Settled Once And For All.

Things are almost never settled once and for all, however (when they are it is doubtful whether anyone writes poetry to celebrate the event), and one evil result of a criticism which keeps going out for such a settlement is that it tends to cut down on the variousness and individuality of the pleasure always offered by works of art; it does this by a constant implication that works of art are rationally perfectible, whereas the truth of the matter is that works of art succeed not quite in spite of and not quite because of their defects, which they simply and rather heroically drag along with them: Milton's pomposity, Proust's tediousness, Melville's unseemly lust after "symbolism" and Mann's impression that he is being funny, are not traits which can be rationally detached from their great works for improvement's sake. But a certain species of criticism, not altogether unknown where verse is reviewed, continually speaks of poetry as though it had an officially derived set of objectives, which by themselves had invented a great poet yesterday and would by themselves invent a great poet day after tomorrow. While these people are climbing trees to see what happens next, it appears that very few people, even of those professionally connected with the art, read poems for pleasure.

These three volumes pleased me a good deal; they illustrate, and help to form, an art which is alive and working, not by bitter exclusions, and which many readers might enjoy, taking time off for this purpose from the invention of a monolithic, eternal criticism on the Plain of Shinar.

I hope this will not be read as a plea for tolerance. If there is a type of poetry your soul detests, you should do your best to kill it off—honestly, if possible, otherwise, if necessary. But surely it remains as a consequence that there must be, here and there, things that you admire? For me, three of them have accidentally come together here. Chekhov's Laevsky, pacing up and down his room, mutters to himself, "We must define the position and run away!" It will do for a motto.

On Longfellow

Great reputation is perhaps the most curious as well as the most volatile product of civilized society; lives of great men very often remind us, Longfellow's celebrated "Psalm" to the contrary, what a vast deal of illusion their energy sustains around them while they live, and how perishable a commodity it proves to be after they die. William Blake put the matter with characteristic clarity:

> When Sir Joshua Reynolds died
> All Nature was degraded:
> The King drop'd a tear into the Queen's ear,
> And all his pictures faded.

But the fame of a great poet in the nineteenth century seems to us, a hundred years after, peculiarly productive of the grotesque and absurd, and of a nature extremely ready to be degraded. Here, for example, is Queen Victoria's comment on Longfellow's visit to Windsor Castle (this happened, with more or less tact, on the Fourth of July in 1868): "I noticed an unusual interest among the attendants and servants. I could scarcely credit that they so generally understood who he was. When he took leave, they concealed themselves in places from which they could get a good look at him as he passed. I have since inquired among them, and am surprised and pleased to find that many of his poems are familiar to them. No other distinguished person has come here that has excited so peculiar an interest. Such poets wear a crown that is imperishable."

Alas.

And here is a description even more revealing, in my opinion, of the strangeness of this kind of fame. I am quoting an early biographer and critic, George Lowell Austin, writing in the year after the poet's death:

"It is about seven inches in height, and is broad, stout, and capacious. It holds, when filled to the brim, about five pints; has an honest handle; and is, of course, of the usual color of Wedgwood ware. . . . The jug exhibits two panels, one presenting a most admirable portrait of Mr. Longfellow, and the other the following familiar verse from the poem 'Kéramos':

> Turn, turn, my wheel! Turn round and round
> Without a pause, without a sound:
>   So spins the flying world away!
> This clay, well mixed with marl and sand,
> Follows the motion of my hand;
> For some must follow, and some command,
>   Though all are made of clay!

"One is tempted to say of the portrait, that it is one of the best, if not the best, that has been made of the poet. The remaining decorations of the jug comprise scrolls intertwined with flowers, on which are imprinted the titles of some of Mr. Longfellow's most popular poems: 'The Golden Legend,' 'Hiawatha,' 'Evangeline,' 'Psalm of Life,' etc. As a specimen of art production, the jug is certainly one of the most beautiful and desirable, and will immensely please all lovers of Mr. Longfellow's poetry."

Alas for the jug, the specimen of art production!

Even the beard, the universal and encyclopedic beard behind which, in our childhood, half the poets of the world seemed to be hiding, is only falsely and as it were "historically" characteristic of Longfellow, who grew it only when in his fifties, as a consequence of burns suffered in the fire which killed his wife; these burns made it impossible for him to shave. As simple as that!

And so it is possible, barely possible, that behind the jug, the world-renown, the official beard, there exists another poet, smaller but truer than the impressive representations of his time would allow.

It would not be quite true to say that no one nowadays reads Longfellow. A while ago, between the halves of a football game, some fifty thousand persons—I was one of them—heard great swatches of "Hiawatha" droned out over the public address system while several hundred drum majorettes twirled their batons; this was, to be sure, in Minnesota, which is Hiawatha country.

But it is probably true, as this example suggests, that Longfellow is not fashionable among literary people, is in fact regarded by them slightly, scornfully, or not at all; and in this situation I find a problem or two, which I shall try to describe in these pages.

I am certain that the last thing Longfellow wanted was to be a problem. He was a man of very settled dispositions, and what he wanted from very early days was to be a poet—as he put it in a letter to his father, written while he was still an undergraduate at Bowdoin College, "I most eagerly aspire after future eminence in literature." In the course of a long, honorable career at teaching and writing he then achieved this eminence step by step, in a steady upward progression, until, nearing the end of his life, he was clearly one of the great poets of the world, not to America only but to England and all Europe—admired, as we have seen, by Queen Victoria and by her servants; by Saintsbury and by King Leopold of Belgium; by Baudelaire and the Princess Royal of Russia. Greater even than these, the heroine of a novel by Charles Kingsley, on her way to the Crimea to be a nurse with Florence Nightingale, took with her two books, *The Bible* and *Evangeline*.* Longfellow's "eminence in literature," then, was in every way comparable with that attained to by his contemporaries (and acquaintances), Browning, Tennyson, and Dickens. Nothing problematic in that!

And yet—and yet. Fifty years after his death in 1882, the writer of a popular history of American literature disposes of Longfellow in a few pages of severities, breaking off in the midst to ask himself, "Am I slaying the thrice slain? Who, except wretched schoolchildren, now reads Longfellow?" And he supplies this justification for going on: "The thing to establish in America is not that Longfellow was a very small poet, but that he did not partake of the poetic character at all." (Ludwig Lewisohn, *The Story of American Literature*, first published 1932, Modern Library Edition, 1939.)

That is more or less how the matter stands at present. The world went a long way, from the schoolgirl of the seventies who unhesitatingly chose Mr. Longfellow's *Poems* as "the book that all good people loved to read," to the wretched schoolchildren of 1932, and long ways, where the world is concerned, have a trick of curving back; but it is doubtful that Longfellow will ever again achieve his past eminence. It is all very well to think of the fluctuations of the literary market as the whirligig of time brings in his revenges, but in this

* I am indebted for this information to Professor Charles Shain of Carleton College.

instance we must content ourselves with a more limited revision of judgment. Possibly, indeed, the appropriate lesson to be drawn from this history has less to do with rehabilitating Longfellow than with imposing a certain missing modesty and reasonableness upon contemporary pretensions in the same line of work.

There are at least two problems here, though they are closely related ones. First, there is the question of a violent change in literary fashion between the Victorian period and the period, if it is one, which with a prolonged optimism keeps calling itself "the modern." Second, and symptomatic of this change in literary fashion, there is an increased distance, perhaps a near-absolute separation, between what I shall have to call, having failed to find any noninvidious terms to convey my meaning, popular poetry and good poetry. Longfellow's renown, spread, like that of Browning and Tennyson, through all classes of society, suggests that for the Victorian era the two terms were very nearly synonymous, or could become synonymous, at least, in the case of these poets who were thought of, surely, as "broad" as well as "lofty" and "deep." This kind of reputation, compared with that accorded, say, Ezra Pound or William Carlos Williams on the one hand, and Edgar Guest, Ella Wheeler Wilcox, or Robert W. Service on the other, suggests the magnitude of the change, the definite nature of the separation between what have become two quite different arts, whose audiences exclude one another.

The kind of difference involved, and the tension produced, are well expressed by Cleanth Brooks and Robert Penn Warren in their influential handbook *Understanding Poetry,* where they begin a detailed and destructive analysis of Joyce Kilmer's "Trees" by writing: "This poem has been very greatly admired by a large number of people. The fact that it has been popular does not necessarily condemn it as a bad poem. But it is a bad poem." The essay which follows, brilliant as it is, cannot of course get around the difficulty that the more "objective" determinants you bring up to show that "Trees" is a bad poem, the more you must convince your readers, so far as you convince them of anything at all, that the popularity of this bad poem rests on a sentimental popular misconception of what poetry is and does; and a similar demonstration might be made, with the same justice and the same implications about popular taste, upon certain of Longfellow's "best-loved" poems.

My object in this discussion of Longfellow's work is to exhibit a poet somewhat different from the one who wrote, e.g., "A Psalm of Life," "Hiawatha," "The Wreck of the Hesperus." Without trying to present him, in the result, as anything like a great poet (there are fewer of these than formerly thought), I shall claim for some of his productions an interest other than historical, scholarly, or biographical—an interest truly poetical, and undiminished by time.

Longfellow was a good minor poet, at times a very good one indeed, who succumbed to the characteristic disease of minor poets especially of the nineteenth century (it would be invidious to speak of the twentieth in this connection), the fevered wish to be a major poet, accompanied quite often by the hallucination that he was. Why this kind of thing happens and goes on happening will perhaps never be altogether clear: we may remark that the ambition in itself is not blameworthy, and that knowledge, in this of all endeavors, is precisely what comes too late to be of any use; but in attempting to say why it happened to Longfellow I find that three sorts of cause become visible. These do not exist in isolation but are much interwoven, yet they may be broadly named as the encouragement of history, the encouragement of popularity, and the encouragement of literature.

1. *The Encouragement of History.* "Surely," writes Longfellow to his father, from Bowdoin College, "surely there was never a better opportunity offered for exertion of literary talent in our own country than is now offered. To be sure, most of our literary men thus far have not been profoundly so, until they have studied and entered the practice of theology, law, or medicine. I do believe that we ought to pay more attention to the opinion of philosophers, that 'nothing but nature can qualify a man for knowledge.' " In other words, America in the eighteen-twenties is thought to have so far entered civilization as to be able to support poetry; and not only so, but to support a poetry which is not merely the by-product or graceful accompaniment of the practical life of the professions, but a something in itself—a true art, and "profoundly so."

Still quite early in his career, in 1849, through the mouth of a character in his novel *Kavanagh*, Longfellow invests his wish with the questionable authority of the *Zeitgeist:* "We want a national literature commensurate with our mountains and rivers . . . a national epic that shall correspond to the size of the country . . . a national drama in which scope shall be given to our gigantic ideas and to the unparalleled activity of our people. . . . In a word, we want a national literature altogether shaggy and unshorn, that shall shake the earth, like a herd of buffaloes thundering over the prairies."

This has a pathos in the midst of its generous absurdity, "shaggy and unshorn" being perhaps the qualities we are least likely to think of in connection with Longfellow's poetry, for which, as Howard Mumford Jones has said, the canonical adjective is "gentle." Such a program for literature will sound to some like Walt Whitman, whom it anticipates, and to others like a pronouncement of the Supreme Soviet; it had been, in fact, an extremely popular idea since the formation of the Republic (on this point, see R. W. B. Lewis, *The American Adam,* pp. 79-81), and it continues to be heard among us year by year, despite our extreme modernity. Though Longfellow is capable of viewing the matter with some detachment—"a man will not necessarily be a great poet because he lives near a great mountain," says another character in the same novel—the subjects he chose for the larger works of his middle period seem to show the American theme as equivocally appealing and summoning, a desire and a duty at once ("Evangeline," "Hiawatha," "The Courtship of Miles Standish," "The New England Tragedies"), while his treatment of these —the hexameters, the measure of the *Kalevala,* the imitation Elizabethanism, a generally pervasive atmosphere of almost scholarly caution—suggests the strain attendant on becoming a great national poet and harmonizing Europe and the past with America and the future.

His solution, or one of his solutions, to this problem is quite simply to become universal and do everything, and so he writes, over a long period of time, *Christus: A Mystery,* of which the three parts, "The Divine Tragedy," "The Golden Legend," and "The New England Tragedies," are designed to represent the theological virtues of Faith, Hope, and Charity as respectively characteristic of Antiquity, the Middle Ages, and modern times. But the connection of the parts seems, unhappily, more accidental and arbitrary than the grand design of this program would indicate, nor do the parts themselves come off so much better if considered as separate pieces. "The Golden Legend" is the most attractive, as it is the most fully imagined of the three; even so, the influence of Goethe's *Faust,* especially upon Longfellow's conception of Lucifer, is quite plain to be seen. "The Divine Tragedy" seems a mere mechanical repetition of the sources shuffled into verse, while "The New England Tragedies" sufficiently illustrate that Longfellow shared with many poets of the nineteenth century the inability as well as the desire to write dramatically.

2. *The Encouragement of Popularity.* Given the ambition of making a national literature, and given the response of all sorts of readers not only to the idea but to the productions, such as "Hiawatha" and "Evangeline," which embodied the idea, we can scarcely blame Longfellow for accepting success as it came. His earnest sincerity, and somewhat simplistic spirit, are not in question; he was neither writing down to his audience nor posing as a prophet among the people. But he was stretching a relatively small gift over a very large frame.

This was indeed noticed, not at all uncertainly, by Edgar Allan Poe and Margaret Fuller among others. Poe, varying between a carefully limited admiration of Longfellow and a bitter resentment extending as far as a reckless and unproven charge of plagiarism, yet noted something essential: "didacticism is the prevalent tone of his song." Margaret Fuller, in an essay which Longfellow privately described as "a bilious attack," wrote an appraisal very judicious in some points, and the more damaging for the impression it gives of deep hostility straining to be fair: "Longfellow is artificial and imitative. He borrows incessantly, and mixes what he borrows, so that it does not appear at the best advantage. He is very faulty in using broken or mixed metaphors. The ethical part of his writing has a hollow, second-hand sound. He has, however, elegance, a love of the beautiful, and a fancy for what is large and manly, if not a full sympathy with it. His verse breathes at times much sweetness; and if not allowed to supersede what is better, may promote a taste for good poetry. Though imitative, he is not mechanical."

But the detractors died; Longfellow and the admirers lived on, and presently the poet's fame was beyond effective question in his day: "surely," he heard from a friend, "no poet was ever so fully recognized in his lifetime as you."

An immense, a world-wide reputation must be a difficult thing to bear gracefully; it is my impression that Longfellow took it all with a beautiful modesty so far as the personal life was concerned. If he was (and he was) a trifle vain in trifles, he had never been swollen with pride, never been self-idolatrous, and was not so in the time of his greatest fame. But professionally, in the image of the poet at his work, he may have succumbed and received the enormous reverberations of his worth for the thing itself; at all events, his very success involved him in a relation with the public, a commitment to the public, to its idea of what a poet is and does, which to later judgment appears as a misfortune. The same over-encouraged ambition of an obvious fame, where largeness is taken for greatness, profundity for accuracy, importance for truth, also affected his great contemporaries Tennyson and Browning, and seems to be responsible for those large, facile gestures which we now find so oppressive in the works of those poets. The situation of Victorian poetry ought perhaps to be construed as in large part the result of a false idea (one still very common) of the poet's relation with his audience: the idea that, instead of seeking patiently the truth of the matter at hand, the poet is a repository of "values," which he affirms "in beautiful language" *pour encourager les autres.*

This is not to say that the poet, on this view of him, is insincere. But there exists a curious and even tragic tension between poetry and value. In the work of very great poets we seem to find ideas of order, harmonious articulations of our experience, inextricably involved with the poetry; these poets are admirable not because they present values (though they do) but because they *become* values. I mean by this simply that after a certain point in our reading we cease to judge them in the light of our experience and begin instead to judge our experience in the light of their poems.

Lesser poets, in attempting to attain this distinction, are deceived into philosophizing, or poetizing philosophically, and when time has worked a little on their poems it comes to seem as though their finest poetry escaped them by accident, when they had forgotten for some reason to conclude the poem by orienting it with explicit reference to their beliefs, their values, or when the poem had somehow evaded the censorship of "ideas." This may be one meaning of a phrase from the *Kena Upanishad* which Yeats renders so beautifully: "The living man who finds spirit, finds truth. But if he fail, he falls among fouler shapes."

This may or may not be essential among Longfellow's difficulties; I think, myself, that it is. But it is not the business of criticism to practice preventive medicine by saying Thou Shalt Not to anyone's future; so that the poet's attempt to exceed his limitations is always necessary, and knowledge, after all the returns are in, always too late.

3. *The Encouragement of Literature.* Longfellow was from the beginning of his career as a teacher a learned and a studious man, who became accustomed to viewing the world of experience with an immediate, almost automatic reference to a wide range of books, a range much extended by his study of languages, his travels in Europe, his love of history, and his work as a translator. A few samples, drawn

from among many, will show not only his scrupulousness about giving sources, but also his positive delight in doing so; the following are the opening lines of the poems in which they occur:

> Have you read in the Talmud of old . . . ?

> In Mather's Magnalia Christi,
>   Of the old colonial time,
> May be found in prose the legend
>   That is here set down in rhyme.

> Saint Augustine! well hast thou said . . .

Another poem, "The Discoverer of the North Cape," is prefaced with the subtitle "A Leaf from King Alfred's Orosius"; and in his diary he notes about "My Lost Youth" his particular pleasure at "the bringing in of the two lines of the old Lapland song." It is also observable in this connection, about the "Tales of a Wayside Inn," that the interludes between tales not infrequently resemble seminars in criticism and comparative literature—for example:

> "A pleasant and a winsome tale,"
> The Student said, "though somewhat pale
> And quiet in its coloring,
> As if it caught its tone and air
> From the gray suits that Quakers wear;
> Yet worthy of some German bard,
> Hebel or Voss or Eberhard,
> Who love of humble themes to sing,
> In humble verse; but no more true
> Than was the tale I told to you."

The Theologian (who had told the pleasant and winsome tale) replies "with some warmth":

> "That I deny;
> 'Tis no invention of my own,
> But something well and widely known
> To readers of a riper age,
> Writ by the skilful hand that wrote
> The Indian tale of Hobomok,
> And Philothea's classic page. . . ."

That is, by "the folk."

Now there is nothing wrong with this in itself. Poets have always taken their stories from past literature and history and tradition. Dante and Shakespeare no less than Longfellow relied on what they read; people who believe otherwise, and think that poets write out of some simple, untutored relation with nature, are making a mistake. But the point scarcely needs to be insisted on, I hope, that when Dante read Ovid or Statius, when Shakespeare read Cinthio or Plutarch, something quite new happened; while with Longfellow, all too often, no transformation takes place in the passage from source to poem, and the result is a mere mechanical "putting into verse," a patient but routine setting down of the external facts of the matter, with nothing problematic about it, no inwardness, as though the transaction between the poet and his subject were primarily a measuring-out of feet and rhymes to be applied to something already in all essentials existing.

This doesn't by any means happen all the time, and the reference to literature is responsible for some of Longfellow's finest things as well as some of his worst; but the point here is that his love for literature, his knowledge of it, his piety toward it, may have suggested to him that the achievement of poetry was after all a simpler matter than it is generally thought to be, and may have encouraged him in a facility which by nature he already amply had.

Our attempt to find a workable relation with poets of the past is always likely to produce embarrassment at the start—and we might in charity admit that if it were possible the embarrassment would be on both sides. Words change, and the habit of speech changes. Dr. Johnson, for example, can no longer commend Dr. Levet to us by calling him "officious," because officious has ceased to mean "kind; doing good offices," which is what it meant to Dr. Johnson. In the same way, when Longfellow calls this life "a suburb of the life elysian" our dismay probably has less to do with our view of immortality than with our view of suburbs. When he continues, however, writing of his dead daughter:

> She is not dead—the child of our affection,—
> But gone unto that school
> Where she no longer needs our poor protection,
> And Christ himself doth rule,

we may have to see our difficulty, if we dislike the lines, as a difficulty of attitude, and that it is somewhat snobbish in us to refuse from Longfellow what we should gladly accept from Dante, who also speaks of heaven as a school: *nel quale é Cristo abate del collegio,* "where Christ is abbot of the college" (*Purgatorio* xxvi. 129).

It will be helpful to be as clear as possible about such distinctions, lest on the one hand we reject our poet altogether and uncritically because we do not share his beliefs, or are embarrassed by the form in which he expresses them, lest on the other hand we admire him uncritically for things he cannot truly give us. So, for example, I have seen Longfellow praised as a pioneer Imagist for the following lines:

> In broad daylight, and at noon,
> Yesterday I saw the moon
> Sailing high, but faint and white,
> As a school-boy's paper kite.
> —"Daylight and Moonlight"

Whether these lines do in fact anticipate the practice of Amy Lowell, or whether anyone ought to be praised for the anticipation, I am uncertain; but I am quite certain that this sort of imagery is uncharacteristic in Longfellow's work. Nor is he a poet of brilliant or subtle or elaborated metaphor, though there are occasional miracles of fused vision like this one:

> A memory in his heart as dim and sweet
> As moonlight in a solitary street,
> Where the same rays, that lift the sea, are thrown
> Lovely but powerless upon walls of stone.
> —"Torquemada," from *Tales of a Wayside Inn*

His more usual practice is to limit his metaphors immediately by an application, by drawing out their meaning, by moralizing upon them; and this is of course what most offends against the taste of the present age, and makes us look with especial disfavor upon the conclusions of many of his poems as being comically reductive in their insistence on pointing the moral:

> By the mirage uplifted, the land floats vague in the ether,
> Ships and the shadows of ships hang in the motionless air;
> So by the art of the poet our common life is uplifted,
> So, transfigured, the world floats in a luminous haze.
> —"Elegiac Verse vi"

I suppose that the attitude of many modern readers toward what is represented here would be in favor of the first two lines and against the last two; substantially the attitude of Longfellow himself in the fourth and fourteenth of these same "Elegiac Verses":

> Let us be grateful to writers for what is left in the inkstand;
> When to leave off is an art only attained by the few.

And

> Great is the art of beginning, but greater the art is of ending;
> Many a poem is marred by a superfluous verse.

Now it is certainly true that some of Longfellow's poems are spoiled for us by their endings which are so explicit and sententious; and this is especially sad in poems which otherwise attain to a considerable and convincing eloquence, such as "The Lighthouse" and "The Golden Milestone." As to the former in particular, after an achievement of the following order,

> Even at this distance I can see the tides,
>   Upheaving, break unheard along its base,
> A speechless wrath, that rises and subsides
>   In the white lip and tremor of the face,

it is very disappointing to be brought down to the conclusion in which the lighthouse "hails the mariner with words of love" which turn out to be platitudes.

Yet, when I consider the general question involved, of morality and statement in poetry, I am not altogether convinced of the absolute rightness of the modern attitude, or that it ought to be applied, without many reservations, to such a poet as Longfellow. He is perhaps most immediately impressive, or at any rate most accessible to us, in those relatively few poems, such as "The Harvest Moon" and "Chaucer" and "Aftermath," which remain steadfastly with their minute particulars. "Aftermath" especially seems to me to have a very moving sort of melancholy, a music in which more is suggested than said. The aftermath is the second mowing of the fields, in late fall; beyond this, perhaps, the poet's work in old age; and the second of the two stanzas deals with it this way:

> Not the sweet, new grass with flowers
> Is this harvesting of ours;
>   Not the upland clover bloom;
> But the rowen mixed with weeds,
> Tangled tufts from marsh and meads,

> Where the poppy drops its seeds
> In the silence and the gloom.

I shall risk saying that that is first-rate writing. It is not typical of Longfellow's style or way of concluding; yet there are more examples of the kind than people nowadays incline to acknowledge.

And in the other kind, the explicit and moralizing kind of verse, the standard idea of his being "gentle" ought not to blind us to a sometimes considerable strength. For example, in "The Challenge," the "ancient Spanish legend" he begins with is a mere excuse, an occasion only, and the poem exists as a sermon on riches and poverty, as he sees

> The living, in their houses,
> And in their graves, the dead!
> And the waters of their rivers,
> And their wine, and oil, and bread!

The challenge is from the poor, who "impeach us all as traitors, / Both living and the dead," leading to this decisive and not especially gentle conclusion:

> And there in the camp of famine,
> In wind and cold and rain,
> Christ, the great Lord of the army,
> Lies dead upon the plain!

Generally, then, though Longfellow is not a poet of great dramatic powers, he does have in good measure the essential lyrical equivalent of those powers, the ability to make his moral reflections arise out of experience, emerge from the substance of the stories he tells, the images he presents. Though he is sometimes sentimental, and though it is true that "didacticism is the prevalent tone of his song," yet the substance of his teaching is often poetically just, that is, relevant to the material. Though he is more explicit about drawing the moral than is now the fashion, it may be a false romanticism in the present taste, a desire to indulge the spirit in pseudo-mysteries, which is embarrassed by plain statements and wants everything "left implicit."

This justice, indeed, is the virtue of Longfellow's poetry that I most wish to call attention to. It seems to me the constant element common to good poetry everywhere and always, and I would define this justice as the poet's acceptance of the consequences of his poem,

his will to submit his will to the matter at hand, and follow where
the thought will lead him. This quality will demand, no doubt, the
sacrifice of incidental beauties, spectacular surprises, especially toward
the end of a poem, where the consequences are most powerfully to be
felt; and a poet subjected to this discipline will incline to finish his
poems rather formally, definitely, explicitly, even with "a message"
if that seems an appropriate result of the pressure of what has gone
before. When this is properly accomplished, the reader should feel
the force of the formal close as rather conventional and distant, bring
the measure and the meaning to a resolution together; as in the conventional endings decreed for eighteenth-century music.

Consider in this connection "The Fire of Drift-Wood." The
friends sitting before the fire rehearse their memories, and this naturally leads them on to think of themselves as changing in their relations with one another, and to feel "The first slight swerving of the
heart, / That words are powerless to express." Then, looking into the
fire, they think of the driftwood feeding it, thus of "wrecks upon the
main, / Of ships dismasted, that were hailed / And sent no answer
back again."

Outward and inward images come together now, in "The long-
lost ventures of the heart, / That send no answers back again." And
the close of the poem is a very simple placing of the one against the
other:

> O flames that glowed! O hearts that yearned!
>   They were indeed too much akin,
> The drift-wood fire without that burned,
>   The thoughts that burned and glowed within.

It is quiet, but it does its work, it exactly resolves the elements of
the poem, and does so without any gorgeous or spectacular fussing.

The same is true of a much better poem, "The Ropewalk," where
the spinners are seen in a figure subtly involving time and fate:

> In that building, long and low,
> With its windows all a-row,
>   Like the port-holes of a hulk,
> Human spiders spin and spin,
> Backward down their threads so thin
>   Dropping, each a hempen bulk.

It is not going to be a "metaphysical" or conceited poem; its development will be more diffuse than that; but the quality of the world is

here nevertheless a quality of thought; the wheel going round suggests that "All its spokes are in my brain."

> As the spinners to the end
> Downward go and reascend,
>   Gleam the long threads in the sun;
> While within this brain of mine
> Cobwebs brighter and more fine
>   By the busy wheel are spun.

In the development, which is perhaps over-extended and too catalogue-like, the rope being spun is related metaphorically to experience, as to gallows-rope and dragging anchor-cable; again the conclusion is deliberate, conventional, quiet:

> All these scenes do I behold,
> These, and many left untold,
>   In that building long and low;
> While the wheel goes round and round,
> With a drowsy, dreamy sound,
>   And the spinners backward go.

Here the reminder of the spinners going backward throws retrospectively a mysterious air, almost of paradox, over the details of the poem, life having been seen simultaneously as remembered, as lived, as spun, or fated, in the spinning of the rope.

Nor does even "The Ropewalk," good as it is, define the limit of Longfellow's achievement. On the one hand, I have not touched on his humor, which is often much livelier than his present reputation allows us to believe, and shows especially well in some of the *Tales of a Wayside Inn*, e.g., "The Monk of Casal-Maggiore," "The Cobbler of Hagenau," and the Landlord's final Tale of Sir Christopher Gardiner, Knight of the Holy Sepulchre,

> The first who furnished this barren land
> With apples of Sodom and ropes of sand.

On the other hand, this "gentle" and melancholy Christian poet now and then, though rarely, touches simultaneously on tragedy and greatness. "The Chamber over the Gate," simple, reserved, yet, at its end, passionate quite beyond sentimentality, is a lyric poem of the first rank. And in the vast meditation "Michael Angelo," which Longfellow left unfinished at his death, the relation of art and mortality produces, in addition to a sardonic and critical humor not felt in his poetry before, moments which have a claim to be considered the equal of the best in nineteenth century poetry:

> All things must have an end; the world itself
> Must have an end, as in a dream I saw it.
> There came a great hand out of heaven, and touched
> The earth, and stopped it in its course. The seas
> Leaped, a vast cataract, into the abyss;
> The forests and the fields slid off, and floated
> Like wooded islands in the air. The dead
> Were hurled forth from their sepulchres; the living
> Were mingled with them, and themselves were dead,—
> All being dead; and the fair, shining cities
> Dropped out like jewels from a broken crown.
> Naught but the core of the great globe remained,
> A skeleton of stone. And over it
> The wrack of matter drifted like a cloud,
> And then recoiled upon itself, and fell
> Back on the empty world, that with the weight
> Reeled, staggered, righted, and then headlong plunged
> Into the darkness, as a ship, when struck
> By a great sea, throws off the waves at first
> On either side, then settles and goes down
> Into the dark abyss, with her dead crew.

This entire scene, indeed, the meditation on the Coliseum in the fourth section of Part Three, is a study of art and life of a profound beauty rare not only for this poet but for any.

Unfashionable Longfellow is a poet of allegory rather than of symbol, of personification rather than of metaphor, of anecdote rather than myth. His ways are plain so far as he can make them so. I have tried to suggest in these prefatory observations what the differences and difficulties are which will make the modern reader impatient very often with this poet, but also what the rewards may be for those who, sick of the fashion, are willing to take a fresh view of the matter, and who may find, as I have found, that Longfellow, gentle as he is, maintains beneath his gentleness a fair share of that unyielding perception of reality which belongs to good poetry wherever and whenever written.

The Generation of Violence

The Collected Poems of Dylan Thomas. New Directions, 1953.

The idea, the not altogether clear and distinct idea, that poetry should be "organic," seeks to emphasize this distinction between writing in poetry and writing in prose, that poetry wants an order other than the narrative order in which argument and reasoned discourse commonly proceed, that the poem must make this order by radical rather than linear progressions, seeking so far as it may to be somehow simultaneously present in all its parts, overcoming so far as it may the disability, which language shares with all else produced in time, of one thing's happening *after* another. It is a very appealing and beautiful idea, for even if in poetry one thing must happen after another, nevertheless if the poem is brief enough and the relation of its parts made clear enough we may presently come to hold it, tenuously, in its entirety as a system not bound to the temporal order: only through time time is conquered. Poetry, it can be argued, is the best means in language to this end because of its brevity and compactness, because of its metrical nature which imposes a unity of suggestion on the most diverse materials, because of the patterning and echoing of like sounds whereby the poet's art furthers the cause of this unity, and at last by the images and figures, which set up cross-relations and resonances and tensions between parts of the poem too distant from one another for grammatical relation and so make a new syntax of the elements of the poem, an order other and more immediate than the narrative.

A beautiful, and really a religious idea. What is questionable, though, is whether, or how far, the narrative, linear progression can be dispensed with in aiming at this end. If we favor getting rid of that order entirely, as some surrealists attempted to do, who printed

Reprinted by permission from *The Kenyon Review*, Vol. XV, No. 3, Summer 1953. Copyright 1953 by Kenyon College.

their poems more or less without grammatical relations at all, as compositions in space rather than time, we may or may not enjoy our results but we inescapably disparage not most but all the poetry of the past, which proceeded by means of reasoned discourse, by one thing after another. This is a quite possible attitude, so long as we understand and accept its consequences, which will rid us of Donne no less than of Tennyson, and of Chaucer and Edgar Guest together. If we return from the surrealist optimism to a tragic view of human activities, including human speech, we may perceive that this attempt to overcome the order of time without going through it is rather like the attempt to have a human action without human actors, which Aristotle thought would be a fine thing but, regrettably, impossible. Nevertheless, perhaps something can be done toward freeing poetry from this bondage—a suppression, to some extent, of consequential relations in time and reason, and a playing-up on the other hand of the specifically metaphorical or associational, the leap of likeness poetry shares with and derives from magic.

Most of the poetry of Dylan Thomas, both as it succeeds and as it fails, is characterized by this attempt to make the order of association do the work of and in part replace the order of narrative. I say most of the poetry, for interspersed among the difficult poems which have made his distinctive fame is a number, more considerable than I had thought, of brief, relatively simple poems, quite straightforward and of rational progression and almost without metaphorical elaboration. Some of these are competent, e.g., "The Hand That Signed the Paper" and "In My Craft or Sullen Art," while one at least, "This Side of the Truth," seems quite good; others again are flat and uninteresting, like "Ears in the Turrets Hear." But however one may compare the qualities of these poems one with another, they are on the whole not very distinguished in their means and of less interest than the more difficult sort, so I will leave them out of this consideration.

Not a great deal of Thomas' poetry does succeed, to my mind; and when he is bad I believe he is very bad indeed. But there are a few poems, and few poets have more, which strike me as perfected results, and very beautiful. These are: "Hold Hard, These Ancient Minutes in the Cuckoo's Month," "After the Funeral (*In Memory of Ann Jones*)," and "Over Sir John's Hill." As it is more pleasure to deal with what one likes than with what one doesn't, I will say something of the shortest of the three, and reserve until later my reservations about a large part of his poetry.

> Hold hard, these ancient minutes in the cuckoo's month,
> Under the lank, fourth folly on Glamorgan's hill,
> As the green blooms ride upward, to the drive of time;
> Time, in a folly's rider, like a county man
> Over the vault of ridings with his hound at heel,
> Drives forth my men, my children, from the hanging south.
>
> Country, your sport is summer, and December's pools
> By crane and water-tower by the seedy trees
> Lie this fifth month unskated, and the birds have flown;
> Hold hard, my country children in the world of tales,
> The greenwood dying as the deer fall in their tracks,
> This first and steepled season, to the summer's game.
>
> And now the horns of England, in the sound of shape,
> Summon your snowy horsemen, and the four-stringed hill,
> Over the sea-gut loudening, sets a rock alive;
> Hurdles and guns and railings, as the boulders heave,
> Crack like a spring in a vice, bone breaking April,
> Spill the lank folly's hunter and the hard-held hope.
>
> Down fall four padding weathers on the scarlet lands,
> Stalking my children's faces with a tail of blood,
> Time, in a rider rising, from the harnessed valley;
> Hold hard, my county darlings, for a hawk descends,
> Golden Glamorgan straightens, to the falling birds.
> Your sport is summer as the spring runs angrily.

I have to make the damaging admission that there are places about which I am still unclear: why the south in stanza one should be the "hanging" south, for instance; and "the sound of shape" in stanza three, worry it how I will, remains a little empty of suggestion; but the poem, on one reading after another, continues to grow in power and in the accuracy of its relations, so perhaps these details too will sooner or later find their places.

It is composed upon repetitions: hold hard (hard-held); four, fourth (forth)—the seasons, the four-stringed hill, the four months of the year which intervene between December and May, the four feet of the fox whose tail, in stanza four, will blood the children;

ride, rider, ridings (rising); folly; the opposition of country and county. Time, in the imagery of hunting, is the figure to which these several relations relate.

Easy enough to say that this poem is about *process;* some maintain that all his poetry is, and I have heard it said in disparagement that "he is a very narrow poet; all he can write about is life and death." But unless we are content, as I suspect some of Thomas' louder admirers are, to take the love of process for the love of a poem on that subject, we shall have to do better than that. The particular process here described is the *fall* (another key word) from nature into history, from the timeless to the organic: "the deer fall in their tracks," "down fall four padding weathers on the scarlet lands," "a hawk descends," "the falling birds," April's breaking-open of new life "Spill(s) the lank folly's hunter and the hard-held hope." *Folly,* itself a tonal variation on *fall,* holds also the suggestion of bankruptcy in its connection with the "county man" riding to hounds; while, behind this, Time is remotely glimpsed ("the lank folly") as the skeleton death, riding. (And perhaps a long way behind that, then, the "snowy horsemen" would be those other four of the Apocalypse.) Life is seen as the hunt; time is the hunter, he "drives" before him "the green blooms" as well as "my men, my children." Against time we are to "hold hard," in vain, hopefully and hopelessly, to the moment's or the season's eternity, to "the world of tales." At the climax of the poem the children are blooded with the brush of the slain fox who, as he is now become an emblem of time, is also seen as the hunter, "stalking my children's faces with a tail of blood." Accepting the invitation to the pun, we see that the "world of tales" has changed, with the children's initiation into manhood and the hunt, into "a tale of blood." There is a good deal more, but so much will do.

What I find admirable in this is the complexity of controlled relations, upon which the attention is everywhere (almost everywhere) sustained; an imitative polyphony so made that richness and economy go easily and unforcedly together in a world where composition and generosity become one. The resonances, however distant, come to be clearly heard after a little study, and they constantly direct the mind from place to place within the poem, establishing the web of oneness among many separated points, much as the imagination makes constellations by drawing invisible lines among separate stars. In this way the poem achieves the quality which I have called "organic," making a syntax of its parts other than the narrative and grammatical syntax which is, for better or worse, the condition of its being read at all. Other than, and not "opposed to" or "independent of."

This success, and that of the other two poems I have mentioned, is made, as I believe, by means traditional to a large part of English poetry, means used, for example, by Shakespeare, Donne, Hopkins; or by a relatively slight, personal, and particular emphasis on one side of the balance; not (as some seem to claim) by a new means altogether. In these three poems—and several others perhaps less fully accomplished ("The Hunchback in the Park," for example, and "Lament") but still impressive—a *subject* indisputably engages the poet's full attention, and in its perfectly prosy way *holds things together while the poem is being made.* That Thomas, or another, can do away with the subject entirely, or obscure it by the generation of violence among its particulars, and achieve an equal success, is disputable.

There is, there always is, a second side to the matter. I read once, in Baron Schrenk-Notzing's book, that even those psychic mediums who, as he believed, possessed perfectly genuine powers, did not have these always at their command; and on such occasions were willing to work by sleight of hand as much as the most arrant charlatan. I am afraid this is a parable about poets.

Dylan Thomas' poetry, when it is not at its best, tends to degenerate more rapidly and completely, it seems to me, than any sort of poetry I have read; wanting the Muse, he is quite capable of filling in with:

> I dreamed my genesis in sweat of sleep, breaking
> Through the rotating shell, strong
> As motor muscle on the drill, driving
> Through vision and the girdered nerve.

This is stuff quite worthy of his numerous imitators, and might have been written for the commencement exercises at a school of dentistry. As verse it will scarcely bear discussion, and it cannot be admired for its difficulty, since it is not difficult. It may be noted in general here, that when the characteristic violence, become rather mechanical than muscular, does not cast its fine cadence over the whole, and allows the disparate objects of which it is composed to become clearly visible, the result is sometimes very funny:

> They suffer the undead water where the turtle nibbles,
> Come unto sea-stuck towers, at the fibre scaling,
> The flight of the carnal skull
> And the cell-stepped thimble;
> Suffer, my topsy-turvies, that a double angel
> Sprout from the stony lockers like a tree on Aran.

The art of sinking in poetry is not dead; and there is an art of rising, too, like a paper bag in a high wind.

The opinion is sometimes to be heard that Thomas is not only a great poet but also a great master of verse: not only does he pour out an immense wealth of song in careless exuberance, but he is also, and at the same time, it seems, rigorously precise about formal and technical considerations. Such an opinion might seem at first sight to be warranted by "Vision and Prayer," which has its stanzas shaped into diamonds and hourglasses, but a closer look reveals that as the metrical and riming requirements of this poem are by no means very rigorous the trick could not have been so hard after all and, moreover, that a fair portion of the art belongs not to the poet but to the linotypist; so that now and again there has been some Procrustean stretching of short lines to look longer than long lines, or perhaps the other way around. Though this may be thought a quibble, it does not need to stand alone:

> The heavenly music over the sand
> Sounds with the grains as they hurry
> Hiding the golden mountains and mansions
> Of the grave, gay, seaside land.

The technical qualities of this passage would be hard to describe. It certainly has few virtues, and probably no vices at all; it lives, if it does, in a very humble way.

In some of the most recent poems the scansion seems to have become entirely accentual, the tone rhapsodic, the gesture very large and sweeping; the verse proceeds by leaping from one epithet to the next over an emptiness of uncounted small words:

> The leaping saga of prayer! And high, there, on the hare-
>   Heeled winds the rooks

Cawing from their black bethels soaring, the holy books
Of birds! Among the cocks like fire the red fox

Burning!

My objection to this as verse—I believe further objections are possible—is that the energy has nothing to hold it back, it is under no pressure from the theoretical pattern of the line (which it has almost but not quite destroyed), so that the tension and sinuosity are lost, and the energetic impulsion which begins the line either cracks up or proceeds merely as shouting; nor does any intensification of assonance and so forth overcome this difficulty. The best poetry in English, I think, secures its tones of violence and force (like its other tones) working through the mutually opposed pressures of the scansion, which is accentual and syllabic at once, and in a sense also working against both, but always in a perceptible relation not only to the stress but also to the placement of the stress.

In the matter of metaphor, too, though there are very fine ones, I am uncertain whether it is not the tendency of Thomas' method to disintegrate the idea of analogy altogether. If it is first in virtue of a likeness that we compare two objects, there remains the other side of it, that we can so compare them because they are, after all, two objects, and not one. Thomas in his figure-making obeys his subject—the cyclical transformations of life into death and death into life—to such a degree that any thing may be compared with any other thing, for the sole reason, sometimes, that any thing may be supposed to become any other thing: "Imperious Cæsar, dead and turned to clay, / Might stop a hole to keep the wind away." But Cæsar for Thomas may further become almost anything else in the world, and without warning. It is rather metempsychosis than metaphor, and between feathers and iron he frequently takes no steps at all, and allows the reader the mere conjunction of the two for evidence of a likeness. Though there are fine hits, that does not ennoble the misses. The following, for instance, seems to me a near miss:

> I make this in a warring absence when
> Each ancient, stone-necked minute of love's season
> Harbours my anchored tongue, slips the quaystone,
> When, praise is blessed, her pride in mast and fountain
> Sailed and set dazzling by the handshaped ocean,
> In that proud sailing tree with branches driven

Through the last vault and vegetable groyne,
And this weak house to marrow-columned heaven,

Is corner cast. . . .

I feel, and perhaps I simply am reading it badly, that this is almost beautiful but finally doesn't jell. There is too much of it (here and in the poem of which it is a part), and its languages do not so much compose as they mechanically combine, under a very considerable pressure which badly shows the effort; too much of the syntax seems merely additive, so that in the last three lines the stanza becomes labored and a little breathless.

Finally, there is an emptiness to a considerable part of this large rhetoric ("the lovely gift of the gab") by which the poet excites at first and bores presently. Many of these poems go nowhere, fail to develop a subject, their gesture cannot conceal that the world of this poetry (which uses half our language and mostly lets the Latin alone) is the shifting world of water and air. In it, solid shapes dissolve, and the most energetic rhapsody fails to convince, at the end of some poems, that anything has happened. The great temptation of lyric poetry is to the dramatic posture, the dramatic gesture, unwitnessed by any drama, and many of Thomas' poems succumb constantly.

Bring out number, weight, and measure in a year of dearth. But he has written a few beautiful poems.

The Poetry of Reed Whittemore

The poetry of Reed Whittemore has not, so far as I know, had the attention it deserves at the hands of serious readers. It is occasionally, in reviews, acknowledged to be good work, and otherwise is rather neglected than objected against; its rare candor and integrity of purpose have not been valued as they ought to be.

For this neglect I think there are two reasons: that he is often funny, and that he is often literary. People who either have no faculty of independent judgment or perhaps rightly distrust what they do have, are suspicious and even resentful of new poetry which is funny (the word "wit" has been made safe for democracy, but does not include the idea of actually laughing), because they are afraid of being caught admiring something which will turn out to be light verse. It is correct, on this view, and even elegantly paradoxical, to raise Ogden Nash to a high place as a serious poet, just because there is never any doubt about what he is doing, that is, being funny; but when a doubt arises it is deemed best to be quiet and wait for the next issue of the Laputan Review, which may possibly bring an official opinion. As for poets whose poems take off from other literature, there is a special hell created for them; they are out on that limb, which Van Wyck Brooks keeps lopping off. Whittemore is a most grievous offender in this respect; like Dante, Milton, Pope, etc., he keeps bringing in literature and referring to books. If he looks into his heart and writes, what he writes is still liable to be about a novel by Conrad or Hardy, a poem by Tennyson, or such; what kind of heart is that? and so on. Both these doubts, if I am right in my diagnosis, express something naïve, superficial, and ignobly secure in contemporary taste, which appears to be formed largely by persons who value poetry for its power of making them feel *profound*. To consider Whittemore's poems as a whole is to be convinced of

Reprinted by permission from The Kenyon Review, Vol. XXI, No. 2, Spring 1959. Copyright 1959 by Kenyon College.

a singleness of purpose, growing in clarity, to which both the humor and the "literary" quality are essential instruments. This purpose is that of a great deal of modern literature, it is to illuminate the question of identity, the relation between the self and its election of possible or impossible character to play on the great stage where so much currently is mere confusion.

Whittemore's first book, in 1946, was called *Heroes and Heroines*, and was unusual for a first volume not only in the high degree of accomplishment and consistency of style which it displayed, but also in the deliberation with which the subject announced in the title was explored and developed by examples. The poet in his mid-twenties, having behind him his childhood and the two standard pedagogical experiences of the time, school and war, set out to examine some among the many images of honor and achievement which civilization had offered him to be models for the conduct of life. Though some poems spoke directly from the poet's own situation as soldier, far the greater part were given to the inspection of heroism as it is recommended to us by certain figures of our mythology, among them Sherlock Holmes, the Rover Boys, Lord Jim, Gulliver, Paul Revere; Emma, Hester Prynne, Lady Ashley, and so on.

Though the prevailing tone is light—the author's attitude to his heroes and heroines half affectionate and half ruefully amused—these poems nevertheless are sketches for tragedies, essentially tragic in their dealings with the obsolescence of particular forms of virtue, with the situation of "the best people" whose heroic qualities have been superseded, who have remained in fashion but have lost their function, and who go from bewilderment to defeat as they try to apply to a new world the moral talents which used to work so well in the old one.

Behind each particular experiment, placing the old hero in the new context, the literary hero in the everyday context, lay the more general question: whether literature would do? or rather, how much of it, under new conditions, had become merely "literature" and nothing else? The appearance of parody in part disguised and in part perhaps alleviated the painfulness of this inquiry. It was not yet a matter of the poet's summoning these instruments to him, trying what each would do, and rejecting them, like Beethoven in the IX Symphony, in favor of "the human voice" (a less literal and a more problematic decision, in poetry), but rather of letting each demonstrate dramatically its limits in action and his reservations about it;

but it is useful to notice, in the light of later poems, that Whitte-more's Sherlock Holmes discovers the arch-criminal to be, after all, Doctor Watson—bourgeois, professional, and the narrator, or poet, of those adventures; a combination germinal in much that followed.

Whittemore's second collection, *An American Takes a Walk*, ap-peared a decade later. It further develops the same inquiry about the relations between art and life, this time from the opposite quarter. Whereas the earlier poems were projected from the consideration of a definite heroic image already established, these later ones arise from the consideration of the self in its situation.

Vestiges of the former mode do remain in a few poems, and these are broadly joking in style, e.g. "Abbreviated Interviews With a Few Disgruntled Literary Celebrities" (Ulalume, Evangeline, the Lady of Shalott), and three on "Fathers and Sons," parables of hero sons who overcame their fathers' dire predictions of failure. These heroes, how-ever, are from life: Clive, Darwin, Tennyson.

But the major part of this book is given to a many-faceted medi-tation on character and poetic vocation, wherein the self confronts its various public definitions as member of this and that abstract class or category: as citizen, as teacher, as writer; and draws from its sit-uations stoical comedies, metaphors for poetry, metaphors for the poet as tourist or guide, as unemployed, always as seeking an identity which shall be not only dramatic but also truthful.

These poems are often funny in their details, in the brilliance and accuracy of their notation; taken as a whole, they witness to an in-wardness immensely somber and moving, sustained over their black abyss by great technical powers, a gaiety and melodiousness consist-ing inherently with whatever is finely done in the arts, so that even at their most serious reach these works do not fall into that "pro-fundity" which Pope so attentively characterizes in the *Bathos*, and which so many contemporary poets evidently regard as an ideal to get down to.

The scene is most often that small room alone, where all our trou-bles come, *pace* Pascal, whether we stay in it or not; by expansion, the waste, the wasteland, the desert, where the mind meets its in-herited culture and is appalled. The conflict represented is that be-tween the validity and immediacy of feeling, and the vulgar distor-tion which results when feeling is mediated through some structure or authority, literature, morals, ideas, the State.

Now that the State I serve has closed its doors
For the night and left its fate
To the char force and the mice and a few industrious
Slaves of the overtime, I make my flight
Through its long and dark dominions towards my own,
Attended by all those feelings of relief,
Release, renewal and restoration
I am disposed to ridicule in romantic
Stories and poems and friends and relations.

On the one hand there is the impulse to poetry, to order the world by viewing it synoptically, symbolically; this impulse is regarded as given and immediate. On the other hand is the critical doubt of poetic function in a world which may no longer be conceived as a stage, a world in which an opaque reality has everywhere replaced the idea of truth, and where every man must contend, not dramatically against evil, but chaotically against irrelevance. This dilemma is particularly acute in Whittemore's work because he is quite the reverse of a "nature poet." No matter what the contemporary situation, the nature poet is always able to feel that he is satisfactorily reaching after some primal condition of relatedness, productive of truth, because mountain, sea, and storm do not yield to history, and by conjuring with the names of those things great pieties are always able to be obtained. The poet of culture, concerned to dramatize the human and historical, has a harder time, though the scope of his ambitions may plausibly be larger.

He who can tell a grosbeak from a grackle,
Red oak from maple, marigold from heather,
May get on. But will that other,
Inward drawn . . . ?

Whittemore does not think it likely, and sees that "other" as "nameless" in a kind of natural hell.

A fairly full relation of the central conflict is given in "A Day with The Foreign Legion," where the poet describes the military situation, the situation of "all those brave / Heroes of all those books and plays and movies / The remorseless desert serves," in a *montage* composed in equal parts of melodrama and the probable reality. The reality, first, is "one of those days with the Legion / When everyone sticks to sofas / And itches and bitches," but then, when the attack is announced, it is "just like the movies," and there follows a very funny description, too long to be quoted here, of how it would be in the movies, the essential seriousness of which is that artistic form, whether believable or not, acts like grace upon human purpose and human action, controlling without destroying the actors' perfect freedom to make all possible mistakes, and bringing things right in the end. "But in this instance nothing from *Beau Geste* / Or the Paramount lot was attempted," and there is a passage again about the reality. But at last the reality is seen also as a movie:

> . . . the lights went on and the audience,
> Pleasantly stupid, whistled and clapped at the rarity
> Of a film breaking down in this late year of Our Lord.
>
> But of course it was not the film; it was not the projector;
> Nor was it the man in the booth, who hastened away
> As soon as the feature was over, leaving the heroes
> Cursing the food and the bugs, cursing the Legion
> As heathendom marched and the Sergeant whirled, hip hip;
> But some other, darker cause having to do
> With the script perhaps, or the art.
> Or not art—
> None of these but still deeper, deeper and darker,
> Rooted in Culture or . . . Culture, or. . . .
>
> Or none of these things. Or all.
>
> What was it?

It was "that the feature had merely run out, and the lights had gone on." The standard heroism purveyed in our mythology will simply not do; the reality and the dramatic representation no longer come into phase, no longer significantly confront one another so that even their differences would form a comparison—yet, as we expect "realism" in our dramas, the corollary is that we helplessly continue to expect the order of drama to pervade our realities. To allegorize, somewhat more strictly perhaps than the poet's figure will at all points give warrant for, the "feature" is history, or the legend of it we have been brought up to believe in as we sit, alone among many, in Plato's cave where images flicker on the limiting wall. The man in the booth, who runs the "projector" (a word belonging both to Swift and to Freud), may in passing be seen as the poet, who does his job and leaves when his job is done. This figure may be viewed as a parody of various vatic or prophetic ideas of the poet, who speaks not as an individual but as the "voice" of some universal spirit; in this parody his function is a mechanical one, so that it is none of his business if something—the script, the art, Culture, religion ("as heathendom marched"), or force of arms (the Legion)—has failed and the myth is left to end without concluding, simply to trail off in such a way that the audience (readers, citizens) believes the film to have broken down, when in fact it has "merely run out."

This probing of the pieties of a conventional mythology, this severe analysis of all forms of "eternal return," destructive criticism which brings us again and again to what Yeats thought of as "the desolation of reality," is persistently thematic in Whittemore's poetry, and is of course the natural reason of its being "literary." For either Everyman must discover for himself the truth of his inherited fabric of imagery and symbol, or he must find it false and reject it, or destroy it. In the poem about the Legion, the heroes are seen as "aging," and it is observable that in a great many poems this circumstance is central, introducing, as in so many negative rites of passage, the idea of entropy and the irreversibility of time as critical for all mythologies and beliefs formed upon cyclical models (e.g., "Commencement," "Variations on Being Thirty," "After Some Day of Decision"). In several poems, as I said before, the poet figures his role as that of tourist or guide, his book as "a Projected Guide Book," and a possible acceptance of tradition ("Travel is a trick I learned / From my betters") is discussed explicitly in one of these, "Abydos," which begins with the dilemma: "We can't go back to where we were when Time / First chimed in our warm ken," and goes on to argue very ambiguously that we must deceive ourselves by accepting the (deceitful) testimony of the past that this is "a holy place"; so we shall have "green images" instead of "our desert prospect," and so—

> these stones
> And shattered pots, statues and odd inscriptions
> We take as outward evidence of our past.
> And so Osiris and fellow immortal fictions,
> Dug from their deep fallows, reinvest
> The wastes of mankind's memory with pious meaning.

So the poet is a guide, possibly an archeologist; but if he will be a priest he will be perpetuating a fraud, though certainly a pious and perhaps a necessary one. The possibility of this vocation, however, is not often dealt with so tenderly as in the last lines of this poem.

Many examples might be given of this dilemma, of which the result is a poetry become critical of itself, and a poet affiliated almost against his will, surely against his impulse, with a rational, daylight, near-scientific critique, by turns nostalgic and mocking, of the romantic ideals of a dry, secular culture which everywhere imposes itself upon the possibility of a heroic poetry.

I said before that the impulse to poetry is regarded as immediate and given in Whittemore's work, where many of the poems begin simply with that situation, the poet's impulse to write; what stands in the way becomes, often, the subject of the poem. I say further that this impulse, with Whittemore, is to a heroic, representative poetry, a poetry synoptic of history, of culture, making the same claims as the major poems of the past; the evidence for this is his persistent preoccupation with heroism in action, matched, on the technical side, by a preoccupation with epical devices, which he employs, however, chiefly in a mocking or critical sense. What prevents his realizing the impulse is plain from the preceding analysis: the times are out of joint, and so on. And there is a great deal of good evidence that this is so; in fact, the problem thus posed is crucial for much modern poetry, Eliot's for example through *The Waste Land.* Thus, Whittemore, in the title poem of his second volume, strolling through the American scene on his typically diffident quest, is compelled to see the heroic vocations of the past simply as so much "literature":

> In the middle of this life's journey
> He came, like Dante, on a wood
> The notes said stood for error
> But in his case stood for good. . . .

Intellectually speaking, he knows this is Hell, or the road to Hell; at the same time, though, it is extremely comfortable, and feels innocent:

> Nature was awfully kind.
> Hell in that motherly habit
> Put hell quite out of mind.
>
> How in that Arden could human
> Frailty be but glossed?
> How in that Eden could Adam
> Be really, wholly lost?

It is, in effect, present civilization which, even in all good will and with excellent reason, prevents poetry of the sort to which he feels impelled. In honesty and intelligence he is forbidden to write as though he believed what he does not in fact believe; worse than knavery, for a man of sense, this would be absurdity.

The effect of the position is an odd one, given the impulse to write and having the skill to do so: what one writes is necessarily about the difficulty, or impossibility, of a belief which could liberate heroic virtues, and the overt subject of the poems is the attack upon civilization for preventing the exercise of these virtues. But to this attack the poet brings precisely the virtues of civilization: rationality, irony, a balanced and critical understanding. Thus the poems, even at their most sarcastic and satiric, are full of resignation: it must be so. And thus, by a curious transformation nevertheless common enough in life, the poet's own honesty and wit become defenses raised against the impulse to poetry itself.

But to every outside there is an inside. The impulse is taken for granted in the poems, so far as concerns the overt structure, argument, substance; the subject of discussion is apparently the obstacle presented by contemporary life, the obstacle, that is, imposed from without, and from within only so far as the poet consciously acknowledges his own views as penetrated by those of the world. Yet if we look again at the poems, attending this time to the imagery which is dominant over them and comes to his mind often and often in illustrating his predicament, we shall find a somewhat different view of the problem, suggestive of the poet's having reached a balance between the heroic and the critical, between impulse and defense; possibly in this balance already, as it is finely said by the analyst Fenichel, "The defense is invaded by the impulse."

This dominant imagery has to do with isolation, and characteristically takes one of two forms: being locked up or walled in, or being buried. Though with exceptions and reservations the tonality of this motif, its "feeling," is one of relief, of security; imagery of heights, burstings forth, liberations, is contrastingly associated with danger and fear, usually in connection with some idea of "authority."

There are doors everywhere in these poems, and most often they are closed. When a door is open, the fact is regarded not only as an accident but as ominous: that "the latch on the broken door to the backyard is broken" is a "sign." "Authority," on the other hand, enables a man "to open and shut at will all private doors."

Being thus sequestered against experience is the identifying condition of "the self," which resists the seasons, "the weather's fingers caressing it lewdly," and "bolts the door double, and draws up the covers, and frowns," or has fantasies of being "a pale rosy pear-shaped eunuch / Walled up tight in some shah's Himalayan chalet." By further epithets in the same poem ("Moving Among the Seasons"), this self is characterized as "like a virgin or prude": as "illiterate, / Proud, insensible, righteous, / and most of all, worst of all, pure. It knows not / Amour."

Apart from this literal solipsism, the feeling induced may properly be called religious, as in "Still Life," where the poet's compulsion to whisper when alone in the house at night is referred to either "devotion" or "fright." Here he sees "all the inanimate things of my daytime life" come alive, in a "still life" which he would translate into art: "I wish I might somehow / Bring into daylight the eloquence, say, of a doorknob." We should not make too much of the doorknob in this one poem, yet it is curious how aptly it comes in, despite the casualness of "say," as the key illustration of what the process of art is, for a poet whose indecisions are so often represented by doors, for whom doors, whether as inviting the self out into the world or as letting the world in upon the self, are ambiguously opportunities or threats, and sometimes both together.

The extremes are simple; taken together they form a paradox. At the benign extreme, this withdrawal is restful, fecund, pleasurable, as on a Midsummer Sunday "of naps, birds, children and slamming doors / The mind withdrew to its den in a green wood." This green wood is the Arden or Eden of the title poem, but given here without any sarcastic reservation, and

> Into the den
> Shakespeare and Dante and soft furry poets slipped
> And lay down; out of it sauntered
> Miscellaneous nonsense in stocking feet,

(that is, the poet's own works?), and generally the experience is one of "deep but delicate distances," at the end of which "the doors were still." But at the other extreme, "After Some Day of Decision," the poet contemplates his having "adjusted to society"—

> He doesn't know when it was that the last door closed,
> But now it is closed for good. What he is doing
> He will continue to do, and what he has not done
> Will not be done.

He accepts, though satirically and with some self-contempt, the identity imposed upon him: "It is called settling down"; but finally, in a figure curiously combining the medical and legal, "He dreams of being tried and pronounced—'Dead.' "

The paradox is this: poetry comes from the silences of the self immured; even in the second poem he assures himself sarcastically that one can go right on doing this sort of thing "stanza by stanza" (that is, incidentally, room by room, as in Donne's "We'll build in sonnets pretty roomes")—but this security is regarded as ignobly passive, and is possibly to be thought of as death.

Consistent with the terms of the dilemma is the distinction of day and night, waking and sleeping. In a poem called "The Girl Friend," waking is "wisdom, ungodly, civil," a state in which the doors may safely be open and one can walk "through kindly halls and offices"; but night is warlike and dangerous "in old General Terror's tenement," where sleep is a "wall." The resolution here is the girl friend herself, "Sylvia," described as combining "sleeping, waking," equated with "reality," and religiously seen as an essence in "fire or cloud or bush or whirlwind." In some sense the poet's ambiguous approach to the condition of being immured or cloistered seems to represent a struggle with narcissism, to which the solution may be either love or death; the poems, in dramatizing this struggle, necessarily participate in the values of either side, and since the overt question at issue is so often poetry itself, the subject of style, manners, or manner, is not infrequently affiliated with the prevailing imagery. An earlier poem, taken in this context, seems to give a riddling, sibylline answer, which may perhaps have provoked the later poems into asking the appropriate questions:

> Only the dead have manners; they alone
> Are never trapped between The Lady and The Door. . . .

Sometimes the place of confinement is not a room or house, but a pit, a grave. One poem, "A Treasure," mediates the two images:

> Up in the attic, down in the cellar, and under
> The sagging old porch in back lies the treasure.

This treasure, sought by a scholar "on a generous grant," consists of the literary remains of someone who "will be led / Out in due time from this timeless house of the dead," while the scholar himself in his turn sinks into "these depths, in this dust," himself now a forgotten treasure "For later scholars on generous grants to discover." Again in an earlier poem there occurs a similar diffident and riddling image of history: at the grave of an American draftee in Africa strangers pause, reading his name and "possibly dreaming of heroes." This view of "eternal return" or the futility of process is strangely brought into relation with writing by a poem wherein an author dreams up a story ("for Fantasy Fiction") about how spring failed to come one year:

> So ran an author's thoughts in that season of brown,
> Thoughts of a new Jeremiah looking for something
> Salable even as shoots of green began groping
> Their way in the dark to the surface of things,
> And robins appeared on schedule, and buds swelled.

The decisive, balancing emblem of this imagery of womb or tomb occurs in a subtle and beautiful poem which is not primarily a satire, though announced as one: "Lines, Composed Upon Reading an Announcement by Civil Defense Authorities Recommending that I Build a Bombshelter in My Backyard." Here the poet first remembers "a dugout we dug in the backyard as children," where the children were "thoroughly squashed, / But safe, with our chins on our knees, from the world's hurt"; it was "our self's damp stronghold among the selfless dead." This memory he now thinks of as a scene from "a marathon play," "with the lost hero / Preferring, to death, some brave kind of decay." Now, an adult, "under the new and terrible rules of romance," he is told by "authorities" that he is to do it again, but he refuses to

> go back
> And lie there in that dark under the weight
> Of all that earth on that old door for my state.
> I know too much to think now that, if I creep
> From the grown-up's house to the child's house, I'll keep.

The combination is powerful, and puzzling. This "burial" is recommended to the adult as security; for the child it was heroism, part of a "marathon" play (both an "endless" play and one involving heroic virtue); the child accepts life (a "brave form of decay") in preference to death, while the adult fears death less than the attrition of time, and rejects the offered security of a bombshelter perhaps because, on the literal level, he believes it to be ineffectual, but, in the allegory, because it will not save him from corruption; he will not "keep." "I know too much," he says, and this is directly related to poetry ("romance," "play"), so that an undercurrent of the poem seems to be making the point, though nostalgically, that poetry too is childish and may have to be given up: the world is no longer a stage.

To sum up. This imagery seems to equate modest security with death, possibly a living death, with notions of narcissistic independence, and with the thought, rarely explicit but somehow dominant all the same, that if one lives small one may be overlooked. Its corollary, not so numerously expressed but readily seen to be present, is a defensive, sarcastic, even fearful rejection of heights, of journeys upward and outward, to which "authority" is often related. Thus in the first poem in the book, thinking of Julien Sorel's "social climb" to Mme. Reynal's bedroom by means of a ladder, "I am frightened by ladders, Freud, by ladders," and "My soul, Freud, my soul sinks in the ground." In another poem, "A Projection," a voyage to Mars by rocket (it is sponsored by authorities, but lands on Venus "through some slight error") is contrasted with "the walled-up, balled-up self." And there are some satires rejecting the idea of progress, which is characterized as "onward and upward."

Possibly the most comprehensive and accomplished use of this body of images and associated ideas appears in the following wonderful poem or totem-image:

THE KAYLAVASI

First there came the Kaylavasi (iguana), the animal of the Lukulabuta clan, which scratched its way through the earth as iguanas do, then climbed a tree, and remained there as a mere onlooker.
                                                                    —Malinowski

> We,
> Rooting where our fathers sleep,
> Or borne or bearing outward, creep
> Golden in our season from below.
>
> Above us, lost in leaves to us, a few
> Down upon our sunning glare

As if for that they were not there
Too.

But when we past our growing grow
And wander withered down and in,
They from their gaunt perches soon
Follow.

Great riches in this little room, whose somewhat intricate organization I shall not attempt to unravel. In an early poem about another lizard, the poet inquires cryptically about ambition and necessity:

How is it this green lizard
Climbs the climbless wall?
And when to where he goes he
Comes, why fall?
Surely he who crawls so
Far against the law
Can crawl a lawless minute
More. With awe
I watch the conduct of green lizards.

Poetry, then, would take place in that lawless minute?

In themselves these poems of Whittemore's represent a considerable accomplishment. I am more concerned, however, with what problems they pose, and what developments they suggest, for his future work.

The poet speaks about the world, and about himself, simultaneously, and in the same words. I have tried in my analysis to show something of this janual congruence, or identity, in the works of a poet whose writings very often become quite overtly the subjects of themselves, in which the debate whether poetry is possible now, in this world, is also the debate whether poetry is possible for this poet. The result so far appears to be a number of finely made and reckonable poems which are nevertheless critical of themselves, express dissatisfaction with themselves.

It is perhaps very presumptuous in the critic to introduce a subject of this sort, concerning which his remarks must run inevitably beyond what he has been able to demonstrate; my excuse must be that Whittemore has opened the question himself, with reference to his own poetry, in an essay, "A Few Ways of Pulling Apart a Poem" (*New Republic*, December 9, 1957). Here he examines a poem of his own according to the canons of several kinds of criticism (the element of parody, even of self-parody, appearing here just as it does in the poems) variously oriented to internal and structural criteria or to criteria of social meaning and significance. He finds the poem deficient in various ways which I need not describe, but what seems to him finally most useful, most helpful to himself as a poet, is the application of a remark of Shaw's to the effect that the most serious intellectual concerns might be just "a mere middle-class business." Poetry, his own first but not by any means alone, may be viewed as "a mere middle-class business." This is something of a revelation in prose, but I think it is what his poems have been worrying for a long time.

The poet *is* a man of the middle class, and among his middle-class virtues, rationality, common sense, sincerity, is a keen sense of the limits of what it is to be middle-class, that is, middling. It is the class whose members say to themselves over and over that they are not Prince Hamlet nor were meant to be, just as they are not Macbeth or Antony. Poetry, though, seems to demand something different, having to do with great heights and great depths. On the other hand, the virtues instrumental in writing the poetry down—wit, learning, eloquence—are virtues (when they are not vices) which properly belong to the middle class, which is why, it may be, so many great poets have been of that class instead of being princes, farmers, or workers.

Poetry demands the dramatic, not structurally but as its gesture—flair, elegance, *panache*. The poet must pretend to be what he is not, that is one way of saying it, and it may be that the poet, being middle-class, has so powerful a sense of what he is (look at those tweeds, that crew-cut, not to mention the wife and kids) that he is overcome with embarrassment at what seems the hypocrisy of speaking in voices not his own; what will his friends say? In the result, it appears, poetry becomes reserved, critical, somewhat dry—"a mere middle-class business." It is not a new problem:

> *Hic.* And I would find myself and not an image.
> *Ille.* That is our modern hope, and by its light
> We have lit upon the gentle, sensitive mind
> And lost the old nonchalance of the hand;
> Whether we have chosen chisel, pen, or brush,
> We are but critics, or but half create,

Timid, entangled, empty and abashed,
Lacking the countenance of our friends.

—Yeats

It is a major virtue in Whittemore's work that he has constantly brought himself face to face with this dilemma; the fineness of the best of his poems has intimately to do with their rejection of the theatrical, oracular, and "significant," their refusal to be "important" and "deep" by faking up an irrelevant heroism. Yet in honesty and criticism there remains the problem, deep in the poetry, whether goodness is not closely allied with timidity and a failure to presume. Nietzsche speculated on the good man as "a poison, a narcotic, by means of which the present battened on the future." And on the other hand, it was honest Iago who was "nothing if not critical." Perhaps, then, the poet must presume, because his job is rather to make the future than to understand the present. High talk. How can a *bourgeois gentilhomme* make the future? John Keats offers comfort:

As to the poetical Character itself (I mean that sort of which, if I am anything, I am a Member; that sort distinguished from the wordsworthian or egotistical sublime; which is a thing per se and stands alone) it is not itself—it has no self—it is every thing and nothing—It has no character—it enjoys light and shade; it lives in gusto, be it foul or fair, high or low, rich or poor, mean or elevated—It has as much delight in conceiving an Iago as an Imogen. What shocks the virtuous philosopher, delights the camelion Poet. It does no harm from its relish of the dark side of things any more than from its taste for the bright one; because they both end in speculation. A Poet is the most unpoetical of any thing in existence; because he has no Identity—he is continually in for *—and filling some other Body—the Sun, the Moon, the Sea and Men and Women who are creatures of impulse are poetical and have about them an unchangeable attribute—the poet has none; no identity —he is certainly the most unpoetical of all God's Creatures.

At this point surely, and probably long before it, the critic reaches his limit. The poet's choice between what I have roughly distinguished as heroism and critique must be a matter of temperament and history; not a subject of conscious election; no matter what his

---

* It has been conjectured Keats wrote "informing"; see Buxton Forman's edition of the *Letters*, 228n.

awareness of the dilemma he can add no cubit to his stature by taking thought. Yet it has seemed clear to me that Whittemore, through all difficulties and self-questionings, is strongly and increasingly impelled to those heights and liberations which his poetry has been suspicious of so far, toward the heroic extreme. His first book taught him it was absurd; his second, that it was impossible. Thus far at any rate his evident rationale. But the dominating image of his predicament suggests a third characteristic of the heroic, that it may also be necessary and impossible to avoid. Thus the conclusion come to by the hero of his "Closet Drama" which takes place, piously, in a closet:

> Nothing is safe, nothing secure,
> From powers and passions I store
> In a secret room behind a secret door.

The Poems of Weldon Kees

The Collected Poems of Weldon Kees. Edited by Donald Justice. The Stone Wall Press. Iowa City, Iowa, 1960.

It was a good thought on Mr. Justice's part to collect as fully as possible and make available again, even in so limited and expensive a form, the poems of Weldon Kees. I share his hope that a larger edition may soon follow. For surely the great beauty of the work must arouse wide interest among readers of poetry, if there are some still around.

That last clause of reservation comes up as part of some rueful-ironic reflections about this handsome publication; I can imagine the poet, if by chance he still lives, looking wryly at the leather binding, the rich paper, the Romanée and Lutetia types, and perhaps writing a characteristically sardonic poem about it; then I reflect sadly that he might not be able to afford a copy.

But probably Weldon Kees is not alive. The circumstances of his disappearance in 1955 suggested suicide, and though one keeps an uncertain hope it is more likely that this fine book is a monument and a memorial. As a friend of the poet, I am filled with regret for the despair which must have possessed him, and do not regard this review as a proper occasion for those elegant literary comparisons with Rimbaud and Hart Crane, which I doubt would have delighted him. He was a man not greatly patient of clichés.

A few words, then, about the specific excellences of the poems, and the characteristic voice of the poet.

He is in a special sense a poet of the city, and though he lived the last several years of his life in California the city of his poems is always New York, a grim and somber yet loving abstraction of that metropolis of the mind, with place names like invocations: Tenth Street, Avenue A, Chelsea, Astor Place, Brooklyn Heights . . . and

Reprinted by permission from *The Carleton Miscellany*, Vol. II, No. 2, Spring 1961. Copyright 1961 by Carleton College.

summers on Fire Island or the Cape. The rest of the world is most often a matter of indifference:

> We are in Cleveland, or Sioux Falls. The architecture
> Seems like Omaha, the air pumped in from Düsseldorf.
> —"Dead March"

What is special about his work is the degree to which the city invades the poems, becomes the poems, the way in which he feels himself into the textures of the city, slowly perceiving the fragments of a huge fact which is also a fate; the poems are the process of this perception, which he sums up in the title of one of them: "The City As Hero." It is a scene which dominates the actors in it, and invents their actions: the sidewalks, buildings, roofs, chimneys, lights and shadows and resonance of stone, "the rouged and marketable glow / Beyond Third Avenue"; "Far down on Lexington, / A siren moans and dies." Above all, the lonely apartment room of despair and disrepair, where "the crack is moving down the wall," "the fissures in the studio grow large," "a drunk is sobbing in the hall," where the mirrors reflect nothing and the phone rings only when Robinson is not at home. Robinson is Weldon Kees' lost citizen, his nearest approach to a hero, and a horrifying explanation is suggested for the ringing phone:

> It could be Robinson
> Calling. It never rings when he is here.

It is with items of this sort—architecture, garbage, furniture—that Weldon Kees works his magic; and it is of the nature of this magic, too, that for all the grimness of its properties the result is also somewhat gay, a courageous assault on the deep melancholy of self-doubt which guarantees the public and satiric gesture.

There is another way in which Kees' is a distinctively metropolitan consciousness, a way which I should like to characterize as Alexandrian, without any feeling that Alexandrian is a disgraceful thing for a human mind to be. He is not afraid of erudition, and doesn't have delicate lyrical qualms about culture. It is in fact central to the understanding of his poems that the city is above all a place of compositions, of *collages*, inheriting the beautiful junk of the ages from all over the world, making one thing relevant to another for the simple but adequate reason that the two things happen to be in the same place, the two thoughts happen to come into the same head together.

So a fair number of his best pieces have to do with the idea or form of a catalogue; they list and vary items which have at first a merely arbitrary look, then grow into strange relations:

> Santayana, who had stomach trouble
> As a youth, once shook the hand
> Of Henry Wadsworth Longfellow. Professor Norton
> Lingered on. "No comfort, not a breath of love,"
> Wrote Nietzsche, going mad. Booth Tarkington loved art.

This technique, this view of what form is, I find always at least engaging and immensely instructive. It looks easy, perhaps, but it isn't. In which it a little resembles Cubism. Often he employs it for an effect of flatness to set off and prepare his revelations; the parody of a scholar fumbling among his sources and finding, suddenly, the horror of himself:

> *Vide Master,*
> Muzie, Brown and Parker on the hypoplastic heart.
> Culpin stressed the psychogenic origin. DeCosta
> Ruled out syphilis. If we follow Raines and Kolb,
> We follow Raines and Kolb. . . .
> —"The Clinic"

Eclectic? Of course. Technique of prose? Certainly. Yet it will happen that a piece of deliberate pastiche, a putting together of elegant cultural snippets, rises to be sublime poetry. The subject is women, and I quote the last of three stanzas:

> Their bowels almost drove Swift mad. "Sad stem,
> Sweet evil, stretching out a lion's jaws," wrote Marbode.
> Now we cling together in our caves. That not impossible she
> That rots and wrinkles in the sun, the shadow
> Of all men, man's counterpart, sweet rois
> Of vertew and of gentilness . . . The brothel and the crib endure.
> Past reason hunted. How we die! Their pain, their blood, are ours.
> —"A Pastiche for Eve"

So, for this poet, any collocation of data may become available as a form: a diary, a detective story, program notes for a symphony, "Abstracts of Dissertations," "Report of the Meeting." Nor may this be thought of, or dismissed, as a technical trick only, for it finds its exact equivalent in the poet's view of his city and his world—a place where one lonely human mind, witty in its worst despair, strives to assert necessary connections among a million pieces of random information, seeking its own image in one sliver after another of the world's shattered mirror. It is greatly to the honor of Weldon Kees' memory that he understood and demonstrated so well what kind of thing, in these days, a poem is: a piece of language with which nothing else can be done.

Now it is too late, one reads in these poems the record of a terrible and increasing despair. The hitherto uncollected poems at the end of the volume (though I have no assurance they are all necessarily late ones I am certain that some must be) are full of hopeless distances, flood, fire, ruin, regret for "the marvelous cities that our childhoods built for us"; in one, a ghostly murderer with "moulting beard and ancient stare" pursues the speaker to a fated and fatal encounter; another is a mocking account of burning books to keep warm; a third imprecates a final flood upon "this room" which is "our world." Here is another, "Covering Two Years," which I shall quote in full for a testament of excellence as well as anguish:

> This nothingness that feeds upon itself:
> Pencils that turn to water in the hand,
> Parts of a sentence, hanging in the air,
> Thoughts breaking in the mind like glass,
> Blank sheets of paper that reflect the world
> Whitened the world that I was silenced by.
>
> There were two years of that. Slowly,
> Whatever splits, dissevers, cuts, cracks, ravels, or divides
> To bring me to that diet of corrosion, burned
> And flickered to its terminal.—Now in an older hand
> I write my name. Now with a voice grown unfamiliar,
> I speak to silences of altered rooms,
> Shaken by knowledge of recurrence and return.

But it is too late, I guess, even for that uncertain hope I spoke of before; seven years, one is told, is the statutory limit, beyond which an unidentifiable existence cannot legally be continued; and those years are gone: subject for a poem by Weldon Kees. Still, out of some more and more marginal sense that life is better than death, one does hope. My hope founds itself on nothing more solid than one of these poems, "Relating to Robinson," in which the story is foretold:

> Somewhere in Chelsea, early summer;
> And, walking in the twilight toward the docks,
> I thought I made out Robinson ahead of me.

Maybe, I think for a moment: maybe. I remember Browning's "Waring"; comparison no less inconsequent than the one about Rimbaud and Crane. In Vishnu land what avatar? And I consider walking in Chelsea early in the summer.

But even if one had the generous folly to believe in poems, this poem would give no guarantee, and comfort scant enough:

> Under a sign for Natural Bloom Cigars,
> While lights clicked softly in the dusk from red to green,
> He stopped and gazed into a window
> Where a plaster Venus, modeling a truss,
> Looked out at eastbound traffic. (But Robinson,
> I knew, was out of town: he summers at a place in Maine,
> Sometimes on Fire Island, sometimes the Cape,
> Leaves town in June and comes back after Labor Day.)
> And yet, I almost called out, "Robinson!"
> There was no chance . . .

And though the speaker does meet someone, a terrified accuser who says, "You must have followed me from Astor Place," the meeting is inconclusive, and the poem disappears into the blue distances of Weldon's legendary city, New York:

> I had no certainty,
> There in the dark, that it was Robinson
> Or someone else.
> The block was bare. The Venus,
> Bathed in blue fluorescent light,
> Stared toward the river. As I hurried West,
> The lights across the bay were coming on.
> The boats moved silently and the low whistles blew.

The Careful Poets and the Reckless Ones

Decembrist. By Joseph Bennett. Clarke & Way, 1951.
The Sorrows of Cold Stone. By John Malcolm Brinnin. Dodd, Mead, 1951.
Selected Poems. By Richard Eberhart. Oxford, 1951.
The Seven-League Crutches. By Randall Jarrell. Harcourt, Brace, 1951.
Night Sky. By Bernice Kenyon. Scribner's, 1951.
First Poems. By James Merrill. Knopf, 1951.
The New Barbarian. By Winthrop Palmer. Farrar, Straus & Young, 1951.
The American Fantasies. By James Schevill. Bern Porter Books (P. O. Box 222, Agana, Guam, M. I.), 1951.

Of these eight volumes I shall deal first with four which are altogether less ambitious than the others and which, despite their individual differences, are much alike in a number of ways both as they succeed and as they do not. Three of these poets—Mrs. Palmer, Miss Kenyon, and Mr. Bennett—write usually in rimed stanzas and with a certain caution, as though their poems were in danger of getting out of hand; the fourth, Mr. Schevill, at first glance looks more rebellious but gets, I think, similar results.

Joseph Bennett, in his first book, shows that he has one of the good gifts, he cares for words, and so far as it is better for the poet to be at the start rather foppish than earnest, fair enough; his choices are at many places elegant, particular, what they used to call "curious"; for instance, of his "Tombstone Man":

> Outfitter to the credulous,
> Treasurer of dust,

First published in *The Sewanee Review*, Vol. 60, No. 2, Spring 1952. Copyright July 7, 1952, by The University of the South.

Your chisel, flagrant, sedulous,
Elaborates a crystal crust.

It is disappointing to have to note about the poems in this book that
with all their minute and pleasing surprises they do not seem to come
to much.

He writes in general strictly as to rime and meter, often in octo-
syllabics and quatrains, perhaps too strictly and closes off the form
before it is well begun; sometimes the meter falls too into a perfunctory regularity which belies a little the effect of hard choice in individual words. In poems like "Quatrina" and "News from the Rear"
it seems the formality becomes ridiculous as, by reiterating his end-
words, he imitates the idea of the sestina in a monstrous cramped
space (the latter poem adds rime to all this); I find I do not have
this objection, though, to "And Then the Woman Spoke," a combination of villanelle and roundel, which is one of the two best poems
in the book; the other being "Pointillism," a witty melodrama in
which the mere number of characters to be accounted for happily
suppresses the poet's will to nostalgic reverie, while the frequent occurrence of their odd names is perhaps what prevents him from riming.

The problem is to keep the elaboration of particulars from stopping
the poem, or from allowing the poem to exist only as an elaboration
of particulars; it must move through its action too, and be able to
carry with it the repetitions and refrains and returns-to-the-beginning,
which, however attractive in themselves, achieve what they do of
elegance and ceremony at very great expense; here, for example, the
note (there are notes) describing the background and theme of the
poem "Pharos" seems to me for these reasons to be a better poem
than the poem itself.

Bernice Kenyon does not appear to care for words very much at
all; she writes with very considerable skill what may be called, with
a nod to the sociologist, the normative English poem, which is strong
and tender and weeps easily. It is a sad poetry, and takes place
mostly in autumn or winter, at night; summer and spring, and daylight, appear only as charming villains do in the movies, admitted to
a temporary triumph already seen in the melancholy-virtuous after-
glow of the bad end the producer's code has doomed them to.

> . . . in the high hours of May,
> At noon I can believe the lovely sight,
> Green-gold and bright, might yet contrive to stay
> Forever. . . .

The development of this poetry is not hard to follow: characteristically it sets up the beauty of nature, in which for a moment it takes a plausibly epicurean delight; knocks this over for being ephemeral; finds stoical acceptance of nature's sad god, whose permanence is suspiciously like death; emerges with a synthesis about the enduring but indefinable qualities of *love*:

> One must have love. One must forever reach,
> Nor hold too much to the light. Night is too near.

There is no objection at all to this program for poetry except its being programmatic; after I read several of these poems they come to seem somewhat wearily foreordained with a weariness that affects the imagery, which is neither freshly observed nor usually particularized at all, and severely affects the diction—as though the poem, being predestined to its feelings, had simply to reach its end with as little fuss as possible; in six lines of one poem occur the following phrases: the loud morning, the swift descent, our most intimate star, the vast planes of space, the purple dark, the high vaults of time, the low regions of distance.

This is too bad, because there is certainly much technical ability here, especially in the setting of the rhythm over against the meter; a good way of talking, in places suggestive of Frost. But surely the excellence of Frost is in being always surprising not only in technical matters but in attitude; and even when he takes this melancholy line (and he does sometimes) the poem is likely to turn it rather shrewdly back upon him: "There may be little or much beyond the grave, / But the strong are saying nothing until they see." It is this shrewdness, debating with the feeling too easily and too often evoked, that is lacking in Miss Kenyon's otherwise attractive work.

James Schevill, in *The American Fantasies*, appears at first very different from the two poets so far discussed, but his proletarian and somewhat gamin recklessness is perceptibly, at its worst, as much a stereotype as Miss Kenyon's standard poeticism or Mr. Bennett's elegant caution. His is a species of poetry rebellious, "unofficial," marked by social protest in which the achievement of "savage irony" becomes occasionally much too easy (the voice of Mr. Patchen); but marked also and more happily by vigorous imagination, the production in a great many lines of very strong and apt effects. Titles of a few of the poems will suggest their general character: "The Strange Case of the American Mirror Which Reflects Only the Ever-Present I," "An Interview with the Devil by the Editor of Time Magazine," "Confidential Data on the Loyalty Investigation of Herbert Ashenfoot," the last in my opinion the best poem in the book.

The satirical tone is the least attractive in Mr. Schevill's range, probably because his subjects, for all their homely titles, are so abstract that they do not evoke much more than a standard, negative reaction a little illuminated sometimes, as in the following example, by the poet's way with images; this is from "The Burial, With State Honors, Of the Unknown Physicist":

> "My life was smoked in cheap cigars.
> I lived within the clip of compromise.
> My wholeness was a hole through which
> The moon, submission, peered."

Rime and regularity of meter also appear to disturb this poet; from time to time he seems to want to show that he can do those things with the rest, and he has even one poem remotely like a villanelle; but one feels the excitement of language depends for him on its jaggedness, its eccentricity, and the compulsion to write a couplet may produce this:

> And in the awful necessity of time
> The innocence of love is often the mask of a crime.

The beauties of this poetry are largely the beauties of its imagery, which is often strange and startling with an effect of reaching deeply hidden connections, as in these examples from a fine poem called "Hermanski, the Hobo, and the Hotel of Death":

> By the sea's eye stands the hotel of death
> Where lamps glow like bandaged heads. . . .

and

> . . . defeated eyes are sunken
> Jacknives in a desert of the mind.

Now and again, as in the first two parts of "Lament for a Man Who Loved God," Schevill reaches a serious exaltation of tone without sacrificing, as he does in the third part of the same poem, his dramatic way of isolating and accenting particulars.

Winthrop Palmer's first collection, *The New Barbarian,* displays the results of an intention "to regard the contemporary world without nostalgia, to discover its heroes, its gods, its rites and games, its triumphs and its defeats. . . ." Though the subject is roughly that of Mr. Schevill the aim of these poems is different, not to depict but "to regard"; this they do, with a witty eye and in the long light of history, proposing a sad but angry resignation to the new barbarian as to the Rome that requires his nasty services. It is not, I think, as the portrait of an age or a culture that these poems have their value; their dry asperities would be good at any time, and would doubtless be given occasion under the most flourishing polity as in our sad decay; while their more ambitious and general resonances would not be good at any time. The mere summoning of Christian authority—

> The agony of power will begin
> In the suffering of life, the state of sin.

—will suffice perhaps to conclude a general poem but not a particular one. The charm of the best of these poems, cast for the most part in a plain, intelligent speech, is the charm of shrewd lucidity staying with the point, and Mrs. Palmer shows this virtue again and again. I would mention in particular "Metamorphosis," "Noble Savage," and the two villanelles, "Storm" and "Positivism"; and for a demonstration, "Music Hall" is short enough to be given in full:

> "One line." Stragglers shuffled in the stony street.
> The centurion and his command are curt.
> (But citizen, the world is at your feet.)
> A section advances, halts. "A short wait
> For all seats." (To behold colossal man
> in captivity, with his mate.)

In *The Sorrows of Cold Stone,* John Malcolm Brinnin exhibits two sorts of poetry. Ten poems reprinted from his volumes of 1942 and 1945 illustrate an early style in which the language is relatively plain, the progressions simple and the conclusions pointed, as in "Views of the Favorite Colleges" and "Rowing in Lincoln Park"; the opening of the first will be a fair sample:

> Approaching by the gate, (Class of '79,
> All dead) the unimpressed new scholars find
> Halls of archaic brick and, if it is April,
> Three dazzling magnolias behind bars, like lions.

This manner continues to be developed in a few of the more recent poems, e.g., "Nuns at Eve," and "American Plan"; and whether the attitude at any moment be satiric or elegiac the tone is usually light and somewhat remote. Most of the poems in this book, though, show a very violent change in subject and treatment, which it will be my not very easy business to characterize.

The wit of the earlier work is not lost in these poems, so much as it is overgone, greatly elaborated, and used for another purpose, to liberate passion and energy at any cost. Sometimes the cost is very great, and the wit precipitated out in highly conventional puns delivered with odd earnestness, such as "guilt-edged beds" and "what is chaste is caught" and the wry acknowledgment of the master's celebrated hymn, "Have done with John's thin image and have Donne." Yet it is so that the surface of these poems is often intensely interesting; the brilliancy and fervor of the diction over and over strike off impressive lines, whose particular beauties, however, do not always unite with the poem in which they appear.

The mood of these poems is one of religious excitation in the thought of death, and to any sort of aroused feeling in poetry much may be allowed, but perhaps not so much as sometimes happens here, particularly in the long and central poem called "The Worm in the Whirling Cross" and in the series of acrostic poems where the added formal requirement seems so often to be met at the expense of the subject. It will be noted that the diction owes something to Dylan Thomas, but the end intended, the kind of poetry, remains very different from Thomas's; it is more rational in seeming than his and rather closer to the point of paraphrase, though, like his, subject also to the vice of decoration, the elaboration of ornament at the expense of progression.

Now in a queer way the greatest peril for this kind of poetry, which creates so tremendous and immediate excitement, will be the bathos that comes if this excitement be too readily reducible to plain sense; there is a real danger in being easily intelligible. Mr. Brinnin is not always easily intelligible by any means, but he does, not infrequently, allow us to perceive that the fuss is being blown up over precious little indeed; the lines

Does he not fix his dark Silurian eye,
Stark ebony, on the revolving day,
His mechanism pulleyed and well-strung,
And with precise antennae cautiously
Tuned all a-twitch to his predaceous wing,
Drink the charged space with vast humility?

would be, though not greatly impressive, more so if I could forget
that they were occasioned by the question: "How does the mantis
pray?" and that this question itself was brought up by the dark hint
that "O, perhaps we know— / More than we know. . . ."

"May I not," he asks in the same poem, ". . . From troubled
meanings strike the singleton?" But does it seem as though that is his
true attempt? Is he not rather delighting in the ambiguous elaboration of possibilities, and is it not from this very elaboration that his
poetry gets its great but often undirected verbal force? With this
poem, "The Worm in the Whirling Cross," the poet has allowed to
be reprinted from John Frederick Nims' analysis the pages dealing
with the first stanza—five pages to fourteen lines—and this analysis
contains almost nothing but the spreading-out of portmanteau words:
the three meanings of "green," the three meanings of "apple-wise,"
and so on. Mr. Nims typifies a certain interpretative enthusiasm in
that it never occurs to him to doubt that this sort of thing is wonderful or to think that the discourse of the poem may not be improved
by this means. One egregious example will suggest that the union of
poetry and the colleges is not always a happy one; Mr. Nims, dealing
with the phrase, "Wild Tigris at full spring," interprets as follows:

> The Tigris [is] a recollection (of course anachronistic) of a center of
> man's early activity, but, as *spring* indicates, there is also intended a
> pun on tiger, which has a powerful symbolic force in itself and is im-
> measurably reinforced by recollections of two of the great tigers of lit-
> erature: Blake's beautiful terror in the forests of the night and Eliot's
> tiger in "Gerontion." . . .

Well, is it? Immeasurably reinforced, I mean. As a line of poetry it
is, I should have thought, immeasurably reduced by the comparisons,
neither of which has visibly to do with Mr. Brinnin's discourse at
that place in his poem; and why our computer-like brains should respond to "Tigris" with these two tigers alone and not with, say, "The
herd hath more annoyance by the breese than by the tiger," or with
Mr. Milne's Tigger, remains mysterious.

But the poetry cannot be asked to bear the added burden of Mr. Nims' exegesis except insofar as its compositional practice makes it seem so easily available to that exegesis, as though it had been built up precisely by exegetical methods itself and were not at all an effort to "strike the singleton" but leaned heavily instead on multiple and often random possibilities. Yet there are many fine things about Mr. Brinnin's way, and at least one thoroughly admirable poem, "Cradle Song"; with the kind of power he shows in brief passages and single lines brought to more severity of conception the result must be good.

James Merrill's *First Poems* are certainly very good for first poems; probably some of them would do even for second poems. He has the delight in language, in the play of it, and accordingly language serves him well; beyond this his poems, elaborate as some of them are, have a plain consecution, a development, which is pleasing to read.

One of his best manners is to be somewhat portentously casual in the opening:—

> "One is reminded of a certain person,"
> Continued the parson, settling back in his chair
> With a glass of port. . . .

—and to carry on at some length with this amusing and appropriate novelistic parody; then to conclude swiftly and with a certain roughness, as here, where the parson's daughters, after absorbing his fable about the man who climbed up on a kite,

> fled to their young men
> Waiting in the sweet night by the raspberry bed,
> And kissed and kissed, as though to escape on a kite.

A poem similar in structure, "River Poem," because it has not this careless speed at the close, seems in comparison loose and uninteresting.

I do not think anyone would claim even the best of these poems to be without fault; for me the faults are, trivially, the giving-in now and again to a misplaced cleverness (the peacock which "trails / Too much of itself, like Proust") and, more fundamentally, an appeal to irrelevant and general beauties as a way out of trouble (in the final stanzas, for instance, of the same poem). But this last is the defect of considerable virtue, in proof of which I cite the opening of one of the poems I like best, "The Drowning Poet."

> The drowning poet hours before he drowned
> Had whirlpool eyes, salt at his wrists, and wore
> A watery emphasis. The sea was aware
> As flowers at the bedside of a wound
> Of an imminent responsibility
> And lay like a magnet beside him the blue day long
> Ambiguous as a lung.

It is my opinion that the last comparison is one too many, though if one were to be suppressed I should choose the one before it. But all the same it is very good, and the ending of this poem is better:

> And turning to the sea he entered it
> As one might speak of poems in a poem
> Or at the crisis in the sonata quote
> Five-finger exercises: a compliment
> To all accomplishment.

The poems are slight but fully accomplished; preciosity is the vice of this exactitude, but he is not often precious. It is a part of my pleasure in some of this poet's work that he does not appear to regard it as a duty to spend all or even most of his time being angry at something; the indignant scream has so nearly become the poet's stipulated tone that this is quite a relief; but doubtless this is an extraneous and *uncritical* consideration. Nevertheless, Mr. Merrill has the gift of *looking* at things, and even sometimes speaking well of them—as he calls it, "a happiness / Bound up with happenings." In another good poem he writes a quatrain that could serve for a motto:

> To kill the bull would be to spoil the game.
> The French pluck roses back from the bull's black shoulder.
> And this, I mean, is delicacy, a name
> For the fighter less than for the skilled beholder.

With the recent poems of Randall Jarrell I have had my difficulties, and have been reading him more than the other poets so far discussed; this is probably a desirable result for a poet to get out of his readers, and better by far than the resounding laudation and the closed book. His work brings up acutely a problem which has been implicit in all the foregoing discussion, the problem of distinguishing form and formality. The six poets already noticed, even including Mr. Schevill who does not always rime, appear to operate with overweening caution in this matter, desiring in some sense that the shape of the poem should be predetermined; the extreme degree of this desire is expressed in the villanelle or somthing like it. The fear of criticism constipates.

In comparison, a good deal of Mr. Jarrell's poetry deliberately invites you to say it is slovenly; a number of these poems are long, they look silly on the page, they meander and sometimes read rather like a novel, even with rows of dots . . . they don't look "well made," or "closely knit," or any of those fine things. The invitation is so open as to be a warning; one becomes cautious about calling anything slovenly that looks so slovenly as all this. For when we ask, in our hopeless way, what is *form*, what is it that at all holds poems together, echo answers; it appears that poems are held together by people's opinions of what holds poems together. Hopkins gives, perhaps, the objective minimum: "The artificial part of poetry, perhaps we shall be right to say all artifice, reduces itself to the principle of parallelism." No more than that, and we are already beyond the simply technical, we are at the point at which the form cannot be discussed apart from the subject, and we must talk, if we talk at all, not about sonnets or villanelles and so forth, but about the working-out of whatever is in hand to be worked out.

Mr. Jarrell tells stories, fairy tales, dreams; recounts experiences, conversations, meditations; makes drama and dialogue a large part of his means; is often informal, rhapsodic, sentimental. Given a number of readings several of these poems come to seem beautiful. And even in failure, for I will stick to it that some of this work is slovenly, the direction of his attempt is admirable; he perceives (as many do, but how few act upon it) that one cannot go on being neat, finished, well rounded, in poems whose success is inversely proportionate to their ambition; that there must be a next phase, in which the fear inspired by criticism is at all cost overcome. The cost may be here and there excessive, as in the dozen or so pages of "The Night before the Night before Christmas"; elsewhere admirable things are liberated in the breakthrough.

The ironic, witty poems, and the plain funny ones like "Nollekens," reveal themselves more immediately, to me, than the rest; "A Conversation with the Devil," with its witty reminiscence of similar interviews in Dostoyevsky and Mann, was at once attractive, and remains so; one finds very little poetry as intelligent as this. Then I came to like "A Quilt-Pattern," strange combination of fairy tale and the fantasy of a child; and even came to consent to "A Girl in a Library" down to and excluding the last figure, where the anthropology ("The Corn King beckoning to his Spring Queen") seems horribly dragged in. And "The Knight, Death, and the Devil," after Dürer's picture, is also good.

And as for what is not good, I incline to leave it out of account, out of this account anyhow. Much in this poetry is still in the course of change, some virtues have been thrown out with the vices, and judgment upon it is likely to be plain, unsupported predilection on the reader's part; but it is a poetry which opens out possibility beyond its present respectable achievement, and that is a satisfying thing.

Richard Eberhart, too, works toward freedom and increased possibility, but by another means; in their metrical practice, for example, he and Mr. Jarrell compare somewhat as do Yeats and Eliot, the one roughening and straining the formality of verse until he works with a great freedom that is yet in technical relation to the quatrain or other stanza, the other beginning in the utmost freedom and developing dramatically his own rituals of restraint. Mr. Eberhart's cadences, his combinations of sound, often wrenched and twisted to a deliberate awkwardness, remain attached to the artificial part of poetry by the minimum means, and produce from the old forms a special and new energy.

In this strict selection from his work I admire most a number of brief lyrics; the longer, discursive poetry seems to me very often diffuse and turgid, operating either by too many particulars too little imagined ("The Brotherhood of Man") or by a rhetoric too enlarged for the feeling ("The Soul Longs to Return Whence it Came"). But there remains such a great deal that is fine, "New Hampshire, February," "The Moment of Vision," "Four Lakes' Days," "Dissertation by Wax Light," "This Fevers Me." And there is, of course, "The Groundhog" (now matched by a charming groundhog on the dust jacket), but the celebrated beauty of that poem ought not to obscure for us one that is in my opinion far better, the one called "In a Hard Intellectual Light." It is unfortunately too long to be quoted here, and I did not bring it up in order to discuss it—this is very nearly absolute, this poem, and the only thing proper to be said is that you must read it.

Altogether this book has been a source of great pleasure to me; a difficult, unfashionable poetry which is above all things alive and intelligent. One example (the poem has no title other than its first line) will suggest his quality:

> When golden flies upon my carcass come,
> Those pretty monsters, shining globules
> Like tautened oily suns, and congregate
> Fixing their several gems upon one core
> That shines a blossom then of burning gold,
> 'Tis as the sun's burning glass and diadem
> They work, at the first chance of rotten flesh,
> And, senseless little messengers of time,
> Some beauty keep even at the guts of things,
> Which is a fox caught, and I watch the flies.

Seven Poets and the Language

The Monument Rose. By Jean Garrigue. The Noonday Press, 1953.
The Green Loving. By Dorothy Hughes. Scribner's, 1953.
The Anathemata. By David Jones. Faber and Faber, London, 1952.
More Clinical Sonnets. By Merrill Moore. Twayne, 1953.
The Year One. By Kathleen Raine. Farrar, Straus and Young, 1953.
To Lighten My House. By Alastair Reid. Morgan and Morgan, Scarsdale, N. Y., 1953.
Europa and the Bull. By W. R. Rodgers. Farrar, Straus and Young, 1952.

Here, first, are a couple of first volumes whose differences, looked at together, define a kind of problem. Alastair Reid's book, *To Lighten My House,* can be taken as a compendium of style and even attitude for the beginner at specifically Modern Poetry. It is all here, the loneliness, the carelessly sauntering verse, wry humor, eccentric epithet, the grave and testamentary reverence about the treasures of the self as reflected, usually, in the sea. Guilt, love, childhood, the want of a tradition, are approached with a delicate and *raffiné* recklessness of speech and a clear innocence of eye which are, however, almost entirely literary in origin. The late Dylan Thomas is clearly the master: "Not now for my sins' sake, / Nor for Adam or anyone / a memory might wake, / do I take this breaking day to grieve, / not for today's Eve / perpetually weeping in the nibbled apples, / and not for all the lost or too alone." But Mr. Reid's breath, or his intention, won't run to those enormous inwoven complexities of cadence and syntax, so he is usually more simply declarative, as well as more restrained in epithet. In his poems about the sea, which occupy a third of the book and are easily his best, he shows affinities, perhaps simply on account of the subject, with, for example, W. S. Graham and

First published in *The Sewanee Review*, Vol. 62, No. 2, Spring 1954. Copyright ©
April 21, 1954, by The University of the South.

Vernon Watkins. Here is the concluding section of "Four Figures
For the Sea":

> Over the walking foreshore cluttered
> black with the tide's untidy wrack,
> and pools that brimmed with the moon,
> I trespassed underwater.
> My feet stained seabed sand.
> The night wore guilt like a watermark;
> and down the guilty dark,
> the gulls muttered to windward.
> Far out, the tide spoke back.
>
> Across the morning clean of my walking
> ghost and the driftwood litter,
> singly I walked into singing light.
> The rocks walked light on the water;
> and clouds as clean as spinnakers
> puffed in the sea-blue sky.
> A starfish signed the sand. Beyond
> I faced the innocent sea.

The effect is delicate and mild, the manner carries it without strain;
a series of descriptive notes whose irony and reservation consist in
their being casually given; the idea that these details are thematic
is, however, somewhat explicitly labored. Where it is deficient is in
the action; the guilt is merely assumed to be present, assumed to be
purged. Whence it came, where it went, how or why all this happened, we are not told; we are simply given the outer change as warrant of the inner one. It is all quite well done, ending deliberately
enough with the naïve colors of a child's painting, but despite the
elegant maneuvering with puns which hint a metaphor ("the tide's
untidy wrack," "guilt like a watermark," "singly . . . singing"), it is
the pictorial surface which is pleasing. As to more serious implications, the tone of the passage tells us we may take it or leave it, and
if we are pleased by its easy diffidence we will probably take it, but
with our own reservations about how much it will be allowed to
matter.

Dorothy Hughes, in *The Green Loving*, writes quite skillfully a very
recognizable sort of verse, personal, sometimes sentimental, frequently shrewd. The failures belong to ladies' magazines; probably
the successes do too, and are distinguishable from the failures chiefly

by intelligence, sharpness of perception, a dry snap in the last line which picks up the form. This verse is technically competent, and for that reason technically not very interesting; it is not imitative so much as taken for granted, and, by a paradox which might become a law, the effect is personal by so much as the idiom is not; the language keeps departing from the matter at hand to wax poetical:

> For this I hated you. You turned your face,
> And there I saw such loneliness on guard,
> The terror of a child in some dark place.
> Thinking again of fear, I could not tell
> Who are the brave: who seize life, breath and bone;
> Or dare its dry revenge, and walk alone.

Or rather, the matter at hand is poetical to begin with, and the language is skillfully appropriated to feelings which are themselves literary from having been too frequently poetized upon in this or something like this manner. The gesture of the last line is nicely made, it was a beautiful gesture and still pleasant to see well done—the theatrical pause before it, the fine, intensifying alliteration, the stretched vowel on the verb, the marked caesura before the slower but decisively chiming conclusion—it is the very stuff of poetry, and that is its trouble.

These are vast and terrible reservations, and no amount of saying "But she does it well" will help my credit with the poet's friends; yet Miss Hughes does it well enough that, having offered her up on the altar of theory and rigor, I should allow her a happier demonstration, from a poem called "The City and the Book." Here the City is described in conventionally vague language, but not so the Book:

> Out of it issue the shapes of Chancery,
> Tulkinghorn, dealer in disgrace, and Krook,
> The great house, and the slum's obscenity.
> The strangers fade. Swarming, innate, these come,
> Down Chancery Lane vulgar and proud of face,
> Caddy, and Mr. Snagsby, Jo with his broom,
> Roistering and sad, the creatures of the place. . . .

Particulars, how they help! even if, as here, they are literary particulars. How the verse hulks with Tulkinghorn and snags on Snagsby!

The point in all this is certainly not revolutionary. It has nothing to do with free verse, imitated Greek meters, logoaedic rhythms,

amphisbaenic rimes, or any of all that there; our common English
line has in it individuality enough for another few hundred poets if
by wrestling they can get it out. The point is, probably, that when
the poet names things they must stay named, which means that his
names must be more like Tulkinghorn than like, say, "interminable
ridges of loneliness." This may be a matter of elegance and fastidi-
ousness carried to the point of parody—where the art begins—but
it remains that if you begin a poem with "Acknowledge now the wine
of weariness" it doesn't make much matter how good you get later on.

As for the problem. Readers of *Modern Poetry* would immediately
feel at home with Mr. Reid, and immediately throw out Miss Hughes.
The reasons given for all this would be interesting reasons, but would
they have anything to do with the case? It seems to me that the fault
in both poets is the acceptance of a literary manner which has precipitated out certain characteristic shapes and gestures. In both, these
shapes and gestures may now operate quite independently of any
imagination whatever. The ones favored by Miss Hughes are roughly
of the nineteenth century, while Mr. Reid's are currently fashionable;
yet if I compare a poem of his with a nineteenth century poem on the
same subject I do not find that the difference in handling the language more than superficially affects the real action of the poem.
Here is the last section of Mr. Reid's "Directions for a Map":

> A globe-eyed child finds first a map for wonder.
> Her sea is scribbled full of ship-shaped fish.
> Playing with all the names like spells, she tells
> the time in Spain, and sails her fingers south.
> Europe is torn: the world has no dimensions.
> America is half the size of Rome.
> Also, since here is now, all maps are nowhere.
> This is a wishing world, where towns are home.
>
> She marks a cross for luck, and lastly colors
> a puff-cheeked cherub in the bottom corner—
>
> > which terrifies a folded fly
> who, tired from crawling foodless over Europe,
> was crouching in the margin, contemplating
> the little cipher of the maker's name.

The following is "Letty's Globe" by Charles Tennyson Turner, and
to be found in *The Oxford Book of English Verse*:

When Letty had scarce pass'd her third glad year,
And her young artless words began to flow,
One day we gave the child a colour'd sphere
Of the wide earth, that she might mark and know,
By tint and outline, all its sea and land.
She patted all the world; old empires peep'd
Between her baby fingers; her soft hand
Was welcome at all frontiers. How she leap'd,
And laugh'd and prattled in her world-wide bliss;
But when she turned her sweet unlearned eye
On our own isle, she raised a joyous cry—
'Oh! yes, I see it, Letty's home is there!'
And while she hid all England with a kiss,
Bright over Europe fell her golden hair.

Any difference not superficial between these two poems belongs not so much to poetry as to international relations during the past hundred years. And as for the revolution in modern poetry, and its results, I am reminded of Naphta's saying about Settembrini's *carbonaro* ancestor: "He consecrated his burgher's pike on the altar of humanity in order that salami might be taxed at the Brenner frontier."

W. R. Rodgers' second volume, *Europa and the Bull,* shows a poet who clearly knows, most of the time, what effect he wants: naturalness, energy, ease. His prayer on this subject begins: "Lord, if I had a lathe / To turn out words as fine / And fit as any turd / That ever fell behind. . . ." And he does bring into poetry a tone which has, for better or worse, been missing for some time, since Browning, but is even more reminiscent of the later poems of Lord Byron; a genial robustness full of detail and with something of the air of improvisation. This quality makes, as it were, agreeable conversation in such a poem as "Summer Journey," which describes a Basque festival, and makes his "Journey of the Magi" run along quite pleasantly, its generalizing digressions very much à la Byron:

Caspar got blind one night, Melchior met a lady,
Balthazar was involved in something shady;
Strange that, in lands, and countries quite unknown,
We find, not others' strangeness, but our own;
That is one use of journeys; if one delves,
Differently, one's sure to find one's selves.

But his ambitions, of course, far exceed this kind of thing, and it is the ambitious poems which I found oddly disappointing. They divide, as to subject, into Pagan and Christian poems, the two major ones, "Europa and the Bull" and "Resurrection: an Easter Sequence," being antithetically balanced also as to style.

"Europa and the Bull" amounts to fifteen pages of descriptive elaboration on that swim and the majestic copulation which followed. Some of all this seems quite beautiful, but there's a great deal of it and not much besides. The verse is a very liberally conceived blank verse, rambling when not swaggering; the intensity dissipated in this freedom is perhaps supposed to be supplied by the alliterations and internal rimes, which hiss and bang most infernally and have naturally caused half the tin-eared reviewers of the United Kingdom to mention that the poet "sings":

> Hour after hour
> The rhyming furrows met them, sweetly-timed
> And chiming to their mood; hour after hour
> Miming the dipping dolphin-backs that swelled
> And fell in swathes; slide and divide, divide
> And slide.

But this is not singing; it is practicing arpeggios. And the entire poem gets along in this way, presumably on the idea that this kind of activity in the language will make up for the dramatic interest that is missing from the spectacle of girl and bull ("O fructifying friction, furthering both!"), which it will not.

"Resurrection," on the other hand, is characterized by a simplicity and sobriety of language, a stern tone not exactly suppressive of detail but dead set against any boisterous elaboration of it. This may seem to satisfy an idea of what is appropriate to the subject, or it may seem to confess the serious failure of the other style; anyhow, I like it better than the other style, but find all the same that much of this sequence quite fails of the magnificence which its tone clearly intends, and puts a serious flatness in its place:

> Jesus did not belong to this time;
> Their clocks all said he came before his chime,
> All the lamps of the city declared him a stranger,
> A nobody come out of darkness, and therefore a danger
> To law and to order.

Even here, Mr. Rodgers' other self now and then breaks through with a pun: Peter hears the cock crow in the "petering" hour; and in another religious poem, "Nativity," we have—what must have been hard to resist—"And hark! the Herod-angels sing to-night." Among the lyric simplicities of this poem, too, occurs the following:

> And here, most meek, most eager and most hushed,
> The angelic agents hover,
> A great prudential company, all come
> To offer him life-cover.

We are instructed now, and we know—Criticism has told us for twenty years—that this is metaphysical wit, and really deepens the seriousness of the poem. But is it? and does it?

Acknowledged that Mr. Rodgers is a gifted poet; here and there in this volume the gift emerges, in a couple of stanzas of "Armagh," in his "Carol," which is beautiful all the way through, in the very end of "Europa and the Bull," where he finds a seriousness and authority which, unhappily, the poem until then has done nothing to support. It is probably out of the critic's province to say of a gifted poet, "He *ought not* to use his gift in this way," since such things are seldom the result of the poet's deliberation anyhow, but rather of his nature. Nevertheless, it is disappointing that a poet so evidently interested in the sound of poetry should use, out of the enormous range of sympathetic resonance in the language, chiefly the blatant effects; that he should be highly praised for it suggests what one has long suspected, that this matter of the poet's "ear," of *music* in poetry, is made much of mostly by people who have not listened carefully enough and regard a phrase like "the dragonfly's gonfalon" in Mr. Rodgers' "Evening" as somehow the height of musical invention.

Though his publishers, seeing a good thing and having an eye to the medical trade, have done their best to present him as a funny man—"Try *this* one in your waiting-room; patients will love it!"— Dr. Merrill Moore's *More Clinical Sonnets* * is not a funny book but a witty and sad one, thoroughly and unheroically concerned with our daily dreariness. The mood is one of dispassionate irony, reserved commiseration. It is not satirical; one feels that satire or sarcasm,

---

* Half a dozen or so of these sonnets are reprinted, some with minor changes, from Moore's earlier collections, *The Noise That Time Makes*, 1929, and *Six Sides to a Man*, 1935. As the present volume shows no acknowledgment of this fact, and the poet's other works are not available to me, I do not know how much of *More Clinical Sonnets* is new.

for Dr. Moore, would be themselves products of the illusions he coldly and a little flatly delineates, would be, in effect, hitting Man when he is down.

The idiom he has made, of which he is thoroughly the master, is itself impersonal, the language of newspapers when they are quoting witnesses to a disaster, the language of clinical interviews or of conversations only a little less distant than that; the abysmal revelations of suffering and stupidity and humiliating absurdity which form the theme of so many of these poems gain a good deal of force from being given in this tone of voice which amounts to the indifference of desperation, and from the studied, casual sketchiness with which the verse refers to the form of a sonnet.

ESCAPE FROM ESCAPE?

Sometimes a man does something that is an escape
Knowing full well that it *is* an escape
And in spite of that he keeps on doing it—

(*In spite*, I say; perhaps I should say *along with*:
Knowledge is not always power, of course.)

Like drinking. Drinking is an excellent example
(Although I could mention many other things.)
I believe that in certain situations
That might otherwise be intolerable, alcohol
Is as much an adaptation as an escape,
A way of holding on where there is no hold;

For example, the drinking of certain fighter pilots
And of pleasureless old people in dark rooms
Before they are sealed again in their metal wombs.

This example shows his typical tone, reserved, discursive, critical; the effect at the end, of choice given with one hand to be taken away with the other, is characteristic, but allowing the poem to finish on an image is not; more usually the end simply announces the conclusion to the argument, e.g., "She said: I tried hard, but it didn't work," or, "So finally he migrated to Tasmania." The relaxed, informal, yet sufficiently distant quality to the language makes these poems fun to read; or perhaps *fun* is not the right word and it may be that they are simply habit-forming—after coming at the book with some repugnance, not seeing any reason to read sonnets in quantities of fifty and over, I read on and on, not seeing any reason to stop either.

Only a very few of these poems make a strong individual effect, or
have the absolute completion that would stop you at the end of one
from immediately proceeding to the next, with a pleasure which is
likely to contain something patronizing and unfair. The work, you
feel, is good, solid, and of its own sort, but pretty much at a dead
level; it has in common with the best of modern poetry just about
every virtue except that which the best of modern poetry has in common with the best of the past, variety and range of feeling; here replaced, perhaps, by variety and range of subject. What you have in
the end is an informally versified chronicle of an intelligent, learned,
ironic sensibility, turning attention to this and that in the world,
which it speaks of wittily and well; and there is never too much of
that around, no matter how much or how fast Dr. Moore writes.

The Anathemata, by David Jones, gives little ground of comparison
with the other books this review is about, being no collection of lyrics
but a long poem in eight sections. The conception it displays of what
a poet is, and what his tradition, is in some sense ancient and bardic;
he is the personified voice of a particular culture. But because there
are now so many cultures, none of them intimately known to the
others and none which can be commanding except in despite of its
particularities, the voice of the bard is now attended by a long, intelligent preface and a myriad footnotes. It is a poem, with all this
apparatus (and illustrations by the author), capable of exercising an
antiquarian rather than a poetic fascination; and I ought to confess
at once to having fallen into this trap, if it is a trap, and liking, on
the whole, the explanations better than what they explain.

First as to the title. In antiquity the word had a double sense,
referring equally to holy and accursed things, the common element
(as in a word like *sacer*) being that the things were *set apart.* Only
the second meaning is preserved in our "anathemas," but Mr. Jones
draws for his purpose on the other English plural form, "anathemata," which preserves the ancient ambiguity and which he uses to
mean "the blessed things that have taken on what is cursed and the
profane things that somehow are redeemed . . . things that are the
signs of something other, together with those signs that not only have
the nature of a sign, but are themselves, under some mode, what they
signify." The poem, subtitled "fragments of an attempted writing,"
"has no plan, or at least is not planned. If it has a shape it is chiefly
that it returns to its beginning. It has themes and a theme even if it

wanders far." It is about "one's own 'thing,'" which *res* is unavoidably part and parcel of the Western Christian *res*," further modified by the author's being "a Londoner, of Welsh and English parentage, of Protestant upbringing, of Catholic subscription." The poem is written to be spoken aloud. About the poet's function Mr. Jones has this to say:

> Rather than being a seer or endowed with the gift of prophecy, he is something of a vicar whose job is legatine—a kind of Servus Servorum to deliver what has been delivered to him, who can neither add to nor take from the deposits. It is not that that we mean by "originality." There is only one tale to tell even though the telling is patient of endless development and ingenuity and can take on a million variant forms.

The poet, on this view, is the reciter of the ritual which keeps the world in being; but because the ritual these days has either fallen in disuse or is used for limited purposes (religion, ironically, having become a limited purpose), the poet must also be a rediscoverer, re-edifier who causes the purified and idealized history recited in the ritual to be freshly seen as penetrating and modifying our secular or supposed secular concerns—which is, after all, exactly what was proposed, and achieved, by Dante. Mr. Jones is aware of the immensity of the task, of difficulties which Dante faced and overcame, but also of many which, at this distance, it does not appear that Dante had to deal with. But it is a question, beyond that, whether the attempt in its nature may ever be unplanned or random, whether the assumption, to begin with, of *ruins* does not in a degree dishonor or make unavailing whatever fragments may be shored against them.

This poem, a continuous meditation in free verse and prose, presents us with an enormously detailed world chiefly composed of those artefacts nearest to the heroic life of the past; with an easy familiarity the poet or his anonymous characters talk the honorable craftsmen's languages of old techniques neglected or lost: architecture, shipbuilding, manufacture of sieging engines. Thematically, through all this, the ancient Mediterranean *res* is absorbed into the matter of Britain, pagan antiquity into Catholicism—*Teste David cum Sibylla*, as it is written at the head of the poem. By the familiar Catholic argument that anything which is not Catholic is merely a natural prevision and inadequate vision of what is Catholic, even the geology of Great Britain is pictured as preparing itself for a sacred task as the matrix of the cultural form: "This is how Cronos reads the rubric, *frangit per medium,* when he breaks his ice like morsels, for the therapy and fertility of the land-masses," a figure explained by the following note: "See the rubric directing the celebrant at the point of the Mass called the Fraction: 'he . . . takes the host and breaks it in half (*frangit per medium*) over the chalice.' Cf. also Psalm CXLVII. xvii, Bk. of Com. Pr. version. 'He casteth forth his ice like morsels: who is able to abide his frost?' "

Now it is perfectly part of Mr. Jones' business in the poem to present us with this connection, if he can, as a *fait accompli*; and, facing an audience which cannot unaided make such connections, to explain them in a note. He splendidly, unfailingly, anticipates our great ignorance, but does not care to anticipate our resistance. So far as his poem is a religious testament, that is entirely up to him, but so far as we may speak of poetry I'd contend that this connection, and others like it, is arbitrary and does not strike, when understood, as an illumination; and that the poem largely fails of conviction because it is undramatic in small things as in general outline—which doesn't prevent it from being often very interesting, but with, for me, as I said before, an antiquarian and rather epicurean interest.

The distinction defines itself pretty precisely in the language and the verse. The book brings back into use, in great numbers, weird and wonderful words:

> Carlings or athwart her
> horizontaled or an-end
>   tabernacled and stepped
> or stanchioned and 'tween decks.
>   Stayed or free.
> Transom or knighthead.
> Bolted, out in the channels or
> battened in, under the king-plank.
> Hawse-holed or lathed elegant for an after baluster
>   cogginged, tenoned, spiked
> plugged or roved
>   or lashed.

But it does not always appear that all this is doing much more than "talking the way a shipwright (or his hardware catalogue) would be expected to talk." Nor is it particularly convincing, on the same line, that the Goddess should be represented as a Cockney girl if she must also be a Cockney girl philologist, folklorist, antiquarian, much in the manner of the historical novelist: ". . . on m'own name-day captain, the day the British Elen found the Wood—Ceres big moon half ris beyond her own Cornhill, behind de Arcubus as chimes *I do not know*. . . ."

And the verse, or verse-and-prose, with all its beautiful things, suffers similarly from arbitrariness and want of dramatic tension; its particular beauties want a common rhythmic beauty to play against. The incantatory tone, which when one reads aloud is seen to be a sort of substitute for a formal verse, is for all its interspersed erudition and colloquialism capable of no great variation, nor does the considerable amount of informal riming and chiming (if, as the notes warn us, we pronounce the Welsh aright) make up for a certain inherent want of energy in the verse and syntax.

Still, the explicit intention is to write "fragments," and if you take it that way there is a great deal here to wonder at and care for, though housed, perhaps, more in a museum than in a poem; a particular freshness, delicacy, and clarity now and then emerges from a speech that is by nature and intention somewhat pedantic:

> so Iuppiter me succour!
> they do garland them with Roman roses and do have stitched
> on their zoomorphic apparels and vest 'em gay for Artemis.
> When is brought in her stag to be pierced,
> when is bowed his meek head between the porch and the
> altar, when is blowed his sweet death at the great door, on the
> day before the Calends o' Quintilis.

Unlike the poets so far considered, Jean Garrigue and Kathleen Raine write poems rather than versified thoughts, philosophical rhapsodies, poetical equivalents to something else, something pre-existing the poem. The fact that both are women does not, perhaps, have much bearing on the matter, unless it be that women more easily than men find and define their gift and remain within it, writing poems which may be slight but are remarkably accomplished, illustrating a small world but one absolutely brought into being . . . but I do not altogether believe in the force of this fine generality. These two poets, however, very different one from the other, Miss Garrigue ornate, elaborate of tongue, and somewhat lightly, ironically impassioned, Miss Raine simple, of a strength of feeling sober even perhaps to sullenness, have the one splendid thing in common, that they speak in verse as a native language, while the others, barely excepting, for conversational purposes, Dr. Moore, give an impression of more or less laboriously translating into it.

Jean Garrigue's ways can be, to get the carping over with first, very irritating indeed; the following passage, beginning of "The Opera of the Heart: Overture," has successfully resisted my ardent pursuit of sense, especially as to the references of "this," "your," and "you" and the reason why it is all posed as a question:

> Music at this, for whom the kings throw dice
> Or favor your wild beauty by that sky
> They know the gods appareled white with stars
> Who stung and pale, indifferent as those maps you rule,
> Are then appointed by our passioned wills, know you?

But this doesn't happen often, so I'd take it that I've simply missed something, which is not unheard of, and go on.

The world of *The Monument Rose* is romantic in its richness and strangeness and curious elaboration of detail—"Flesh of timber wrung through / As lilac enflasked in its smoky color / Gives up on the white alphabet of the river"—but to speak of Keats in this connection would be to neglect the energetic wit that checks this tendency to linger, and keeps it under pressure sometimes suggestive of Pope, as in this about Valentine's Day: "For this is heart's ease day, when dear-my-loves / Blood-bright or velvet-sewn, adorn the door / Or smash their pretty triumphs on the floor." Most of all, though, and for all the elegance in particular words, the character of this poetry is just where it belongs, in the play between rhythm and syntax, the wave-motion, so to say, which makes the identity of passage after passage and makes all one and most fine. This thing, the weaving and stitching, is the most neglected part of poetry at present, but attention to it is a mark of mastery, and the gift for it, the melodiousness which is, as Coleridge claimed, the final and distinguishing sign of a poet, is something Miss Garrigue wonderfully has:

> If you should wander by the ports and parks
> Where goes my mistress, say for me
> When greet the flowers her sumptuous head more sumptuously
> Than clouds bringing their rain by distant steppes
> To the green turfs of sieges dust has wrought

Or by the fountains where the light has spent
Its elements by archways lavishly—

Here, as elsewhere, with a certain consciousness and deliberate slight
mockery, the verse refers to the madrigalists, and to the tradition out
of Italy; in general her idea of meter goes back to a time when the
English line was a lighter and slighter thing than the dramatists made
it, with more hesitations, charming uncertainties of stress, the time
of Wyatt, and in Miss Garrigue's hand is capable of fine surprises
and syncopations:

Love is the friend whose faithfulness is wit,
Is best your mimic when you tongue-tied vow,
Aloof when you win and surly when you stammer,
Cries I do not understand you, and
Corrects your right answer.

Kathleen Raine's new poetry shows a mastery of the most difficult
simplicities. This is a thing seldom done—Blake did it, and in some
of his poems Yeats, who is generally more elaborate—nor do I know
how it is done. A gift, yes, but I imagine it to be given only to persons altogether free of sentimentality, and probably it is a gift which
imposes loneliness as a condition of its being given; the technical
equivalent of its purified feeling must be that "line of rectitude and
certainty" which Blake spoke of as the distinguishing mark of honesty. Miss Raine, anyhow, can say "Lonely dreamer on the hill" and
make it stay that way, and make it seem as though never said before.

The Year One differs also from the books so far discussed in that
it ought to be read straight through, as a sequence, or a series of pro-
gressing variations. The dust-jacket reads, *The Year One and Other
Poems*, but as there is no title poem I take it that the title refers
generally to the theme, which is the debate of birth which must take
place before history, or even autobiography, can begin.

These poems, then, are altogether formed of Nature and Dialectic,
in a world which has time but no history; although they center precisely about the mystery of incarnation, that most famous Example
never appears on the scene. As befits a world which has time but no
history, the world of these poems does not include the sharply or
eccentrically characterized individuation of particulars—Tulkinghorn,
or Madame Sosostris—which is commonly supposed the measure of
excellence in modern poetry; particulars there are in plenty, but they

are themselves generic, deliberately not localized or detailed—"Flowers and trees and skies and running burn," and "Scales irridescent, cells, spindles, chromosomes." When she does pause to elaborate into metaphor, the result is the more beautiful for being rare:

> . . . the white kid, the calf,
> Their newborn coats scarcely dry from the natal waters.
> Each hair lies in its place, ripple-marked
> By the rhythms of growth, the tides
> That washed them up onto the shores of time.

The pivot of these poems is our double allegiance to spirit and earth, the major and ambiguous image is *home* as both the mortal, earthly house of memories and the home of the spirit in death—"Home, with not one dear image in the heart." Between these, incarnate, are the living:

> I weave upon the empty floor of space
> The bridal dance, I dance the mysteries
> That set the house of Pentheus ablaze.

The first poem, the long "Northumbrian Sequence," places the problem of separateness which is then prayed against magically in a series of "spells," explored to the depths in poems meditating on death and on illusion, and resolved in acceptance in the final poems. Everywhere, the image of *home*, with its fine and final doubleness, is the key to these meditations: so the "Spell to Bring Lost Creatures Home" gets its pathos from this ambiguity, the warmth and security of home being played over the idea of home as death; so the image of the last "Poem of Incarnation" describes existence as a house, the child unborn standing before the door, "on the threshold of being." And the final poem of the book, "Message from Home," a rhapsody of remembered immanence and future reconciliation, plays steadily upon the image, and concludes:

> Earth sends a mother's love after her exiled son,
> Entrusting her message to the light and the air,
> The wind and waves that carry your ship, the rain that falls,
> The birds that call to you, and all the shoals
> That swim in the natal waters of her ocean.

Miss Raine, too, is the poet as ritualist; hierarch and victim; but her spells splendidly work, showing us again, as the good poet always does, that it is magic which, beyond its mechanical purposes, invents and liberates the feelings, and gives them their proper occasions.

Younger Poets: The Lyric Difficulty

A *Case of Samples*. By Kingsley Amis. Harcourt, Brace, 1957.
Letter from a Distant Land. By Philip Booth. Viking, 1957.
Adam's Footprint. By Vassar Miller. New Orleans Poetry Journal.
Poems. By Marcia Nardi. Alan Swallow. Denver, Colo., 1956.
Uncertainties and Other Poems. By John Press. Oxford University Press.
London, 1956.
Hot Afternoons Have Been in Montana; Poems. By Eli Siegel. Definition Press, 1957.
The Green Wall. By James Wright. Vol. 53 of the Yale Younger Poets
Series.

This piece was to have been something more ambitious than a review, was to have offered some general survey of new poets and an opinion, from their practice and what was revealed of their intentions, as to "where we are now." This project proved too ambitious, and had to be given over. First, the mere quantity was too great; from more than twenty books I have made a rather drastic selection which nevertheless may be thought arbitrary. Second, great as the quantity is, it is not enough; almost every book gives notice of others which might have an equal claim to consideration at this time, and I cannot be at all confident that what I have before me is honestly representative of any tendency or movement. I can see, on the other hand, that in or around or behind many of these books something about tendency and movement seeks expression. The lyric difficulty —the difficulty of continuing to see lyric poetry as an art by itself, the preference or compulsion to see it as the expression of strong emotions or fashionable opinions, the insistence on communicating as *opposed* to making—this difficulty seems to affect very severely a number of the poets whose work I discuss in the first part of what follows, as well as a larger number whose work I have omitted from consideration. So if this essay is, after all, a review, one of those omnibus reviews in which no one is done either justice or even the proper injustice (for which there isn't room), I have nonetheless put down some general reflections on the theme, usually (I hope) in connection with the examples which provoked them. As I am dealing mostly with the work of young poets, I will take from one of them the motto that seems appropriate; Mr. Philip Booth, prosing along to Thoreau in a homey New England way, says it: "I still defend the new growth with an axe."

Eli Siegel is not a young poet, but *Hot Afternoons Have Been in Montana* is his first collection. These poems were written, according to the author's notes, in two periods, the late 1920's and the early 1950's. I could not myself have distinguished between specimens of the two. The poems are ecstatically introduced by William Carlos Williams, who tells us among other things that Siegel "belongs in the very first rank of our living artists" and "has outstripped the world of his time in several very important respects. Technical respects."

When Dr. Williams says these things, adding that the title poem (which won *The Nation's* prize in 1925) "secures our place in the cultural world," and goes on with "I make such a statement only after a lifetime of thought and experience, I make it deliberately," he is clearly not in a mood for any backchat from "our critics (what good are they?)" or " 'authorities' whom I shall not dignify by naming." I must respectfully say to the above remarks about Mr. Siegel's quality that I don't think so. But to argue with Dr. Williams would mean being provoked into undervaluing these sometimes charming pieces. There has been some debate over that word "charming"; I do not use it as a cautious way of implying something much better; it does not mean either "beautiful" or "first-rate," and perhaps avoids only by a little the word "cute."

Siegel's subject is easily described; it is *experience,* or everything. The manner is sometimes rhapsodic and repetitive, sometimes dry and quite funny. He can say sensible things, and say them prettily: "Even in our dooms / The graces lie, shy and unperturbed." (That is an entire poem, by the way, entitled "Even.") He is in love with experience, all experience, and is sometimes so taken by the consideration that Montana or Idaho are no worse places than Athens for having experiences and writing poems about the experiences, that he forgets to write the poems; and he clearly assumes that the mere mention of any detail makes that detail revelant: "Was not Lydia born of a mother who had, once, $400 in her right hand?" A Philadelphia sky which may be seen by Alfred is "an Alfred-seeable sky." He is impressed by history, or perhaps bemused is the better word, in a vague way which is sometimes very pleasant, as in "The Best Surmises about the Feelings of Louis XV"—"(It is well to consider eighteenth century trees)"—and his exaltations achieve sometimes a pantheistic ecstasy, as in "The Lord has Stolen her Whims," but more often a pantheistic coziness: "Worms fit in. / They fit in, and everything is nice, and that takes in worms."

With all this goes a deal of critical theory: a preface, pages of notes, a poem on "The Siegel Theory of Opposites." It is not easy, these days, to develop a theory of opposites so original as to bear one's own name, and Siegel doesn't. In the preface he says that his poems "took the form" of "Aesthetic Realism," which "is about how the having-to-do-withness or relation of people, is they, is themselves." A "Society for Aesthetic Realism," whose members he names, sponsors the publication of these poems, which therefore, I suppose, must represent Aesthetic Realism.

It is a difficulty of the art that a great many people know how it ought to be, how it ought to go, and tend to regard the statement of these beautiful aims as synonymous with their achievement; in our grand perennial logomachy the statement of beautiful aims is perhaps, judging merely by volume, more desirable than the production of poems. And no doubt poetry can be discussed about as well under the heading of Aesthetic Realism as under other headings; "relation" and the "coincidence of opposites" are beautiful things to think about. But Mr. Siegel's poems mostly do not do their work, they are too easy, assume too much of what is to be demonstrated, and substitute too often the splendid intention for the thing made. As to the content, "Reality is that / Which everything / Is an instance of." As to the style, "Free verse is when / You're at ease with something / You mean with your whole heart." It takes in a good deal, or nothing much, about equally.

What Marcia Nardi is up to in her poems I should be hard put to say. Her own *note* explains that men, or, anyhow, male poets, are chiefly to blame: "If a woman wants to write genuinely out of a strictly female emotional world, she has to strike out for herself not only in subject matter but technically as well." She herself acknowledges that the attempt, as here represented, seems in retrospect fumbling and tentative, and I can only agree. It is a poetry singularly soft and self-indulgent, by turns rhapsodic and "cultured," e.g.,

> Here, now,
> Your life
> Real and unknown
> As the shapes in a Tanguy.

Such things may indeed be the products of a good deal of conscious thought and study, but they seem never to impose any decisions, and never for a moment to recognize the existence of objects, situations, persons as other than an opportunity for one warm delicious feeling: "To take my soft breath / And fold it / Around my mind's chilly shoulders." So anything she deals with becomes a kind of characterless mash of impression, sometimes cleverly phrased but at no time tending to anything that I could see but one statement after another, about circumstances which remained extremely vague, though almost always very somber and portentous.

John Press's *Uncertainties* shows practically all the external signs of poetry, and practically none of the essentials. He is both thoughtful and knowledgeable, he has a number of fine subjects, and he writes like a man who has heard poetry described but never read any.

It cannot be true that he has not read any, not only because he is highly praised, in England, for his criticism, but also because there are in his poems some startlingly clear indications of just what poems he has most especially read; this is something much balder than "being influenced by" Eliot ("And I have wondered has it been worthwhile . . .") or Yeats:

> Yet I have talked with Newton and with Wren. . . .
>
> Body's decreptitude
> And glory in that dance. . . .
>
> It was the spirit's laceration,
>   Animal lust and rage
> Spurred him to song that still re-echoes
>   On the unfading page.

In fact I should say he has scarcely been influenced by Eliot or Yeats at all; in that last example (which is about Catullus—and Lord, what would *he* say?) he has contrived to take those sanctified phrases from "The Spur" (*Last Poems*) and make them into nothing at all; besides introducing, at the end, a fairly nonsensical metaphor, which however becomes merely ordinary beside the following piece of egregious nonsense:

> for we men are here
> As blind and transient as a tennis-ball
> That stains the ground with pale and futile smear.

He is speaking there in the character of the Earl of Rochester; no doubt scholars will tell me that seventeenth century tennis balls had eyes painted on them and were colored in such a way as to leave stains on the court; meanwhile I shall keep to my opinion.

These are extremes of inadequacy. But most of Mr. Press's poetry is simply competent in dulness; metronomically regular, woefully poeticized, utterly undramatic. He cannot or will not dramatize or present, but simply proses, or versifies, *about* things, and postures before his subjects like a tourist on a postcard, moralizing turgidly. A very few things I found which make exceptions in some degree to these remarks; and one exceptional enough to be worth naming, "To a Dead Lady," where a serious anger overcomes the gentility.

Of the poetry of Philip Booth I have not got much to say. There is a kind of modern lyric as recognizable as a new Chevrolet and perhaps as efficient; Mr. Booth writes it with very fair skill, and his volume has been accorded recognition as the Lamont Poetry Selection of the Academy of American Poets for 1956.

Mr. Booth's manner is gentle, grave, stoical, ironic; he appropriates to his poetic uses the Maine seacoast, with some of the language of sailing and fishing, and leaves us in no doubt that all this is *poetry*:

> I wake to call
> the osprey, tern, the slow-winged gull,
> say all the sea's grave names, and build
> with words this beach that is the world.

Perhaps he thinks too much about poetry; and its magical transmutation of experience, instead of being accomplished in the poem, becomes merely the subject of the poem; anyhow, after a set of skillfully seen details he frequently fades out on the image of himself being a poet and contemplating his world:

> six black shags shagging;
> August fog, me, a Maine ledge,
> and the seventh shag, lagging.

I can only say that the miracle, for me, does not take place as advertised. These poems don't have enough to do, and get reduced to talking about themselves; seeing a pair of jet planes he says, "I know no metaphor / for them except to say they are great sharks / with silver fins that plane the ocean air . . ." (So he does know a metaphor for them after all, sort of.)

There are some pretty poems made out of all this, and at least one which stands out from the rest, "First Lesson," about teaching a child to swim. Here is the finish:

> Daughter, believe
> me, when you tire on the long thrash
> to your island, lie up, and survive.
> As you float now, where I held you
> and let go, remember when fear
> cramps your heart what I told you:
> lie gently and wide to the light-year
> stars, lie back, and the sea will hold you.

Even here cleverness obtrudes itself: not "stars" but "light-year stars," as if some brisk Georgian poet in him had decided that things had better get a touch more "evocative" just here; but what is evoked, in its vagueness, nearly destroys the fine close.

Mr. Booth has a good deal of talent, which perhaps in future work he will treat with less reverence. I imagine that, like the sailor he praises, "he knows the chart is not the sea." But there is not much demonstration of the knowledge in this book.

Kingsley Amis writes a clever, neat sort of verse whose major visible ambition, not to be taken in, is well expressed by the cheerful vulgarity of the title, *A Case of Samples* (the literal sense being that this book is only a selection from among the author's poems). It is as though he had decided that the world exists only as literature, that he and his readers are too wise to be fooled any longer by so much literature, and that, in consequence, the remaining job for poetry (aside from cleaning up after the Grand Ball of History) is to be more or less benevolently amused at itself and its former pretensions. Here, for instance, in his "Ode to the East-North-East-by-East Wind," he shows how determined he is not to be made anyone's lyre:

> You rush to greet me at the corner like
> A cheery chap I can't avoid,

And blow my hair into one leaning spike
　　To show you're never unemployed.
You sweating, empty-handed labourer,
You bloody-rowelled, mailless courier,
　　　Before you rush off somewhere new,
　　　　Just tell us what you do.

Notice the fine ambiguity of "mailless courier," which is good, like
"mobled queen." Mr. Amis goes on about what the wind does
("Sometimes you pump up water from the ground; / Why, darling,
that's just fine of you!") and finally decides as follows:

Well now, since blowing things apart's your scheme,
　　The crying child your metaphor,
Poetic egotists make you their theme,
　　Finding in you their hatred for
A world that will not mirror their desire.
Silly yourself, you flatter and inspire
　　　Some of the silliest of us.
　　　　And is that worth the fuss?

The sense of this as I read it is that people like Shelley and Shakespeare have actually succeeded in diminishing the wind-force to a
point at which it will turn no poem; because, after all, nature is only
literature, one is tired of poets drawing their dreary conservative morals from nature (or literature), the wind blows in the most meaningless manner, and so on. It may be that there is no natural religion,
but the belief may not be extended to say that there is no nature
either; or it may, and that is Mr. Amis' own business, but why then
prose along about it so, and have all one's delicate irony fetch up,
as so much of this book does, in parlor verse? The ladders Mr. Amis
delights in kicking over have been rungless, I suspect, these many
years; and even when they're down there remains that foul rag and
bone shop we have been told of.

Much of the poetry I have touched on until now rests one way
or another on the idea that certain things have become impossible,
in technique, in attitude. Mr. Siegel, for instance, appears to reject
some formal and melodic virtues because they have been used before (this is one of the things that so pleases Dr. Williams); Miss
Nardi throws away most of what poetry at any time has to be about
because she sees all that as pre-empted by "male poets"; Mr. Amis,

while retaining "form," dismisses from his poetry great ranges of seriousness in favor of an exclusive, somewhat negative "honesty," or self-limitation. These one-sided choices have an effect on *making*, and I think it is a bad effect almost always; it substitutes for *making* some more or less poetical assertion about the poem which ought to have been made.

Since religious poetry is, of all things, the one most commonly supposed to have become impossible, it is doubly a pleasure to come upon the work of Vassar Miller. The poems in *Adam's Footprint* rely in subject and theme very often on traditional erotic-religious figures ("Nor ever chaste unless Thou ravish me"), but what they finely demonstrate is that this doesn't matter and that doesn't matter, but only the making matters. These pieces, though they have sometimes what I see as faults—they sometimes sentimentalize a little, sometimes lapse in generality, now and then echo Donne, Hopkins, Empson—are at their best brilliant works of language, with a fine energy flowing through one passage after another, the hard-working vocabulary, rich, strange, accurate, beautifully paced by the rhetorical and rhythmic organization, the harmonies of sentence and stanza brought into unity by the kind of freehand control which is technically the first sign of a poet. I mean that these are poems you can read over many times—as against that other kind which, like Kleenex, is meant to be used once and thrown away—because they are not only things said, things meant however intelligently, seriously; they gain, above all that, a quality as objects really existing, with a solidity of specification which comes from strong feeling already taken into the mind and consequently not afraid of argument and demonstration. I have room for one example, complete:

CONSOLATIONS OF RELATIVITY

Quicksilver nerves awry, you inch
Your wheelchair on from here to yonder
With muscles like a fist whose clinch
Keeps itself captive. Yet why squander
Your admiration to aver
My feet are heeled with lightning's wings,
My hands merged into moth-gray blurs
Of harpist fingers over strings!

The stars competing in their race,
With one another for sole measure,

Flash neither gaucherie nor grace,
Neither celerity nor leisure.
Galactic seas stagnate unrippled,
For—being deadlocked in the groove
Of their own motion—more than crippled,
Even the fleetest never move.

It has, as well as virtues, faults; the last three lines of the first stanza give me the kind of twinge I associate with ladies' poetry (not all of it by any means written by females), and lines three and four of the second seem to come too pat and a little dead. But how admirably, even including these lines, the poem stays kept up together, and with what a fine economy and precision it works the subject through the two stanzas. And in general Miss Miller's poetry shows, much talk about "modern" poetry to the contrary, that force and form are not really antagonistic, or are so only for bumblers who understand neither; that power increases in a strait place—what Shakespeare meant, maybe, in having Hamlet speak without distinction of "form and pressure" as indissolubly the same thing.

James Wright, in *The Green Wall,* says that he has elected his tradition (Robinson and Frost), and that he has "wanted to make the poems say something humanly important instead of just showing off with language." This last sounds like little more than being against sin, but I think it is a false dilemma for so good a poet, which luckily doesn't often embarrass him in his poems. These I found generally intelligent, elegiac, beautifully formed, and finely spoken in their compound of colloquial ease and intensely developing metaphor. He is, like Miss Miller, a poet in the understanding that the durable force of one's convictions belongs to the developing figure of the poem, and is therefore not to be arrived at by shouting, but by finding, in tradition, nature, history, the right revealing situation for one's thought or wish; or else by allowing the thought or wish to arise only from the situation. So in a poem "To a Defeated Saviour" he considers someone who has failed to save a boy from drowning, and how the memory of this transforms itself in sleep:

You see his face, upturning, float
And bob across your wavering bed;
His failing fingers call your boat,
His voice throws up the ruddy silt,
The bleary vision prays for light

In sky behind your frozen hands;
But sinking in the dark all night,
Your charm the shore with bloomless wands.

The last figure seems suddenly most moving because it brings out at a stroke the concealed implications of the title. It is altogether a good poem, I think, and he has others as good, e.g., "A Song for the Middle of the Night," "Mutterings over the Crib of a Deaf Child," "The Ungathered Apples." The defect of so much virtue is the usual one, that when the situation doesn't define and choices fail to be imposed, Mr. Wright will rhapsodize as calmly and develop his diffused portentousness as nobly as any poet in the world, and bring himself down from dominant to tonic most gravely at the close —because that is what a poem must do, if it does nothing else. When this happens, the development outgrows its poem, the general relaxation of tone becomes dull, and the grand resignation seems too easily won, as it does also in poems by his admired masters, to mention no others. But altogether this is a most reckonable first book.

If this review of a few more or less arbitrarily selected volumes of recent verse reveals anything at all beyond the prejudices of the reviewer, it might be put (though by the same reviewer) as follows:

The aim of the poet is to write poems. Poems are arrangements of language which illuminate a connection between the inside and the outside of things. The durability of poems, as objects made out of language which will be around for some time because people experience this illumination and therefore like reading them, results from the clarity, force, and coherence with which this connection is made, and not from anything else however laudable, like the holding of strong opinions, or the feeling of strong emotions, or the naming of beautiful objects. Because of the oddly intimate relations obtaining between the inside and the outside of things, the poetic art is always with us, and does not decay with the decay of systems of philosophy and religion, or fall out of fashion with the sets of names habitually given, over more or less long periods of time, to the relations between the inside of things and the outside. With all the reverence poets have for tradition, poetry is always capable of reaching its beginning again. Its tradition, ideally, has to do with reaching the beginning, so that, of many young poets who begin with literature, a few old ones may end with nature.

The lyric difficulty also is always with us, but our sense of it these days comes most poignantly from publicists (who may on other occasions be critics, or poets) and people who, intending to be poets, do not yet write poems. This difficulty is usually presented to us as a series of pairs of opposites—e.g., form and having something to say, grace and passion, control and urgency, etc. Thus equipped, any man may make his own battlefield, not to mention that he may also, and probably will, make his own side win. What such warriors of the abstract fail to take into account is that any poet, any at all, is aware that these opposites exist. He is further aware that writing poetry does not mean choosing one side against the other, but achieving the maximum intensity and the greatest harmony of both sides. And he is painfully aware, from the experience of writing, that his own temperament (which irremediably belongs to him, and cannot be subordinated to any ideal however fine) is constantly pushing him toward one side or the other. But poetry is one of those human activities in which it is not the object to identify oneself exclusively with the right or the left, though it is hoped that the result will look more like tightrope-walking than fence-sitting.

Part III

Composition and Fate in the Short Novel

The writer attempting for the first time a short novel must face, I should think, nothing but problems, the first, though probably the least, of which is, What are short novels? For the writer who is by habit of mind a novelist they must represent not simply a compression but a corresponding rhythmic intensification, a more refined criterion of relevance than the one he usually enjoys, an austerity and economy perhaps somewhat compulsive in the intention itself. For the writer who habitually thinks in short stories—a bad habit, by the way—the challenge is probably greater: he will have to learn as never before about the interstices of his action; he will have to think about a fairly large space which must be filled, not with everything (his complaint against the novelist), but with something definite which must be made to yield in a quite explicit way its most reserved and recondite ranges of feeling; he will have to think, for once, of design and not merely of plot. To both writers it must soon become apparent that a short novel is something in itself, neither a lengthily written short story nor the refurbished attempt at a novel sent out into the world with its hat clapped on at the eightieth page.

I am speaking, perhaps, ideally, and about the ideal; it is difficult not to. For quite apart from technical considerations, the tradition of the short novel—perhaps because for so long it was commercially useless and unacceptable—is a tradition of masterpieces; further than that, the composers of this tradition of masterpieces are almost without exception the composers of still greater works, such as *Moby Dick*, *War and Peace*, *The Possessed*, *The Magic Mountain*, and so on,

Reprinted by permission from *The Graduate Journal*, Vol. 5, No. 2, Fall 1963. Copyright 1963 by the Board of Regents of the University of Texas. This essay was presented as a lecture before The English Institute at Columbia University, September 7, 1956.

from which their short novels differ, in fact, by a kind of intensification of art, by a closed and resonant style of composition suggestive of the demonstrations of mathematics or chess.

The writer proposing to himself a short novel probably ought not to scare himself with the thought that he is entering that kind of competition; once he begins, of course, he will resolutely forget all about those great men and their works, and pay his exclusive attention to the business in hand. Again, though, the game is scarcely worth playing without an acknowledgment of its specific difficulties; the specific difficulties, if they can be identified, are what define the form—without them it is not a form but only so and so many thousand words—and in a discussion like this one I see no way of approaching the matter at all except by attending to the ideal so far as it can be deduced from great examples.

The material economy of the short novel, and its strict analogical style of composition, seem to be functions one of the other. The epitome of the first point, material economy, I must fetch from far away; it seems brilliantly expressed in a discussion of variety in the creation, by Thomas Aquinas, who says that although an angel is a better thing, objectively considered, than a stone, yet a universe composed of two angels is inferior to a universe composed of one angel and one stone. A variousness so strictly limited and identified as that characterizes, as though by satiric exaggeration, the universe of the short novel. As to the strict and analogical style of composition, I shall quote a somewhat extended but very rewarding anecdote from the autobiography of a most admirable novelist, Vladimir Nabokov:

> The place is . . . Abbazia, on the Adriatic. About the same time, at a cafe in nearby Fiume, my father happened to notice, just as we were being served, two Japanese officers at a table near us, and we immediately left—not without my hastily snatching a whole *bombe* of lemon sherbet, which I carried away secreted in my aching mouth. The year was 1904. I was five. Russia was fighting Japan. With hearty relish, the English illustrated weekly Miss Norcott subscribed to reproduced pictures by Japanese artists that showed how the Russian locomotives—made singularly toylike by the Japanese pictorial style—would drown if our Army tried to lay rails across the treacherous ice of Lake Baikal.
>
> But let me see. I had an even earlier association with that war. One afternoon at the beginning of the same year, in our St. Petersburg house, I was led down from the nursery into my father's study to say how-do-you-do to a friend of the family, General Kuropatkin. To amuse me,

he spread out a handful of matches on the divan where he was sitting, placed ten of them end to end to make a horizontal line and said, "This is the sea in calm weather." Then he tipped up each pair so as to turn the straight line into a zigzag—and that was "a stormy sea." He scrambled the matches and was about to do, I hoped, a better trick when we were interrupted. His aide-de-camp was shown in and said something to him. With a Russian, flustered grunt, Kuropatkin immediately rose from his seat, the loose matches jumping up on the divan as his weight left it. That day, he had been ordered to assume supreme command of the Russian Army in the Far East.

This incident had a special sequel fifteen year later, when at a certain point of my father's flight from Bolshevik-held St. Petersburg to southern Russia, he was accosted, while crossing a bridge, by an old man who looked like a grey-bearded peasant in his sheepskin coat. He asked my father for a light. The next moment each recognized the other. Whether or not old Kuropatkin, in his rustic disguise, managed to evade Soviet imprisonment, is immaterial. What pleases me is the evolution of the match theme; those magic ones he had shown me had been trifled with and mislaid, and his armies had also vanished, and everything had fallen through, like my toy trains that, in the winter of 1904-05, in Wiesbaden, I tried to run over the frozen puddles in the grounds of the Hotel Oranien. The following of such thematic designs through one's life should be, I think, the true purpose of autobiography.

—*Speak, Memory*, 1951, pp. 15-17.

A good deal that characterizes the composition of short novels is summed up and lightly demonstrated in this passage, even to a certain ruthlessness: "Whether or not old Kuropatkin . . . managed to evade Soviet imprisonment, is immaterial." And "the evolution of the match theme," with the problems attendant on it, is my proper subject here. But before going on to discuss examples I will try to suggest, without wasting time on attempts at unexceptionable definition, some of the things, other than length, which seem to set the novella apart from the short story and the novel. For the term "short novel" is descriptive only in the way that the term "Middle Ages" is descriptive—that is, not at all, except with reference to the territory on either side. And just as historians exaggerate the darkness of the Dark Ages and the brightness of the Renaissance, I shall exaggerate some elements of the short story and the novel, to make the middle term more visible.

The short story at present is a way of transacting one's fictional business which is shiny, efficient, and inexpensive; consequently it has become very attractive to non-artists. If publishers tell us despite this that collections of short stories rarely succeed, that is probably because everyone is too busy writing his own to be able to read anyone else's. To write a fine short story may be harder now than it has ever been, but there is no indication that large numbers of short story writers are aware of the fact. There are many honorable exceptions, perhaps, submerged in the flood of junk—commercial junk, high-literary junk, undergraduate junk, much of it competent and even attractive, but bearing too much the mark of the machine to give, even at the best, any deep pleasure. Short stories amount for the most part to parlor tricks, party favors with built-in snappers, gadgets for inducing recognitions and reversals: a small pump serves to build up the pressure, a tiny trigger releases it, there follow a puff and a flash as freedom and necessity combine; finally a Celluloid doll drops from the muzzle and descends by parachute to the floor. These things happen, but they happen to no one in particular.

Of many possible reasons why this fate has overtaken the short story, one must be the vast quantity of such stuff produced every day of every week and published in newspapers and magazines, on radio and television (for those "dramas" are either adapted from short stories or made up with the same requirements in mind). That so much of our experience, or the stereotype which passes for it, should be dealt with by means of the short story is perhaps the symptom, not unnoticeable elsewhere in the public domain, of an unlovely cynicism about human character, a propensity to see *individual* behavior as purely atmospheric—*colorful*, as they call it—and accordingly to require stereotyped behavior for everything having to do with the essential action. To invent an example: our hero is individual to the point of eccentricity, he is weirdly named Cyrus Pyracanth, he suffers from hemophilia, keeps pet snakes, and smokes a nargileh; but when it comes to the point, none of this has anything to do with the action his author requires him to perform, for the sake of which he might be called Mr. X and live in Bronxville on an average income and a moral equipment supplied by *Time* magazine or some other leading wholesaler. What has happened to him in the short story is not that he has lost his inwardness; only that for all practical purposes (the writer's purposes) it has ceased to matter.

It is natural that the mass production of short fiction should exert great pressure to bring the story down to its mechanically imitable elements, so that it provides solutions at the expense of problems, answers to which no one has asked the question; there is, indeed, a certain aesthetic pleasure to be gained from the contemplation of simple and pretty combinations purified, as in the detective story, of human complication and human depth; but it is a pleasure easily exhausted. The story gets its power from a whole implied drama which it does not tell aloud; its neglect of that implication reduces it to clever trickery. There is much to be said for clever trickery as a contributing means to great works, nor do great novelists often neglect this part of art which is purely artifice—but when there is little or nothing else, and when in addition all the tricks have been played so many times . . . ?

This is not simply a question of length, but much rather a question of depth; when a short story's action comprises, by brilliant symbolic reflection, the whole of a life, it becomes novelistic. I think in this connection of two stories by Kay Boyle, "Keep Your Pity" and "Dear Mr. Walrus." Neither exceeds thirty pages, but those pages are written throughout with the kind of attention sometimes held to be proper only for poetry (I do not mean what is called "poetic prose," rather the reverse), whereas short stories such as I have been talking about usually betray themselves as having been written only with a view to the ending.

The word "novel" will cover a multitude of sins. I can think of an author "writing" a novella, but this simple term will not do for a novel, where I have to think of him "sitting down at his desk" and "addressing himself to the task." I think of lavish productions, casts of thousands, full technicolor, photographed against authentic backgrounds, and so on. Not all of this is accurate, or it need not be, but I emphasize it for the sake of a contrast; besides, when faced with the need for a commanding generality on this topic, I find myself to have forgotten all the novels I have ever read. The contrast I want to bring out is this: for many novelists, all but the simplest element of compositional art (the plot) is destroyed by observation, by detail work, by reality which keeps poking its head in. The leisure, the "warm earthy humanity," of the novel owes itself to this consideration: people read novellas, but they tend to live in novels, and sometimes they live there very comfortably indeed: thus you have descriptions which are nothing but descriptions, thus you have philosophical excursions, set-pieces, summaries, double plot, and full orchestration, not to mention that all the chairs are heavily upholstered and even the walls padded. Stendhal provided benches for the reader to sit down on, but many novelists erect hotels for the same laudable accommodation.

Let me try to bring this distinction back down to the ground. The master novelist is Shakespearean in combinative skill, if not in language: he handles actions which are long, complex, serious, and explicitly generalized through the social and political fabric, e.g., *The Possessed, War and Peace, The Red and the Black, Remembrance of Things Past*. The authors of such works are masters in parable and reality simultaneously. Then there are masters in parable, and I would only indicate the range of this art by mentioning together the names of Jane Austen and Franz Kafka; if I say that *Emma* and *The Trial* are, for me, like short novels in spite of their length, that will suggest my feeling that the name "short novel" does not exactly discriminate, and that some such terms as "simple" and "complex" novels might be used instead. A few lesser examples may help here: Mrs. Compton-Burnett writes short novels at whatever length, as do Graham Greene and Henry Green and Virginia Woolf. I need hardly say that the distinction is not one of quality any more than it is one of length. *The Counterfeiters* means to be a novel, so does *Point Counter Point*, so does *Nostromo*, so does *Tender is the Night*, but I do not prefer them before *Lafcadio's Adventures, After Many a Summer Dies the Swan, The Secret Agent*, or *The Great Gatsby*, which are examples of the other kind.

I favor this distinction of the simple and complex, the Greek drama and the Shakespearean, over the other which seems to be based purely on length. Simple novels will normally be shorter than complex ones anyhow, though not always—I notice for instance that Cyril Connolly refers to *Gatsby* and *The Spoils of Poynton* together as short novels, and I, sharing his feeling or mistaken memory as to the latter, was surprised to find it just twice as long as *Gatsby*. But I shall not insist on these terms, simple and complex, and will draw my illustrations in the following discussion from novels generally allowed to be *short* ones.

We have, after all, only two ways of thinking about literary composition. In one, general ideas are illustrated by appropriate particulars; in the other, the contemplation of particulars produces general ideas. Perhaps neither of these species can ever be seen in purity and isolation in any given work, especially since the work as we read it offers no certain guide to the means of its composition, so that all literary composition appears as a combination of these extremes, possibly to be characterized by the dominance of one or the other. The pure state of the first kind, in which the author determines first upon a more or less systematic arrangement of general notions, then devises particular appearances for them, would be allegory of the most rigorously scientific sort, like an equation; literary allegories can never be quite that rigid, because every particular does more than illustrate, it modifies the general idea. The pure state of the second kind would exist only if the contemplation of particulars quite failed to produce general ideas and systematic meanings, but produced only the intense view of particulars as themselves the *irrational* demonstration of the nature of things: symbolism is a way station on this road which runs further to expressionism, surrealism, dada, and the riddles of the Zen Koan.

It is fashionably believed at present that the artist belongs finally to the irrational, that his is the ecstasy of the unique, the individual and irreducible, the opaque detail existing in and for itself; conversely, that reason, construction, architecture of general ideas, will destroy him as an artist. It is a theme which I shall not develop at large in this place, but the tradition of the short novel offers a good deal of evidence for the opposite view. The most striking element shared by almost all the great pieces in this genre is their outright concentration upon traditional problems of philosophy, the boldness of their venture into generality, the evidence they give of direct and profound moral concern. We are not entitled to suppose, of course, that such works were composed from the point of view first of general ideas and philosophic problems and paradoxes, even though sometimes—as with the *Notes from the Underground*, for example—it is tempting so to suppose. What we may insist is that these works combine with their actions a most explicit awareness of themselves as parables, as philosophic myths, and almost invariably announce and demonstrate the intention of discursive profundity—the intention, it is not too much to say, of becoming sacred books: final instances, exhaustively analyzed, of a symbolic universe of whose truth we can be persuaded only by fictions. The result for composition is that problem becomes the center of the short novel, which with a peculiar purity dramatizes conflicts of appearance and reality (*Benito Cereno*), freedom and necessity (*Notes from the Underground*), madness and sanity (*Ward Number Six*); all these are of course forms of a single problem essential and not accidental to the genre, which I shall try to illustrate by describing and giving examples of one theme which is pervasive to the point of obsession in the short novel.

The theme is broadly speaking that of *identity*, and the action deriving from it may be generalized as follows: the mutual attachment or dependency between A and B has a mortal strength; its dissolution requires a crisis fatal to one or the other party; but this dissolution is represented as salvation.

It is clear from many examples that the story of the Passion itself, with its suffering and dying Redeemer, sin-eater, scapegoat, is explicitly thought of in connection with this theme, which may be told as a religious parable, an adventure story, a fantasy, a psychological novel, often with strong homosexual or narcissistic emphasis.

1. The most literal form of this attachment occurs in the conclusion of *St. Julian the Hospitaler*, which Flaubert adapted from the *Gesta Romanorum* (though the story embodies even older materials, such as the legends of St. Hubert and St. Christopher). Julian's final penance is to lie down in the embrace of the leper, who turns into a bright angelic being and takes him to heaven.

2. In *The Private Memoirs and Confessions of a Justified Sinner*, by James Hogg, the self-righteous man is seduced and destroyed by the Prince of Darkness who appears as his double; whether his repentance speaks much for self-knowledge may be doubtful enough, but there is a redemptive note in the circumstance that he ends his life in a manger, "a byre, or cowhouse . . . where, on a divot loft, my humble bedstead stood, and the cattle grunted and puffed below me."

3. Melville's short novels, those combinations of the most baldly stated symbolism with the most mysterious ambiguousness of resolution, explore this theme. Captain Delano in his benign unworldliness and innocence becomes responsible for Benito Cereno, through whose sufferings and death he is enabled to perceive, beneath appearances, how things really are. The Master in Chancery becomes liable personally, morally, religiously, and at one point legally, for Bartleby. His final phrase of sorrowful commiseration—"Ah, Bartleby! Ah, humanity!"—gains a certain force of revelation from being compared with some of his earlier statements, e.g., "I am a man who, from his youth upward, has been filled with a profound conviction that the easiest way of life is the best." *Billy Budd* is a somewhat more complex rendering. Billy and Claggart are represented as eternally fated to one another; beyond that it is Captain Vere who suffers

the "mystery of iniquity" of this predestinated encounter. Billy suffers as Adam tempted and fallen, as Cain whose brother (Claggart) is preferred before him, as the Son of God whose death redeems to order an unruly people (the mutinous Navy), but who is publicly misrepresented in history (the newspaper article) and art (the ballad). Other, less religious interpretation is possible, but enough has been said for the present purpose.

4. In Conrad's *The Secret Sharer* the story is told with a particular purity as well as a rare optimism (in other examples where the disappearance of one party is allowed to do for his death, that disappearance is usually into an insane asylum). The young captain, irresolute and uncertain in his first command, comes face to face with his double: "It was, in the night, as though I had been faced by my own reflection in the depths of a somber and immense mirror." By protecting Leggatt (a legate from the darkness of the sea outside and the self within), by sharing his identity, by experiencing in homeopathic amounts the criminal element in his own nature, by at last liberating, or separating, this other self from his own at the risk of shipwreck, the young man gains a "perfect communion" with his first command.

Marlow says of Kurtz, "It was written I should be loyal to the nightmare of my choice," and he is loyal to the final extent of lying for him, though "there is a taint of death, a flavor of mortality, in lies." The view of Kurtz as scapegoat, as evil or fallen savior, is generalized throughout, notably in what Marlow says to his audience, those nameless masters of the world, the Director of Companies, the Lawyer, the Narrator: "You can't understand. How could you?—with solid pavement under your feet, surrounded by kind neighbors ready to cheer you or fall on you, stepping delicately between the butcher and the policeman, in the holy terror of scandal and gallows and lunatic asylums—how can you imagine what particular region of the first ages a man's untrammeled feet may take him into by the way of solitude—utter solitude without a policeman—by the way of silence —utter silence, where no warning voice of a kind neighbor can be heard whispering of public opinion. These little things make all the great difference." So Kurtz is an instance of absolute power corrupted absolutely, yes, but this power is further characterized as that of the impulsive, archaic life liberated, which no man can bear and live, which Marlow himself nearly died of the briefest and most homeopathic contact with, and which in some sense is the force that makes history and makes civilization.

5. The theme we are describing is of the first importance to Dostoevsky, who intensifies both the psychological penetration of the treatment and its ultimate religious or metaphysical expansions. The typical bond, between the worldly man and his sinister, underworld, epicene counterpart—his "poor relation," as the Devil is called in *The Brothers Karamazov*—occurs in the major novels in such double figures as Ivan and Smerdyakov, Ivan and the Devil, Christ and the Grand Inquisitor, Stavrogin and Pyotr Stepanovich, and, with a quite different tonality, Muishkin and Rogozhin. Two of the short novels concentrate exclusively on the development of this theme. *The Eternal Husband* ties together the seducer and the cuckold in a relation characterized as ambiguously homosexual and sadistic, a comedy agonizing enough but hardly more so than that of *The Double*, which relates how poor, stupid Mr. Golyadkin, portrayed from the outset as suffering symptoms of paranoia, comes face to face with his double, Golyadkin, Jr., who behaves insufferably, calls him "darling," pinches his cheek, embarrasses him in every way public and private, until the original Golyadkin, what remains of him, is driven off to the asylum. In this last scene several people run after the carriage, shouting, until they are left behind, and "Mr. Golyadkin's unworthy twin kept up longer than anyone . . . he ran on with a satisfied air, skipping first to one and then to the other side of the carriage . . . poking his head in at the window, and throwing farewell kisses to Mr. Golyadkin."

6. Without giving any further examples in detail I may merely mention a few more short novels in which this theme is developed: in Chekhov's *Ward Number Six*, Andrew Ephimich and the young man Ivan Dimitrich Gronov; the young soldier and his captain in Lawrence's *The Prussian Officer*; Aschenbach and Tadzio in Mann's *Death in Venice*, Mario and Cipolla in his *Mario and the Magician*; the condemned man and the officer in *In the Penal Colony* by Kafka; Howe and Tertan in Lionel Trilling's *Of This Time, of That Place*; Wilhelm and Dr. Tamkin in Saul Bellow's *Seize the Day*.

My intention is to discuss composition in the strict sense, rather than to consider the interpretation and historical placement of this thematic insistence. Yet it is worth pausing here to observe in how many of these stories the theme is employed to show the man of the middle class, rational, worldly, either rather stupid or of a somewhat dry intelligence and limited vision, plunged into the domain of the forbidden, extravagant, and illicit, the life of the impulses beneath or the life of compulsive and punitive authority above, both of them equally regions in which every detail gains fatal significance, every perception is excruciatingly intensified, and every decision for salvation or doom: so it happens, in various ways, to Captain Delano, the Master in Chancery, Ivan Ilyich, Gustave Aschenbach, Velchaninov, Gregor Samsa, the Woman Who Rode Away, Andrew Ephimich. . . . And it is remarkable, too, how often, by the device of the double, the incubus as it were, their sufferings and perceptions seem to invade them ambiguously from the world outside and the self within. I am tempted to think that the characteristic economy of the short novel, its precisely defined space, the peculiar lucidity and simplicity of its internal forms—two or three persons, a single action, equal tension among the persons, each of whom has a fate —tends to involve the artist more overtly than usual in trying to expound by fantasies what he himself is and what he is doing in his art. Indeed, this is perhaps cryptically hinted to us by Flaubert, when he makes his Félicité suffer the lash of a coachman's whip on the road between Honfleur and Pont l'Eveque, where he himself, riding in a carriage, suffered his first attack of epilepsy, or serious hysteria. And by Melville, who sees his scrivener—unwilling to copy the writings of others—as having had the previous job of handling dead letters "and assorting them for the flames"—this in the year after a fire at the publishing house had destroyed the plates for Melville's own works. Less cryptically by Mann, who sees his artist-heroes by turns as diseased aristocrats, confidence men, and monstrous tyrants (Savonarola, Cipolla). For the fullest meaning of the theme, most minutely expounded, we should have to refer to Proust, who by the most intricately woven analogies throughout his immense work characterizes the moral isolation of the poet as, on the one hand, that of the invalid, the pervert, the criminal, the Jew, the traitor, and, on the other hand, that of the hero, aristocrat, doctor or surgeon, and commander of armies in the field.

Whether what I have tried to describe is the product of a limited historical tradition or of a tragic circumstance as near eternal as that witnessed to in Greek tragedies or in the Book of Job I am unable to say certainly and must not stop to debate here. So far as the theme results in actions typical of the short novel—actions simple and decisive, generally mortal in fact, and involving few persons—the following points of compositional interest arise.

Whereas the short story tends to rest upon action, a combination of circumstances to which the characters must very readily conform, while the novel, especially in English, goes toward the opposite pole and tends to produce "characters" as an independent value, the short novel strikes a very delicate and exact balance between motive and circumstance; its action generally speaking is the fate of the agonists, and this fate is regarded as flowing demonstrably and with some precision and in great detail from their individual natures, which accordingly are developed at considerable length. I need barely mention examples: the portraits, as distinct from the stories, of e.g., Aschenbach, Captain Delano, The Man from Underground, Gabriel Conroy, John Marcher . . . What happens to all these persons, and ever so many other protagonists of the short novel, happens expressly to them and because they are as they are; perhaps the simplest instance is that of Captain Delano, whose innocence is represented precisely as the condition of his survival in a naughty world: "a person of a singularly undistrustful good nature, not liable, except on extraordinary and repeated excitement, and hardly then, to indulge in personal alarms, any way involving the imputation of malign evil in man. Whether, in view of what humanity is capable, such a trait implies, along with a benevolent heart, more than ordinary quickness and accuracy of intellectual perception, may be left to the wise to determine."

The same balance is maintained by the authors of these compositions, in the exact division of their attention to the inside of things and the outside, between knowledge of the ordinary, undramatic world, and imagination of the drama which takes place under its exacting conditions. How this is so may be seen most simply from *Notes from the Underground,* where the argument and its dramatic equivalent are given separately; oftener, however, the two strands are concurrent, and occasionally, in very sophisticated and elegant works, they are identical; as in *Un Coeur Simple,* which may be read as the plain product of observation, as though a "sketch of provincial life," and read again, or simultaneously, as a structure of great intricacy and density, entirely musical and contrapuntal in the laws of its being, and consequently forming a world all its own, rhythmic, resonant, symmetrical, in which every detail balances another so as to produce great riches of meaning not so much symbolically in a direct sense as by constellation and patterning, the method James called the figure in the carpet. In this connection I would mention once again Kay Boyle as possibly the foremost modern practitioner of this subtle style, especially in two short novels, *The Crazy Hunter* and *The Bridegroom's Body*.

It is this balance, so like that of the poetic drama, the balance between the appearance and the motive, the observed world and the world of law, which I conceive to be more exactly drawn and maintained in the short novel than elsewhere, that gives to works in this genre the characteristic of ruthlessness I referred to before. The ideal, that every detail should at once seem freely chosen by probable observation, and be in fact the product of a developing inner necessity, confers on these tales something of the air of demonstrations; so that, for example, when Andrew Ephimich is first drawn to visit Gronov in the asylum it is as though the chess master announced mate in twelve—we neither doubt the result nor see at all how it is to be accomplished. In this sense we sometimes feel the protagonists of short novels to be the victims not of fate or of the gods so much as of literary styles and laws of composition—that strict style of composition discussed by Adrian Leverkühn, himself such a victim, in Mann's *Dr. Faustus*.

This again is a subject I must be content to leave implicit: whether the idea itself of the "art work" any longer has anything to do with anything; whether, being based at last on religious valuations, magical sanctions, and the sense of a universe at once "real" and "symbolic," a universe of signatures, the work of art can continue to interpret human experience. I merely note that this theme is disturbingly *there*, and pass on to safer ground.

The characteristic balance I am speaking of reflects itself very distinctively in the treatment of detail in short novels; more so, or more perspicuously so, than in long ones. A few instances will serve to conclude this discussion.

There are two kinds of relevance in literary composition, and I think they are both readily observable in principle although it is doubtful whether they can always be distinguished in the work itself. One kind has to do with the temporal succession of events, as though the single point of the idea must be viewed in an added dimension as a straight line: in order to tell how a distinguished German author dies in Venice we must get him to Venice, keep him there, and supply a disease for him to die of. He will doubtless see many things, and think many things, on his journey—what things? We need another kind of relevance, having to do with association, symbol, metaphor, as well as with probable and realistic observation; while the distinguished author is in Venice it occurs to him, waking, that his situation is like that discussed in the *Phaedrus*, and, dreaming, that his situation is like that of King Pentheus in *The Bacchae* of Euripedes.

The first kind of relevance you may call external, the second internal; or, better, the first is linear, and progresses in time, while the second is radical and comes at every instant from the central conception. The difference between them, practically speaking, is that the story could be told without the contribution of the symbolic details and could not be told without the succession of events. It will be objected, perhaps, that without the symbolic details, or with other symbolic details, it would be a different story and an inferior one, and that is true enough but for compositional purposes irrelevant. What is more important is that neither kind in itself accounts for the story, what makes it worth our while to hear that the distinguished German author went to Venice and died there—for that we require something that binds both sorts together, and makes the temporal and ideal situations the subject of the same decision: in this instance the figure of the boy Tadzio, who according to the first kind of relevance is the motive for Aschenbach's remaining in Venice long enough to contract his fatal disease, and according to the second kind plays Dionysus to his Pentheus, Phaedrus to his Socrates, inspires highly relevant reflections on love and morality, beauty and disease, form and corruption, aristocratic control and chaos, and so on.

The tensions of these two criteria of choice in the short novel tend to make the selection of details extraordinarily fateful; especially it seems that everything which is symbolic, associational, metaphorically relevant, is multiply determined, as the details of a dream are said to be, and thus gains a dramatic prominence and a kind of luminous quality. I will try to illustrate by a few examples.

When Aschenbach dies, there by the shore, we are told that the weather was autumnal, the beach deserted and not even very clean; suddenly we are given this: "A camera on a tripod stood at the edge of the water, apparently abandoned; its black cloth snapped in the freshening wind." That is all, our attention is given to Tadzio, Aschenbach's death soon follows, the camera is never mentioned again.

Crudely speaking, this camera is unnecessary and no one could possibly have noticed anything missing had the author decided against its inclusion; yet in a musical, compositional sense it exquisitely touches the center of the story and creates a resonance which makes us for a moment aware of the entire inner space of the action, of all things relevant and their relations to one another.

Our sense of this is mostly beyond exposition, as symbolic things have a way of being; but some of its elements may be mentioned. About the camera by the sea there is, first, a poignant desolation, the emptiness of vast spaces, and in its pictorial quality it resembles one of the earliest images in the story, when Aschenbach, standing by the cemetery, looks away down the empty streets: "not a wagon in sight, either on the paved Ungererstrasse, with its gleaming tramlines stretching off towards Schwabing, nor on the Föhring highway." Both pictures are by Di Chirico. The camera's black cloth reminds us of the gondola, "black as nothing else on earth except a coffin," and the repeated insistence on black in that description; also of the "labor in darkness" which brings forth the work of art. For we perceive that the camera stands to the sea as, throughout this story, the artist has stood to experience, in a morally heroic yet at the same time dubious or ridiculous or even impossible relation of form to all possibility, and that at the summer's end, in the freshening wind, the camera is abandoned. It would be near forgivable, so full of Greek mysteries is this work, if we thought the tripod itself remotely Delphic.

Here is another example. At the beginning of *The Secret Sharer* Conrad gives us an image which at that time, perhaps, we cannot see as anything but pictorial: the young man, looking out across the sea, sees "lines of fishing stakes resembling a mysterious system of half-submerged bamboo fences." But when we have finished the story we may see even that image in the first sentence as compositionally resonant, as a cryptic emblem set up at the gateway of the action. This emblem suggests to us how the conscious distinctions, the property rights, of reason and society, extend also beneath the surface (of the sea, of the mind) and are in fact rooted down there: precisely what is learned by the narrator who before his adventure "rejoiced in the great security of the sea as compared with the unrest of the land, in my choice of that untempted life presenting no disquieting problems, invested with an elementary moral beauty by the absolute straightforwardness of its appeal and by the singleness of its purpose"

—fine phrases, on which the story, like its opening image, comments in sympathetic, pedagogic irony.

Another example. In *The Death of Ivan Ilyich*, Tolstoy shows us the funeral service and a colleague of the dead man going in to visit the widow, who is under three several necessities which exclude one another: of showing terrible grief, of passing ashtrays to prevent the guest's spoiling the rug, of discussing the payment of her husband's pension. The visitor sits down "on a low pouffe, the springs of which yielded under his weight." The widow, however, catches her shawl on the edge of a table, so "Peter Ivanovich rose to detach it, and the springs of the pouffe, relieved of his weight, rose also and gave him a push. The widow began detaching her shawl herself, and Peter Ivanovich again sat down, suppressing the rebellious springs of the pouffe under him. But the widow had not quite freed herself, and Peter Ivanovich got up again, and again the pouffe rebelled and even creaked." A page later, as the widow approaches the subject of the pension, "Peter Ivanovich bowed, keeping control of the springs of the pouffe, which immediately began quivering under him."

This comically autonomous pouffe represents not merely the social obliquities of the interview, nor merely that inanimate objects continually mutter their comments to the detriment of human dignity and solemnity, but also how such objects may tend actively to push us where we do not wish to go, to represent some implacable hostility in the world of objects, especially those meant for our convenience. Death occurs with just the same independence of human volition, and we are emblematically informed—"As he sat down on the pouffe Peter Ivanovich recalled how Ivan Ilyich had arranged this room and had consulted him regarding this pink cretonne with green leaves"—of something we learn more explicitly later, that Ivan Ilyich's interest precisely in such things, in "decoration," caused his death: "when mounting a stepladder to show the upholsterer, who did not understand, how he wanted the hangings draped, he made a false step and slipped . . ."

This species of inner determination produces, in the short novel, not single details only but chains and clusters of iterative imagery also, such as we usually identify with the poetry of Shakespeare; and sometimes, as in *Un Coeur Simple*, it is the elegant patterning and constatation of such groups of images which alone, implicitly, supply the meaning, or meanings: an interested reader may trace on his own, for example, the provenience of the parrot-paraclete Loulou, not in the action alone, but in the far-ranging associated imagery—how it is gradually prepared for before its appearance by much talk of jungles and far places, by the geography book given the children by M. Bourais, by Félicité's childish ideas of distant places and times, by Victor's voyages and death, by Mme. Auban's dream after the death of Virginie, and so on.

I have tried to describe the short novel, according to the examples I am most familiar with, not as a compromise between novel and short story, but as something like the ideal and primary form, suggestively allied in simplicity and even in length with the tragedies of antiquity, and dealing in effect with equivalent materials. No doubt in dealing with this subject I have slighted somewhat the complex novel and, even more, the short story; that has to do in part, as I said, with making the middle term visible, but perhaps in even greater part with my lasting delight in short novels, which I will even go so far as nearly to identify with tragic art in our fictional tradition. What is accomplished by the works I have been speaking of may be given the sanction of science as well as magic or religion in the following words of Sir D'Arcy Wentworth Thompson in the introductory chapter of his work *On Growth and Form:* "Like warp and woof, mechanism and teleology are interwoven together, and we must not cleave to the one nor despise the other; for their union is rooted in the very nature of totality. We may grow shy or weary of looking to a final cause for an explanation of our phenomena; but after we have accounted for these on the plainest principles of mechanical causation it may be useful and appropriate to see how the final cause would tally with the other, and lead towards the same conclusion." It is this double exploration which, I have contended, is undertaken in the short novel more than in other sorts of fiction. Even the matter of the length or brevity of such works ought not to be beneath discussion as "merely" mechanical; in the book I quoted from before, Vladimir Nabokov says something which I shall repeat for a conclusion to this matter. Discussing ways of seeing—the lantern slide, the microscope—he says, "There is, it would seem, in the dimensional scale of the world a kind of delicate meeting-place between imagination and knowledge, a point, arrived at by diminishing large things and enlarging small ones, that is intrinsically artistic."

Calculation Raised to Mystery: The Dialectics of Light in August

The novelist's technical relation with common reality allows him to make an impression of continuous life by discontinuous means; his selection and arrangement of events give as though naturally the idea of their being brought into prominence from a matrix of being large enough to support them comfortably and, if not indifferently, at least without fatal disturbance; particulars gain intensity from our being made to look at them, but our preoccupation is as it were legitimized and given ironic balance by extensions and indirections suggestive of what remains outside the focus of our immediate concern, and to this great remainder the issues of the story itself make some relation. So, in a peculiarly striking example, the hunters of the White Whale suspend their oars to watch rising from the sea "the vast, pulpy mass, furlongs in length and breadth," of "the great live squid," emblem of all that their exclusive and single-minded chase will leave not only undefeated but unaffected as well.

From the matrix of beings both possible and actual, then, the novelist elevates his human action, "one and entire," as has been said, and from this point the technical and the philosophical become involved together, so that no judgment concerning the one can fail to affect the other; the very fact of his having "a story to tell" directs him to criteria of coherence, unity, and the closest relevance, all to be based, however, on the appearance of the materials as uncoerced and freely existing. We need not push this double commitment to the point of paradox—unless or until we are forced to do so—for the world will certify to us in equal measure ideas of order and ideas of chaos; it is only necessary to note that the novelist, insofar as he has an art, predisposes himself to an order which is at once a question of technique and a question of belief about human actions.

That the novelist has an art, by the way, is still not universally allowed, and even where it is allowed he is very infrequently admitted to have, for the exercise of that art, a compositional language that differs from the language used, for example, by his reviewers. Those who worship formality rather than form are always on hand with their beliefs that the composition of prose is mysteriously less difficult than that of couplets or blank verse; that novels are diffuse, sprawling affairs incapable of a poetic concentration (it is so often the reader who is thus incapable), and the novelist is admired by some, as he is suspected by others, on the grounds of his "realism" —which now and then is revealed as meaning the fidelity of his details to those recorded in other novels. Mr. Auden's sonnet, "The Novelist," with its lugubrious portrait of the creature who "in his own weak person, if he can, / Must suffer dully all the wrongs of man," emphasizes the pathos of this businessman of letters at the expense of the profound, fate-laden, and doubtless a little sinister possibilities open to him, which constitute the comedy of his art, whatever its preoccupation with detailed perception and the illusion of exact report. It is my general contention, in fact, that it is precisely the novelist's "realism," his detailed portraiture from life, which presents to him the subjective problem of the validity of his formal operations. His work is comparable to a "doctrine of signatures" not less than that of the poet, and there is a sense in which his arrangements and analogies have an existence as demonstration, which while it is said to lead to truth has about it an air notoriously cold, directed —what some will call "cynical contrivance" and others "elegance" —and in this sense he may be said to begin from a unity of destiny and the technical to which his "realism" must contribute; he is the spider, who strengthens his web with the bodies of his victims.

I suspect it is time for the very real features of Mr. Faulkner to show through this lay figure of "the novelist"; and from two admirable essays on his work I take the following quotations to establish my theme, giving both to illustrate a striking difference of attitude on this matter.

> *Polarity.* To what extent does Faulkner work in terms of polarities, oppositions, paradoxes, inversions of roles? How much does he employ a line of concealed (or open) dialectic progression as a principle for his fiction? The study of these questions may lead to the discovery of principles of organization in his work not yet defined by criticism.*

* Robert Penn Warren, "William Faulkner," in *Forms of Modern Fiction*, Ed. William Van O'Connor, University of Minnesota Press, 1948.

My second author, equally perceptive, is considerably more uneasy:

> But just as he has deprived his characters of the capacity to make a moral decision, so he has removed from their various squabbles an essential or at least an important ingredient in our concept of Conflict: indeterminacy. That either side may win . . . is normally a possibility, and therefore a source of curiosity, suspense. It is not in Mr. Faulkner's works. His conflicts might more properly be called performances or exhibitions, since both sides take orders from the same headquarters, and since the reader, and most commonly the characters themselves, have been so advised.*

It is right to begin by acknowledging the wealth, brilliance, and diversity of detail displayed in *Light in August,* an impression of fullness and vitality exuberant to the suggestion of chaos; this is half the truth of the matter, and the half most generally emphasized, but the subject of our inquiry is the existence and character of the laws governing this turmoil and violence.

The parable itself is multiple and not easy to abstract with justice, but we may enter it by way of a moral which is clearly and continually emphasized: that the good man profits by evil, and cannot help doing so. Hightower, as the overscrupulous man, dies of this circumstance; Byron Bunch (his name a mocking combination of the individual and society) is aware of it, but his scrupulosity cannot prevent at last his marriage to Lena. Further, in an almost whimsically delicate way, he must participate in evil by way of acknowledging its place; and though he does not *sin,* he is forced to the point of deciding that is what he ought to do, and accordingly makes a halfhearted effort to sleep with Lena before marrying her. For as he has said earlier to Hightower, "there is a price for being good the same as for being bad; a cost to pay."

This "price" cannot be thought of as offering alternatives, to pay or not to pay; or if alternatives seem to be offered, Byron's career consists in his education to the necessity of payment, for the marriage itself is presented as a formal necessity of the novel, its longest suspension, from the first to the final chapter, and as the marriage can clearly not be accomplished without the "price," that too is necessary. Here one sees an illustration of the deliberate crossing of life with composition, destiny with form; the lesson of life is to be one with the requirement of art, or, in the grammarian's terms, the first

* Reed Whittemore, "Notes on Mr. Faulkner," *Furioso,* Summer 1947.

and second impositions have been mixed—not to confusion, however, but rather to the asserted effect that syntax and statement shall be one, a heroic presumption, perhaps, of human likeness to the author of form generally.

This necessity, equivocally fate and aesthetics, is powerfully present throughout. Toward the end of the novel Gavin Stevens briefly appears. He is perhaps the one man Mr. Faulkner fully trusts, for reasons which may appear nostalgic, naïve, and insufficient ("the District Attorney, a Harvard graduate, a Phi Beta Kappa"), and he enters this tale for one authoritative moment, putting Joe Christmas' grandparents on the train for Mottstown and giving an account of Christmas' last hours, during the course of which he says about Mrs. Hines's interview with her grandson at the jail:

> "But of course I dont know what she told him. I dont believe any man could reconstruct that scene. I dont think that she knew herself, planned at all what she would say, because it had already been written and worded for her on the night when she bore his mother, and that was so long ago that she had learned it beyond all forgetting and then forgot the words." (424)

This appears to be a key statement both in and about the novel; that is, about the lives it depicts and at the same time about the principle of its composition. Event ineluctably creates event, there is no escape from the assigned role, the idea of freedom consists in our having forgotten that we learned the part we must play. God, or destiny, or luck, or life itself, is inherently novelistic, as the terms of the statement suggest, and proliferates in most gorgeously libertine effects by the strictest and most reflexive economy of means, to such a degree that coincidence itself has no longer any real existence but is unabashedly faced up to as necessity—the similarity of the names Bunch and Burch, for example, is set forth as a coincidence to begin with, but proves to have no significance to the meeting of Bunch and Lena, which like his immediate love for her is regarded rather as fated and inevitable.

In the same way, the language, the terminology, of *Light in August* multiplies complexities from the elaboration of a basic distinction simple and pure as a proposition or an equation; the almost inexhaustible riches of the particular flow violently and as if chaotically from the primary division of the work's vocabulary. But in all the violence there is no chaos, unless at last we are to perceive that the exhaustive balance, comparison, and contrast of analogies have no center to refer to, are themselves chaos and the abyss, that life (and *a fortiori* the novel) is the endlessly intricate and meaningless labyrinthine design of an idiot god.

This primary division, whose ultimate words are perhaps unspeakable, has many incarnations, accommodations, translations to human speech, of which two pairs of opposed terms appear particularly important. We come to know about them quite early in the book, and well before we can say with any certainty what are the relations between them. Our first task is to elaborate the bare notation of these terms according to the imagery and action of the novel.

1. *Black: White.* The everlasting "civil" war is not the War between the States so much as it is the war of Negro and white man, a combat which is also a marriage. Joe Christmas, the illegitimate and orphaned son of a white mother and a black father, is caught between the lines, and it seems significant of his point of precarious balance and definition that his weapon (also his only possession) is a razor; although he carries an ancient double-barreled pistol for several days before his death, he never fires it.

Christmas, walking at night, is lost, then "finds himself" in Freedman town, the Negro section of Jefferson; he sees himself here "as from the bottom of a thick black pit," "as if the black life, the black breathing, had compounded the substance of breath so that not only voices but moving bodies and light itself must become fluid and accrete slowly from particle to particle, of and with the now ponderable night inseparable and one." And then, "On all sides, even within him, the bodiless fecundmellow voices of Negro women murmured. It was as though he and all other manshaped life about him had been returned to the lightless hot wet primogenitive Female." Running away, out of the "black hollow" and uphill, he comes a moment later to "the cold hard air of white people." And, looking back on the black pit, "It might have been the original quarry, abyss itself." (106-108) So, in his first sexual experience, Christmas, leaning over a Negro girl, "seemed to look down into a black well and at the bottom saw two glints like reflection of dead stars." (147)

Later, Miss Burden, presented as a double figure, man and woman by day and night, appears to Christmas as "two moongleamed shapes struggling drowning in alternate throes upon the surface of a black thick pool," one striving "to drown in the black abyss of its own creating that physical purity which had been preserved too long now even to be lost." (246)

Blackness for Christmas has the quality of disease; on learning, in the North, that "there were white women who would take a man with a black skin," he became "sick" and for two years "lived with Negroes, shunning white people . . . trying to expel from himself the white blood and the white thinking and being." (212) At last, after the murder, when in flight he trades shoes with a Negro, he looks down at "the black shoes smelling of Negro: that mark on his ankles the gauge definite and ineradicable of the black tide creeping up his legs, moving from his feet upward as death moves." (321) And at his death, from the wound of his castration "the pent black blood seemed to rush like a released breath" from his "pale body." (440)

These examples will be sufficient to suggest the character of the ratio in this form, the black being both womb and grave, the white all that lies between; the black being feminine, material, and prior to all distinction, while the white is cold, hard, masculine, and the very principle of distinction, seen in terms of the conflict itself as racial "discrimination."

Miss Burden and her ancestry present this "discrimination" in three ways. Her grandfather, drunk, interrupts a wedding to declare "that Lincoln and the Negro and Moses and the children of Israel were the same, and that the Red Sea was just the blood that had to be spilled in order that the black race might cross into the Promised Land." But she herself "thought of all the children coming forever and ever into the world, white, with the black shadow already falling on them before they drew breath. And I seemed to see the black shadow in the shape of a cross." And her father tells her: "Escape it you cannot. The curse of the black race is God's curse. But the curse of the white race is the black man who will be forever God's chosen own because He once cursed him." (238-240)

It will be appropriate to note parenthetically at this point the strong accent characteristically placed on ancestry, especially grandfathers, as a means of locating essences with respect to this matter of black and white. Christmas' grandfather, Doc Hines, has an unofficial vocation to preach white supremacy before Negro congregations. Miss Burden's grandfather, a Northerner, was killed in Jefferson by Colonel Sartoris "over a question of Negro voting." And Hightower's grandfather was killed in Jefferson while raiding General Grant's stores. The primary division of vocabulary is in this way carried back to the War, which for Hightower at least is clearly a localized expression of the War in Heaven and the Fall of the Rebel Angels.

Woman: Man. This relation is seen throughout the book not in the least as natural and unequivocally acceptable, but in general, though to Christmas particularly, as potently, profoundly disturbing, a fatal and tragic flaw in the wholeness of things, a problem to be solved just as his being white or black is a problem to be solved.

In childhood he is unwillingly present at the amorous conjunction of a dietitian and an interne. He has gone to her room to steal toothpaste to eat, and being trapped there behind the curtain of her closet, he eats too much and is discovered when he vomits "in the rife, pinkwomansmelling obscurity." The violence following discovery makes the first connection between sex and brutality, while in the deceptively phallic toothpaste we may permissibly be intended to find his later horror of the menstrual flow, "liquid, deathcolored and foul," the idea of which again causes him to vomit.

Woman, for Christmas, is, like blackness, the mortal pit, the secret, "the soft kindness which he believed himself to be forever victim of and which he hated worse than he did the hard and ruthless justice of men." (158) In his mistress, Joanna Burden, he sees by day and by night in turn a man and a woman—"the woman . . . a horizon of physical security and adultery if not pleasure; the other the mantrained muscles and the mantrained habit of thinking. . . . It was as if he struggled physically with another man for an object of no actual value to either, and for which they struggled on principle alone." (221-222) The woman is time-bound, is life precisely because committed to death, and the struggle acquires a ritual and symbolic character, "as though he entered by stealth to despoil her virginity each time anew. It was as though each turn of dark saw him faced again with the necessity to despoil again that which he had already despoiled—or never had and never would." (221)

It will be well to note here the close connection that is constantly maintained between lust and brutality. The two are not only inseparable but form almost an identity, one will do for the other and replace it; the sexual meeting of man and woman (like the meeting of black and white) is seen as an occasion of violence, bloodshed, death. The central event in the book is the slaying of Miss Burden, whose relations with Christmas are put in terms of violence and struggle; other sexual experiences regularly and as a matter of course involve beating and kicking as an accompaniment of carnality if not, as in Christmas's first approach to a Negro girl, the substitute for it. Christmas' father is killed for his lust as well as for his blackness, Hightower's wife's death is referred to her sexuality, and Christmas murders his stepfather over a whore. Even the gentle Everyman, Byron Bunch, must offer at least the show of violence before he can win his wife. Conversely, brutality may have a specifically sexual nature, as Percy Grimm castrates the dying Christmas. The treatment of this pair of terms throughout the book is an intensive reduction and concentration of the traditional values of love and war; the cynicism of Thersites speaks in the terms of the huge revulsions of Hamlet and Lear.

It is already noticeable that the pairs of terms are not strictly isolable, but mingle and mutually interpenetrate to form a combinative, intricate imagery of which the general characteristics, however, clearly refer to a central relation which is at once marriage and conflict. Man, as one pole of the dialectic, is seen as white, spiritual, rationally divisive, hard, cold, a principle of justice and calculation; Woman, as black, material, mysterious, soft, warm, a principle of secrecy and capriciousness. The marriage combat of these opposed and mutually indispensable forces, which relate somewhat as works and grace, creates the world of the novel, and this primary division appears to be a major law of its composition, one of its generating principles. I know that some, out of a sentimental regard fcr inspiration, for "realism," will complain that novels are not written that way; and doubtless they are perfectly correct so far as that goes, but I would simply remind them that our subject here is a novel which has already been written, and that a principle is not necessarily a method.

We have been speaking thus far as though *Light in August* were almost exclusively the story of Joe Christmas, which it is not; but it will be necessary to return to his story because it is exactly by their contact with him that the others—Miss Burden, Bunch, Lena, Hightower, Brown, the Hineses, and Percy Grimm—achieve whatever consummation is stored up for them: marriage, or death, or vicious heroism, or just going away. Christmas, rejected and rejecting, appears as the touchstone by which life knows itself; at his approach potencies hasten to become actual. Yet the story of his life, from the fifth year to the week before his death—one third of the entire work—is enclosed in a dreamlike, actionless parenthesis so placed as to suggest a comparison with the period during which Lena is in labor, as though to say that the ruinous travel of thirty years is going on in her womb; when the birth is accomplished, Lena's son is taken by Mrs. Hines to be Christmas born again—a delusion not altogether a delusion—and Lena herself is for a moment half-convinced that Christmas is somehow the child's father ("I am afraid she might get me mixed up, like they say how you might cross your eyes and then you cant uncross.")

The others, out of love, or hate, or opportunism, find their need in Christmas; their relation to all that is not self, and sometimes to self also, must somehow pass through that implacable form, which they may use but cannot change. For Byron Bunch he is the possibility of marrying Lena; for Brown he is a thousand dollars. For Joanna Burden he is her own lust after her own corruption, and paradoxically he represents to her also the possibility of improving the status of the Negro in the South. For Doc Hines he is a sacrifice and a vindication of white superiority, for Mrs. Hines a newborn babe again; for Hightower the chance of affirmation, the true "price"; for Percy Grimm the feared and envied power of sex, the darkness of blood.

And only Lena and Byron Bunch, with her child—only the ones who have had no direct contact with the contagion of Christmas—emerge with what they want. Miss Burden is killed; Hightower tells the ennobling lie uselessly, too late, and dies; the Hineses go back to Mottstown; Brown is forced to run away without the thousand dollars; Percy Grimm takes from the dying man the dead and impotent symbol of sexual power.

Of all these lives, which despite the fullness of detail in which they are displayed are nevertheless dialectically and almost schematically developed, that of the Reverend Gail Hightower, D.D., will perhaps be best suited to stand as an example of the compositional method, whereby character itself, so generally allowed the product of observation, is as it were synthesized from the distinctions of the imagery.

Hightower upon his ordination had "pulled every string he could" to be sent to Jefferson; it appears much later that his grandfather had been shot there during the War, and only in this grandfather does Hightower have any life—he keeps recurring to this sole event,

"and the dogma he was supposed to preach [was] all full of galloping cavalry and defeat and glory just as when he tried to tell them
in the street about the galloping horses, it in turn would get all
mixed up with absolution and choirs of martial seraphim." (57) It
is rumored that he is inadequate to the demands of his wife, who
takes trips to Memphis and presently dies violently there, falling or
jumping from a hotel room where she had been staying with another man. Hightower, forced to resign from his church, refuses to
leave town, is beaten up on the suspicion of practices "contrary to
God and nature" with the Negress who is his cook, and finally is
more or less forgotten as even the street on which he lives loses its
former importance in the town.

His real life, then, his only force, is located in the War and produced rhetorically from the pulpit as the War in Heaven; as a man
he is incomplete, and in a way suffers carnal violence and brutality
vicariously, in his wife, just as he suffers later because of the Negress.
Alone, he becomes womanish, doing his own cooking and house-
work, and, in an emergency, acting as midwife. And even this martyrdom, "bought and paid for" with ridicule, ostracism, and physical pain, is at last seen as unacceptable because based on "Satanic"
pride, on a lie, that is, on his real motive in coming to Jefferson—
the image of his grandfather's triumph in heroic death, the vision
that he himself is permitted to have at the moment of his own
death.

He is obscurely Christmas' opposite number; they are remotely
comparable by means of the razor which is Hightower's instrument
as midwife and Christmas' as murderer; also by the fact that Hightower and his wife conveyed messages through a hiding place in a
hollow tree just as Christmas and Miss Burden did. These are resemblances of the slightest kind, to be sure, yet perfectly definite
and even emphatic. In line with Hightower's continual emphasis on
"the price," on the most scrupulous morality, in line also with the
suggestions to be taken up next, it may be that Christmas' replacing
Hightower in the latter's own house is to be regarded as a curious
parody of "driving the money-changers from the temple."

Christmas and Christ. The connection is of course in some sense
indicated, and I shall now list some of the striking points of resemblance. Christmas' father is mysterious and unknown, a black man
in a black night, "a stranger or a neighbor for all [Hines] could have

known by sight and hearing." Christmas is as it were born into manhood in a stable, where he is beaten, recalling later, "On this day I became a man." His feet are washed by a woman. He has a very brief career at preaching, in a Negro church which he afterward wrecks. His preaching consists in cursing God, it is, e.g., a scandal and an offense, and this episode ends on a highly biblical note ("But they could not see him when he departed, nor which way he went") which does not however appear to be a quotation. He is, one may say, crucified, in that of his own will, or his own apathy, he turns himself over from the law to personal violence, which he bears passively; and he does go through an ascension—on the black blast of his blood he seems "to rise soaring into their memories forever and ever. They are not to lose it, in whatever peaceful valleys, beside whatever placid and reassuring streams of old age, in the mirroring faces of whatever children they will contemplate old disasters and newer hopes. It will be there, musing, quiet, steadfast, not fading and not particularly threatful, but of itself alone serene, of itself alone triumphant." (440) And then there is his name, of which more presently.

But this is, it would seem, the point at which we are invited to blind ourselves on the brilliancy of our insight; the indiscriminate statement of this relation on the basis of superficial resemblances ("Muishkin is Christ!" "Stavrogin is Christ!" "Alyosha is Christ!" and so, let it be added, are Julien Sorel, Taras Bulba, Chichikov, and Emma Bovary) is the critical equivalent of eating the haystack to find the needle, and ought to be the source of a more innocent merriment than it generally is.

The ranges open to the author in the imitation of Christ are extensive indeed, but like the painter on this theme he may be emphatic either on the God or the man, on the suffering or the glory, the criminal or the king. If we are to say in any meaningful fashion that Christmas has clearly to do with Christ, we ought to say whether we mean, for example, the Christ of Dürer, of Simone Martini, or Mathias Grünewald, for this will certainly reflect on the world and the work in which this image of Christ lives and dies; and we ought to be careful about basing our statement on the resemblances noted above, which have an altogether plausible and worldly air of wishing not to be overlooked. The proposition, in itself, that a character in a fiction "is" Christ is insufficient because it expresses no more than the enormous possibilities of dialectical exploitation in the Word made flesh, the God who dies; that any particular may exemplify a generality does not alone isolate the particular as itself. "But may I live in hope?" asks the King. "All men, I hope, live so," replies the lady.

Christmas is, indeed, the scapegoat; he is the sheep he sacrifices, washing his hands with the blood, in extenuation of woman's menstrual uncleanness; he may be ironically likened to Isaac, his life rather rented than redeemed by this sacrifice; he has to do with the goat for that obscure demon Azazel, who in the Book of Enoch appears as a Promethean figure bound down in a pit as punishment for having taught mankind the art of war and womankind the use of cosmetics. So Christmas is driven into the wilderness after his life has brought other lives to what actuality they have in them and are able or unable to bear. The aspect of Christ that is depicted here is purely sacramental, purely suffering, dying in demonstration of grace abundant, to which works are as nothing. He is the criminal, the despised and rejected who in his turn despises and rejects, who offers only himself, without forgiveness, kindness, or love. The hero's business is to die for his people, to give his blood for their continuance. Christmas gives his blood, which is black, and as for himself, he has said, while meditating murder, "All I wanted was peace."

He was named Joseph after Mary's husband ("Joe, the son of Joe") and Christmas because he was left on the orphanage step on Christmas Eve; also, as Doc Hines records the word of God, "in sacrilege of My son." According to the same source he is doomed for a sacrifice from the beginning; he is "My abomination," and the Lord tells Hines, "I have set my will a-working and I can leave you here to watch it." As Christmas later sacrifices the sheep, so he too is predestined a sacrifice to the "abomination and outrage" of woman, who is in turn "a instrument of God's wrathful purpose."

There is in this something that is Christian, much that is older, and a little that is more new-fangled. God the Father (speaking now through Heaven Knows What the Grandfather) is vengeful and cruel, hard, powerful, incredibly devious. Not that he is, in man's language, unjust; but his justice is elaborate, formal, reflexive, economical of its materials, and takes precisely a life to happen in. That Christmas in his last days should be displayed, after thirty years, to his aged grandparents, is not extenuated as a coincidence but baldly and awfully put by God the Father (speaking now through God the Novelist), Who put the masculine doom form on the liquidly elusive and feminine sea of matter, and put it there to stay, so that all through this book the masculine image is "angelic," "monastic," with "a rapt, calm expression like a monk in a picture" as it kneels in rigorous prayer, or aims the automatic, or waits for the beating; even the woman, when she kneels to pray, becomes a man, "talking to God as if He were a man in the room with two other men." But they kneel only to Power, and they are its transmitters as well as its victims as it runs through the whole range of the distorted hierarchy that has produced in Christmas and his father its own necessity for that daily renewed and continuing salvation which is, however, but the affirmation and signature of what happens, what things are like. "Why should not their religion drive them to crucifixion of themselves and one another?" asks Hightower, and in the church music he seems to hear "the declaration and dedication of that which they know that on the morrow they will have to do," that is, crucify the man Christmas, who in local circumstances may be called an image of Christ but who is in terms of the novel's form the principle of mediation, progression, movement between one and other. Perhaps the wisest word on his identity is spoken by an anonymous body working in the yard of the orphanage, to whom Christmas said:

> "I aint a nigger," and the nigger says, "You are worse than that. You dont know what you are. And more than that, you wont never know. You'll live and you'll die and you wont never know," and he says, "God aint no nigger," and the nigger says, "I reckon you ought to know what God is, because dont nobody but God know what you is."

The violence, the appearance of freedom, of "realism," can be seen as dialectically produced, as formal necessity which is affirmed as the image of living necessity; not therefore unreal, though quite possibly meaningless; not "something performed in a region without dimension by people without blood," but, quite simply, the imitation of a human action, in which the necessities of fiction analogically represent the necessities of life. And if "both sides take orders from the same headquarters," that need not cause us the suspicion that the fix is in so as to be fatal to the work of art; for the Protestant tragedy differs from the Greek precisely in respect of its attitude toward necessity. Its motives cannot be altogether self-produced or self-contained, nor can its ambiguities, as it shifts from world to world, ever be altogether resolved. And perhaps its power lies rather in ambiguity than completion, as from the visible and sensible world it darkly reads signatures, looking not to "progress and social improvement" but, with equal irony and faith, to the resurrection.

> And we are put on earth a little space
> That we may learn to bear the beams of love;
> And these black bodies and this sunburnt face
> Is but a cloud, and like a shady grove.
>
> For when our souls have learn'd the heat to bear,
> The cloud will vanish; we shall hear his voice,
> Saying: 'Come out from the grove, my love & care,
> And round my golden tent like lambs rejoice.'

The Morality of Art

Lolita. By Vladimir Nabokov. 2 Vols. Olympia Press, Paris, France, 1955.
Pnin. By Vladimir Nabokov. Doubleday, 1957.

My admiration for the writings of Vladimir Nabokov began in college, when I read for the first time *The Real Life of Sebastian Knight* and thereon determined to spend my own more or less real life in writing Sebastian Knight's novels: *The Prismatic Bezel, Success* ("the probing of the aetiological secret of aleatory occurrences"), and most of all *The Doubtful Asphodel* ("A man is dying. . . . The man is the book; the book itself is heaving and dying, and drawing up a ghostly knee"). Of many reasons why I did not carry out this notable project, the best is that Nabokov, who had occupied the field first—immediately after inventing it, in fact—went on to write, if not those books, books very much like them, books about lonely, scholarly heroes a little insane, in situations more than a little absurd, heroes who at the same time "are what can be loosely called 'methods of composition' ": *Bend Sinister*, the *Nine Stories*, the wonderful essay on Gogol, and now *Pnin* and *Lolita*, the latter of which is, I suppose, bound to deepen the odd silence around its author's name.*

I do not know how to account for this silence (which I should be glad to be told I exaggerate), unless it be that among intelligent persons (I mean critics) there exists a prospectively competitive resentment of so much intelligence; or that even the most burning devotee of "irony" has the uneasy suspicion as he reads that Nabokov has gone one irony further and is standing behind him; or that the Freudians will not grant advancement to a writer who has torn from the very stuffing of the couch and the central casting office of dreams

* Prophecy!? (1961).

some absurdities not admitted by the Establishment; or that the con-fraternity of novelists, obeying perhaps some edict of the Council for Creative Writing, cannot abide a practitioner whose relations with his narrators and theirs with their characters are so irregular as to make the sacred "point of view" emit rabbits like a hat. I do not know, and (wearing now my ruthless critical hat) do not much care; it may be that Nabokov, like Stendhal (whom he seems not to con-sider an artist), is already the object of a cult whose members gloat in secret over those "signatures" which turn up, like a cartouche on a Chinese painting, in remote corners of his paragraphs: a moth, a butterfly, or a cloud-reflecting mud puddle. But I don't know that either, and must get to business.

The later of the two books at hand is a collection of anecdotes about a White Russian whose declining years are spent teaching Rus-sian at Waindell College in the United States. We read of Timofey Pnin's good nature, his dithering, his sufferings (teeth, lost wife, job), his troubles with timetables, back roads, and rented rooms. The vari-ous episodes are charmingly told, by turns funny and pathetic, some-times though rarely falling into that rich, warm humanity so ad-mired by certain book reviewers and detested by Nabokov, who wrote of Gogol's death that "the scene is unpleasant and has a hu-man appeal which I deplore" (*Nikolai Gogol*). As a novel, this book looks somewhat accidental, though held together (if it is) by one pretty device emerging at the finish, where the first-person narrator appears on the scene to take Pnin's job and incidentally reveal that most of what he knows about Pnin is gathered at second hand from people who impersonate him.

The earlier work, *Lolita*, may well be the funniest tragedy since *Hekuba*. That it is published abroad is possibly on one of two ac-counts: that it comes under some statute about pornography and/or obscenity; or that no American publisher, if any were asked, was willing to take the chance; but I am unable to confirm either of these conjectures. The mock preface—"Lolita, or the Confession of a White Widowed Male, such were the two titles under which the writer of the present note received the strange pages it preambu-lates"—does, in speaking of scenes that "a certain type of mind might call aphrodisiac," mention Judge Woolsey's 1933 decision about "an-other, considerably more outspoken, book," but I do not know cer-tainly whether *Lolita* does or does not come under the stipulation which forbade the importation of *Ulysses* (Section 305, Tariff Act of

1930, Title 19, US Code, Section 1305). To be on the safe side I rowed out into extra-territorial waters, where a kindly naval gentleman handed me his copy, which I read all during a sunny afternoon, taking certain notes, and handed back after.

Some literal-minded persons doubtless believe that the problem of pornography in the novel had to do with a particular sort of word (which I had best not mention here, since a review is not somehow as expectably sexy as a novel), and that this problem has long since been solved by the New Enlightenment, which knows all about how soldiers talk and how fundamentally harmless it all is. But that is not quite so. As Nabokov's prefator (John Ray, Jr., Ph.D.) says of *Lolita:* "Not a single obscene term is to be found in the whole work; indeed, the robust philistine who is conditioned by modern conventions into accepting without qualms a lavish array of four-letter words in a banal novel, will be quite shocked by their absence here." On this same point I recall the troubles of an acquaintance of mine who in one of his novels employed the word "semen," drawing from his publisher a response which began: "Dear ———, I hope you will not consider me a 'Nice Nellie,' but, frankly, we feel. . . ." The author, who had not considered the publisher a "Nice Nellie" or near it, insisted and won the day; but the occurrence taught him (he said) a lesson, that the "obscenity" of a word consists not in the number of its letters (*those* words have all been made safe), but in the sensitivity of the feelings touched by that word; and there we arrive at something which goes deeper than the public morality, we arrive at the principle whereby language itself is (or more often is not) kept alive. It was perhaps in this sense that Shelley wistfully spoke of incest as "a very poetical circumstance."

Lolita is the story of the love affair between a gentleman in his forties, Humbert Humbert (pseudon.), and a twelve-year-old girl named Dolores Haze (var. Dolly, Lo, Lola, Lolita). Humbert Humbert, a European of somewhat inclusive national antecedents (his father "a salad of racial genes"), writes this memoir from prison, where, the preface tells us, he died awaiting trial (not, however, for the offense we should expect). He recounts to begin with something of his early life and, in particular, of his carnal predilection for certain female children whom he calls "nymphets"—girls between nine and fourteen (but not all such girls: "otherwise, we who are in the know, we lone voyagers, we nympholepts, would have long gone insane") whose true nature is "not human, but nymphic (that is, demoniac).'' He partly believes the singularity of his desires to have been fixed by an episode in his early adolescence, one summer on the Riviera: an unconsummated passion for a girl named Annabel who died shortly afterward: "In a certain magic and fateful way Lolita began with Annabel," and, on first seeing Lolita, "It was the same child." This flair for recurrence represents, however, the piety not of Freud, whose views and school the narrator holds in some contempt, but rather of Proust—"another internal combustion martyr," says Humbert Humbert. And in any event it doesn't much matter; by the time he arranges to possess Lolita at the seashore, in reminiscent circumstances, "the search for a Kingdom by the Sea, a Sublimated Riviera, or whatnot, far from being the impulse of the subconscious, had become the rational pursuit of a purely theoretical thrill. The angels knew it, and arranged things accordingly"— that is, as a common, uncommonly comic, disaster.

To be near Lolita, Humbert Humbert marries her widowed mother, his landlady in a small New England town where he has come to rest after a somewhat odd career rhythmically marked by nervous breakdowns. The mother, who disgusts him both sexually and culturally, dies in the absolute convenience of an automobile accident exactly one minute after discovering the truth of his relations with her daughter. He then abducts Lolita from her summer camp, and the middle part of his narrative tells of the wild fugue from motel to motel of Humbert Humbert and his daughter-mistress, over a period of some two years. At last she escapes him and goes to another person (whose pervasive presence near the scene has been indicated throughout by indirections as slight as the Brownian Movement); when he finds her, much later, she has left that person, too, and is married and about to have a child. Leaving her peaceably with her husband, Humbert Humbert, in what must certainly be the funniest murder scene in literature, destroys his successor, and it is for this crime, presumably, that he is about to be tried at the time of his death. He concludes his memoir with a word of fatherly advice and blessing to Lolita, who, however, as we know from the preface, has since died in childbirth.

That, more or less, is the action, which can be viewed as remorseless, simple, and inevitable, like a Greek tragedy; or else as a mass of absurdities, coincidences, and perverse exfoliations, like a Greek tragedy. The sense of that major coincidence, for example, of the mother's death, is that it purifies the moral demonstration, making the poor sinner's bondage develop directly out of his unthinkable freedom, with all civil limits removed. But I suppose it is necessary, so as not to seem to be shirking, to speak a little about the morality of this book, which does in fact share some tonalities, some brush-work—let us be eloquently vague—with books which, in my youth, were sold to children secretly and at connoisseurs' prices by elevator boys and the proprietors of candy stores.

Nabokov's editor, John Ray, Jr., Ph.D., does us the service of de-fending the manuscript in his charge by means of some red herrings, for instance:

> "H.H." 's impassioned confession is a tempest in a test-tube; . . . at least 12% of American adult males—a "conservative" estimate accord-ing to Dr. Blanche Schwarzmann (verbal communication)—enjoy yearly, in one way or another, the special experience "H.H." describes with such despair.

But "Dr. Blanche Schwarzmann" is a peripheral character in the story, and the statistics, true or false, do not matter. So also with his moral conclusion:

> . . . in this poignant personal study there lurks a general lesson; the wayward child, the egotistic mother, the panting maniac—these are not only vivid characters in a unique story: they warn us of dangerous trends; they point out potent evils. "Lolita" should make all of us— parents, social workers, educators—apply ourselves with still greater vig-ilance and vision to the task of bringing up a better generation in a safer world.

This attitude, in Nabokov's opinion, would be like that of those Russian critics who saw Gogol's *The Government Inspector* as "so-cial criticism" and his *Dead Souls* as a species of documentary: not merely that it falsifies experience, but also that it is quite irrelevant to experience.

Humbert Humbert, of course, is deeper and subtler than that. His attitudes toward himself and his desires and actions are very various. Sometimes, in an access of cultural relativism, he tries to justify him-self: "Lepcha old men of eighty copulate with girls of eight, and nobody minds." Sometimes he is scientific: "I am not concerned with so-called sex at all. Anybody can imagine those elements of animality. A greater endeavor lures me on: to fix once for all the perilous magic of nymphets." More often, and without losing a certain air of pride and cunning, he is horrified: ". . . lanky, big-boned, woolly-chested Humbert Humbert, with thick black eyebrows and a queer accent, and a whole cesspoolful of rotting monsters behind his slow boyish smile." Sometimes he is pathetic: "Humbert Humbert tried hard to be good. . . . But how his heart beat when among the innocent throng, he espied a demon child, *'enfant charmante et fourbe,'* dim eyes, bright lips, ten years in jail." . . . and appealing: "Please, reader . . . try to imagine the doe in me, trembling in the forest of my own iniquity; let's even smile a little." And his view is somewhat complicated by the added circumstance that Lolita, at the age of twelve, turns out to have been thoroughly corrupted already, elsewhere, by someone else: "I am going to tell you something very strange: it was she who seduced me."

Nonetheless, toward the end his dilemma becomes more critical, bringing Humbert Humbert to the question of wickedness itself, which is ultimately the question of meaning in the universe, and which he puts in somewhat the same way as did Ivan Karamazov:

> Unless it can be proven to me—to me as I am now, today, with my heart and my beard, and my putrefaction—that in the infinite run it does not matter a jot that a North-American girl-child named Dolores Haze had been deprived of her childhood by a maniac, unless this can be proven (and if it can, then life is a joke), I see nothing for the treatment of my misery but the melancholy and very local palliative of articulate art.

Nabokov's own artistic concern, here as elsewhere, I should say, has no more to do with morality than with sex; with either or both only incidentally, as problem, as offering poignant particular illuminations of what it is to live. His subject is always the inner insanity and how it may oddly match or fail to match the outer absurdity, and this problem he sees as susceptible only of *artistic* solutions. He may well be the accountant of the universe—in *Pnin,* the narrator recalls a speck of dust extracted from his eye in 1911: "I wonder where that speck is now? The dull, mad fact is that it *does* exist somewhere"—but he is not its moral accountant, and his double entries seek only the exact balance between inside and outside, self and world, in a realm—"aurochs and angels, the secret of durable pigments, prophetic sonnets, the refuge of art"—to which morality stands but as a dubious, Euclidean convenience; that balance is what in the arts is traditionally called *truth.*

Lolita is nevertheless a moral work, if by morality in literature we are to understand the illustration of a usurious rate of exchange between our naughty desires and virtuous pains, of the process whereby pleasures become punishments, or our vices suddenly become recognizable as identical with our sufferings. In some dream-America, *Lolita* would make a fine test case for the Producers' Code, for if Humbert Humbert is a wicked man, and he is, he gets punished for it in the end. Also in the middle. And at the beginning.

But I don't care to pursue the general question just now. I have so often heard it said that Shakespeare's humor is grand because though it is often coarse it is never vulgar. Lately I have read in a book by Edith Hamilton (*The Great Age of Greek Literature*) that Aristophanes' humor is grand because though it is often vulgar it is never degenerate. And now here is Humbert Humbert, who is also very funny. Rather than push the great argument one step further to the inevitable prat-fall—though it is always degenerate it is rarely dead?—I had better stop here.

The Ills from Missing Dates

Nabokov's Dozen, A Collection of Thirteen Stories. By Vladimir Nabokov. Doubleday, 1958.

In trying to fix the quality of experience dominant over these stories I thought of some famous lines by William Empson:

> It is the poems you have lost, the ills
> From missing dates, at which the heart expires.

Thus Mr. Nabokov also; where are the poets, governesses, girl friends of yesteryear? he asks over and over. More precisely, *who* were they? People like Nina ("Spring in Fialta"), Perov ("A Forgotten Poet"), or the wife of the narrator in "That in Aleppo Once" slip in and out of their stories as they slip in and out of their identities—identities for a long time nebulous, "historical," dependent upon the capriciousness of memory, then suddenly precise and unforgettable for an instant.

If that abused (and ordinarily abusive) word "experimental" may for once apply to something, these pieces exhibit Mr. Nabokov's experiments on the identities of his characters, on his relations with them, and on the questionably theatrical symbolisms, or styles of presentation, of Life, who is seen as "an assistant producer." These identities and relations are multiple, fluidly shifting; few of the persons involved are so simple as to be merely doubles, like the one in "Conversation Piece" ("a disreputable namesake of mine") or the poor, prize-winning traveler in "Cloud, Castle, Lake," who is, says the author, "one of my representatives." The result is the depiction of a world by now familiar to Mr. Nabokov's readers, a world of objects fragmentary and allusive, elusive, illusive (all three will have to do), suggesting more or less fleetingly their relation to some lost whole; a world in which the possible immanence of meaning is either

Reprinted from *Venture*, Vol. 3, Nos. 1-2, 1959.

a stage trick on the part of the assistant producer, or else the disastrous visionary madness of the perceiver. For illustration, let one story stand for all, as by its title, "Signs and Symbols," it seems to want to do. Here the sort of world I have ascribed to the author is compressed into eight pages which come as near the absolute of art as anything I have seen in the short story.

An old couple, refugees, are going to the sanitarium to take a birthday present to their incurably deranged son; they have chosen "a dainty and innocent trifle: a basket with ten different fruit jellies in ten little jars," and this choice has cost them much thought, since the young man's malady is such that almost any object in the world achieves for him a frightening, hostile significance, or else is simply meaningless and useless.

At the sanitarium they learn that their child has again attempted to kill himself; he is all right, but a visit is out of the question. They go home, they think about the past, they torture themselves, and, after midnight, decide they must bring the boy home, no matter what the inconvenience, what the danger, since until they do so life is impossible.

The decision makes them happier, and at this moment the telephone rings, frightening them; it is a wrong number, "a girl's dull little voice" wanting to speak to "Charlie." The telephone rings again, right away, and the old woman tells the girl "you are turning the letter O instead of the zero." The old people sit down to "their unexpected festive midnight tea," the man examines with pleasure the birthday present, the ten little jars; and the telephone rings again.

Readers who think first of "plot" will quite properly say, "but that isn't a story"; and so, in my description, it isn't. Yet in this simply articulated space a vast and tragic life works itself out, presenting the tension between meaning (which is madness) and the meaningless (which is the normal, or sane, condition of present life). The system of the young man's delusions has the high-sounding name of "referential mania," and might as well be called "Poet's Disease":

In these very rare cases the patient imagines that everything happening around him is a veiled reference to his personality and existence. He excludes real people from the conspiracy—because he considers himself to be so much more intelligent than other men. Phenomenal nature shadows him wherever he goes. Clouds in the staring sky transmit to one another, by means of slow signs, incredibly detailed information regarding him. His inmost thoughts are discussed at nightfall, in manual alphabet, by darkly gesticulating trees. Pebbles or stains or sun flecks form patterns representing in some awful way messages which he must intercept. Everything is a cipher and of everything he is the theme. Some of the spies are detached observers, such are glass surfaces and still pools; others, such as coats in store windows, are prejudiced witnesses, lynchers at heart; others again (running water, storms) are hysterical to the point of insanity, have a distorted opinion of him and grotesquely misinterpret his actions. He must be always on his guard and devote every minute and module of life to the decoding of the undulation of things. The very air he exhales is indexed and filed away. If only the interest he provokes were limited to his immediate surroundings—but alas it is not! With distance the torrents of wild scandal increase in volume and volubility. The silhouettes of his blood corpuscles, magnified a million times, flit over vast plains; and still farther, great mountains of unbearable solidity and height sum up in terms of granite and groaning firs the ultimate truth of his being.

Over against this hostile and sinister truth (the universe does mean something, and if you are able to perceive it you will go insane and die) is set the life of the old couple, displaced persons with their hopes and memories (a pack of soiled cards and old photograph albums), with the near-absolute, meaningless chaos which twenty years of history have made of their lives. And the two halves into which the universe has thus split are mediated (not put back together) by those telephone calls. Just here, where the Satevepost reader waits for his satisfaction (it will be the doctor, announcing a sudden cure by miracle drug), and the reader of rather more artsy-crafty periodicals waits for *his* satisfaction (the young man has finally done away with himself), comes the exact metaphor for the situation, as the telephone, the huge, mechanical system whose buzz relates everyone to everyone else, has the last word: "you are turning the letter O instead of the zero."

Detail for detail there's a great deal more, but that is more or less how it goes. Not all the stories are that good (which would be asking a great deal), but this is a wonderful book. It is good that the (wildly improbable) success of *Lolita* could exert enough leverage to raise its author's short stories once more over the horizon, and all Mr. Nabokov's readers, the new ones and the others who will remember much of the present volume from the New Directions edition of *Nine Stories* (long out of print and hard or impossible to come by), ought to be grateful.

The Discovery of Cozzens

By Love Possessed. By James Gould Cozzens. Harcourt, Brace, 1957.

The public acclaim given James Gould Cozzens' novel was extraordinary even in a land where great books appear steadily, two and three in any week. The earnest professional enthusiasm of so many reviewers, the air of relief pervading their notices ("Here at last is something we can really be *for*"), their readiness to turn this book into a weapon against other sorts of book, are matters interesting in themselves, though possibly of greater interest for sociology than for letters.

By Love Possessed is "a masterpiece," "the chief literary event of the year," "a rich and wise novel," "a grown-up novel by a grown-up man for a grown-up audience," "the best American novel of the year," "deserving national praise and international consideration," and so on. The market responded to all this rapidly, and after only a few weeks Mr. Cozzens' book arrived at the top of the best-seller list. It has been proposed as the proper candidate for the Pulitzer Prize and the National Book Award, and its author nominated by at least one reviewer for the Nobel Prize.

It is characteristic of modern literature that the first-rate and the popular do not typically come together; what is immediately accessible is not often enduringly useful. That this is so has been on occasion of regret and sometimes rage to many reviewers, especially those who write chiefly for middlebrow journals of large circulation, and who, it may fairly be said, despise comic books and confectionery fiction on one hand as much as they detest little magazines and "modern poetry" on the other. In the very high praise these writers accord Mr. Cozzens, the claim is explicit that he is to be regarded as the champion of the right, in literature, as against the wrong, or left; that the Establishment, white, Protestant, Republican, may find in him a defender who has expropriated the weapons of the other side (analytic intelligence, candor, disillusion), and made them, in his fable, harmless if not altogether benign. Consequently, much of this criticism is somewhat shrill, tendentious, prospectively defiant, as though anticipating objection, and much concerned with lambasting a number of abstractions, or idols, got up for the purpose of being knocked down.

Many reviewers, generously indignant over the corruption of our times, have composed a drama about literary reputation. In this morality play Mr. Cozzens represents patient merit spurned by the unworthy, and his success with this book is not merely *his* success, but an allegory, also, of quiet worth triumphing over gaudy show, of solid virtue at last imposing itself by force of character upon the pretensions of fashionable literature. Mr. Cozzens, as the hero of this play, has remained obscure because he does not do the things which are supposed responsible for literary fame: "He is never seen at literary parties, rarely has been interviewed, seldom stirs from his farm." Cozzens, in one of the rare interviews, adds that he regards himself as "more or less illiberal," that his preference is to be left alone, and that he does not go to movies, concerts, plays, or art shows.

Some reviewers complained of the mass audience, which they saw not as villainous but as unenlightened. Despite praise from critics, three previous Book-of-the-Month Club selections, one Pulitzer Prize, and the fact that most of what Brendan Gill calls "the canonical novels" are still in print, several in paperbacks, "no Cozzens novel has ever become a really big seller." This condition seems in a fair way to be remedied.

Then there appears the wicked intellectual, whom a number of reviewers savagely held responsible for keeping Cozzens all these years from the critical esteem which properly should have been his —"the most lordly of the academic critics," "the magisterial critics whose encyclicals appear in the literary quarterlies and academic journals" (John Fischer, in *Harpers*). "Critics and the kind of readers who start fashionable cults have been markedly cool to him" (Brendan Gill, in *The New Yorker*). "The interior decorators of U.S. letters—the little-magazine critics whose favorite furniture is the pigeonhole—find that Cozzens fits no recent fictional compartments, and usually pretend that he does not exist" (Anon., in *Time*).

This sort of wrist-slapping, these hurt sneers and offended frowns, which give to literary criticism something of the scholarly air of a proxy fight, suggest the very grave accusation of a conspiracy in restraint of trade, and should therefore perhaps be documented or else not made at all. For the defense, I may mention that I have seen only one intelligent, ordered, and exhaustive appraisal of Mr. Cozzens' body of work: Stanley Edgar Hyman's "James Gould Cozzens and the Art of the Possible," in the *New Mexico Quarterly*, Winter 1949. Nothing I have read about *By Love Possessed* comes remotely near its quality.

The tensions of the biographical and social drama were duplicated in the reviewers' aesthetic and moral judgment about the composition of the novel and the character of its protagonist. Of those who touched on the matter at all, most reached substantial agreement on Cozzens' qualities as a writer and their relation to qualities now admired in literature: "Cozzens is dry, classical, cerebral," "a classic mind, operating in a romantic period," "a man closer in spirit to Samuel Johnson than he could ever be to Samuel Beckett," "a degree of professional responsibility that few young writers even try to acquire; Cozzens would no more deform a character to meet the demands of his plot than he would steal from his Delaware Valley neighbors" (a comparison piously appropriate to the novel itself). "In contrast to Faulkner, say, a moralist who writes by ear and accident, Cozzens has developed an almost forbiddingly finished technique."

Similarly, the character of Arthur Winner defined itself, for some, with reference to its opposite. This middle-aged, successful, intelligent, and responsible lawyer, honest not quite to the limits of possibility, shows Mr. Cozzens as heroically opposed to the fashion in heroes: the novel is "a bold presentation, in the face of the current craze for the unrelated man, the drifting man, the outsider, of the ignored and undervalued but still existent related man" (Jessamyn West, in the New York *Herald Tribune*). "Arthur Winner is a rational rather than a traditional conservative . . . reasonable enough to recognize the limits of reason" (Granville Hicks, in *The New Leader*). "He is the quintessence of our best qualities" (Brendan Gill). Similar claims of fidelity to contemporary life are made for the other characters and the action: "[Cozzens] has created recognizable people with recognizable problems in a recognizable world."

Of reviewers who regarded the book as a masterpiece or near it, almost all had minor reservations, chiefly to do with style: "a little weedgrown and murky" (comparison of the mountain stream), "frosted with parenthetical clauses, humpbacked syntax, Jamesian involutions, Faulknerian meanderings" (comparison of glass). "Henry James in his most intense writing never . . . wrote longer, more involved sentences." This resemblance to James, which I was nowhere able to identify, came up frequently, and it may have been on this account that several reviewers, right in the midst of their enthusiasm, revealed that they were bored and wished the book might have been cut: "You may come away from the reading of this novel with a certain degree of tiredness." John Fischer had two other objections more or less explicitly shared by some other reviewers: "(1) Several women, of sound taste and judgment, tell me that they find the story disconcerting. They are not used to seeing love handled in such an unsentimental fashion, and they are not sure they like it. . . . (2) Other people, by no means prudes, have suggested that *By Love Possessed* is not a suitable book for the young. They may be right."

I have seen only one adverse notice. Sarel Eimerl, in *The New Republic*, glancingly attacks the novel for its style, the complications of its plot ("it is nonsense to claim that a writer who uses such methods is giving us a slice of Life as it Really Is"), its tendency to lecture and, especially, for the concentration in time and place of such a quantity of violence and crime, asking whether a typical American community "would prove, if analyzed, to consist predominantly of sadists, nymphomaniacs, embezzlers, and suicides." This is something like the argument Sainte-Beuve used on *Madame Bovary* (some Norman housewives—he had met them personally—did not deceive their husbands, were virtuous, hard-working, etc.). So, no doubt, there are in real life Republican lawyers and Episcopalian vestrymen who do not cuckold their best friends or countenance embezzlement, however reluctantly, on compassionate grounds. It was an odd argument about *Madame Bovary*, and it is odd still. But I sympathize with the writer's feeling that objections may be made, and exceptions taken, to the general view.

I liked *By Love Possessed* more for its discursive qualities than for any other reasons. The narrative had a kind of arbitrary, cumulative quality which a little resembled the movement of a detective novel or a radio serial. I enjoyed quite well in themselves the speechifying of Julius Penrose and the meditations of Arthur Winner, being pleased with the combination of colloquial wit and learning easily displayed, but always feeling that the author spoke for, rather than through, his characters, of whose individual existence I was never convinced. Penrose, for instance, is a type figure who, in a romantic novel of the last century, would have been seen—crippled, and with a luminous intelligence running to cynicism—as related more or less theologically to Satan or Prometheus; while in a movie he might be portrayed à la Lionel Barrymore as a heart of gold under a gruff exterior. So in fact he is portrayed in the novel, in a piece of not uncharacteristic psychological analysis, as Arthur Winner thinks that "both Julius and common consent erred, too easily taken in by harshnesses of manner and sharpnesses of speech which, in fact, manifested that Julius was a sensitive man, not an insensitive."

Arthur Winner seems both stereotyped and impossibly idealized: from one point of view a man of fair ability and average honesty, whose tragic flaw will be a want of self-awareness; from another point of view, a man deeply knowledgeable about himself and others, and vastly (unbelievably) cultivated, who habitually thinks in tags from literature (Shakespeare mostly, though a crisis brings at once to his mind phrases from Donne and Swift). The author's conception of the character requires the most penetrative self-scrutiny and a near-absolute wisdom about human motives, while the action requires the same character to be crucially unaware; between the two ideas a gap remains.

In the same way, I was disturbed by what seemed a paradoxical double necessity for the novelist: to produce a tragic action, from which the protagonist, by reason of the faith we are told to place in him, should be withheld. Like most of Mr. Cozzens' novels (making some exception for *Castaway*), *By Love Possessed* suffers from a want of essential drama: though all the great rites of tragedy are prepared and invoked, the demonstration remains at last unmade; as though the author had some reservations—possibly about "real life" and "the way things really work out"—which protect his major actors from their ends. I cannot help thinking that the book, in this respect, functions as a kind of secular apologetics, the defense of an image of life, much idealized, which is regarded with so much reverence and nostalgia that its exemplars may not and must not be brought down from their high places; as though some Producers' Code forbade that a dignified professional man, kind father, dutiful son, prop of the community, should go the way Oedipus went, and Antony, and Julien Sorel. The mere acknowledgment of the possibility will do instead, so that in the end honor, wealth, position, are saved at the expense of honesty, on the stated ground that considerations higher than honesty (charity, compassion, expedience) are involved, a shift of justifications not without its Jesuitical quality.

Some such reservation produces typically, I think, the dubious inner nature of Cozzens' novels, in which everything gets said—brilliantly said sometimes—and nothing, finally, gets done. His persons perceive, with every refinement of stoical *apatheia* matched by intelligent epicurean compromise, that man does not deserve to be saved and will not be saved from his folly or his wisdom—they are humorously contemptuous of the young and foolish, who do not understand this axiom ("You shall know the truth, and the truth shall make you sick")—and they go on discussing the matter until they are saved. Dr. Bull in *The Last Adam*, Abner Coates in *The Just and the Unjust*, Colonel Ross and Captain Hicks in *Guard of Honor*, and now Arthur Winner, all, to Mr. Cozzens, are the salt of the earth, to whom nothing may happen. They simply go on, their awareness of life's melancholy pointlessness substituting for their crucial experience of it. And their immunity is, as it were, made up for by any number of incidental deaths and disasters in the minor people surrounding them: the paratroopers in *Guard of Honor*, victims of typhus in *The Last Adam*, most of the passengers and crew of *S.S. San Pedro*, etc. In *By Love Possessed*, as in *The Just and the Unjust*, the hero is surrounded by sacrifices, victims of crime and victims of the law, victims of disease and victims of medicine, who seem to offer up his vicarious atonement. Perhaps it is for this reason that a Cozzens novel characteristically involves a huge complex of persons and institutions; not so much a plot (though he always begins as if there were going to be, this time) as a fund which may be drawn on (or added to) at will, and out of which a few elements form the possibility of a resolution.

Toward the end of *Guard of Honor*, Colonel Ross considers that life "seemed mostly a hard-luck story, very complicated, beginning nowhere and never ending, unclear in theme and confusing in action." Though *By Love Possessed* is more thoroughly composed than the other novels, this epitome seems to hold of it also; not, I should think, from inability on Mr. Cozzens' part but rather from a conscious and willed decision about both life and art—that tragedy, for the man of reason, can only be illusion, and that a rational despair can no longer be met by the traditional resources of art.

I respect the view, though I do not share it. I respect and admire the somber intelligence illustrated in Mr. Cozzens' sermons on reason, futility, and the will. I also am impressed, and a little amazed, at the obedience of a large reading public which, having heard for years from its popular critics that the Great American Novel would be optimistic, sane, cheerful, and full of positive values, now accepts from the same critics, as the same Great American Novel, this work of a mind whose cold temper and grim austerity and firm conviction of despair make existentialists look somewhat cozy and Rotarian, if not evangelical.

Fiction Chronicle

The Rack. By A. E. Ellis. Atlantic-Little, Brown, 1959.
The Optimist. By Herbert Gold. Atlantic-Little, Brown, 1959.
Men Die. By H. L. Humes. Random House, 1959.
Saturday Night and Sunday Morning. By Alan Sillitoe. Knopf, 1959.
The Cave. By Robert Penn Warren. Random House, 1959.

Alan Sillitoe's first novel, *Saturday Night and Sunday Morning*, is strong and modest work. The two qualities seem essentially related: one's sense of the story's truth, that is, owes a good deal to the author's avoiding any discussion of its Truth.

The narrative is about a young factory worker, Arthur Seaton, who is drunk when we meet him, sober when we leave him. At the outset he is carrying on an affair with the wife of a fellow worker, an older man; at the end he is planning to get married to a young woman of his own. In between he endures some of the consequences of his mode of life: assists at an abortion, is beaten up. But this is not a novel about sin, repentance, and redemption, and therein lies its chief virtue, that it gives a serious impression of how society, by equal measures of seduction and exaction, stabilizes its relations (whether these be wicked or not) with a human being.

The first thing to notice about Arthur Seaton is that he is not a young man of the middle class, and has not got the intention of climbing into that class, either, any more than he has any practicable intention of overthrowing society by revolution. Upon this simple observation, which may occasion us some little dismay as we reflect to what extent, and in how many examples, the novel is absolutely presupposed to be a middle-class business, we may go on to note some other attractive things about this young man: that, as he is not a member of the middle class, it is not necessary (not novelistically necessary) for him to hate or fear his parents; that, in fact,

Reprinted by permission from *Partisan Review*, Vol. XXVII, No. 1, Winter 1960. Copyright 1959 by *Partisan Review*.

he enjoys and thrives on family life; and that he does not wish to improve his situation by becoming a novelist. All very different, considering the degree to which the novel has become populated with the many if not various progeny of Stephen Dedalus, Paul Morel, Monk Webber.

So instead of a sensitive young man, you have here a very clear-sighted one, who pursues his selfish and illicit pleasures with considerable courage, honesty, and kindness, who gets what advantage he can from the licentious Saturday night of his youth, enduring its pains as well, and understands that its inevitable passage into the Sunday morning of marriage and sobriety does not mean the repentant acknowledgment of any higher justice, but simply his acquiescence in a process which his own nature compels him to desire no less than the nature of society commands him to submit to it. His self-reliant stoicism, compounded of impudence, shrewdness, and vanity, is neither adolescent nor solipsistic; as he says to the husband he has cuckolded (and who has been instrumental in his being beaten up by two soldiers): "You don't need to tell me what's right and what ain't right. Whatever I do is right, and what people do to me is right. And what I do to you is right, as well." It is an engaging thing about Arthur Seaton, that in deciding to change the course of his life—to swallow the bait and be hooked, as he puts it—he does not go back on this ruefully funny and melancholy attitude.

Mr. Sillitoe writes his story most attractively, accepting its humor with its seriousness and blessedly not playing it for laughs: this is especially true of a remarkable account of an abortion procured by gin and a hot bath, where pathos and absurdity beautifully combine; and of the depiction of family life at Christmas, a scene whose rich impression of kindness and confusion, of abounding goodness in a bad world, is subtly influential in turning Arthur toward his own marriage.

Mr. H. L. Humes' somewhat starkly titled *Men Die* is in some ways the simplest of the works at hand, a kind of allegorical fantasy; at the same time, though, it is a technical achievement of dazzling virtuosity. Though put off at first by some of its mannerisms, I finished by being almost altogether fascinated.

The story draws its materials from one blinding instant, the explosion of a Navy munitions dump on a Caribbean island, shortly before the Great War of 1939; in this blast all personnel are destroyed except for five Negroes imprisoned pending their trial for mutiny, and the young Lieutenant Sulgrave who is responsible for them. The novelist, with an ingenuity reminiscent of that displayed in the demonstrations of topology, explores the antecedents and consequences of this instant in a series of scenes and meditations. Thus there are revealed, for example, not only the madness of the Commander, Hake, which the moment of the explosion puts in the past, but also some of the circumstances surrounding that madness, the past of that past, told to Sulgrave by the Commander's widow, Vannessa, at a time which the moment of the explosion puts in the future; past and future, by this means, come into a very elegantly patterned and classical relation with motive, prophecy, idea.

I don't think it's any part of the reviewer's business to tell over the plot in detail (since I have been unable despite all instruction to give up a simple pleasure in stories, which I hope some of my readers share), and so I shall confine my comment to some generalities about the narration.

The dramatic novel, the one which by largely implicit means seeks to relate time and idea, time and fate, which reveals the most widely separated actions as radically bound to a single center, is a crucial instance at present for any debate about the continued existence of the novelist's art. At one extreme, you have the cheesy classicism of the detective story, where purity of form is exactly equivalent to poverty of imagination; at the other, the grand peripeties and recognitions of tragedy. The conduct of this business, when it is brought into intimate relation with a certain realism of tone and detail, as in the novel it must be, is invariably risky; we seem to watch great ingenuity struggling to defeat itself, and our admiration for the superb predestinations of the design is brought into conflict with our feelings that real people do not behave in this way, that real people could not possibly be related in these hidden and devious ways, &c. A crucial instance, as I say—because it puts any assertions about form right where they ought to be, in relation to assertions about destiny. The beauty which is sought is, to my mind, the greatest beauty of all, that to be derived from a closed situation apart from the world and thus comparable to the world: the parable of composition itself as the law of nature. So it is, for instance, in *The Tempest*, which, like Mr. Humes' book, takes place on a magic island.*

* Cp. also William Golding's *Lord of the Flies*.

At the same time, owing to the novelist's concern for "realism," that is, for a convincing triviality in the manners and details, the execution of this design is often attended by absurdities.

Mr. Humes' parable is essentially, I think, a grand one: the explosive island, stored (by Negroes regarded as expendable) with the powers of death, commanded by the insane and sexually impotent superego, who is in turn advised by a subordinate representative of intellect and art (helpless, kindly, cynical); the young man Sulgrave, brought in as bewildered and hurt mediator between the cold, white, punitive authority and the black, enslaved power (the Negroes and the explosives)—all this is compelling and convincing in the implacable simplicity of its relations and the inevitable, driving motion to fulfillment of its design. I may mention especially two splendid scenes, one in which a surprise fire drill in the midst of inspection brings on disaster, and another in which the Commander exposes to Sulgrave not only himself but an uproarious exegesis of history as a mystical and prophetic cipher. A marvelous talent is at work in these places.

About other matters I am less happy. The introduction of the woman Vannessa brings about a loss in clarity, a certain queasily erotic sentimentalizing of the story, and the making of some connections which strike me as forced.

I should mention, though, that I am *not* criticizing the style in which the woman's reflections are set forth, that is, in a series of double-column thoughts and comments on the thoughts which indeed at first resemble the poetry of a mad bookkeeper. On first seeing these, I was prepared to be outraged. But since we seem to be at present in a period of automatic condemnation of anything that looks like a "device," I had better record my later impression that all this worked out quite well as a convincing imitation of the process of her distracted thoughts.

Mr. Humes has attempted something very wonderful indeed. My feelings against the accomplishment have to do with some few signs of looseness and padding, and with a certain trailing away toward the end, a weakness of resolution attendant on his concentration on the love affair between the widow and the young man. These faults, however—and they may be faults only, or mostly, to that strict view one takes when called upon to "criticize" something—scarcely diminish my admiring appreciation of his beautiful work.

Robert Penn Warren's *The Cave* resembles Mr. Humes' book in one essential way, that is, that people apparently unrelated, or related in apparently superficial ways, are brought into radical relation with one another by means of a single situation, in this instance that of a young man trapped in a cave. It is an incidental resemblance, perhaps, that the single situation has to do, in both books, with something underground, with ideas of mortality and mystery associated with the earth. But here the differences begin.

Mr. Warren has here, as always in his novels and his narrative poems, a strong, almost religious sense that he is telling a parable, not just a story in which we may find more or less meaning; this sense he betrays in a portentous anxiety lest we miss the profound import in what is going on. At the same time, though, he has an immense, almost uncontrollable gift for those details which bring to the reader the conviction that what is going on is, after all, nothing more nor less than "real life" itself: To hear him describe, as he does to begin with and thereafter again, a pair of boots ("They were number X-362 in the Monkey Ward catalogue"—and though I haven't looked, I bet they are), is to feel oneself at once in the real, trivial presence of everyday American life. But even before the beginning, Mr. Warren's other side has got in by prefixing to the whole an epigraph from the "Allegory of the Cave" in *The Republic*, whence we understand that we are in the presence not only of everyday American life but also of something a good deal more serious and profound—*Myth*.

I am sorry to find myself responding in this way, for I think Mr. Warren a vastly gifted writer; a good poet, and a novelist whose only problem seemed to be the management of those great powers of the imagination which enabled him to produce *Night Rider* and (not less admirable) *All the King's Men*. But it is my response, and I am stuck with it. *The Cave* seems to me to represent his specific virtues as having reached a point of overripeness: his tragic concern with the search for identity become a kind of mass-produced mechanism; his ear for dialogue and eye for detail, a glib sleight-of-hand; and his meditative lyricism, an embarrassment.

It ought to be said that with all this he is still terribly good, and this remark has no idea of condescending: he is simply not as good as he has shown himself able to be. He tells an interesting story, perhaps too many interesting stories. The situation at the center—the young man in the cave—involves him, before he can arrive at

it, in a number of life histories, which he tells in characteristic fullness (even with a very minor figure far from the action and related
to it mostly by telephone, we have to hear, as a prelude to his slight
involvement, a page and a half about his housing problems, the
bourbon he drinks, his acid stomach, his dead daughter, his wife's
varicose veins); consequently the drama itself sometimes gets left in
rather ridiculous postures. The book opens at the mouth of the cave,
it is over a hundred pages and several life stories later before we
hear why one of the major persons is concerned; a girl who starts
running to town with news of the disaster is left running for chapter after chapter while the sight of her produces the full-scale portraits and biographies of several persons.

There remain qualities that reveal some of the reasons for Warren's being, at the best, so convincing a novelist: for one, his sympathetic recollection of the pains of adolescence; for another, his
feeling for the sorrow in people, and their terrible isolation, even,
or especially, when they are ludicrous people. Of this latter trait, a
quotation may serve to show both the extent of the virtue and the
extent to which it has become a mannerism:

> He was so burly he always seemed on the verge of popping a seam.
> His thighs were so tight-packed with muscle that he wore slick places
> on his trousers, halfway between knee and crotch, where the bulge of
> muscle on one leg wouldn't clear the bulge on the other when he
> walked. You knew he would have a black pelt on his belly like a buf-
> falo robe, and have a scrotum like two doorknobs stuck in a chamois
> bag. His hands were excessively white—as though the dishwater of the
> years of his apprenticeship in his chosen vocation had had permanent
> efficacy—and were sprigged with coarse black hairs, with square-cut nails,
> strong and sharp-edged like the business end of a three-quarter-inch
> chilled-steel wood chisel. And in that deep, dark, angry secret center of
> his being tears fell without ceasing.

The book in fact is full of mannerisms, though the name of them
is "real life": for example, the endlessly repeated *leitmotiv* of Jack
Harrick's holding up the head of the slain bear; the stereotype comic
figure of the henpecked husband who as a result of the main action
turns on his wife; such passages as the following:

> He must have been aware, for if he was aware now he was aware with-
> out looking, and the looking must have occurred some other time, and
> the awareness that came with the looking must have been there, some-
> where, all the time. In any case, the awareness was here now. . . .

There is something overwrought, hysterical, movie-like about the whole, including the insistence on archetypal and mythical depths: not only the Cave, but the sacrifice of Isaac: not only that, but the Redemption ("He is suffering for me. Jasper Harrick, he is in the ground suffering for me").

On arriving at Herbert Gold's *The Optimist,* I am tempted to the following generality. Mr. Humes' book represents one extreme, the dramatic novel whose meaning is implicit in the action; Mr. Warren's book represents the same notion, essentially, about the novel, but qualitatively altered by the compromise with "real life" and a consequent immense expansion of detail (not to mention the quantity of meditation which goes on); while Mr. Gold's book represents the interest in real life itself, without other form than that conferred by the sequence of events, the hero's career, with no single action, and thus suggests another extreme view of what the novel may be. This generality is perhaps no better than most, and I do not mean it as an apologetic suggestion that I dislike *The Optimist* simply as the example of a type, for I believe I dislike it for itself alone; yet the differences do also strike me as typical ones, and as involving the writer of fiction in difficult decisions.

The Optimist takes sections through its hero Burr Fuller at three stages: college, the war, a decade after (married, lawyer, running for public office, unfaithful). The outer sections are in the third person, the center one in the first. This first-person episode, a wry and funny account of the college boy soldier's life, is for the most part brilliantly recorded and entirely appropriate, in its tone, to the theme of the young man's education recollected. Retrospectively, though, the third part made it seem as if the young man's education had been recollected not dramatically, by himself, but by that far wiser person the novelist, who now took off the mask of this identity to reveal himself as entirely doubtful of his creation, whom he had set up to begin with as something of a hero however ironically regarded, or at any rate as a person of conspicuous individual interest, and who was now turning into a shapeless and helpless bore, along with the novel in which he figured.

It may be, indeed, that this was the theme of the narrative, and that Mr. Gold's procedures, or the collapse of them, represent the artistic imitation of what was happening to Burr Fuller; but I don't quite believe it, or in it.

The first part, at college, among the fraternity brothers and the young man's two loves of comfort and despair, was pretty much a waiting game between me and the novelist. I kept grudgingly allowing that though I didn't care for it he had to start somewhere, and that my interest would properly be in what followed from all this. The second part, as I said, I enjoyed very much in itself. The third part seemed a sprawling disaster, trailing off into the open uncertainties of the future, as perhaps this sort of novel has to do, and into a species of composition which suggested the author's preliminary notes about his characters, which I don't think any sort of novel has to do.

The manner of writing—this particularly applies to the last major division, amounting in length to more than half the book—belongs to that species of irony which may be called "the knowing"; there is no doubt that Burr Fuller, or Mr. Gold, or someone who is more than both and less than either, *knows* what life is in the United States, and has taken the exact measure of its worth if any, and knows especially how important it is to take a knowing tone about it:

> For a few parents it was a night out, their baby sitters safely embedded in pop, potato chips, tangerines, and the U. S. Steel Hour; the Young Marrieds would have the luxury of a real movie together instead of a spliced 1940 epic with Clark Gable eighteen inches high, not needing his belt (they saw *Band of Angels*, 1956, Clark Gable fourteen feet high, cinemascope, sash hiding the belt which tucked in the honorable summers of his age). The girls went by in their Basic Black dresses, the men wore summer suits, and some, proudly, narrow lapels and belted rumps. Burr reached back to touch his Ivy strap. *Trousers*, he thought. I am a proper young man and I shall wear the back of my trousers belted.

This wise air of sophistication and culture sometimes, in the course of preening itself, reveals the simple reverse of the poetics of advertising, as automobiles become "Detroit's grinning chromium colossi." So too in epigrams: "Love is a consumer product for certain marriages, like a detergent or new can opener," introducing a passage of psychological generalities of the textbook type, "Consequently these women feel a driving impatience, an anger and thrill of mighty assertion. . . ." Indeed, the ambition of wisdom becomes sometimes so overpowering that the author cannot resist introducing his scenes with the universal maxim that each one will exemplify: "There is one time in a man's life when he can do anything; there is one time when he can do nothing. For Burr Fuller these two times came on the same day." And so into the episode? Not quite. Into pages of reflections which, by this time, have more and more the apparent function of providing a *résumé* which will tell the author where he has got to.

Despite some demonstration of narrative skill, this book is upon the whole dull and pretentious, overweighted with its commentary on itself, and exasperatingly smug in an attitude of moral rightness which the author is unable or unwilling to state unequivocally or bring into any relation with his story.

I may introduce here a brief scholium on sex in the novel at present. Mr. Warren and Mr. Gold, and to a much less degree Mr. Humes, exhibit their characters as preoccupied in the most explicit way with the sexual equipment of men and women, especially women.

Let us note, first, that they are perfectly free to do this. And let us note, second, that I do not dispute their right to do it. And, third, that I do not deny that human beings, and perhaps especially male human beings, are very often thus preoccupied.

All these disclaimers because any hint that one might even accidentally sympathize with the Postmaster General in any way on these matters will bring up quite naturally—dear God, naturally!—the suspicion of one's being either impotent or in some more complicated way queer. Accepting this risk, there is another element I should like to consider.

It is that all these thoughts of lust, feelings-up, and copulations take place not in real life but in an ideal realm, the realm of the novel, which is as far removed from everyday human life as would be something taking place under the sea. Their vividness, or the quantity of detail in which they are described, may provoke but never satisfy our desire (leaving to one side masturbation, which is a remedy neither more nor less outside the realm of fiction than a man's being moved by a novel to go in to his wife). Since our technologists have not yet enabled us to feel every hair on that bearskin rug, the criterion of sensuous vividness is brought into question, and with it is brought into question also the part played by detail of all sorts, not only sexual, in fiction. As to sexuality in particular, it is the monstruosity not only in love, but in writing about love, that the will is infinite and the execution confined, that the desire is boundless and the act a slave to limit. The writer's freedom to indulge himself in these descriptions—which have, most often, a remarkable similarity one to another—may or may not be good for him. But my impression is that it is not altogether good for the art he practices, that the increase in the quantity of sexual detail is but a special case of the proliferation of detail throughout (flawing Mr. Warren's book, destroying Mr. Gold's); and that the development of a separate art form of nipple-description, or tit-wit, while it will probably not be the death either of sex or the novel, is not necessarily in itself the demonstration of great artistic powers, and may even become a great bore.

Nothing I have said, of course, should be taken as intending the least infringement on the artist's right to do just as he damn pleases.

The Rack, by A. E. Ellis (I have been told this is a pseudonym), portrays the long sufferings of a young student, Paul Davenant, in a French tuberculosis sanatorium called Les Alpes. It is a very grim book, having often the air of being not so much a fiction, and also a very funny one. In this unfamiliar area, the massive support of medical detail (not of sexual detail, though there is a love affair) seems entirely relevant and functional; and, in fact, though massive in its effect of authority and knowledge, this detail is not quantitatively so much, it is only exact.

Through Paul Davenant's sufferings, which owe as much to the treatment as to the illness, or more, through his reflections and feelings, his conversations, even through the varying condition of his finances, which make a difference to his accommodations (first a charity patient, he becomes a private patient on a small legacy, which eaten through he goes back on charity), we are made the witnesses not only to illness itself, and not only to the demeanor of society toward this illness, but also of an appalling, final, and heroic self-revelation.

Beyond this, a certain allegorical intent becomes visible now and then. The illness and its treatment are a religious experience, the hospital and its equipment are seen as in catacomb or cathedral. At the same time, historical and sociological considerations are brought to bear on the nature of the illness, which is for many patients, on the one hand, a result of the War (malnutrition, ill-treatment in concentration camps), but, on the other hand, especially for Paul

Davenant it seems, a disease ironically obsolete, like himself a characteristic phenomenon of Romanticism, of nineteenth century Europe. Within the remorseless literalism of the account things of this sort are for the most part allowed to be implicit; but one of the doctors remarks to Paul, on finding Proust, Stendhal, Dostoyevsky; among his books: "You're a century behind, *cher monsieur.* You see yourself in front of a *décor* of samovars and racing droshkys or dining by candlelight *chez la Princesse de Noailles,* whereas in reality you're just another of Chekov's dreary, eternal students."

I've not got much to say about this extraordinary book. On the jacket, in addition to numerous ecstatic but brief encomia from England, there is quoted a substantial part of a review by V. S. Pritchett, and though it is a pleasure to agree for once that all the shouting is about something, my agreement leaves me without any impulse to expand these remarks. A very gloomy and a very courageous book. Though its technique is novelistic, sometimes amateurishly and sometimes brilliantly so, its readers will understand me if I say that it comes as a great relief after all those novels.

Themes and Methods in the Early Stories of Thomas Mann

The art work has, to begin with, its own form, its own finish, and represents an achievement in itself. Retrospectively, however, each work by a master has an additional significance as an episode or chapter in the development of his art; that voyage of discovery whose three-fold goal is to liberate, elucidate, and universalize the author's characteristic obsession with certain figures, materials, means of composition.

The reader's retracing the steps of this journey, though he profit, like any historian, solely from the wisdom of hindsight, is a process not without interest; one gets a view, even if it is a fictive view, of things which had seemed deep and hidden in each individual work, but which now become apparent in the whole series; one gets a view of the necessity within what had looked arbitrary; it is an exercise in the "reading of destinies." The reader is privileged to make, rapidly and with some ease though at greatly diminished intensity, some of the discoveries which his author must have made painfully and laboriously over many years; and he thus participates vicariously, as well as he may, in the idea of creation. For the author himself does not begin with "a world," ready-made and waiting only to be described; he begins rather with an impulse, a tendency, a secret which is secret also from himself and can express itself only indirectly, in the work, by means of the work.

Rapidly and very generally resuming Thomas Mann's career in fiction, from the somber naturalism of *Buddenbrooks* through the symbolic and allegorical fabrics of *The Magic Mountain* and *Doctor Faustus*, the triumphant "God-invention" of *Joseph and His Broth-*

Reprinted by permission from *The Carleton Miscellany*, Vol. II, No. 1, Winter 1961. Copyright 1961 by Carleton College.

ers, the miracle tales of *The Transposed Heads* and *The Holy Sinner*, to the satyr play of *Felix Krull* which crowns and in a sense redeems the entire *oeuvre*, we are struck not only by the immense reach of this author's development, but also by the great constancy at all times dominant over it. Beginning, as it were, with original sin in the shape of the artist's expulsion from a nineteenth century bourgeois Eden, the fatally corrupting flaw of knowledge, the reflexive splitting-off of consciousness from self, becomes the dialectical instrument for re-creating history, gradually expanding to take in the furthest realms of power, politics, and the practical life. To say something of the beginnings of all this, of how much of it, to hindsight at any rate, is already present at the start, is the object of this essay.

Disappointed lovers of life and the world, those whose love has turned to hatred or to cynicism, those whose love is an abject and constantly tormenting surrender in the face of scorn, those whose love masquerades as indifference and superiority which a chance encounter will destroy—such are the protagonists of Mann's early stories.

Perhaps the simplest expression of the type occurs in "Little Herr Friedemann" (1897). Deformed by an accident in infancy, Friedemann learns by the age of sixteen that love is not for him. Very well, he will settle for what remains when that is subtracted: the innocent pleasure one takes in nature; the almost equally innocent pleasures afforded by books, music, and especially the theater. And so he lives quietly until he is thirty, when he meets a woman whose beauty becomes his obsession, and whose scorn for his humpbacked, pigeon-breasted self causes him to take his own life. But her scorn can gain this final power only after her kindness has broken through his carefully constructed defenses:

> "Thirty years old," she repeated. "And those thirty years were not happy ones?"
> Little Herr Friedemann shook his head, his lips quivered.
> "No," he said, "that was all lies and my imagination."

With the help of "lies and imagination" he has composed for all these years a disciplined, critical life not without elegance, a life based precisely upon his infirmity and what it has forbidden him. In this life, love is characterized as "an attack," and associated with physical symptoms of fever and fatigue. It is not so much the woman

Gerda who destroys Herr Friedemann, as it is what she evokes from within him in the way of the forbidden, the long-buried will-to-live which is for him a mortal sickness. There is in this figure, with his masochistic stoicism, his deliberate self-limitation, his rigid intelligence, already much of Aschenbach, whose more elaborate destiny in "Death in Venice" is similarly grounded on the clash of archaic impulses with the prohibitions of civilization, art, and intellect, to say nothing of a certain physical debility.

The same revelation, the same knowledge of scornful betrayal on the part of the beloved, destroys the hero of "Little Lizzy" (1897), the lawyer Jacoby, whose disability in life it is to be enormously, grotesquely, painfully fat, and to despise himself on this account. His life is an endless apology, a will to humiliation (in this he a little resembles, as he does also in some physical respects, Chekhov's Andrew Ephimich in "Ward No. 6"; and compare the figure of Wehsal in *The Magic Mountain*), and he is most abject in his love for his wife, who betrays him with a musician, Alfred Läutner. It is the sudden knowledge of this betrayal which brings about Jacoby's death, as his wife and her lover compel him to participate in some amateur theatricals as "Little Lizzy," "a *chanteuse* in a red satin baby frock."

It is worth dwelling in some detail on the crisis of this story, because it brings together a number of characteristic elements and makes of them a curious, riddling compound obscurely but centrally significant for Mann's work.

The wife, Amra, and her lover are both savagely portrayed, she as incarnate sensuality, "voluptuous" and "indolent," possibly "a mischief maker," with "a kind of luxurious cunning" to set against her apparent simplicity, her "birdlike brain." Läutner, for his part, "belonged to the present-day race of small artists, who do not demand the utmost of themselves," and the bitter description of the type includes such epithets as "wretched little poseurs," the devastating indictment "they do not know how to be wretched decently and in order," and the somewhat extreme prophecy, so far not fulfilled: "They will be destroyed."

The trick these two play upon Jacoby reveals their want not simply of decency but of imagination as well. His appearance as Lizzy evokes not amusement but horror in the audience; it is a spectacle absolutely painful, an epiphany of the suffering flesh unredeemed by spirit, untouched by any spirit other than abasement and humiliation. At the same time the multiple transvestitism involved—the fat man as girl and as baby, as coquette pretending to be a baby—touches for a moment horrifyingly upon the secret sources of a life like Jacoby's, upon the sinister dreams which form the sources of any human life.

The music which Läutner has composed for this episode is for the most part "rather pretty and perfectly banal." But it is characteristic of him, we are told, "his little artifice," to be able to introduce "into a fairly vulgar and humorous piece of hackwork a sudden phrase of genuine creative art." And this occurs now, at the refrain of Jacoby's song—at the point, in fact, of the name "Lizzy"—a modulation described as "almost a stroke of genius." "A miracle, a revelation, it was like a curtain suddenly torn away to reveal something nude." It is this modulation which reveals to Jacoby his own frightful abjection and, simultaneously, his wife's infidelity. By the same means he perceives this fact as having communicated itself to the audience; he collapses, and dies.

In the work of every artist, I suppose, there may be found one or more moments which strike the student as absolutely decisive, ultimately emblematic of what it is all about; not less strikingly so for being mysterious, as though some deeply hidden constatation of thoughts were enciphered in a single image, a single moment. So here. The horrifying humor, the specifically sexual embarrassment of the joke gone wrong, the monstrous image of the fat man dressed up as a whore dressing up as a baby; the epiphany of that quivering flesh; the bringing together around it of the secret liaison between indolent, mindless sensuality and sharp, shrewd talent, cleverness with an occasional touch of genius (which, however, does not know "how to attack the problem of suffering"); the miraculous way in which music, revelation, and death are associated in a single instant —all this seems a triumph of art, a rather desperate art, in itself; beyond itself, also, it evokes numerous and distant resonances from the entire body of Mann's work.

When I try to work out my reasons for feeling that this passage is of critical significance, I come up with the following ideas, which I shall express very briefly here.

Love is the crucial dilemma of experience for Mann's heroes. The dramatic construction of his stories characteristically turns on a situation in which someone is simultaneously compelled and forbidden to love. The release, the freedom, involved in loving another is either terribly difficult or else absolutely impossible; and the motion toward it brings disaster.

This prohibition on love has an especially poignant relation to art; it is particularly the artist (Tonio Kröger, Aschenbach, Leverkühn) who suffers from it. The specific analogy to the dilemma of love is the problem of the "breakthrough" in the realm of art.

Again, the sufferings and disasters produced by any transgression against the commandment not to love are almost invariably associated in one way or another with childhood, with the figure of a child.

Finally, the theatrical (and perversely erotic) notions of dressing up, cosmetics, disguise, and especially change of costume (or singularity of costume, as with Cipolla), are characteristically associated with the catastrophes of Mann's stories.

We shall return to these statements and deal with them more fully as the evidence for them accumulates. For the present it is enough to note that in the grotesque figure of Jacoby, at the moment of his collapse, all these elements come together in prophetic parody. Professionally a lawyer, that is to say associated with dignity, reserve, discipline, with much that is essentially middle-class, he is compelled by an impossible love to exhibit himself dressed up, disguised—that is, paradoxically, revealed—as a child, and, worse, as a whore masquerading as a child.* That this abandonment takes place on a stage, during an "artistic" performance, is enough to associate Jacoby with art, and to bring down upon him the punishment for art; that is, he is suspect, guilty, punishable, as is anyone in Mann's stories who produces *illusion,* and this is true even though the constant elements of the artist-nature, technique, magic, guilt, and suffering, are divided in this story between Jacoby and Läutner.

It appears that the dominant tendency of Mann's early tales, however pictorial or even picturesque the surface, is already toward the symbolic, the emblematic, the expressionistic. In a certain perfectly definite way, the method and the theme of his stories are one and the same.

Something of this can be learned from "The Way to the Churchyard" (1901), an anecdote about an old failure whose fit of anger at a passing cyclist causes him to die of a stroke or seizure. There is no more "plot" than that; only slightly more, perhaps, than a news-

---

* We may compare the sufferings of Leopold Bloom in Nighttown.

paper account of such an incident would give. The artistic interest, then, lies in what the encounter may be made to represent, in the power of some central significance to draw the details into relevance and meaningfulness.

The first sentence, with its platitudinous irony, announces an emblematic intent: "The way to the churchyard ran along beside the highroad, ran beside it all the way to the end; that is to say, to the churchyard." And the action is consistently presented with regard for this distinction. The highroad, one might say at first, belongs to life, while the way to the churchyard belongs to death. But that is too simple, and won't hold up. As the first sentence suggests, both roads belong to death in the end. But the highroad, according to the description of its traffic, belongs to life as it is lived in unawareness of death, while the way to the churchyard belongs to some other form of life: a suffering form, an existence wholly comprised in the awareness of death. Thus, on the highroad, a troop of soldiers "marched in their own dust and sang," while on the footpath one man walks alone.

This man's isolation is not merely momentary, it is permanent. He is a widower, his three children are dead, he has no one left on earth; also he is a drunk, and has lost his job on that account. His name is Praisegod Piepsam, and he is rather fully described as to his clothing and physiognomy in a way which relates him to a sinister type in the author's repertory—he is a forerunner of those enigmatic strangers in "Death in Venice," for example, who represent some combination of cadaver, exotic, and psycho-pomp.

This strange person quarrels with a cyclist because the latter is using the path rather than the highroad. The cyclist, a sufficiently commonplace young fellow, is not named but identified simply as "Life"—that and a license number, which Piepsam uses in addressing him. "Life" points out that "everybody uses this path," and starts to ride on. Piepsam tries to stop him by force, receives a push in the chest from "Life," and is left standing in impotent and growing rage, while a crowd begins to gather. His rage assumes a religious form; that is, on the basis of his own sinfulness and abject wretchedness, Piepsam becomes a prophet who in his ecstasy and in the name of God imprecates doom on Life—not only the cyclist now, but the audience, the world, as well: "all you light-headed breed." This passion brings on a fit which proves fatal. Then an ambulance comes along, and they drive Praisegod Piepsam away.

This is simple enough, but several more points of interest may be mentioned as relevant. The season, between spring and summer, belongs to life in its carefree aspect. Piepsam's fatal rage arises not only because *he* cannot stop the cyclist, but also because God will not stop him; as Piepsam says to the crowd in his last moments: "His justice is not of this world."

Life is further characterized, in antithesis to Piepsam, as animal: the image of a dog, which appears at several places, is first given as the criterion of amiable, irrelevant interest aroused by life considered simply as a spectacle: a dog in a wagon is "admirable," "a pleasure to contemplate"; another wagon has no dog, and therefore is "devoid of interest." Piepsam calls the cyclist "cur" and "puppy" among other things, and at the crisis of his fit a little fox terrier stands before him and howls into his face. The ambulance is drawn by two "charming" little horses.

Piepsam is not, certainly, religious in any conventional sense. His religiousness is intimately, or dialectically, connected with his sinfulness; the two may in fact be identical. His unsuccessful strivings to give up drink are represented as religious strivings; he keeps a bottle in a wardrobe at home, and "before this wardrobe Praisegod Piepsam had before now gone literally on his knees, and in his wrestlings had bitten his tongue—and still in the end capitulated."

The cyclist, by contrast, blond and blue-eyed, is simply unreflective, unproblematic Life, "blithe and carefree." "He made no claims to belong to the great and mighty of this earth."

Piepsam is grotesque, a disturbing parody; his end is ridiculous and trivial. He is "a man raving mad on the way to the churchyard." But he is more interesting than the others, the ones who come from the highroad to watch him, more interesting than Life considered as a cyclist. And if I have gone into so much detail about so small a work, that is because it is also so typical a work, representing the germinal form of a conflict which remains essential in Mann's writing: the crude sketch of Piepsam contains, in its critical, destructive, and self-destructive tendencies, much that is enlarged and illuminated in the figures of, for instance, Naphta and Leverkühn.

In method as well as in theme this little anecdote, with its details selected as much for expressiveness and allegory as for "realism," anticipates a kind of musical composition, as well as a kind of fictional composition, in which, as Leverkühn says, "there shall be nothing unthematic." It resembles, too, pictures such as Dürer and Bruegel did, in which all that looks at first to be solely pictorial proves on inspection to be also literary, the representation of a proverb, for example, or a deadly sin.

"Gladius Dei" (1902) resembles "The Way to the Churchyard" in its representation of a conflict between light and dark, between "Life" and a spirit of criticism, negation, melancholy, but it goes considerably further in characterizing the elements of this conflict.

The monk Savonarola, brought over from the Renaissance and placed against the background of Munich at the turn of the century, protests against the luxurious works displayed in the art shop of M. Bluthenzweig; in particular against a Madonna portrayed in a voluptuous style and modeled, according to gossip, upon the painter's mistress. Hieronymus, like Piepsam, makes his protest quite in vain, and his rejection, though not fatal, is ridiculous and humiliating; he is simply thrown out of the shop by the porter. On the street outside, Hieronymus envisions a holocaust of the vanities of this world, such a burning of artistic and erotic productions as his namesake actually brought to pass in Florence, and prophetically he issues his curse: "*Gladius Dei super terram cito et velociter.*"

Hieronymus, like Piepsam, is alone, withdrawn, a failure, ugly, dressed in black; a representative of spirit in the sense that one manifestation of spirit is pure negation based on the conviction of one's own and the world's utter sinfulness. He is like a shadow on "radiant" Munich—again it is early summer, the time belongs to Life—with its elegance, unconventionality, loose morals, its emphatically Renaissance and Italianate ambition of viewing life altogether as "art." On this scene he cannot fail to appear graceless, awkward, depressing; nor can any remark of his, in this context, be other than ridiculous. To a salesman he says that the painting of the Madonna "is vice itself . . . naked sensuality," and that he has overheard how it affected two simple young people and "led them astray on the doctrine of the Immaculate Conception"; to which the salesman replies: "Oh, permit me—that is not the point," and goes on to "explain" that "the picture is a work of art."

This parable is similar to that of "The Way to the Churchyard" in posing against the brilliant, careless commonplace of the world a rebellious figure who insists with all his being that all around him is a vicious sham, and that the truth of life consists in suffering, misery, failure. But in the figure of the monk this attitude is much enriched, complicated, and, accordingly, compromised.

Like Friedemann's life, and Jacoby's, that of Hieronymus is based with Freudian piety on what is forbidden, on denial; and his catastrophe amounts to a return of the repressed. The painting of the Madonna, which he objects to as blasphemous and tending to the corruption of morality, has become his erotic obsession: always with him, even in church, "it stood before his outraged soul." "And no prayer availed to exorcise it." (Compare the treatment of the theme in "Fiorenza," where Savonarola's religious hatred of Lorenzo's mistress is depicted as the consequence of his unrequited lust.) The ambiguous reference of beauty, to the ideal on one side, to the flesh on the other, to the spiritual and the sexual equally, is the stumbling-block for many of Mann's characters: "Beauty alone . . . is lovely and visible at once . . . it is the sole aspect of the spiritual which we can perceive through the senses, or bear so to perceive." Thus Aschenbach, in "Death in Venice," feverishly recollecting Socrates in the *Phaedrus* and characteristically stressing the implication that the spiritual, in becoming visible, also becomes compromised and corrupted.

Hence the problem of art, with its double allegiance to the spirit and the senses inextricably and at once. Hieronymus' rage is not inchoate like Piepsam's; at first, anyhow, it is orderly, eloquent, as well intellectual as impassioned, and directed especially against the affinity of art for elegance, decoration, illusion, laxness and luxury; he would reject that art in favor of an art bent on spiritual knowledge, "in which the passions of our loathsome flesh die away and are quenched." For him, "art is no conscienceless delusion, lending itself to reinforce the allurements of the fleshly. Art is the holy torch which turns its light upon all the frightful depths. . . ." One notes that this definition equably accepts it that art is in the service of knowledge, and that knowledge in turn is in the service of negation and utter annihilation: illuminate to destroy. The agon upon this question continues to be played out, in varying forms, with varying results, through all Mann's works.

An element of composition, of method, also of enduring significance, makes its first appearance here. The central figure is as it were not an "individual" at all, but is based on a prototype from history; he is Savonarola, somewhat clumsily taken over in all his features and attitudes from fifteenth century Florence; and this identity is accented: "Seen in profile his face was strikingly like an old painting preserved at Florence in a narrow cloister cell whence once a frightful and shattering protest issued against life and her triumphs." This circumstance raises some odd questions about the relation between character and deed, will and fate, the actor and his part; it introduces for the first time that further question, so poignant for Mann's art, whether and in what sense the work has to do with life, how the one is fitted, if it is, to interpret the other; how far the idea of destiny, for example, is nothing more than a law of literary composition, having no more status in reality than the device of a magician. For the moment, it is enough to note the early presence of this question, deferring the discussion of it until we shall have collected other examples, in which this "taking over" of the historical, legendary, or literary extends beyond the persons to the action of the drama itself.

The examples we have so far considered share one dominant trait, and that is the doomed impotence of the lonely protagonist against a world which is cruel, mocking, or indifferent; a world in which the inevitable end of his attempt either to live more fully or to overcome life is defeat: his humiliation, followed three times out of four by his death. Whether this death be literally suicide, as with Friedemann, or the result of a stroke of some sort, as with Piepsam and Jacoby, it comes from within; it is a product of self-knowledge, and somehow suggestive of a fulfillment of a wish; one might say that the suppressed erotic nature in these persons reaches out and forces the world to destroy them. For the solitude in which they live is an absolute one; their efforts to break the charmed circle of their isolation appear as impulses to self-destruction.

There is another, and somewhat more fruitful, sort of isolation exhibited in these works, and the examination of some instances of this sort may serve to conclude our discussion of the early stories and sketches.

This is the isolation of the artist, the being who has some not altogether satisfactory yet not necessarily fatal way of responding to the world. Like the other kind, that of Piepsam, Friedemann, etc., it is an enforced loneliness often associated with disease and death; it ends not in violence, however, but rather as a dream, distancing itself and losing itself in the distances; its tonality is different from that of the other. The suffering protagonist may be viewed with some mockery, may even view himself with contempt ("Disillusionment," "The Dilettante"), but upon the whole he is regarded with sympathy by the author, perhaps because he has some insight into his own sufferings ("The Hungry," "A Weary Hour").

In "The Wardrobe" (1899), Albrecht van der Qualen, though still a young man, is mortally ill; doctors have given him only a few more months to live; we scarcely need his name to relate him with agonies and torments. Traveling on the Berlin-Rome express, he yields to impulse and gets off at a way station, a town whose name he does not know. Here, he reflects, he is free; he experiences what Hans Castorp will later know as "the advantages of shame": "Honest unhappiness without charity," thinks Van der Qualen, "is a good thing; a man can say to himself: I owe God nothing."

In this nameless town he rents a room; in the room is a wardrobe; from the wardrobe appears to him at night a girl * who tells him sad, ballad-like stories, and also, in a fevered phantasy somewhere between dream and reality, sweetness and shame, becomes his mistress . . . and that is all, there is no more "story" than that. But that any of it ever "really" happened is a matter of doubt to the author. "Would any of us care to take the responsibility of giving a definite answer?"

This lonely traveler, diseased, bemused, on a journey without beginning or end (he never gets to Rome and we are specifically told that Berlin had not been the beginning of his trip), is the embryonic form of the artist hero; more exactly, the bourgeois artist hero. One observes that Van der Qualen has a first-class compartment, just as his fellow artists and fellow sufferers do: the writer-narrator of "Railway Accident," Tonio Kröger, Gustave Aschenbach. Tonio Kröger supplies the reason, which is that "anyone who suffered inwardly more than other people had a right to a little outward ease." While Tonio Kröger goes North "to the polar bear" and Aschenbach South "to the tiger," Van der Qualen gets off somewhere in between, where nothing has a name . . . and he vanishes, is without issue. His muse of eros, pathos, pathology, tells him stories, but he doesn't write the stories down; and his status in reality is that of a dream, a nineteenth century dream reminding us of lonely streets in the lost cities of Balzac and Stendhal.

Though Van der Qualen's isolation, like that of the others, is as-

---

* She appears from the wardrobe. Piepsam hid his bottle in the wardrobe and went on his knees before it. One might thoughtfully continue to look for wardrobes, cupboards, closets, which turn into tabernacles. Consider, for example, the cupboard from which Hans Lorenz Castorp reverently takes the christening basin.

sociated with melancholy, illness, boredom, disgust, and though it is once again primarily the inwardness of the character which is stressed, the idea of art, however ineffectual, unreal, fevered, is represented as an alleviation of his condition; it is identified with erotic fulfillment, though also with guilt (his mistress-muse, after yielding to him, tells no more stories for some time); and by the sweet remoteness of its melancholy this little sketch seems to hint that art, a kind of ideal equivalent or substitute for sexuality (perhaps at once the equivalent and the antithesis of masturbation?), is the possibility of escape from the world, a transcendence of it if not its redemption.

Together with and over against this portrait of the artist as sufferer there must be placed the antithetical figure of the artist as illusionist, cynic, or even charlatan; the artist as virtuoso and actor. While we see such persons as Van der Qualen, Spinel, Detlev, Kröger, Aschenbach, and the anonymous protagonists of "The Dilettante," "Disillusion," "Railway Accident," as almost invariably alone, or at most engaged in private conversation, the Greek boy, Bibi, of "The Infant Prodigy" (1903), is depicted in the fullest glare of publicity, giving a concert. He is of course not less alone than the others; but his loneliness is public, aggressive, confident, and assured of mastery.

This most interesting piece is scarcely a story in any usual sense; instead of plot we have a kind of rudimentary musical organization of anecdote. Several themes are introduced and dismissed, only to return in variations. The major contrast of the work is between Bibi's thoughts about his own performance and the thoughts evoked by this performance in the minds of selected members of the audience. These latter take the form of variations on the theme which connects the idea of art simultaneously with the secret-erotic and the composition of society: Bibi's virtuosity arouses in his hearers sexual and forbidden thoughts, while his innocence, or the innocence which they presume in the fact that he is a little boy, makes these thoughts permissible and even rather religious.

Just at the finish a decisive point is made in the confrontation, after the concert, of an elegant young lady accompanied by her officer-brothers, and a bohemian, or early beatnik, couple, a gloomy-looking youth and "a girl with untidy hair." This girl has just said, "We are all infant prodigies, we artists," causing an old gentleman who overhears her to think that "she sounds very oracular"; now, however, she looks after the beautiful and aristocratic girl ("steel-blue eyes," "clean-cut, well-bred face") and her brothers: "she rather despised them, but she looked after them until they turned the corner."

This compound of eros, art, delicate envy, and social climbing is not arbitrarily introduced at all, but forms the climax to a number of preparatory references. Bibi's performance, which he himself regards with a cold pleasure from the technical point of view, in terms of cleverness, calculation, intelligence, virtuosity, arouses warmer sentiments in his hearers, from the old gentleman who compares Bibi to the Christ child, thinking that one could kneel before a child without being ashamed, to the young girl who thinks of kissing the little musician because what he is playing "is expressive of passion, yet he is a child." And she asks herself, "Is there such a thing as passion all by itself, without any earthly object, a sort of child's play of passion?"

The meaning of such reflections is brought out when the impresario climbs on the stage and, "as though overcome," kisses the little boy, "a resounding kiss, square on the mouth." "That kiss ran through the room like an electric shock, it went direct to people's marrow and made them shiver down their backs. They were carried away by a helpless compulsion of sheer noise." A music critic thinks: "Of course that kiss had to come—it's a good old gag. Yes, good Lord, if only one did not see through everything so clearly—." And when Bibi finishes with a piece incorporating the Greek national anthem this critic goes on: "I think I'll criticize that as inartistic. But perhaps I am wrong, perhaps that is the most artistic thing of all. What is the artist? A jack-in-the-box. Criticism is on a higher plane. But I can't say that."

This remarkable composition plays with great though quiet effect on subjects which remain central to the author's work throughout his career. "The Infant Prodigy" is Mann's first representation of some sinister qualities belonging to the underside of the artist nature. A figure like Van der Qualen, with his fever, near to death, and with his sexual muse, might be thought quite sinister enough, but in comparison with Bibi and his like he looks innocent and sympathetic. Here for the first time art is explicitly related to childhood, to perverse sexuality, to a kind of cynical innocence, and to power. Also to criminality, fraud, and imposition. For though Bibi is not a fake, he really can play the piano, we have only to compare his concert to the fake violin concert given by the child Felix Krull on a fiddle with greased strings, to see that the latter is but an intensification of meanings already present in the former: Krull's parents, for instance, profit socially by their son's "little joke." And the "realism" of Krull's performance does depend, we are told, on his being truly inspired, "enchanted" by music. Thus the fraudulent is not completely so, but rooted in real feelings; and the artistic performance, however real, is to a degree fraudulent, depending on illusion; people applauded, we are told, before Bibi played a note, "for a mighty publicity organization had heralded the prodigy and people were already hypnotized, whether they knew it or not." Art, then, takes place in a mysterious realm where nothing is either true or false; the realm of Van der Qualen's dreamy, nameless town, the realm of the theater where in some sense only the child is at home, while the adult must suspect in himself those real feelings which are evoked by means of illusion, and subject these to criticism, that is, to the reservations of shame and guilt.

This relation of art to the theatrical goes very deep in Mann's work, and develops very far. We may observe, about the stories we have been considering up to this point, that the theater is in some way always present. Some of them, like "The Infant Prodigy" and "Little Lizzy," have theatrical performances for their subject. But the ambulance men take Piepsam away smoothly and efficiently, "as in a theater"; Friedemann "loved the theater most of all," and he falls in love at a performance of *Lohengrin*; "Gladius Dei," though chiefly concerned with painting, contains several references to the theater, and Hieronymus' vision of doom has for a background Theatinerstrasse, Theater Street.

Anticipating, it is possible to see the relation of Bibi to the development of those artist figures most involved with evil, with "the questionable" and the powers of darkness: Cipolla, artist and illusionist of the political-erotic; Leverkühn, the artist as Faust, compacted for his powers to the devil; Krull, the artist as criminal, working directly on life. Many minor episodes and vignettes deal with the same compound of beauty and its dubious beginnings: for instance, Tonio Kröger's anecdote about the banker whose talent for short stories emerged only when he served a prison sentence; Felix Krull's horrifying sketch contrasting the actor Muller-Rosé's appearance on stage and off; the ambiguous characterization of art in *The Magic Mountain* and in *Doctor Faustus* as "alchemical," as inorganic imitation of the organic; as bound up with the *illusory* (or *spiritual*: the doubt is everpresent) transmutation of lower into higher: of nothing into matter; matter into life; life into thought; those successive quantum jumps of creation which are characterized also as intensifications of shame and guilt.

There are thus already revealed two views of the artist. In one he is the lonely sufferer of the dark horror of the world; in the other he is the cynical magician whose illusionistic powers enable him somewhat coldly to exploit his own suffering and that of others, for ends which may possibly be redemptive but which are always regarded by the author with much misgiving, at the least because they are remote from the ends of practical life—"poetry is a kiss one gives the world," says Goethe in *The Beloved Returns*, "but kisses get no children"—and at the worst because it is the nature of art to lend a certain prospective reality to dangerous and impermissible phantasies.

Over against both views of the artist there is the commonplace view of "the beautiful," relating it to amusement, entertainment, health; as with the lieutenant in *Tonio Kröger* who "asks the company's permission to read some verses of his own composition." The disaster, says Kröger, was the lieutenant's own fault: "There he stood, suffering embarrassment for the mistake of thinking that one may pluck a single leaf from the laurel tree of art without paying for it with his life."

Thomas Mann's Faust Novel

Thomas Mann's *Doctor Faustus* may be seen as a magnificent grotesque, a final parody perhaps not only of the novel but of art generally; it may be likened to a cathedral whose proportions strain so to the overt and exact, to an ideal elegance, as to witness of a god at least as mighty as the one worshipped inside. The long allegiance of Mann's art to music, to the expressly "pure" and solely "formal," has here issued in the story of the musician-hero Adrian Leverkühn, where the tension between Apollo and Dionysus may be localized as that between Bach and the Bacchic; yet the essence of the dialectic was already present in the story of Gustave Aschenbach, the "morally valiant" hero whose art took for its ideal the figure of St. Sebastian: "The conception of an intellectual and virginal manliness, which clenches its teeth and stands in modest defiance of the swords and spears that pierce its side." Pain and disease disguised in form —form as itself the noble concomitant of disease, they are already here in "the aristocratic self-command that is eaten out within and for as long as it can conceals its biologic decline from the eyes of the world." D. H. Lawrence, reviewing *Death in Venice*, spoke of Mann as "the last sick sufferer from the complaint of Flaubert," who, like Flaubert, "feels vaguely that he has in him something finer than ever physical life revealed." This and Lawrence's related complaints (Phoenix, pp. 308-313) seem inaccurate inasmuch as they do not account for Mann's further irony, his understanding of the position, whereby Aschenbach's fate (and Leverkühn's too, I think) is made splendidly implicit in the description of his discipline:

> Was it perhaps an intellectual consequence of this rebirth, this new austerity, that from now on his style showed an almost exaggerated sense of beauty, a lofty purity, symmetry, and simplicity, which gave his productions a stamp of the classic, of conscious and deliberate mas-

Reprinted by permission from *The Graduate Journal*, Vol. 3, No. 2, Fall 1960. Copyright 1960 by the Board of Regents of the University of Texas.

tery? And yet: this moral fibre, surviving the hampering and disintegrating effect of knowledge, does it not result in its turn in a dangerous simplification, in a tendency to equate the world and the human soul, and thus to strengthen the hold of the evil, the forbidden, and the ethically impossible? And has not form two aspects? Is it not moral and immoral at once: moral in so far as it is the expression and result of discipline, immoral—yes, actually hostile to morality—in that of its very essence it is indifferent to good and evil, and deliberately concerned to make the moral world stoop beneath its proud and undivided sceptre?

The fascination and danger of form, of purity, of the rigorous and extreme, is a theme many times debated in Mann's work; it forms a dialectic most productive of paradoxical counterpositions where the individual and the "anonymous and communal," the ideas of "harmonic subjectivity" and "polyphonic objectivity," may change places or be seen as ultimately one, as single nature's double name. In *Doctor Faustus* this theme has so operated as to produce a work that seeks, as it were, to draw all its subject up into form, to leave, as Adrian says, "nothing unthematic"; and in some sense the novel itself develops according to those laws of composition which form one expression of its hero's fate. Just as in music there is something the layman does not hear, an entire dimension not in the least concerned with making pleasing noises and that in fact he would just as lief not hear, so in a "novel" of this sort the expression of internal laws of development entirely takes the place of "psychology," observation of behavior, naturalistic creation of event; the inside is turned outward, like the creatures Adrian Leverkühn's father speaks of, who wear their skeletons like overcoats. And the *leitmotiv* method, whereby in Wagner music vulgarized itself in the direction of literature, now in a fantastic efflorescence becomes a means whereby literature approximates to the condition of music—not a Wagnerian music, however, but a strict counterpoint, a polyphonic objectivity, the solution of a problem.

This extreme, if not in this particular form, not infrequently characterizes the late development of a style, as it does for example in Melville's *Pierre*, where the art to conceal art seems deliberately to have been rejected; as it does in late Shakespeare, where divine revelation is given the figure of artistic management; as it does toward the end of *A la Recherche du temps perdu*, where Proust untiringly insists that the whole business of art is the discovery of general laws governing appearances. Art itself replaces the world it sought to observe, or regards itself lovingly in that world as in a mirror:

> For speculation turns not to itself,
> Till it hath travell'd and is mirror'd there
> Where it may see itself.
> —*Troilus and Cressida* III. iii. 109.

The distinguishing feature of this development is a majestic yet somewhat sinister contempt for the devices by which art customarily pretends to the casualness of life (concealment of technique, apparent liberty of action and development, all effort to make the surface of things look "natural"). The artist, as the god of his world, deliberately exposes the perpetual laws of its being, and suggests by bold analogy how in our "real world" the two great antagonists, freedom and necessity, may move in constant harmony to produce the one result.

To illustrate the method of this late style we may compare the making of certain connections in *The Magic Mountain* with the way in which similar connections are made in *Doctor Faustus*. The relations of spirit and desire, disease and knowledge are imaged in the earlier work as they are in the later; the operation of these images in the life of Hans Castorp is most carefully and circumspectly worked out with a high regard for plausibility and naturalism, in terms of the appearances of life: entire chapters, long meditations, exhaustive recollections of the past, of childhood, are employed to demonstrate a certain predestinated character of life with which the will accords, whence it is clear that Clavdia is the evoked image of the schoolboy Pribislav, that the disease itself is founded on the erotic experience in the then and the now. In *Doctor Faustus*, on the other hand, these relations constitute the given, and not that which is to be shown. They are hurled at the reader in absolute, rigidly jesting and ironical openness, with the most terrible candor not altogether unlike contempt, in terms of a contrapuntal arrangement and variation of similar material in erotic, political, artistic, theological, and pathological realms or, better, voices of a work written in fugue. The Leverkühn house of Adrian's childhood is duplicated in the Schweigestill house where he passed his later years; the dog Suso becomes then the dog Kaschperl; Adrian inherits his father's migraine and also, transmuted into art and intensified, his father's timid concern with that part of inorganic nature that so perfectly imitates the organic; the Devil remarks on the re-entrance of the daemonic into Europe simultaneously under two forms: the Reformation and the spirochetes. The operation of law, then, is here to be made visible and explicit, according to the idea expressed by Adrian (p. 191) that freedom "becomes the principle of an all-round economy that leaves in music nothing casual, and develops the utmost diversity while adhering to the identical material. Where there is nothing unthematic left, nothing which could not show itself to derive from the same basic material, there one can no longer speak of a 'free style.' " It will be apparent that the essential question of aesthetic here has clearly political resonances, and I propose that the general subject of this work properly may be spoken of as the relation of subject and object, of freedom and necessity. This relation is for Mann extremely subtle, complicated, and liable to inversion; irony, far from being, as Settembrini would have it be, a direct and classical device of oratory, becomes the end, or at least the last known objective, and man's nature is seen as a "between" nature whose best choices cancel out each other. Now the in-betweenness of irony is on the one hand "sane, noble, harmonious, humane"—it is the golden mean of wisdom—but again it has in it something of the cruel and contemptuous (as in the portrait of Goethe in *The Beloved Returns*), of being too good for both sides, refusing to involve oneself with either party out of a feeling of pride and absolute superiority; and again it may be seen as contemptible also, as a craven refusal to join the eternal war, a refusal masquerading under this "above the battle" superiority—thus Dante's feelings about the trimmers, *a Dio spiacenti ed a nemici Sui*, and thus it was said to the Laodiceans, "I know thy works, that thou art neither cold nor hot . . . So then because thou art lukewarm, and neither cold nor hot, I will spew thee out of my mouth." And thus in the hell described by Mann's Divel, in a brilliantly ironic image, the sinners have their choice only between extreme cold and extreme heat, they fly from the one into the other and can never quite get between; yet the tension between their wish and their reality makes out that they are always between.

As for a detailed analysis of the fabric of this novel, this metaphysical poem, fugue, theology, or whatever, it is difficult even to find a way in; should one start with the "utmost diversity" or with the "strictest economy," the "basic material" from which it is produced? If my notion has anything right about it, the analysis of a work in which there is "nothing unthematic" will be impossible short of an exposition of the entire contents of the work according to a different order of presentation, an abstract schema something like the synopsis of Burton's *Anatomy*; but I hope without going to that length to show at least something of the method of composition. And this method itself in a way makes the job possible, for in a texture so closely and relevantly woven one might conceivably start at any point and by firm probability reach any other, assembling on the way some picture of the whole.

Though the narrator, Serenus Zeitblom, pretends to naïveté perhaps more than is properly his, and especially about the length and order of his chapters, pretending them to be disposed more or less in a random order within a loose frame of necessity, one nevertheless detects some attraction to the magical and formal quality of numbers; the work is divided into forty-seven chapters and an epilogue, the acknowledgment of the covenant with the Divel coming pretty closely in the center, and Schleppfuss, that early Satanic "incarnation," is with reverent propriety given the thirteenth chapter all to himself; probably no number in this work, however, has anything like the importance of the number seven in *The Magic Mountain*. But I do think to discover six "voices," each carrying the theme in a different realm of experience, each relating with the others so as to produce the theme (which it is our business so far as may be to define) as an existence independent of any voice; and I like to be fancifully (and not very relevantly) reminded of the great second Ricercar of the *Musikalische Opfer*. These six voices may be named as follows: biological-chemical, or the relation of the organic and inorganic; pathological; theological; erotic; political and historical; aesthetic.

It is only seldom possible to hear these voices in entire isolation; the texture is generally too complicated. But simple combinations of two are very frequent: the identification already mentioned of the spirochete and the Reformation as "daemonic," Adrian's syphilitic corruption of speech referred to his archaizing fondness for the old German of Luther's time, the repetition of the symbols of Hetaera Esmeralda in musical notation as an example of the strict style—in such instances we recognize the most elementary effects of this resonant, echoing, and musically conceived manner of composition. To explore a little further into the last example: Hetaera Esmeralda first appears in Jonathan Leverkühn's "speculation of the elements" as the name of a butterfly "in transparent nudity, loving the duskiness of heavy leafage." The discussion here is generally about camouflage and concealment in nature, a question is asked about the purpose of such devices, and a new example is introduced, of a butterfly not only large but strikingly colored, highly visible, which is "tragically safe" because its secretions are so revolting no animal would eat of it: "We . . . asked ourselves whether this security had not something disgraceful about it, rather than being a cause for rejoicing." And the reader learns that Adrian could not control his laughter over this perverse manifestation. But Esmeralda is the name he gives the whore from whose body he contracts syphilis, and the brief musical "signature" of this name is found to be of strikingly frequent occurrence in the fabric of his music, and may be seen as an example of the strict style inasmuch as it elevates an extraneous and literal consideration into a first principle of composition. In this syndrome we perceive a harmony based primarily upon polyphony, where continuing voices allude to each other and so produce passing chordal effects, the erotic, the aesthetic, the pathological, the question asked of nature about the design of things: these momentarily meet and form a nexus of meaning, then continue their many narratives.

For the narrative is at once one and many, the one theme varied by the voices; so that there exists a clear sense in which Adrian is Germany ("the German soul," "the Kaisersaschern soul"), in which the development of his disease and his talent, his pact with Satan and Germany's pact with the daemonic archaism of the Nazi mythology, are one. Adrian is finally stricken in 1935; in 1939 he is all but dead, "a picture of the utmost spirituality, just there whence the spirit had fled"; in 1940 he dies. But his confession and collapse, his withdrawal from the world and from music, express that degree of *contritio cordis* based on absolute despair that is found in his last work, the "Dr. Fausti Wehe-klag," whose text, strictly bound to the twelve tones of the chromatic scale, is formed of the twelve syllables, "For I die as a good and as a bad Christian."

This counterpoint of the musical, theological, and political is nowhere more clearly put than in the conversations of Chaim Breisacher, the German Jew and polyhistor, who by making the worse appear the better reason confounds the conservative and radical, the archaic and the late-decadent together, and makes of history and all development the magic circle and "the crossway in the Spesser's wood." Thus "the softening, the effeminizing and falsification, the new interpretation put on the old and genuine polyphony . . . had already begun in the sixteenth century, and people like Palestrina, the two Gabrielis, and our good Orlando di Lasso . . . had already played their shameful part in it." And "in this decline, right in the middle of it, belonged the great Bach from Eisenach, whom Goethe quite rightly called a harmonist." Dr. Breisacher's audience is confused at this, but more so at his treatment of the next subject:

> King David, King Solomon, and the prophets drivelling about dear God in heaven, these were the already debased representatives of an exploded late theology, which no longer had any idea of the old and genuine Hebraic actuality of Jahve, the Elohim of the people; and in the rites with which at the time of genuine folkishness they served this national god or rather forced him to physical presence, saw only "riddles of primeval time." (p. 281)

Here, and in Dr. Breisacher's characterization of Solomon as "a progressivist blockhead, typical of the back-formation of the cult of the effectively present national god, the general concept of the metaphysical power of the folk, into the preaching of an abstract and generally human god in heaven," one sees, ironically enough, the German implicit in the Jewish situation, the situation which would be "remedied" by the Nazi atavism.

One more illustration will perhaps serve to exemplify the method, and lead on as well to a further consideration: Hans Christian Andersen's tale of *The Little Mermaid*, which Adrian "uncommonly loved and admired," forms the center from which many essential matters radiate. References to her, both direct and extremely devious, occur at many places in the text, but only at the end we learn that the Devil had given her to Adrian for mistress in a "divelish concubinage" in compensation of that *clausulum* in the pact that forbade his love to humankind; we learn further that Adrian regards his sister's son, Echo, as the child of their union, the human-divine child, their Euphorion in fact, and so bound to death by the father's damnation. This liaison, like other elements in Adrian's fate, has amply if indirectly been predicted; for example in the stories told by Schleppfuss (an early devil-avatar) about the relations of young men with succubi. And there are remoter echoes no less important: In Andersen's tale, the world at the bottom of the sea is described, a strange dead world with trees and plants "so supple that they move as if they were alive." And to reach the palace of the witch, the sea-maid must swim through a wood of polyps. These details are represented early in *Doctor Faustus*, in that underwater world, the dead but heliotropic creation of chemistry at which Adrian so laughed when his father displayed it as the result of "osmotic pressure," the melancholy yearning of the inorganic toward life.

But the radiations go further than this, for the Divel speaks thus of the works Adrian will produce under the exaltation of the pact, which is the disease: "Then shall osmotic growths *sine pudore* sprout out of the Apothecary's sowing . . ." and at Adrian's rebuke he says:

> Oh, thy father is not so ill placed in my mouth. He was a shrewd one, always wanting to speculate the elements. The mygrim, the point of attack for the knife-pains of the little sea-maid—after all, you have them from him. . . . Moreover . . . osmosis, fluid diffusion, the proliferation process—the whole magic intreats of these. You have there the spinal sac with the pulsating column of fluid therein, reaching to the cerebrum, to the meninges, in whose tissues the furtive venereal meningitis is at its soundless stealthy work. But our little ones could not reach into the inside, into the parenchyma, however much they are drawn, however much they longingly draw thither—without fluid diffusion, osmosis, with the cell-fluid of the pia watering it, dissolving the tissue, and paving a way inside for the scourges. Everything comes from osmosis, my friend, in whose teasing manifestations you so early diverted yourself.

It will be seen that we are here brought to a center of the work, the question of the alchemy of art ("has the sun better fire than the kitchen?" asks the Divel) and whether it indeed is organic or merely gives the illusion: "What then does 'dead' mean, when the flora grows so rankly, in such diverse colors and shapes? And when they are even heliotropic?" So that our consideration of the role of the sea-maid might from this place be taken anywhere in the work, since it has brought us so rapidly to the essence, the matter of life and death which are called by the names of God and Satan; "for the light shineth in darkness; and the darkness comprehended it not." This figure of Hyphialta, the sea-maid, speaks in all the voices, of lust and disease, of the pact with the Devil and the exaltation thus produced in art, and of the relation of death to life; if the political has not been touched on so explicitly, it may at any rate be seen in the equation of Leverkühn's disease, pact, music, with the rigid and death-bound form imposed upon life—a "strict style of composition," surely—by the Nazi regime, of whose concentration camps the Divel reminds us in his description of hell, the *spelunca*, the *carcer*, where all terrors happen "unrecorded, unreckoned, between thick walls."

"Au commencement était le scandale."

This Faust, in life a cheap-jack charlatan as ever was, according to the sources (and if Rembrandt drew him right), more than Christ has given his name to our modern folk, being the instance and image of an honor rooted in dishonor, a striving to the One but nourished by the Other, man blessed by the blessings of heaven and of the deep that lieth under—there is no end to the possible translations and accommodations of his figure. The parable of Job, according to some, teaches that order is broken up in the depths of being only to be more firmly established in the end, that good can have only evil for material to operate upon; and the Divel, the oldest theologian, says to Adrian, "Life is not scrupulous—by morals it sets not a fart. It takes the reckless product of disease, feeds on and digests it, and as soon as it takes it to itself it is health." But St. Paul asks whether we should continue in sin that grace may abound, and replies "God forbid." This is perhaps the deepest question we ask of Faust's covenant. For morality has about it something of the safe, the mediocre ("Virtue," observes Kafka, "is in a certain sense disconsolate"), and mediocrity, as Adrian says, "has no theological status." The traditional, reasonably supported, and already conventionalized fictions by which man lives are seen, according to the Divel, as unsatisfactory also in music:

The pretence of feeling as a compositional work of art, the self-satisfied pretence of music itself, has become impossible and no longer to be preserved—I mean the perennial notion that prescribed and formalized elements shall be introduced as though they were the inviolable necessity of the single case.

We cannot get by this by calling the devil a romantic expressionist in music and a Manichaean in matters of faith. Shall we continue in disorder that truth may abound? ("Only the non-fictional is still permissible, the unplayed, the undisguised and untransfigured expression of suffering in its actual moment.") Shall we continue in disease that health may abound? (". . . the lads will swear by your name, who thanks to your madness will no longer need to be mad"). It is not possible for Adrian to reply to this with the pious "God forbid."

For the Satan, the questioner, is within and without; before and after his apparition to Adrian we have his avatars and reminders, some overt and direct, some equivocal. I have already mentioned Schleppfuss the theologian, or psychologist of theology (who perhaps did really drag one foot, according to Serenus Zeitblom), and Dr. Chaim Breisacher who could make beginnings appear as ends; and may add to the list not only the porter who leads Adrian to his Esmeralda ("a small-beer Schleppfuss," he is called), and the impresario Saul Fitelberg who comes, he says, "to show you the kingdoms of the earth and the glory of them" (Luke IV. 5-6), and "Professor Akercocke," name of horrible derision; but also those neutral or even benign figures of the biography, one or more of whose characteristics is presently found in Adrian under diabolic auspices: Johann Conrad Beissel, the musician-priest of Ephrata, whose tyranny of the "master" and "servant" notes is found, "ghostlike," in Leverkühn's *Apocalypsis cum Figuris*; Wendell Kretschmar, who told Beissel's story, and whose uncontrollable stutter eventually affiliates itself with Adrian's pathologic and archaistic corruption of speech; and Jonathan Leverkühn, who provided the migraine and the urge to "speculate the elements." It is the effect of the method to make Adrian's life seem extraordinarily fate-laden and significant at every instant, all detail being as in a dream multiply-determined, both a *vis a tergo* and a teleological motivation, so that it is at last difficult enough to say what is will and what is fate, what is harmonic-subjective and what polyphonic-objective; even of the Divel, when he appears, all that can be said is that his real existence, if he exists, is horrible, but not more so than if he exists as a delusion produced by the sick soul.

What is the Divel? He is death, he is deceit as he is death pretending to life, he is himself what he sponsors so theologically, the osmotic growth *sine pudore*. But he is not mediocrity, not Laodicean or trimmer. And therefore, as Schleppfuss was at such pains to emphasize in his lectures, sanctity must take its chance with him: "The temptation that one withstood was indeed no sin; it was merely a proof of virtue. And yet the line between temptation and sin was hard to draw, for was not temptation already the raging of sin in the blood, and in the very state of fleshly desire did there not lie much concession to evil? Here again the dialectical unity of good and evil came out, for holiness was unthinkable without temptation; it measured itself against the frightfulness of the temptation, against a man's sin-potential."

The Divel is deceit, and he, who would not serve, appears to man in the likeness of a servant, a position of unique power because it is at once and already the expression of a wish. It is the wish to go beyond the limitations of the human, the wish for "the breakthrough," an impulsion to freedom which dialectically makes its own chains, since man enslaves himself to his servant and his power becomes his sickness.

The apparition to Adrian Leverkühn plays boldly upon a similar scene, the apparition to Ivan Karamazov (who suffered, one remembers, with symptoms very like Adrian's, though from Dostoevsky's favorite disease, that mysterious "brain fever"), and even contains hints of a dialogue with it; the world for Dostoevsky is a journal to which the Devil must write the "column of criticism," but Mann's Divel denies it outright—"a man of destructive criticism? Slander, and again slander, my friend!" There are more general parallels: the horrible bantering tone, the fact that both visitors are seen as social inferiors, the careful attention given in this regard to their clothing, the recurrent debate about their reality, the use they make of their hosts' secret thoughts. But Ivan's Devil seems by far the less horrible; almost he is merely the Satan of the Book of Job, questioning, "writing the column of criticism," "pre-destined to deny" without much hope of ultimate success—he regards himself somewhat sadly as a scapegoat, and he is to Ivan almost an occasion of salvation: "I shall sow in you only a tiny grain of faith and it will grow into an oak tree . . . you'll wander into the wilderness to save your soul." Whereas in *Doctor Faustus* he is to the full evil, powerful, the antagonist in a still undecided battle, the very Prince of Lies at whom Martin Luther threw the ink-pot.

For Dostoevsky the mystery of Christianity lies in freedom, which necessarily involves the freedom to do evil. Berdyaev works out the dialectic thus:

> Free goodness involves the freedom of evil; but freedom of evil leads to the destruction of freedom itself and its degeneration into an evil necessity. On the other hand, the denial of the freedom of evil in favour of an exclusive freedom of good ends equally in a negation of free-

dom and its degeneration—into a good necessity. But a good necessity is not good, because goodness resides in freedom from necessity.
—Nicholas Berdyaev, *Dostoevsky.*

Mann, too, is concerned with this theme, but entrusts its exposition primarily to Schleppfuss, who sees here "a certain logical incompleteness of the All-powerfulness and All-goodness of God; for what He had not been able to do was to produce in the creature . . . the incapacity for sin. That would have meant denying to the created being the free will to turn away from God." And the Divel too plays upon this freedom and uses it as a temptation: "Have you forgotten what you learned in the schools, that God can bring good out of evil and that the occasion to it shall not be marred?" It is as though Mann, at such points, would take back the vision of Dostoevsky as Adrian would take back "the good and noble . . . what we call the human, although it is good and noble . . . the *Ninth Symphony.*"

Yet not entirely so. Though the "Lamentation of Dr. Faustus" is conceived as the melancholy counterpart, the formal negation, of the Beethoven *Ninth,* it is yet expressly a "religious" work, "a conversion, a proud and bitter change of heart," the "prideful *contritio*" earlier debated with the Divel, and at its end the last melancholy tone becomes "a hope beyond hopelessness, the transcendence of despair—not betrayal to her, but the miracle that passes belief," and this tone "changes its meaning; it abides as a light in the night." And as with the music, so with the novel, when at its conclusion Serenus Zeitblom, whose name speaks of "the fullness of time" (Ephesians I. 10), speaks of the miracle beyond belief, the light of hope out of the utmost hopelessness.

Doctor Faustus is a noble and a melancholy work, and a melancholy hope it expresses there at the end, a hope almost in the strict style of composition—that is, will the dialectic pull us through? The question so long ago debated between Naphta and Settembrini, whether man is "natural" or against nature, in despite of nature, has extended its ground to nature itself: Is nature "natural" even in its perverse osmotic manifestations? Is the sea-maid a monster, or "a complete and charming organic reality" as Adrian held her to be? And so too with art, that "calculation raised to mystery"—can it be organic, or is it Divel's work with magic squares and osmotic pressure? These are questions not to be answered without some sort of intimate relation with the "dubious and questionable"; that they are asked shows the depth of our predicament.

Tragedy exists in tension between ritual and ethic, magic and religion; the hero as he suffers is both punished and sacrificed, and the humanist may well misdoubt himself, in such an ambiguous operation, to be paid by the wrong master. The scapegoat is laden with sin and driven into the wilderness to save the people, as Adrian upon his confession was deserted by his friends, but possibly it is only the scapegoat who is saved out of it all. If the tension cannot be maintained, that is Armageddon or the coming of the Kingdom, either one but in any case the end; for it is with us as it is with music: "Her strictness, or whatever you like to call the moralism of her form, must stand for an excuse for the ravishments of her actual sounds."

Part IV

Across the Woods and Into
the Trees

The Literary Situation. By Malcolm Cowley. Viking Press, 1954.
The Lion and the Honeycomb. By R. P. Blackmur. Harcourt, Brace, 1955.
Creation and Discovery. By Eliseo Vivas. The Noonday Press, 1955.

Malcolm Cowley's *The Literary Situation* has two principal subjects, "an informal history of our literary times" and "a natural history of the American writer," both of which the author discusses at length in a patient, detailed, and usually good-humored way. The style may be called conditionally fair-minded, the condition being that after a fair-minded discussion of any matter we allow Cowley to be right, something he engagingly helps us to do by pointing out with considerable candor those errors which he intends to go right on committing, and those weaknesses of method which cannot, however, be allowed seriously to disturb him in his course. He is quite aware, for example, that all novels are not the same novel, either in the intention or in the result, yet the principle of his discourse requires some such covert agreement to such an extent that we constantly anticipate his coming out with "the average novel" and "the mean annual novelist"; a problem which, when he finally gets to it explicitly, he solves by fictional means: "possibly there is no such creature as an average writer. But if he did exist, and was established in his calling. . . ."

There is no reasonable objection to this kind of composite portrait, or to the means whereby alone it may be represented; only when, as in his "informal history," the same "topographical or taxonomic method" is applied with the object of criticism, some doubt

First published in *The Sewanee Review*, Vol. 63, No. 4, Autumn 1955. Copyright ©
October 20, 1955, by The University of the South.

must be allowed as to whether the critical judgments derive reasonably from the method, which, Cowley admits, "reveals the sorts of qualities, usually faults or foibles, that are common to a group, but not the more important qualities that make a novel survive as a separate work of art." A handsome acknowledgment, but the implicit tendency throughout is to treat the two judgments as one; and on the same page with the above he gives another sample of his propensity for kicking away with one foot what he puts into his mouth with the other: "The postwar period has not produced any novels that the future is likely to call great—only the future is entitled to speak of greatness"—taking, that is, the same liberty with the future which Job's friends took with the ways of the Lord. Given this condition, Cowley is an observant reader of novels (of poems he has scarcely anything to say, though much of the poet's economic situation, which is believed to be poor), he has patiently collected for comparison many examples, and he has produced a readable book with some of whose negative conclusions, at any rate, we may be forced disagreeably to agree.

We live in a period of criticism, Cowley tells us, comparing it with "the Roman Empire during and after the age of the Antonines, which was also the great age of the rhetoricians." Though he does not altogether approve of this situation, neither does he fly into a rage over it, and his treatment of the topic is reasonable beyond the line of the critic's duty as this is set forth, for example, in the editorials of the *New York Times Book Review*. He is favorably impressed by an improvement in the quality of critical writing over the past three decades; he does not make invidiously automatic distinctions between criticism and "creation" (unless inversely: "our critics are now performing the writer's task better than many of the new novelists and poets, whose work by comparison seems timid, formal, and correct"), and he thinks that "the principal creative work" of the period has been, perhaps, "the critical rediscovery and reinterpretation of Melville's *Moby Dick*." Nor does he hold literature responsible for the political attitudes of the time, which he finds "the result of wars and threatened wars, not of books and essays in the quarterly magazines." Of course, these ploughshares may be beaten into swords at any moment: so that the "new" critics are "Alexandrian or scholastic," guilty of a "divorce from life and retreat into libraries," they have a terrible effect on fiction, which has gained "a neo-classical purity and correctness" at the expense of "its force and its common humanity"; and so far as one can make out what sort of literature Cowley ideally would favor the production of, it would be a sort (which he calls "personalism," "affirming the value of separate persons in conflict with social forces") that might very well become responsible for political attitudes and their consequences.

He discusses the fiction of the past decade in three categories: "War Novels," "The 'New' Fiction," and "Naturalism." The war novelists receive a qualified approval; compared with the novelists of the First World War, "more of them reach a certain level of competence or merit," even though none of them has the "separate impact for these times" that Hemingway and Cummings had for the twenties (partly because "the American public has become so familiar with horrors recounted from life"), and even though their competence is conservative in technique; the young men write better because Hemingway taught them to keep their eyes fixed on "actual things." The writers of the twenties were "rebels," whose horrified indignation against war now seems "wrong-headed or simple-minded," but gave their novels "emotional force and a broad perspective," while war novelists at present "have developed an attitude of acquiescence in horror," "have lost the capacity for indignation."

The "new" fiction, which Cowley proposes to discuss "objectively, in the spirit of a foreign sociologist, say a cultivated Hindu," is not let off so easily, being anatomized in all its parts: dust jacket, photograph, epigraph, and contents. It is negative, capable of only a limited number of themes, and "seldom deals with the familiar American theme of social mobility." On the other hand it is very craftsmanlike. It is written by "university men and women," whose careers, in a comically stereotyped description, are said to depend on such factors as being well reviewed in the quarterlies ("he is certain to be made a full professor"), and who are said to revise scenes in their work so as to offend nobody on the board of regents—the imitation of a Hindu sociologist is at this point, I should say, particularly convincing.

Writers of the "new" fiction are also charged with being too much under the thumb of the "new" criticism, too much concerned with "symbolism" and "irony," with "the private experience of a few isolated individuals in some untypical setting—for example, a Back Bay mansion transformed into a brothel" (what won't they think of next, those novelists?)—and with being, finally, "lacking in values."

"Well, then," we think as we turn to the next chapter, "it must be naturalism; what about dusting off that old copy of *Studs Lonigan?*" But Cowley has a surprise for us; it is not naturalism, or not quite naturalism, because naturalism wants a proper respect for language ("I have always felt by instinct that language was the central problem of any writer, in any creative medium"), and because naturalism is impersonal, predestinarian, connected with science by false analogies such as mechanism. What is it, then? It is "personalism": it is Nelson Algren, Ralph Ellison, and Saul Bellow, all three of whose novels have "big" subjects and "are concerned with social forces," but "don't leave us with the impression that the forces were everything or that the characters were 'nothings, mere animalculae.'"

The position, and the complaints that go with it, are familiar; Cowley's distinction is that he does all this "in a nice way." There is a noticeable current of nostalgia for the older, better days with which the author's name is honorably associated—"some of the older men. . . . might have told the young novelists what was likely to happen and is in fact happening today"—and a corresponding predilection for the work of John W. Aldridge, "a young critic but not a 'new' one," who in comparing current novelists with Hemingway, Fitzgerald, and Dos Passos "concludes that the older group was doing much more important work at the same age." Granting the truth of this point, and not quibbling about the relation of "importance" to excellence in literature—nevertheless, what's to be done about it? After we learn that "one could start with the Soviet novel, subtract the bureaucratic qualities, add a greater psychological depth and more attention to form, and the result would be possible masterpieces," it is not much help to hear the candid admission that "novels aren't compounded by a judicious mixture of ingredients." They are not, and Cowley might as well come out of the kitchen.

The second half of his book sketches "a natural history of the American writer," and this often amusing description, like Coleridge's "affectionate exhortation to those who in early life feel themselves disposed to become authors," had the effect on my morale that is so well expressed by an earlier writer:

> O! if this were seen,
> The happiest youth, viewing his progress through,
> What perils past, what crosses to ensue,
> Would shut the book, and sit him down and die.

Coleridge, in the chapter of the *Biographia Literaria* just mentioned, gives us two terms for our subject: "the profession of literature, or (to speak more plainly) the *trade* of authorship." Cowley does not often distinguish these things, and certainly gives little evidence of regarding them as opposites; whereas R. P. Blackmur, sterner even than Coleridge, declares that "the trade of writing is the chief positive obstacle, in our world, to the preservation and creation of the art of literature." That is a very austere sentence, and *The Lion and the Honeycomb*, indeed, abounds in austerities: it is subtitled "Essays in Solicitude and Critique," its standards of judgment may be summed up in the problematic pathos experienced by the literate mind on hearing the name of Dante, and its author is not averse from the divine or pontifical gesture of absolute distinction, as when in speaking of "the humanities in our generation" he takes time out to declare: "I mean of course the official or institutional humanities, not the agitations and deracinations of individuals." But this austerity, too, is what gives Blackmur's book its seriousness, and the seriousness confers a charm; he is in some ways, I suppose, a high priest, or a candidate for the succession, but he is a very good one.

He begins with an assessment of "the situation," reflections produced by a tour of the Middle East in 1954. What he finds, and describes as "the new illiteracy," is by no means new—it was discussed a quarter-century ago, for example, by Ortega y Gasset, and slightly later by Wyndham Lewis—but still with us, and sufficiently frightening. And he ends with a prayerful essay far out in the eternity of dialectic, "Between the Numen and the Moha" (the latter term means "the vital, fundamental stupidity of the human race"), of which the conclusion is the prayer of Platon Karataev: "Let me lie down, oh God, like a stone, and wake like fresh bread." In this progression, the central point in many ways is marked by an essay on "Humanism and Symbolic Imagination," some description of which may serve to suggest the argument of the book.

Humanism, in this piece, is represented by Irving Babbitt, whom Blackmur apologetically resurrects not for his own sake but purely as an emblem, one of those, "quite dead in themselves and whose work is quite finished, who yet survive by implication. . . . as representatives, unusually pure in type, of being and work more wholly achieved by others." In Blackmur's drama, Babbitt (or Humanism) typifies the achievement of an order too narrowly defined, too soon concluded, too rigidly maintained, and incapable therefore of managing, save by arrogant exclusions, the rich chaos of the actual; an order whose powers of statement are entirely confined to the generalized and the intellectual, and thus, at last, incapable of "grace," "the grace indeed that suddenly inhabits all things deeply realized" and that is "expressed if at all through the symbolic imagination." He sees in Babbitt "a mind contaminated by the lust for order, a lust which amounted at times to a trembling bodily infatuation which if it did not destroy order certainly dismantled it, rendering it incapable of the great primary virile act of composition." Something of this sort is what Shakespeare saw in Angelo, and Babbitt, like Angelo, is the character whose sin is precisely the flower of his virtue; he corrupts with virtuous season. "How is it that minds may be so virile in principle and so emasculated in act, so fecund in pattern and so sterile in texture?" The answer to that question is uncertain, but "the decay of Christian imagination, the voiding of religious imagination of any description, has a great deal to do with it."

So over against Babbitt—there where, we might say, the Duke ought to be—is "symbolic imagination," a term in several ways problematical. Symbolic imagination must not be defined narrowly as an intellectual antithesis of Humanism; it must include, extend, and enrich Humanism, and must always remain, like grace, a mysterious overplus rather to be recognized in the event than described in general terms; and, of course, it cannot—or so one would think—be legislated into being. At the same time, it must retain some intellectual content in order to be thought about at all, but this intellectual content must be distinguished from a number of specific forms which it has taken in the past. Thus, though Christian imagination is clearly one of the forms taken by symbolic imagination, the author is not arguing for a return to that form: "Mr. Eliot has his own arguments, which are best read by those of his own persuasion. Here I make no need for a profession of faith, nor for any psychological substitute for the experience of conversion; I do not believe either to be generally possible. . . ." If it is not Eliot, neither is it Arnold: "Poetry is by no means to be understood as anything but an *inadequate* substitute for religion." Nor can it be allowed to be simply pantheism or panpsychism, though it begins, like these, with the animistic and the naturally symbolic: "it is the power of creating or discovering symbols which are the sources as well as the reminders of meaning," and "the man who uses the symbolic imagination must find the most part of his poetry already written for him out of the live, vast waste of disorder of the actual." "The symbolic imagination perhaps can be put as the means of bringing to significance, to order, the knowledge we have above and below the level of the mind. It is, in short, the chief mode of participation in the life common to all men at all times."

Now all this is so put that not to agree with a good deal of it—with its "solicitude" if not entirely with its "critique"—is like not being against sin. Few these days would care to resemble the villainous Babbitt represented to us by this essay, and many will recognize the need for a charity of the imagination—a kind of Pythagorean *harmonia* tempering the soul and the spheres together—which shall not be merely an imaginary charity. And generally, I find much to sympathize with in Blackmur's views in this book; with his diagnosis, for example, of "a society of priests or experts who are strangely alien to the great mass movements which they presumably express or control," and with the corrective ideal, so far as literary criticism is concerned, of the complete scholar-critic who "must be the master layman of as many modes of human understanding as possible in a single act of the mind." But, coming back to the essay on Babbitt, I am a trifle chilled to hear that "it is both necessary and possible that we make a secular equivalent of the religious imagination." We? Who? And which of us by taking thought? I wonder, not that austerity too should have its dangers, but that they should be pretty nearly the same as those which spoil Cowley's practical tips to novelists—the danger in particular of taking the thing talked about for the thing done; and the slight, ineradicable absurdity in lecturing to penguins on the theory of flight. For Blackmur seems to urge (or pray) that all become poets, and behind his argument is the noble view held by Ben Jonson, that the good poet is the good man—also an austerity, since it is probably no easier to be a good poet than to be a good man according to any other ethical arrangement—with the specifically modern extension that the good poet, having finally after all these centuries dropped the mask, is really our new friend the complete scholar-critic. And when I ask myself what sense I am to take from the parable of the lion and the honeycomb as Blackmur uses it, I must conclude that the dead lion is poetry, swarming with critics: from strength shall come forth bees looking like tiny lions—

"So get you gone, Von Hügel, though with blessings on your head."

I think this happens—if I am right in supposing it does happen —precisely because Blackmur is a good poet and, moreover, a very good critic for whom criticism itself becomes a kind of poetry, developing a lyrical absolutism of its own, though "always provisionally within the modes of the rational imagination." There are essays in this volume which enable us to replace that somewhat blank term "symbolic imagination" with the names, for example, of Dante and Henry James, and in those essays Blackmur demonstrates that acute and persevering intelligence with a passion for accuracy which makes him exemplary as a critic. But those great presences do not solve the theoretical *impasse*; they only complicate it further. The complete scholar-critic could probably, at a pinch, invent Dante, but not the *Comedy*; and the lion must do a lifetime's damage, in the wild and in the sown, before the bees can get to work.

Cowley is essentially a journalist making forays into criticism; Blackmur a critic occasionally venturing into journalism but chiefly concerned, in the present work, with generalizing his criticism into an aesthetic. Eliseo Vivas, after giving to begin with some samples of his criticism (on Dreiser, Kafka, the brothers James and *The Brothers Karamazov*), devotes the body of his book to aesthetics, theory of criticism, criticism of criticism, with the kind of purity which can discuss the question "What is a Poem?" for twenty pages without quoting or discussing examples. This purity, of course, is part of the intention, it is what an aesthetician does; and as I am not an aesthetician my judgments about this book must be taken as the judgments merely of a layman interested in poetry.

The title of Vivas' book is *Creation and Discovery*; the keyword, or the disputable one, being "and," for we are told that neither alternative will do: the poet both creates what is not there and discovers what is, "the world is given us *in* as well as *through* the language of poetry." Proper aesthetic apprehension is defined as an "intransitive attention" which we give to the poem, looking at it and not beyond it, at what it is and not at what it says about something other than itself. Yet at the same time "the poet brings forth values with which history is in the pain of labor"; "he is a midwife and uses the forceps of language" (I shall come back presently to the author's metaphors).

To maintain his position Vivas must and does attack the Aristotelian theory of imitation; also Eliot's theory of the objective correlative (which Blackmur takes less absolutely, calling it "an observation put into the form of a notion"); since both these views seem to him predicated upon an already existing reality which is merely discovered by the poem, and with which the poem may usefully be compared—a reality, that is, capable of being described apart from the poem. According to Vivas, the poet both makes reality and discovers it, nor is this paradox allowed to be a paradox:

> But how shall we resolve the contradiction involved in the claim that the artist *creates* novel objects and that he *discovers* the hidden reality of our practical, commonsense world? The contradiction is only apparent, not real, since the two assertions were made from different points of view. From an external point of view, there is novelty in his product and spontaneity is involved in the process. From the standpoint of the artist, however, we grasp a different aspect of the creative process, since what the artist does is not to invent something new but to extricate out of the subject matter at hand its own proper structure or order.

And the upshot of the matter even includes a half-hearted reconciliation with Aristotle: "If this is what the theory of imitation intends . . . it is a valid theory." Moreover, it is difficult for a layman to avoid the suspicion that what we have here is not so unlike what older terminologies quarreled over as matter and form: "the poet divides the light from darkness, and gives us an ordered world." "What the artist does . . . is to wrench from his subject matter something that is not fully realized in it, or that, life being the bungling thing it is, is realized in a different manner than it would be if it were designed to meet the demands of aesthetic order exclusively." "The artist *creates* then, in the sense that he makes a dramatic structure out of subject matter in which the ordinary ungifted mind would not think of looking for it. . . . The writer *discovers* this structure, in the sense that the forms and the substance of his work are found by him in the data of experience which is the subject matter of his art."

Now I do not dispute about the essential thing here, not because I am not an aesthetician, but because I believe Vivas to be quite right: he is talking about the scandal to the Pharisees and the *credo quia absurdum* of poetry, something which poets have so naturally held to be true that they mention it only rather casually, as Dryden does in speaking of "the invention, or finding of the thought" without making any distinction between the one and the other, or as

Wordsworth does when he speaks of the poet (a man "pleased with his own passions and volitions") as "delighting to contemplate similar volitions and passions as manifested in the goings-on of the Universe, and habitually impelled to create them where he does not find them." Habitually, mind you. (See also the passage quoted above from Blackmur, on "the power of creating or discovering symbols.") The danger is only that any long discussion of this mystery becomes a discussion among Pharisees, involving not Vivas alone but all who dispute in circularities where we define literature as "a symbolic construct of what life ought to be like in order to answer the demands of aesthetic apprehension of it," or where we say that "art involves material that possesses an inherent capacity for organization, shaped intentionally by the artist in order to capture a determinate congeries of aesthetic values." In much the same way it has been held that intelligence is a quality tested by intelligence tests, and that sleep is produced by *virtus dormitivus*. Perhaps we shall do best to say of Vivas what he says of I. A. Richards: "a critical examination of his theories will, however, reveal that they often suffer from defects similar to those he has noticed in others." Which might be a suitable epitaph for all of us.

A word, finally, about style. The aesthetician's purity also has its dangers, chief among them the revenge that invading metaphors take upon abstract discussion. While Vivas is speaking rationally about literature, his imagination dwells in dreadful detail upon food: James "pounced on the morsel he selected from the offered tray with the wolfish relish of a starved man"; some poets have tendencies "to feed exclusively from art and to eschew those tougher cuts that come from the rest of life"; ideas may lie heavy in the artist's mind, "like the stones in the wolf's belly in the fairy tale, and not feeding him." In general, "the artistic process does not consist in lowering a bucket into the muddy current of the actual and emptying all one picks up into a book. The artist must wait till the bucket settles before he can catch the elusive silvery animals that shall make his feast." And, worse even than eating elusive silvery animals, "Were we able to put our cognitive teeth on the aorta of Being itself, and were we able to drink the truth directly from it. . . ." Let us be grateful for whatever it is in Nature that prevents the aesthetician from satisfying his ferocious wish.

These three books represent three fairly distinct approaches to "literature," which is, perhaps, no very difficult subject where it can be demonstrated to be a subject at all; that is, where the generality is also *about* the particulars to which it claims to refer, and is not merely a statistical abstract or Platonic archetype resembling none of them. So far as the three ventures may be compared, I think Blackmur's the most excellent kind, not only because he is the most gifted writer of the three but also because the critic begins nearer the center than the journalist or the aesthetician. The critic at any rate has the right Odyssean ambition of avoiding Charybdis, avoiding Scylla, and sailing on; while the journalist has set up a ferry service to shuttle rapidly back and forth between those two now thriving ports; and the aesthetician, I am tempted to think, stays on shore, in that magnificent chess club of the aestheticians, where Ferdinand and Miranda, who do not play well enough, have not been invited.

A Survey of Criticism

The Armed Vision, A Study in the Methods of Modern Literary Criticism. By Stanley Edgar Hyman. Knopf, 1948.

Ola! silenzio, silenzio, silenzio! io son qui per giudicar.—da Ponte.

This is a book of information and criticism. The received opinion about reviewing such books, if I may generalize from contemporary practice, seems to be that the reviewer, who *knows more* than the author, requires the book merely as a stimulus and as a means of directing his attention to the area of discourse under survey, whereupon his qualifications by some miraculous means far exceed those of the author; his function then, still according to contemporary practice, is to inform the public and the author of those things the author did which he should not have done, of those things he did not do which he should have done, and of those things which he did and did badly—the reviewer plays the trump of that small learning he can add to the author's large learning and takes the trick; or, as in the parable of the flea and the elephant, he sits in the author's ear and says to him, "We sure shook that bridge." Having done these things the reviewer, if he doesn't much like the book, is at liberty to make a nasty remark about its thesis if any (whereupon the rules of the game allow the sentence, "Space does not permit me to go into my reasons," etc., or one of its many recognized variants) and then—something that is hardly licensed except in a review —to denigrate The Style, that is, to make use of the wonderful and meaningless conception, left over from a school of polite editorial prose and inherited for some reason by criticism instead of by schools of business English, that Good Writing is Good Writing no matter what. Then the reviewer may go home, having in a manner *written* the book by symbolically triumphing over it.

Having said so much, I recognize how difficult it will be to avoid making the best, or worst, of these public conveniences (as they may be called), which are as attractive as they ought to be reprehensible: they allow the reviewer to evade his proper work, and not only so but seem to congratulate him for it; they suggest, without demonstrating, his qualifications for evaluating the work; they discount what may be in some cases the sole meritorious feature of the work, the effort, learning, study that have gone to composing it; further they make for a tone of contempt designed to show that the reviewer is a superior person who here labors with the left hand.

But any apology this suggests should be taken in a limited and technical sense: honesty and dishonesty may avail themselves about equally of any device; my elders and betters have shown me no very good model for the tone and manners of a review (Mr. Hyman himself being as a reviewer no less querulous and ill-tempered than many among us: see *Accent*, Spring 1948); we do not in these things love the sinner while hating his sin: rather the reverse.

On the one hand I have not the deep and extensive learning Mr. Hyman has. He has read far more than I have, and studied his subject with greater intensity and for a much longer time; where he modestly disclaims sufficient knowledge for a discussion of physics, I as modestly disclaim sufficient knowledge to understand his disclaimer. On the other hand I find myself unable to agree with Mr. Hyman in what seems to me his major intention, the establishment of a "collective criticism," and in many places unable to admire the tone and manners of his book. I shall try as best I can to reason out the nature of my discontents in what follows, describing the plan and procedure of *The Armed Vision* and speaking mostly of particulars, and then describing what I conceive to be the kind, the intention, and the result of the book, and at last advancing my more general differences.

It is with some shame I note that I propose doing exactly what Mr. Hyman's publisher has confidently predicted I (or another, or many others) will be doing: "a book," he says on the dust jacket, "over which rivers of ink will eventually be spilled." Whether this is intended literally or as a trope is not a hard judgment, but if we apply Mr. Hyman's critical method we emerge with the suggestion that the id of at least a hired blurb-writer has not too obscurely had its revenge.

Mr. Hyman intends first of all a critical description of modern literary criticism, which he defines "crudely and somewhat inaccurately" as "*the organized use of non-literary techniques and bodies of knowledge to obtain insights into literature.*" He cites John Crowe Ransom to the effect that "ours is an age of more than usual critical distinction," but, he says, "We cannot flatter ourselves that the superiority lies in the caliber of our critics as opposed to their predecessors. Clearly it lies in their methods." So far as this takes us, it is rather "armament" than "vision" that is to be described, yet the author includes both by treating single authors as exemplary of dominant emphases in method, as his chapter headings indicate, which it will be convenient to list here as showing the outline of the work: an introduction on the nature and ancestry of modern literary criticism; "Edmund Wilson and Translation in Criticism"; "Yvor Winters and Evaluation in Criticism"; "T. S. Eliot and Tradition in Criticism"; "Van Wyck Brooks and Biographical Criticism"; "Constance Rourke and Folk Criticism"; "Maud Bodkin and Psychological Criticism"; "Christopher Caudwell and Marxist Criticism"; "Caroline Spurgeon and Scholarship in Criticism"; "R. P. Blackmur and the Expense of Criticism"; "William Empson and Categorical Criticism"; "I. A. Richards and the Criticism of Interpretation"; "Kenneth Burke and the Criticism of Symbolic Action"; a conclusion, "Attempts at an Integration," composed of two parts, "The Ideal Critic" and "The Actual Critic."

If this organization is factitious (like another) Mr. Hyman does nevertheless a persuasive job of definition and arrangement. Within a chapter he follows, with few variations, a quite intricate pattern treating these factors: a general discussion of the method as employed by the critic who serves as its illustration; a brief outline of that critic's work; a more detailed study of one or more of his major works; a survey of his ancestry in the method; of certain contemporaries who also use this method in one or another variation; a detailed (and often zestful) appreciation of the critic's faults, failings, with, in special instances, a little account of what social and sexual inadequacies and peculiarities are supposed by Mr. Hyman to "underlie" and "explain" the critic's professional work.

We have then (to exclude for the moment the introduction and conclusion) twelve chapters equating men and methods; the arrangement seems to be into an ascending scale of approval not chapter by chapter but in three groups: Wilson, Winters, Eliot, Van Wyck

Brooks, who are on the whole bad; Rourke, Bodkin, Caudwell, Spurgeon, who are on the whole interesting; Blackmur, Empson, Richards, Burke, who are good. I consider that Mr. Hyman is at his best in dealing with people he likes, for he has less incentive to discuss them as problems in personality and thus more time for their work. His essays on Mr. Blackmur and Mr. Burke seem to me ordered and lucid and full of understanding. Where he is offended he has the habit of letting the great ax fall (he notes as one of Mr. Blackmur's weaknesses "an excess of charity to his colleagues"), sometimes with justice and sometimes on his own foot; for controversial ill temper he has substituted a good-humored and superior, though nonetheless tendentious, predilection for epigrams, and I do not see that these, whether they be wicked or coy, do much for criticism. Edmund Wilson has "written his own obituary so effectively that it would be presumptuous for anyone else to kill him off." Van Wyck Brooks is "a narrow and embittered old gentleman with a white moustache." The tone of Mr. Hyman's scorn, in these first chapters at any rate, is too obviously triumphal, and his opinion of Van Wyck Brooks would seem to make the twenty or so pages spent on demolition a matter rather of pleasure than necessity, while the long attack on Edmund Wilson seems to me a buffoonery and an impertinence.

Mr. Hyman's own methods are many, changing with the job at hand. In his critical mood he owes most to Kenneth Burke, but because of the surprising number of his duties in this volume he is not often in that mood. He is by occasion a bibliographer, a scholar, a historian, a man who knows all there is to know about. . . . His best vein, I think, is the one he distinguishes as belonging to Edmund Wilson: he is a popularizer, an introductory critic, a "translator," he gives the "plots" of critical works and excels at concise abstraction and summary of relevant material from voluminous sources. He is also a pedant: "Almost the parody of literary genealogy," he remarks, "is found in the work of an American critic, Joseph Warren Beach," and gives his evidence: Beach has professed to find as influences on Dos Passos "*Ulysses*, Dorothy Richardson, Virginia Woolf, *The Waste Land*, Sandburg, Jules Romains," etc., etc.—a sufficiently ridiculous list, of which Mr. Hyman says, "By this point traditionalism has come a long way." In Mr. Hyman's own judgments it sometimes comes at least an equal distance: the statement that "Wilson's work is traditional in a sense that most contemporary criticism is not" evokes a tradition including Anaxagoras, Anaximander, Stesimbrotus, Glaucus (or Glaucon), Philo Judaeus, St. Augustine, Fulgentius, etc., etc. And while with I. A. Richards he sneers affably enough at "those godlike lords of the syllabus-world, who think that the whole of English Literature can be perused with profit in about a year," his own tempo, especially when dealing with minor authors, has occasionally the speed and terse urgency of the *Outline History* series.

Mr. Hyman has in fact an unhappy gift for pardoning easily in himself what he will by no means pardon in others. Thus he says, "instead of discussing the poem, Wilson reprinted Roger Fry's commentary, surely an unequaled job of shirking in a professional critic." (We are still, I suppose, at liberty to suggest that Mr. Wilson thought Fry had done a good job.) But presently we find Mr. Hyman recommending that "it is about time someone polished off the term 'escape' as a critical concept," and doing it by quoting passages from F. O. Matthiessen and Kenneth Burke published in 1935. And in saying that Yvor Winters' treatment of Henry James "is one of the most completely inadequate in critical writing of our time" is not he doing precisely what he objects to in Mr. Winters? that is, making statements which, whether they are so or not, are not supported in the text. Finally, this ambiguous behavior is erected into a principle of method: "It is always worth doing, as a kind of ultimate test, to turn a man's critical method on himself, his own life and work." This ultimate test issues, so far as I can make out, in a biographical sneer or a pretty compliment. Mr. Hyman is extremely fond of taking statements from the work and applying them to the life, and he seems rather pleased than surprised at being able to record of Mr. Eliot, "The personality that emerges finally is not, as we should expect, that of the triumphant great artist who has achieved, in the *Quartets*, one of the authentic masterpieces of our time, but that of a sick, defeated and suffering man." It may be worth noting in general that whom Mr. Hyman spews out and condemns seem all to have relapsed into the same heretical malady of nerve, being either sick and defeated and suffering, or bitter, or the victims of "a patent and rather frightening insecurity." I suspect that the old despised charge of "escapism" is, for all the exhortations to reform, still doing business at the same stand. What constitutes Mr. Hyman's predisposition to this kind of judgment is not always clear, but vaguely discernible behind the reproach that Edmund Wilson "seems entirely lacking in either humor or human warmth," and unequivocally visible in the statement that Parrington's book "created perhaps the first rounded progressive-democratic-social tradition for American writers to match the reactionary-aristocratic-religious tradition of Eliot, Ransom, Winters, et al." These are key words in Mr. Hyman's war, and there is about their distinctions not only a clear invitation to choose sides but also a description of the reader whose agreement Mr. Hyman perfectly assumes, and to whom I believe he is addressing himself.

A similar "rounded progressive-democratic-social" emphasis and approval characterize Mr. Hyman's conclusions. I will not discuss "The Ideal Critic" since I am able to agree with Mr. Hyman that this personage "is of course nonsense" though not so readily that he is "perhaps useful nonsense as a Platonic archetype." But Mr. Hyman's recommendations to "actual" critics must certainly be put down in part at least.

> With the tremendous growth of the social sciences in particular, sooner or later knowing enough of any one of them to turn it fruitfully on literature will demand a life study, leaving no time for anything else except some acquaintance with the corpus of literature itself.

I am grateful there will be time for some acquaintance. Again,

> A new magazine, calling itself the *Critic* or the *Symposium*, devoted to a detailed collective study of a man or a book or a poem in each issue, acquiring and training a body of specialist critics capable of doing the things it wanted done . . . could solve some of these problems. . . .

Parturiunt montes, nascitur another magazine.

Having come this far I must ask, Why *The Armed Vision?* Here is a work which, whatever I may conceive to be its particular failings with respect to tone and various technical factors, is a learned account of modern literary criticism, together with some conclusions and suggestions about the future and possible organization of this field. I suppose my question to comprise the following divisions: what kind of book this is, and what it has to do with criticism; whether criticism is "autotelic" or (Blackmur) "self-sufficient but by no means isolated"; whether it ought to be; for whom this book is designed; what kind of use different sorts of reader will make of it.

The Armed Vision, though not alphabetically arranged, is encyclopedic, a reference book (the index is more than a twentieth the length of the text); it contains a selective bibliography which would prove of great assistance to any person, however educated, purposing the study of modern criticism. It is a history not only of a period (the past twenty-five years) but of traditions which, its author contends, go back a considerable time. It is a critical work, inasmuch as it describes with intent to evaluate; it is a scientific work, of a sociological sort, inasmuch as it proposes controls, coordinations, integrations which would "bureaucratize" method into methodology and make the kind of knowledge offered by criticism verifiable by experiment that would, ideally, free itself from the personality of the observer. At last, it is recognizably a textbook, and certainly the most complete (if not, indeed, the only one) in its field.

What *The Armed Vision* has to do with literary criticism? This: it shows that criticism is going, and proposes that it ought to keep going, away from "experience" and towards "knowledge." This distinction (whose terms seem to be mine and none of Mr. Hyman's) would be merely ludicrous if its possibilities were limited, but as they are not it describes a real dilemma: naturally experience of a poem and knowledge of it are likely even in the crudest reading to share common ground, and in a good reading they would be as nearly as possible one. But as criticism becomes a science, a "detailed collective study" by "a body of specialist critics" intent on solving "problems," it becomes by so much a means to knowledge, and the work it studies is no longer an experience because it has no experiencing subject (unless the body of specialist critics in full Sorbonne should literally incorporate itself). It is a difficult choice, then: either you read the poem, and like it or dislike it, and reason out however partially and inadequately why; or you interest yourself in "knowledge" and it is right for you to hire an academy which will tabulate the results of the poem for psychology, sociology, botany, history, religion, etc. And a further effect of *The Armed Vision* on criticism is to make the subject educationally legitimate and viable.

"In actual practice," Mr. Hyman writes, "modern criticism has been at once completely autotelic and inextricably tied to poetry. That is, like any criticism, it guides, nourishes, and lives off art and is thus, from another point of view, a handmaiden to art, parasitic at worst and symbiotic at best." Mr. Eliot is rebuked for calling the assumption "preposterous" that criticism is an autotelic art, and I can see indeed that according to present practice the assumption is not preposterous; so many essays in our journals give the impression, and Mr. Hyman's own proposals also seem to suggest, that the destruction unto oblivion of all the art that has ever been would leave criticism staggered perhaps, but milling bravely around all the same.

Whether criticism should be autotelic, or self-sufficient but by no means isolated? The answer, probably, is If it amuses the critic. It has been sufficiently admitted that criticism requires poetry as an occasion at least, but no one has quite said whether it requires good poetry, and in effect that judgment is one that criticism finds itself less than ever able to make or interested in making. If poetry is to be considered mainly in symposium as a means rather to knowledge than experience, I do not see that bad poetry (ah, these outworn and traditional terms) is any less qualified than good, for the Gallup poll of sociologists, the show of hands at the faculty meeting. Mr. Mark Van Doren is severely rated by our author for "the most complete and eloquent attack on modern criticism with which I am familiar." Mr. Van Doren was "eloquent" and, in his melancholy, impassioned, and it may be that he did exercise "a pure obscurantism"; I have affiliations with Mr. Hyman's side of the question but am somewhat impatient of his impatience. And I think it not impossible that Mr. Van Doren was right in saying "Poetry itself can do with silence for a while." It is a kind of criticism that has not recently been tried. But if poetry can do with silence, criticism cannot.

At last, who is to read this work, and what is he to read it for? Do we envision the tired businessman getting around the problem of "modern poetry" by reading a highly rational account of what some people have said about it? Or the undergraduate, cramming for that quiz on the fallacy of expressive form? Or the graduate student, for whose proposed teaching career the book may represent almost the entire critical equipment? Or perhaps the full professor, whose relations with modern criticism will not run to marriage but may include this brief liaison? For if you haven't read the major texts with which the book works you are reading a popularization, of a very educational sort, of course (somehow these doctrines are always considerably easier in Mr. Hyman's version than in the originals, where the train of thought is always being interrupted by the consideration of a poem); if you have read them and studied them you may be charmed with Mr. Hyman or alarmed at him—according, that is, as you are a progressive positivist or a reactionary obscurantist—but you will probably not be instructed by him.

Finally it must be, I suppose, the undergraduate. Modern criticism is unmistakably in business and the tigers of wrath will eat the dung of the horses of instruction. Mr. Hyman with his advanced survey course seems to be on the winning side.

Iniquity It Is; But Pass the Can

A. E. Housman: *Scholar and Poet*. By Norman Marlow. University of Minnesota Press, 1958.

Mr. Marlow contends that his poet, for whom he feels "admiration and even veneration," has been ill-treated, or not treated at all: "Twenty years after Housman's death there is still no comprehensive study of his poetry in English and very little balanced criticism of it." To set this matter straight is a praiseworthy ambition, but Mr. Marlow's performance is unconvincing, though I suppose competent at the routine scholarly duties which occupy two-thirds of the book, and I finished his course more doubtful of Housman's quality than before. Rereading the poems decided me that Mr. Marlow, rather than the poet, was responsible for this sorry result.

After a brief biographical sketch there follow four chapters cataloguing and commenting influences on Housman's poetry; these chapters take up 119 pages out of the total of 179 to demonstrate resemblances to, echoes of, borrowings from, e.g., the Greek and Latin poets, Shakespeare, the Border Ballads, Milton, Tennyson, etc., etc. The excesses of this detective work are sometimes absurd. If Mr. Marlow sees in Housman the phrase "willows in the icy brook," he tells you it is "not unlike" Gertrude's line in describing the death of Ophelia, "There is a willow grows aslant a brook." But it *is* unlike. And if Mr. Marlow sees Housman employ the phrase "eternal bedfellows," he says that "it reminds us of Trinculo's 'Misery acquaints a man with strange bedfellows.'" But it does not remind me, even after the reminder. And if Mr. Marlow reads Housman's lines, "And since to look at things in bloom / Fifty springs are little room," he will have us "contrast" the last phrase with Coverdale's translation of Psalm xxxi. 9: "Thou hast set my feet in a large room." To this contrast I am easily able to agree; the two phrases are indeed poles apart. The climax of this sort of thing is reached with the news that the title *Last Poems* is "probably suggested by Heine's *Letzte Gedichte*." Sometimes, too, wearying himself or anticipating our weariness with so one-sided a relationship, he simply reverses it: "Tennyson can use monosyllabic verbs in the manner of Housman."

These are perhaps quibbles, and I hear a benign professorial voice saying "Harrumph! useful work, useful work." So it may be, but it is disconcerting to have Mr. Marlow in his preface threaten us with much more of it: "I regard this section of the book as merely a necessary basis on which a future critic may build." Without waiting for the future critic, I am convinced by Mr. Marlow alone that "in his search for the forthright phrase Housman draws impartially on all periods of English poetry."

After such knowledge, the next chapter begins: "Confronted with such a collection of reminiscences in Housman's poetry, one might well be pardoned for asking how much is left to Housman himself and whether his poetry is worth much on its own." The answer to this is not easy—"It must be admitted that he had not a creative mind"—and Mr. Marlow asserts his claims on the following page with a judicious moderation indistinguishable from half-heartedness: "But while his architectonic faculty was weak, his poetic sensibility was exquisite. He knew instinctively the kind of thing a poet says, and the early imitations of Swinburne, his own parodies and not least his Latin verses show how perfectly he became attuned to the style of individual poets in English and Latin. His memory was marvelous and together with this ear for poetry made possible his unique work in scholarship." Of this last, by the way, despite the claim of the book's title to consider this area, we hear no great deal; a general encomium of Housman's "savage mockery and devastating wit" is unaccompanied by any example.

It might be supposed that an admiration so narrowly limited in the terms of its praise would be matched by a broad tolerance of other opinions: you, that way; we, this way. Not so. What admiration cannot do, veneration will supply, and in his chapter of eleven pages on "Contemporary Criticism of Housman" Mr. Marlow strikes a good many attitudes in the style of a religious journalist abusing some sect other than his own: lofty disdain, withering scorn, savage irony, contemptuous abuse, sweet reasonableness, and sincere appeal to all right-thinking persons.

Now it is unfortunately not difficult to compile, on any subject whatever having to do with literature, a not so small anthology of the follies of critics, and Mr. Marlow exhibits a few worthy of being ranked with some of his own. My objection is that he doesn't argue with these people, but slangs them, sometimes for brief phrases which seem to have been snipped not without some malice from contexts in which they perhaps would have made better sense. I drew the conclusions from all this, first, that Mr. Marlow does not like modern criticism ("indeed, the earlier critics are vastly superior to the latter," he says, taking us back to 1896 for an opinion), and, second, that Mr. Marlow has a notion that criticism, far from being a matter of opinion supported by evidence, is quite simply a matter of being right, which in the baldest fashion imaginable is identified with being of the same opinion as Mr. Marlow. He cannot bear being disagreed with, but regards the disagreement of other critics among themselves as a mighty blow in favor of himself, listing a paragraph of what he calls "comic contradictions." But since the epithets he quotes are not by one critic but by many, it is difficult to agree that any contradiction is involved, no one of these persons having been responsible for the views of any or all of the others. The differences of opinion, which are indeed extreme, and involve absolutely opposed ideas of Housman's poetry, might have suggested to a more temperate student the possibility of there being something very problematic about the work which inspired such a variety of opinions; but Mr. Marlow does not seem to look at the matter in this way.

For all the demonstration space allows and interest demands, here is Mr. Marlow's *entire* treatment of one writer on Housman; it is not untypical of his dealings with the others:

> Ezra Pound's effort in the *Criterion* for January, 1934, has to be read to be believed; the only way in which one could account for its being printed at all is on the theory that a highbrow journal would at that time print any rant that came from so august a source. Let those who doubt this go to the British Museum and read it.

Now it was a great inconvenience for me to have to go to the British Museum, several thousand miles away, only to read a few pages in a highbrow journal (does Mr. Marlow mean this distinction to convey that he prefers low or middlebrow journals?), but I knew my duty and am able to report that Mr. Pound's piece, "Mr. Housman at Little Bethel," is a review of "The Name and Nature of Poetry." Mr. Pound's writing is a good deal funnier than Mr. Marlow's—"Milton, thou should'st be living at this hour!" he cries, and adds a footnote: "Meaning that he might have lectured at Cambridge"—but his criticism is a good deal more serious than Mr. Marlow's, too. Though expressed with a certain perky and slangy familiarity, Mr. Pound's piece shows throughout the only real respect one poet would think worth having from another, that is, a detailed examination of the arguments set forth, a statement of some differences of opinion *with* the evidence for them, and some praise which is to be valued for being the product of thought, not enthusiasm. If Mr. Marlow regards our difference of opinion on Mr. Pound's piece as improper, let him go to the British Museum and read it again.

I do not doubt, and am only respectful of, Mr. Marlow's sincere admiration for Housman's poetry; but the book he has written scarcely accomplishes its object, and is for the most part, though not simultaneously, trivial, dull, and ill-tempered. Perhaps the best that can be said of it is that it shows a scholarly thoroughness; yet I may risk reminding Mr. Marlow of two essays which I found both pleasant and sensible, and which he does not appear to have come across: John Peale Bishop's, in the *Collected Essays*, on the poetry, and Mr. Edmund Wilson's, in *The Triple Thinkers*, on the scholarship.

The Purgatorio *as Drama*

Dante's Drama of the Mind: A Modern Reading of the Purgatorio. By
Francis Fergusson. Princeton University Press, 1953.

It seems that the highest praise we can give these days to any
literary work (except a play) is to call it a *drama,* and to define its
achievement both substantially and technically as *dramatic.* There is
about these words what we may call, in Lovejoy's phrase, a "metaphysical pathos," and when critics speak of novels, lyrics, and even
essays as *dramatic* we cannot doubt their intention to confer upon
these works not so much a sign of particular distinction in their kinds
as generally a more exalted rank in the nature of things. It is a fashion not unconnected with our contemporary interest in the study
of mythology and what this study suggests as to the development of
the civilized arts from the magical rites of primitive peoples, with
the implication of a dramatic ur-form for the narrative arts generally; so that the peculiar pathos in the idea of the *dramatic* may
consist paradoxically in the achievement of a primitive and elemental motive by means of the most sophisticated devices of form and
thought, a back-to-nature movement in which the Nature sought is
seen to be full of gods.

There is no doubt that the examination of novels, lyrics, etc., for
their dramatic qualities has produced an interpretative criticism of
considerable interest and value; but as every insight induces its proper
blindness, so the idea that excellence in literature must universally
be dramatic is in danger of accommodating altogether too much,
with a consequent loss of useful distinctions and a consequent slight-
ing of works which cannot be accommodated: one sees, for example, how the precarious balance of the terms "creative" and "critical"
has been so overweighted on the one side (with the aid of this very

First published in *The Sewanee Review,* Vol. 61, No. 3, Summer 1953. Copyright ©
August 21, 1953, by The University of the South.

idea, the dramatic) that everywhere, and even in colleges, the writing of a short story (any short story) is held to be a higher and a better thing by far than the writing of an essay, even if the essay happened to be the *Apology for Raymond Sebond.*

These generalities do not of themselves constitute a reason against calling Dante's poem a drama; but two particular difficulties occur to me, neither of them, I admit, altogether convincing, and may as well be mentioned.

First, the *Comedy,* though it has in it many dramatic episodes and though its major and continuing theme of the Pilgrim's ascent may be thought of as dramatic, has one quality which I believe we would commonly speak of as the reverse of dramatic, a quality which it oddly shares with the picaresque romance: that it leaves behind one character after another who will never reappear and who is involved in the action, to use Dante's term, as part of "the setting-forth of examples." There is, then, in the literal narrative a continual novelty of scenes and persons, whereas we are accustomed to think of a drama as proceeding to its resolution by means of a small number of persons who appear over and over. This in itself is no insuperable objection; it means simply that if you wish to show the poem as a drama you must demonstrate above all the bridging and mediating devices of its composition: the way in which certain characters give stability and a larger phrasing to the action by moving with it over a few cantos (Statius, Matelda) or many (Virgil, Beatrice); the way in which certain characters reflect and typify others so as to unify remote parts of the action by analogy (as the *folle volo* of Ulysses, for example, reflects upon Dante's voyage, especially at the end of *Purgatorio* I); the way in which the imagery and metaphors also suggest a unity and continuity of distantly separated episodes (as the rivers of *Inferno* XIV resound behind Guido del Duca's description of the Arno Valley in *Purgatorio* XIV). This pre-eminently must be the critic's work of demonstration, and Mr. Fergusson, where he does it, does it well. I ought to add that it does not seem to me always or even very frequently possible, and this doubt, were there space for it, would raise essential questions about Dante's mode of composition as compared particularly with Shakespeare's, upon which so much of our modern way of reading is based.

My second objection is more nearly theological: that the issues of the poem are never in doubt, just as Dante, but for one or two doubtful places in Hell, is never in danger; the ultimate monism of the vision makes the poet slight theologically what he must intensify poetically, so that the doubt, danger, and evil of the world culminate in a figure which I cannot see as dramatic: Satan frozen in the pit of Hell. It is theologically, and even poetically, a fine solution, the literal result of "*gravezza*," and it is, if you like, ritual, which is half the matter; but not drama—just as it is not drama for the Pilgrim to be protected by angels during his first night on the mountain; where any drama, in the sense of free and open possibility, would be theologically inadmissible. But here it seems to me that the argument is not merely a quibble over the term "drama" but has to do with the more serious question of our appreciation of the poem, with whether we take it as poetry or as in some sense scripture, a prophetic book; and I will come back to this later on.

Mr. Fergusson began explicitly with drama, but even then, in *The Idea of a Theater*, published in 1949, he indicated at many places the crucial importance for his thought of Dante's poem considered as drama; as, in fact, the comprehensive condition of drama: The *Comedy*, he wrote in the introduction to that volume, is the "one work intended to exhaust the possibilities in Aristotle's definition: to imitate all the modes of human action in ordered and rhythmic relationship." And this he held to be particularly true of the *Purgatorio*, where "especially it is evident that, though Dante was not writing to be acted on a stage, he appeals, like the great dramatists, to the histrionic sensibility, i.e., our direct sense of the changing life of the psyche." And in the present work Mr. Fergusson sets himself to describe the dramatic form of the central canticle:

> . . . the underlying subject is always the modes of being and the destiny of the human psyche. The *Paradiso* presents it in relation to many reflections of the transcendent end; but it is the *Purgatorio* which explores the psyche itself—not in terms of its supernatural Goal, but in terms of its earthly existence.

> It is therefore possible to read the *Purgatorio* both as a center of the whole *Commedia*, and as a poem with its own self-subsistent unity. The journey has its beginning in the *Antepurgatorio*, its center and turning-point in the evening of the second Day, its end in the *Paradiso Terrestre*. It is the visionary Fulfillment of the journey of *this* life, moving always, in many figures, toward what the soul may know of itself within its earthly destiny. It reflects Dante's own life, and by analogy, every man's.

This is simple enough, but it suggests one of the major advantages of Mr. Fergusson's commentary: that in all the complications of detail it keeps such simplicities in view; his division of the poem into four acts, corresponding to the four days of the journey, shows the rhythm of the action, its larger phrasings, more evidently than would the usual treatment of the thirty-three cantos one by one. So far as it is the critic's job to demonstrate the reason of the narrative, the motives of action which flow into the narrative sequence, and so far as he does this by pointing to analogy, reflection, and resonance between places in the work which do not follow closely one on another, Mr. Fergusson's book is persuasive because of the coherence and compactness he achieves: he shows the clarity of outline of the poem, not as so many commentators have done, mechanically and "by the numbers," but as flowing from an inward and central motive.

The character he assigns to the four acts of the poem may be summarized as follows: 1. The Antepurgatory (Cantos I-IX), a prologue and in its sentiment a Pathos, in which the Pilgrim, though purified of the journey through Hell, has not yet begun to move to a new knowledge. 2. The "ethical drama" of the Second Day (Cantos X-XVIII), in which the Pilgrim moves through the circles of Pride, Envy, and Anger, first in a moral effort, then in an intellectual effort which is seen as itself a drama of the understanding, phrased from XV-XVIII as Prologue, Agon, Pathos, and Epiphany. 3. The Third Day (Cantos XIX-XXVII), in which the wisdom imparted by Virgil and Marco Lombardo is seen as incomplete and provisional, in which the timeless rationality of that wisdom must be transformed into an acceptance of the mystery of time, which is the Mystery of the Incarnation and is here portrayed in the figure of Statius as an emblem of the risen Christ. 4. The Earthly Paradise; the Fourth Day (Cantos XXVIII-XXXIII), an Epiphany in which by mysterious symbols of the earthly and divine natures Time is seen as redeemed.

The clarity and relative simplicity of this phrasing allow the author a secure liberty to describe the poem without confounding in its particulars the sense of its larger action; by turns he summarizes, examines in detail, generalizes, digresses, without losing the thread. He is a good reader of poetry, with a thorough and deep knowledge of this poem; I was impressed most of all by his detailed readings, and especially that of the dream in Canto IX; and of his more generalized essays I liked best the one on the *dolce stil nuovo,* in which Dante's poetic is compared with that of Aristotle.

If in spite of all this, which surely makes the book an excellent introduction to the *Purgatorio* for the modern reader, I am still uneasy about its success, that is perhaps because the modern, or *poetic,* reading of the work does not seem really able to do the whole job (nor does Mr. Fergusson claim it can: see p. 177). But if it cannot, its use is disturbing; it seems to result from a distrust of allegory and a dissatisfaction with what one may call the impenetrable lucidity of the poem—an opacity and brilliance of the surface which sometimes make the modern reader's most subtle and penetrative insights conclude exactly in what the allegory, or the letter itself, makes obvious. This is a hard judgment, or would be if directed exclusively at Mr. Fergusson; but I believe anyone who has studied the poem seriously with a view to just such a *modern reading*—an accommodation of medieval means to our own, losing as little as possible—will recall having found, time after time, his most inspired perceptions treated rather casually (and made, indeed, rather tedious) in the works of earlier commentators.

It is difficult to disagree with Mr. Fergusson about the dramatic nature of the *Comedy* if drama is allowed to mean simply "our direct sense of the changing life of the psyche"; but it is also difficult to see, on this definition, what would be nondramatic, and it seems as though a useful distinction has been let lapse. I suggested before that the basis of my objection to the term as applied to the *Comedy* was that the issues of the poem (as of the Creation) are never in doubt; that the austerity and grandeur of this work, flowing precisely from its ordained and monistic premise, give it a character of ritual which is half of what we mean by "drama"; the other half being the mystery of freedom. True that this freedom, in works we can agree to call drama, moves tragically to identify itself with necessity: "our peace in His will" is the lesson, finally, of the *Oedipus* plays as of the *Comedy;* but in my view the essentially dramatic fact about these plays, as about the Book of Job, is ambiguity and doubt, the tension of the contest with "His will" in which the protagonist raises himself up in pride. Dante's life may be seen as such a drama, and is retrospectively so seen in the *Comedy;* but then the *Comedy* is but the final scene of such a drama, its Epiphany, and not the drama itself.

The question is important because it involves us (as *Oedipus Coloneus,* at this distance, does not) in doctrinal limitations: the Christian theodicy has always been difficult to maintain for precisely the reason that, if the issues of the contest are not in doubt, and Lucifer is frozen forever at the impotent center, the freedom of the human will may seem at best an academic freedom and its defense in Dante's poem either an unsuccessful defense (since the will forfeits freedom when it acts against necessity) or a defense covertly opposed to the theological conditions of the poem, which would be inadmissible.

Here is the difficulty: if we believe the doctrine upon which the poem is raised we may see the poem as dramatic, but what we mean by drama is recognition only, the progressive revelation of the divine will in the human. If we do not receive the doctrine we must, I think, say that the poem is decisively undramatic at its center, whatever incidental resemblances to drama we may find in it.

Now the great (and continuing) critical quarrel of our time takes place between those readers who claim for poetry a value unique and in its own kind—by analogy, a musical value—and those readers who indefatigably try to show how in every poem they admire there is more truth than poetry. The *Comedy* most poignantly places itself at the center of this debate by its claims upon both sides: a work of such art that it can claim to be considered independently of its own author's explicit claim that it was undertaken "not for speculation but for practical results," "to remove those living in this life from the state of misery, and lead them to the state of felicity." The problem for the "modern reader," the non-Catholic and possibly quite secular reader, if he needs the poem and does not dismiss it as Horace Walpole did ("a Methodist minister in Bedlam"), is how he may take hold of it, and with what accommodations to the particular demands of its doctrine, which claims to be exclusive, explicit, and complete. The excellent "willing suspension of disbelief" may come to seem, confronted with this poem, an evasion.

Mr. Fergusson has a high awareness of this difficulty in theory; in practice he nevertheless tends to suggest that this is a great poem because it is in some sense *true,* but if that is so, I miss in his reading the exclusive and Catholic nature of the truth insisted on, to which all psychological or philosophical or poetical accommodation is held by the poet to fall short. It is Mr. Fergusson's implicit thesis, I think, that just as medieval allegory can be freshly felt by translation as modern "close reading" in a distinctively "poetical" mode, so medieval Catholic doctrine can be freshly felt (in the *Purgatorio* at any rate) as "universal" or "natural" wisdom—"a late natural sanctity," as he says, comparing this poem with *Oedipus Coloneus* and the *Tempest*—without reference to those points at which the specifically doctrinal obtrudes and becomes a cause of dispute. This sort of translation or accommodation works well in many ways; but, perhaps especially where it works best, takes away from the poem something of its stubborn, intricate, and jagged quality, makes it less strange and ancient and of a sort more familiar; a result in which there is both good and bad—good, because if we are to grasp the poem at all it must be according to our own canons in some way; bad, because we understand the poem in vaguer and smoother terms than its own. What we reach here, I suspect, is nothing but the typical and inescapable paradox in all critical adventurings into the poetry of the past. That doesn't prevent the venture, nor keep it from being a desirable one; if, perhaps, our reading does not equal Dante in either subtlety or intricacy of composition, Mr. Fergusson in his analysis of several places—and particularly that of Canto IX which I mentioned before—indicates the way in which one day it might come close to doing so.

Public Services and Pointing Hands

Shakespeare's Tragic Frontier: The World of His Final Tragedies. By Willard Farnham. University of California Press, 1950.
Shakespeare's World of Images: The Development of His Moral Ideas. By Donald A. Stauffer. Norton, 1949.

> "Let both the worlds suffer."—*Macbeth.*

Works of art are sources and centers of energy, or of what used to be called *inspiration*. This statement is, or ought to be, true in the limited, literal sense that when a man writes an essay on a play of Shakespeare he is presumably drawing upon that play; his judgments and the assumptions on which they rest gain coherence from their organization according to the particulars of that play, which holds the mirror up to the nature of his mind, so that within limits sometimes uncertain the man writes his own poem. We are strongly persuaded that this is so by the way in which even the most absolute works of poetry, when reflected from some minds, appear oversimplified, flat, or dull; nevertheless the writing of interpretations is understandably an attractive employment, with the imaginative material already there to be operated on, and especially so with Shakespeare, who is so rich as to offer almost the possibilities that life does. That is one thing. Another is the perfectly routine production of books on Shakespeare which is the result of years of lecturing on him; a mechanism by now so self-perpetuating that the poet's text is hardly needed at all, since the plots of the plays (which must be summarized again) are conveniently to hand in so many books of the same sort. The two works presently to be considered both demonstrate their authors' intimate acquaintance with the Plays, and have certain merits besides; but they are both, as I shall try to show, *in the tradition.* Mr. Stauffer at the end of his book

First published in *The Sewanee Review*, Vol. 59, No. 1, Winter 1951. Copyright March 12, 1951, by The University of the South.

professes gratitude "in varying degrees" to all writers on Shakespeare he has read, "for it is perhaps impossible to write a completely useless book about him; each book is a hand pointing back to Shakespeare, and that is always a public service." This is the conventional language of literary apology (and also does duty for a bibliography), but without taking it very seriously we may mention that it sets, surely, a minimum requirement; as though not one but several hundred citizens had to be thanked for directing you to your destination. And we may puzzle over the kind of interest in Shakespeare that requires numerous books about him only in order to be returned to his text, for it is reasonable to ask what audience is proposed for works of this sort, and what audience they will find, excepting of course those who "must keep up with the literature."

In his new volume Willard Farnham has considered a subject narrower than that of his earlier and more strictly informative work, *The Medieval Heritage of Elizabethan Tragedy*, although his concern here may be seen as a particular instance and development of the general thesis there propounded. In *Shakespeare's Tragic Frontier* he thinks to distinguish a "world" of the "final tragedies" (which he takes to be *Timon, Macbeth, Antony and Cleopatra, Coriolanus*) from the same poet's "early tragic world" and "middle tragic world." The dependence of this notion on established chronology seems not greatly to occupy the author, though he does briefly summarize evidence and conjecture for the view that the four plays were written in the above order "under the influence of a sustained special inspiration." His premise is that "though the chronology of Shakespeare's plays has not been determined exactly, the general course of his development is plain. We may think of a part of that development as producing an early tragic world, a middle tragic world, and a last tragic world." This statement belongs in every notebook.

The basis of the distinction is found in the characters of the last tragic heroes, who are "tainted," "deeply flawed." As it is said of Antony, "His taints and honors / Wag'd equal with him," so, Mr. Farnham proposes, it may be said of Timon, Macbeth, Coriolanus. "Their nobility . . . is one of life's mysteries, for it seems to issue from ignoble substance." This distinguishing feature gains force from repetition: "Shakespeare was creating heroic imperfect humanity for his last tragic world, instead of the imperfect heroic humanity that he had created for his middle tragic world," and, in case this should have eluded the reader (as it very well might), "His middle tragic world . . . shows the imperfect heroic in man, rather than the heroic imperfect, a world in which the flaw of the hero tends to be out of keeping with his nobility rather than paradoxically a part of his nobility." The author's analyses of the four plays include lengthy demonstrations that Shakespeare's use of his sources involved changes ever in the direction of increasing complexity of characterization designed to produce a tragic and paradoxical balance of "taints and honors."

Mr. Farnham's judgment in these matters seems plainly based on a familiar view of Shakespeare's plays as naturalistic, the view to which *character* becomes exclusively important. "There are enigmas in abundance," he writes of *Antony and Cleopatra*, "but all of them that really matter are within the hero and heroine; they are enigmas of personal constitution." I have space here only to disagree; the reader may be interested to compare the essays on this subject of Wilson Knight and the brief but brilliant note of Traversi. It seems to be the rule with adherents of the "character" school that the text, the words of the text, should be used merely as supporting evidence for a view of the play that comes, apparently, from another source; Mr. Farnham sees no need for close reading of the poetry, he is at home in the play but very near the surface of it, and regards ideas as more important than words despite the evident truth, which ought to be commonplace and is not, that our experience of the play is in the first place experience of its language, without which nothing. It is impossible to be sure whether this author is writing about the plays or, "psychologically," about the characters in them; his interest in sources, which occupies so much of the book, leads not seldom to direct speculation: "Did Cleopatra really rise to a true love for Antony when she drew toward the end of her life?" This is, to be sure, of Plutarch's Cleopatra. But here is his final word on Timon: "His paradoxical nobility of spirit is never that of an effective leader of men. Like Macbeth, Antony, or Coriolanus, he is a rare spirit deeply flawed, but unlike those heroes he does not belong among the rare spirits who 'steer humanity.'" What connection this laudable virtue or the want of it has with Shakespeare's play I am very uncertain.

As for the central distinction itself, the matter of taints and honors, is it enough? First, does it distinguish Antony, say, from Othello? Mr. Farnham solves the difficulty as follows: "Othello and

Lear are shown to have faulty substance in them to which evil can be attached, rather than faulty substance that evil can penetrate." Then, if we can grant the thesis to be correct, does it require all this laborious definition which so slights, meanwhile, important questions of the plays? Does it add to our power of reading these plays an instrument, an authoritative idea, or is it merely an observation of some worth which we should do better to take as a pretext or occasion for writing than as an informing concept? The idea itself, it seems to me, is remarkably thin to take up more than two and a half hundred repetitive pages, and even so does not command assent with any blinding clarity but, if at all, with weariness and qualification and a sense that nothing much has happened.

Mr. Stauffer, too, claims Shakespeare for naturalism, and directly declares that "his theory of art . . . was naturalistic." But the word must include a good deal more than one would suspect, for Mr. Stauffer's operations are far more complicated than Mr. Farnham's and for the most part, let me add, more interesting and relevant; he is on occasion a good reader, learned in the connections of metaphor and imagery, though a good deal too seldom concerned with them in this book. I cite his section on Othello as evidence of his powers, but for these brilliant few pages, which seem to me his best, he very nearly apologizes, calling them "this extended consideration."

It would be pleasant to report Mr. Stauffer's volume a piece of virtue, for it has a good deal of solid virtue in it, being the perceptive and coherent account of a theme which he considers to have been much neglected in Shakespeare studies: "the development of his moral ideas." "It is not that Shakespeare had no moral beliefs, but that he embraced so many. His ironical ambiguous attitude, which gives the illusion of suspended judgment, may have misled critics into supposing that Shakespeare's own beliefs cannot be found in his work. On the contrary. . . ." Mr. Stauffer is too good a reader to place the weight of all this on their being *Shakespeare's own beliefs* (the fielder's mitt autographed by DiMaggio), and properly warns us, "If the reader or the writer assumes that the character is a real person instead of a fiction in art, Shakespeare the illusionist is at his work again." I believe I shall be putting the matter reasonably if I say he is concerned with the development of moral ideas in the Plays. But he claims, on the other hand, that when he feels dramatic consistency has been clearly abrogated, he is entitled at least to suspect the poet of speaking in his proper person about his own concerns.

But unhappily the notion is not new; our danger from the "purely aesthetic critics" (whoever they are, for Mr. Stauffer names none, nor even the critics who may have been "misled") seems relatively slight these days, while a list of those authors who without being startled at the presence of moral ideas in Shakespeare have dealt with them intelligently, in the dramatic and poetic context of play or scene or passage, would be a long and honorable one, including for example G. Wilson Knight, D. A. Traversi, Cleanth Brooks, William Empson, L. C. Knights, Francis Fergusson, E. M. W. Tillyard, Kenneth Burke, Colin Still, D. A. Armstrong, Caroline Spurgeon. I do not mean that Mr Stauffer should have made particular acknowledgment of all or any of these ("When a man writes a book about Shakespeare these days . . . there is nothing to say except that his debts are so numerous that they cannot be recorded"), though I am not certain *Hamlet* much requires writing about after Mr. Fergusson's essay and without close consultation of it; only that he should perhaps not so enthusiastically have *discovered* those moral ideas—which also, after all, formed the stock of the Shakespeare scholar (often his entire stock, indeed) for a long time.

And after all, intelligent and "thematic" as it is, this work is another tour through Shakespeare, and subject not only to individual faults but to some of the loathsome requirements of its kind, such as the one that demands the author sustain an interest in all the plays though his best efforts be called forth by but a few. In this respect alone, Mr. Farnham comes out perhaps a bit better; his professorial caution produces an even dullness of tone in which the inadvertencies of wit may easily be overlooked, as in his remark that Lear "possesses that which commands esteem," his optimistic plea that "the Hamlet problem, involved as it is, is not so involved as it might be," or his observation on a passage from *Timon* ("For thy part, I do wish thou wert a dog, / That I might love thee something") that it "does not show Timon, or Shakespeare, as a dog-lover in any ordinary sense."

Mr. Stauffer is graceful and adept at one major problem of the *genre*, that of telling the plot, which he manages to combine with his more particular pursuit (unlike Mr. Farnham, who gives you huge chunks of summary), but cannot always avoid another, the machine-like conversion of good poetry into bad:

The images jet like fountains in Cleopatra's agony over the dying prince of the world. He is "noblest of men," and in his death the crown of the earth melts, the garland of the war withers, the soldier's standard falls. Distinctions are levelled, the odds are gone, all is but naught, and within the great sphere of the moon's orbit nothing is left that is remarkable.

The jetting fountains of imagery, the soldier's pole which has become a standard, the great sphere introduced from earlier in the scene and redeployed from sun to moon, each makes its little contribution to the general ruin and mockery of the magnificent verse. A related disaster is the temptation to the old familiar sermon:

He accepts the physical world in all its earthiness and mixed contaminations. Love itself is always represented in human alloy, with its callousness and quirks and bawdry and cruelties and coarseness and contrarieties. But though Shakespeare never wavers in his belief in the mixed nature of reality, he also never doubts the supremacy of the spirit.

We may add to these the illumination afforded by platitude:

In this history play (*Richard II*) he first finds the way to present a serious problem. The method might be described as the setting up of a dramatic conflict between two points of view, each of which has strengths and weaknesses.

And a gratuitous view of the poet as vaticinator:

He anticipated by a century and a half what the economist Adam Smith considered his masterpiece, *The Theory of Moral Sentiments.*

These are, as I said, examples of generic flaws which not all writers on Shakespeare manage to avoid; they do not nullify Mr. Stauffer's work, but they certainly do not grace it, and they sometimes seem but the surface eruptions of a style inwardly consumed with an embarrassing desire to be familiar, which is also productive of a tone vulgarly jovial or coy ("After the great clean-up campaign the audience is hardly left with a bigger and better Vienna"), not to mention a friendly and tutorial condescension to the poet's earlier works.

Of these faults so common in academic writings on Shakespeare, Professor Limpkin once observed, "But if they were suppressed, I fear you would have very few volumes on Shakespeare."

I fear that is very true.

Part V

A Few Bricks from Babel

The Fables of La Fontaine. A Complete New Translation. By Marianne Moore. Viking Press, 1954.
Dante's Inferno. Translated in Verse. By John Ciardi. Rutgers University Press, 1954.

Offhand I would probably have shared what seems a widespread impression that Marianne Moore was admirably qualified, not only by talent but by sympathy as well, to translate the *Fables* of La Fontaine; this impression appears to have been based on a very rapid summing-up of both poets: "Ah, yes—animals." But there is, I find, a great distance between a Moore jerboa and a La Fontaine rat, and because I enjoy some of Miss Moore's poetry a good deal I am sorry to have to say that the results of this cooperation strike me not as merely inadequate or mediocre but as in a positive way terrible. My fine critical hindsight tells me now, what it didn't warn me of beforehand, that Miss Moore has never been a fabulist at all, that her animals never acted out her moralities; that their function was ever to provide a minutely detailed, finely perceived symbolic knot to be a center for the pattern of her recondite meditations; that what she shares with La Fontaine is a shrewdness and delicacy of the moral judgment, but that the two poets' ways of getting there—their *fables*, in fact—are so different as to be opposed. I still feel, with somewhat less conviction than before, that Miss Moore might have got a happier result by setting herself to *tell* La Fontaine's stories in English, for it seems that a critical factor in the failure of these translations may have been an uncertainty about the ideal degree of her dependence on the French: as poems to be read in English, they are irritatingly awkward, elliptical, complicated, and very jittery as to the meter; as renderings of the French they vacillate between pedantic strictness and strange liberty.

First published in *The Sewanee Review*, Vol. 62, No. 4, Autumn 1954. Copyright © October 28, 1954, by The University of the South.

I began with the intention of reading the volume through without reference to the original—since if the poems could not be read as English it did not seem to matter how accurate they might be as translations—but was at once pulled up by the dedication to the Dauphin, of which Miss Moore has printed the French on the facing page. Inescapably, "Je chante les héros dont Ésope est le père" had come out as "I sing when Aesop's wand animates my lyre." There is nothing necessarily wrong with this: it is precisely the *unnecessary* distance from the original which is odd. And in the last couplet, where La Fontaine's sentiment is rigorously conventional— "Et, si de t'agréer je n' emporte le prix / J'aurai du moins l'honneur de l'avoir entrepris"—Miss Moore has written something much more friendly: "And if I have failed to give you real delight, / My reward must be that I had hoped I might." I read on according to intention but with an occasional uneasy sense of missing things; and presently began turning to the French simply to make certain here and there of what was being said. For example, in the fable about belling the rat (II. ii) the rats hold their meeting while the cat goes courting:

> Now as he climbed, or creeps lengthened his loin
> In his renegade quest for some tabby he'd court,
> Through the witches' sabbath in which they'd consort,
> Surviving rats had seen fit to convene
> In a corner to discuss their lot.

I was struck, or maybe stricken is a better word, by "creeps lengthened his loin." Application to La Fontaine revealed what was behind all this:

> Or un jour qu'au haut et au loin
> Le galant alla chercher femme,
> Pendant tout le sabbat qu'il fit avec sa dame,
> Le demeurant des Rats tint chapitre en un coin
> Sur la nécessité présente.

It is easy to see how "*loin*" became "loin," though not so easy to see why, or what has been gained except a false rime to "convene." But a number of other difficulties come up as a result of this investigation. Granting the necessity of lengthening the first two octosyllabic lines to ten syllables and twelve, is there any other justification for "renegade quest"? Even if the cat has earlier been called "un diable," why should the sabbath be a "witches' sabbath," when the meaning is simply that the rats got a rest? Why confuse the issue with "they," which grammatically seems to want to mean the rats (since "consort" doesn't have to have a sexual meaning)? And why, having expanded the mere suggestion of "au haut et au loin" to the monstrous "as he climbed, or creeps lengthened his loin," does Miss Moore then economize by cutting out La Fontaine's thematic figure—whereby in the moral the rats become "chapitres de moines . . . chapitres de chanoines"—and give us "had seen fit to convene" for "tint chapitre en un coin"? So that she can go on to translate "doyen" once as "doyen" and then later on as "dean"?

Perhaps these are quibbles; I'm sorry if so. And I would give them up instantly if it seemed that the sacrifice of simplicity, accuracy, and sense had resulted in some clear gain in the English version; but it was the oddity of the English that in the first place drew my notice. And while the first line of that passage is outstandingly and exceptionally silly, the general nature of the faults it indicates can be illustrated by numerous examples, of which I shall give a few.

Miss Moore habitually invents metaphors for her poet. La Fontaine talks of people pretending to sophistication and travel, who, "caquetants au plus dru, / Parlent de tout, et n'ont rien vu," for which Miss Moore supplies, "Boasting he's seen this spot and that, / Whereas his alps have all been flat." Gratuitous, probably harmless in this instance, but at least irrelevant and probably destructive when "Les petits, en toute affaire, / Esquivent fort aisément" becomes "modesty anywhere, / Glides in as when silk is sewn." Even when the figure itself is clever, particularly when it is clever, it is disturbing to feel the immediate suspicion that La Fontaine wrote something different.

Miss Moore tends to extremes of latinity, sometimes I suspect because she will do anything for a rime, often a false rime. If a falcon says to a capon, "Ton peu d'entendement / Me rend tout étonné," Miss Moore writes, "Wretched phenomenon / Of limitation. Dullard, what do you know?" La Fontaine begins to consider the head and tail of the serpent with: "Le serpent a deux parties / Du genre humaine ennemies," and Miss Moore brings out, "A serpent has mobility / Which can shatter intrepidity."

The general objection, of which the two foregoing objections are specific instances, is that Miss Moore is so often found going the long way around, making complexities out of simplicities, loading lines with detail until they are corrupted in sense or measure, and writing, in consequence, absurdly bad English. "Une Huitre, que le flot y venoit d'apporter" (to the beach, that is) appears in translation as "an oyster amid what rollers scatter."

It is not much of a compliment to say that there are better things in this translation than these examples suggest; there would have to be. But I give the examples because they seem to me to typify the faults in Miss Moore's practice. Even when things are going well so far as the translation is concerned, the tone and texture of the language remain very uncertain; just as we think we begin to hear in English the modesty and humorous dignity of the fabulist, along comes some monstrous circumlocution or complicated syntactical maneuver to ensure the fall of the rime. And meanwhile the meter is, to say the least of it, very strange; it is syllabic, I think, and Miss Moore in her Foreword mentions "my effort to approximate the original rhythms of the Fables," but what emerges in English is frequently a kind of gallop now and again flattened by a reduction to prose. The following passage seems a fair sample:

> Then he burned bones when they found a roadstead,
> Soiling Jove's nostrils with the noisomeness engendered,
> And said, "There, Sire; accept the hommage I've tendered—
> Ox perfume to be savored by almighty Jupiter.
> These fumes discharge my debt; I am from now on a free man."

I am sorry to be unable to like these translations better than I do; the labor of their preparation must have been long and hard, and the quality of Miss Moore's original talent justified very high expectations. The difficulties of the matter seem to have been faced up to, but rather added to than overcome by the translator's own predilections and powers. One final quotation will perhaps serve as a summary of what appears to me to have gone wrong, as a suggestion, too, that somewhere near a poem of La Fontaine there exists, potentially, a poem of Marianne Moore, but that the two have not come into phase. The Epilogue of Book Six begins thus:

> Bornons ici cette carrière:
> Les longs ouvrages me font peur.
> Loin d'épuiser une matière,
> On n'en doit prendre que la fleur.
>
> Our peregrination must end there.
> One's skin creeps when poets persevere.

Don't press pith from core to perimeter;
Take the flower of the subject, the thing that is rare.

This passage was translated by Elizur Wright in 1841 as follows:

Here check we our career.
Long books I greatly fear.
I would not quite exhaust my stuff;
The flower of subjects is enough.

The general question raised by this comparison is as much concerned with what translators try to do as with what they actually get done; whatever we think of Elizur Wright's version—I hold it to be very fine—we must agree that it shows a detailed deference to the meaning of the original *and* an idea, perhaps a very simple idea, of what English verse is. Now the famous revolution in modern poetry, accompanied by a special uprising in the translation business, destroyed at least the security of that idea of English verse if not the idea itself; but this revolution, product of a few great talents, itself produced no idea of English verse but only the examples of the few great talents, with the stern recommendation: Go thou and do otherwise. It did produce some general notions, what Mr. Pound called his "results," and Miss Moore declares that "the practice of Ezra Pound has been for me a governing principle," but it is doubtful that these general notions, in so complex an affair as translation, ever did more than prescribe avoidances; and a principle cannot substitute for a habit of mind and ear, nor for ease and fluency in the measure or the idiom.

I have observed, too, that modern translations are praised precisely because they are modern translations. Since Mr. Eliot's celebrated remark about Gilbert Murray all those scholarly gentlemen who "did" (often indeed in both senses) "the classics" have been held mightily in disrepute, while recent translators are flattered by critics and publishers (and sometimes preen themselves prefatorily) on writing their versions in "modern, idiomatic English," "the speech of living English, the language a poet would choose for his own work today." But this sort of judgment seems to put an undue strain on the qualities of "living English," and one thinks mournfully of the ghosts of Golding, Chapman, Pope, who never had a chance.

For the translator's problem, a special and poignant case of the artistic problem generally, is that of making flat maps of a round world; some distortion is inevitable. Bearings and distances become accurate at the expense of sizes and shapes, and the end result will never *look* much like the real thing but the hope is that real navigation will be possible with its aid.

John Ciardi, in his version of the *Inferno*, tries for "a language as close as possible to Dante's, which is in essence a sparse, direct, and idiomatic language, distinguishable from prose only in that it transcends every known notion of prose." He does not attempt to imitate the triple rime because he believes the resources of English insufficient for this purpose without serious distortion, but feeling that some rime is necessary "to approximate Dante's way of going" he preserves the three-line stanza and rimes the first and third lines (cf. the version of J. B. Fletcher, 1931).

"Sparse, direct, and idiomatic"—certainly, but in what idiom? Mr. Ciardi's view of Dante emphasizes qualities which he evidently feels have been neglected in earlier translations; nevertheless his necessities are the eternal ones which all translators must live with as they may, and we find him, like the others, juggling sense, measure, and sound until he can reach some more or less pleasing compromise. For example, Mr. Ciardi translates "merda" in the approved modern manner, sparse, direct, idiomatic, and even feels the need of a footnote (the substance of which he repeats on another, similar occasion) to tell us that Dante "deliberately coarsens his language when he wishes to describe certain kinds of coarseness." Very well, but only a few lines before this there appears the word "sterco," which the need of three syllables instead of one causes him to translate as "excrement," without footnote, just like Longfellow. I mean merely that theories of translation spare us none of these decisions.

It is this idea of the idiomatic which is puzzling. I think Mr. Ciardi means that one ought not to be afraid of slang expressions, modern terms, if they make a clear equivalent for the Italian; and among the Demons, the Malebranche, he suddenly finds three modern equivalents in a few lines: "a squad of my boys," "no foul play," "front and center." There is perhaps nothing totally inappropriate in any one of these, but they don't mix very well; and while "tratti avanti" may be rendered "front and center" without violence to the sense, it scarcely helps matters by bringing with it the sudden apparition of a hotel clerk. But, beyond this, what does the translator do when idiomatic equivalents do not come easily to hand? Evidently he must do something else, and what Mr. Ciardi does is become awkwardly literal, so that, for example, Guido da Montefeltro's advice to Boniface, "lunga promessa con l'attender corto," comes out word for word as "long promise and short observance," though this expression is neither an English idiom nor even—there is a difference—idiomatic English. But there is another sense for the idea of the idiomatic, and, I think, a more important one: the idea of the idiom, or style, in which a work is written. This idea deals with the harmoniousness of expression, the rightness of the relations between expressions, in a single passage or a whole work; and in this sense I somewhat doubt if we have here a modern idiom at all, or anything more nearly resembling one than what can be made of a few chance phrases here and there which will give for a moment a modern color to a language otherwise commonplace enough, a language which, seeking an "idiomatic" equivalent for, say, "quella lettura" (the one that seduced Paolo and Francesca), falls back upon "that high old story." The closeness with which the language of poetry refers to the language of common speech must depend upon the qualities of the common speech; if this be characterless, or effective only from time to time and not continuously, the poetry which refers to it is apt to be patchy, uncertain, and shortwinded.

The uncertainty, it appears to me, affects even rime and measure in Mr. Ciardi's translation. "I have not hesitated to use a deficient rhyme," he writes, "when the choice seems to lie between forcing an exact rhyme and keeping the language more natural." "I have not hesitated" may possibly be an understatement of the headlong eagerness which rimes as follows: spirit / summit, author / honor, lamentation / mountain, council / evil, armpits / circlets. We are very free about such things these days; though I should add my impression that this kind of rime nearly disappears in the last third of the poem.

We are very free about meter these days too; an unhappy chapter in the history of modern prosody stands to be written about those people who do not write free verse but a "loosened" iambic pentameter. It may be objected that Dante did not write iambic pentameter but a line which some have despairingly scanned as "eleven syllables and no rules," yet Mr. Ciardi's intention of writing iambic pentameter sufficiently appears in such a specimen as the following:

> Precisely in the middle of that space
>   there yawns a well extremely wide and deep.
> I shall discuss it in its proper place.

It is difficult, then, to know what to make of a line like "What painful thoughts are these your lowered brow covers?"

Mr. Ciardi's formal decision to end each canto with a couplet is also sometimes an embarrassment, an empty formality which might surely have been dispensed with at those places in which Dante makes his effect with a single striking line, e.g., "I am one who has no tale to tell: / I made myself a gibbet of my own lintel," where the first line is entirely Mr. Ciardi's invention. The same fault somewhat mars the close of Ulysses' narrative, which I want to consider somewhat more fully (Canto XXVI, at the end):

> Cinque volte racceso e tante casso
>> Lo lume era di sotto da la luna
>> Poi che 'ntrati eravam ne l'alto passo,
> Quando n'apparve una montagna bruna
>> Per la distanza, e parvemi alta tanto
>> Quanto veduta non avea alcuna.
> Noi ci allegrammo, e tosto tornò in pianto;
>> Chè de la nova terra un turbo nacque,
>> E percosse del legno il primo canto.
> Tre volte il fè girar con tutte l'acque,
>> A la quarta levar la poppa in suso,
>> E la prora ire in giù, com' Altrui piacque,
> Infin che'l mar fu sopra noi richiuso.

> Five times since we had dipped our bending oars
>> beyond the world, the light beneath the moon
>> had waxed and waned, when dead upon our course

> we sighted, dark in space, a peak so tall
>> I doubted any man had seen the like.
>> Our cheers were hardly sounded, when a squall

> broke hard upon our bow from the new land:
>> three times it sucked the ship and the sea about
>> as it pleased Another to order and command.

> At the fourth, the poop rose and the bow went down
>> till the sea closed over us and the light was gone.

This seems to me a fair sample; Mr. Ciardi has better, but he also has worse. It is not a terribly bad translation, by and large, but it is not very good either. "Since we had dipped our bending oars / beyond the world" is Mr. Ciardi's poetical elaboration of "Poi che 'ntrati eravam ne l'alto passo." "Dead upon our course" corresponds to nothing in the original. "Dark in space" is debatable but possible for "bruna / Per la distanza." "Our cheers were hardly sounded" is a solution, but not in my opinion a good one, for "Noi ci allegrammo, e tosto tornò in pianto." "As it pleased Another" has been advanced from its climactic position to one of less importance, while the combination "to order and command," besides the entire absence of any such thing from the original, is redundant, doubly so after "pleased." Finally, the necessity of closing with a couplet forces Mr. Ciardi to supply "and the light was gone" in addition to Dante's "Infin che 'l mar fu sopra noi richiuso." We may sympathize with some of the difficulties of translators as they are revealed in this passage, but Mr. Ciardi's solutions can scarcely be regarded as in any sense triumphant. Longfellow, whose translation nowadays is unread but sneered at, had certain advantages (also sneered at) in this matter, one of which was his firm belief that he knew what a passage of poetry in English ought to sound like; his version at this place is perhaps by no means ideal, but compares favorably with Mr. Ciardi's not least in the allegedly modern virtue of accuracy to the letter:

> Five times rekindled and as many quenched
> Had been the splendor underneath the moon,
> Since we had entered into the deep pass,
> When there appeared to us a mountain, dim
> From distance, and it seemed to me so high
> As I had never any one beheld.
> Joyful were we, and soon it turned to weeping;
> For out of the new land a whirlwind rose,
> And smote upon the fore part of the ship.
> Three times it made her whirl with all the waters,
> At the fourth time it made the stern uplift,
> And the prow downward go, as pleased Another,
> Until the sea above us closed again.

I have no wish to start a back-to-Longfellow movement, nor a back-to-Elizur Wright one either; it may be, indeed, that the powers demanded of a translator are like but not quite identical with those a poet must have. Subordination and fidelity to the text are as much technical as moral decisions, and though it is often said, nowadays, that the poet-translator is by some mysterious means "faithful to the spirit of the original," that is something we can judge of only by his treatment of the letter.

The Golden Compass Needle

Seamarks (Amers). By St.-John Perse. Bilingual Edition. Translation by Wallace Fowlie. Bollingen Series LXVII. Pantheon Books, 1958.

The work before us calls for some descriptive apologies from this reviewer, who is likely to say unfashionable things in the course of his considerations, and accordingly finds it necessary to state first as plainly as possible various doubts and diffidences.

To begin with, is the object of my judgment a poem in French written by St.-John Perse and called *Amers*? or an English translation of this poem written by Wallace Fowlie and called *Seamarks*? My qualifications for reviewing the former are invisibly slight; the small and bookish French I have leaves me helpless with admiration before the sonorities of, for instance, "Toute la Mer en fête des confins, sous la fauconnerie de nuées blanches . . . ," but I get somewhat the same effect from the sonorities of "Malbrouck s'en va t'en guerre." Whereas, about "All the Sea in celebration of its confines, under its falconry of white clouds . . ." I have already some doubts, not all of them concerned with sonorities. That this is not a quibble, and that there exists a serious problem simply in disengaging one text of the poem from the other, may be made clear by the following observations.

Because the poetry of St.-John Perse is not written in a regular measure, it does not impose upon its translator any very rigorous decisions as to the adjustment of sense with meter, rhythm, rime, and syntax such as would ordinarily, in englishing poetry, make formidable demands on the translator's patience and wit; one must attend here only to the meaning and to the characteristic largeness of the cadence. Consequently, translations of this poetry run rather literal. Here are a few random samples:

First published in *The Sewanee Review*, Vol. 67, No. 1, Winter 1959. Copyright © January 30, 1959, by The University of the South.

Solitude! l'oeuf bleu que pond un grand oiseau de mer. . . .
                                                    —*Anabase*

Solitude! the blue egg laid by a great sea-bird. . . .
                                                    —tr. T. S. Eliot

Sifflez, ô frondes par le monde, chantez, ô conques sur les eaux!
                                                    —*Exil*

Whistle, O slings about the world, sing, O conches on the waters!
                                                    —tr. Denis Devlin

Comme l'enterprise (sic) du tour de l'autel et la gravitation du choeur
    au circuit de la strophe.—*Amers*
Like the ritual around the altar and the gravitation of the chorus in
    the circuit of the strophe.—tr. Wallace Fowlie

Whatever the beauties of these phrases in French, it seems plain that
the method of translating them routinely produces an English which
is not often distinguished but very often stilted and unidiomatic. I
do not suggest that the translators should have sought exotic "equivalents" for the poetry of these are the like phrases, after Mr. Pound's
manner of dealing with Propertius; plainness is probably best, where
the original will permit it. But this honest faithfulness to the text,
which one would ordinarily think so great a virtue in a translator,
produces such extremely fancy results as this: "Morganatic is the far-
off Bride, and the alliance, clandestine!" which is not Mr. Fowlie's
fault at all; he is merely doing his duty as he sees it by "Morgan-
atique au loin l'Épouse, et l'alliance, clandestine!" gritting his teeth,
as it were, and going right on through to the literal rendering even
of the exclamation mark.

Over a somewhat longer distance it is the effect of this technique
to spare the poet nothing:

The incorporeal and very real, imprescriptible; the irrecusable and undeniable and unappropriable; uninhabitable, frequentable; immemorial
and memorable—and what, O what, O what else, unqualifiable? The
unseizable and inalienable, the irreproachable, irreprovable and also
this one here: Sea innocence of the Solstice, O Sea like the wine of
Kings! . . . .

What, O what else, indeed? we may think, as turning to the original
we find:

> L'incorporelle et très-réelle, imprescriptible; l'irrécusable et l'indéniable
> et l'inappropriable; inhabitable, fréquentable; immémoriale et mémora-
> ble—et quelle, et quelle, et quelle encore, inqualifiable? L'insaisissable
> et l'incessible, l'irréprochable, l'irréprouvable, et celle encore que voici:
> Mer innocence du Solstice, ô Mer comme le vin des Rois! . . .

Commendable as it may be in the translator to follow his text as
closely as possible, the result is sometimes more mimicry than translation, and unkind, as mimicry generally is. I am not qualified to judge
the original as a passage of poetry, though I do not like it; perhaps
to a native of that language such a catalogue of similarly formed abstractions reads very grand; but I cannot persuade myself that the
English of it is anything other than nonsense.

Katherine Garrison Chapin, writing in the *Sewanee Review* for
Winter, 1952, seems for a moment to offer a solution to my difficulty by advancing the suggestion of the French poet Pierre Jean
Jouve that Perse "has the ambitious dream of creating a universal
language of poetry." Unhappily for me, however, she doesn't believe
it, or she doesn't quite believe it:

> This, I think, is erroneous. The voice is French, in all its nuances, to
> be heard in its special richness of overtone, in its epic music, in its
> delicate inner rhyming, only by ears attuned to French. Yet its breadth
> and power extend beyond the frontiers of language. It is outside of
> time and space, having neither region nor era.

I do not see, myself, how all these things can be true at once. And
I shall say something later about the puzzling language in which the
admirers of this poet generally express their admiration. Meanwhile
I may note that Miss Chapin in the remainder of her essay, as if
to increase my confusion, quotes with apparent indifference passages
in English and passages in French.

So perhaps I am reading, and will be reviewing, a work which is
neither in French nor in English but in a species of both, or in a
not easily definable territory between. When I find Mr. Fowlie using
such remarkable and sometimes beautiful words as *teredo, strigil,
navarch, resipiscence,* and *amphictyony,* I will neither praise him for
his skill as a translator nor blame him for being funny in serious
places, but will simply allow that the special nature of his job involves the acceptance of certain words without convenient synonym,
which exist in both languages, or (one might think) in neither:

Procellarian is the name, pelagic the species . . .
procellaires est le nom, pélagique l'espèce . . .

He means, or they mean, the shearwaters and fulmars (*Procellariidae*).

I am making my way, it is plain, toward the statement of my opinion that *Seamarks* is neither a great poem nor even a very good one; as to its original, *Amers*, I have already advanced some reasons to excuse me from having an opinion at all, or at any rate from recording an opinion which would be so little valuable. I shall now say why it is that I find it somewhat painful to have to say about *Seamarks* that it is neither great nor greatly good.

1. St.-John Perse is a poet of great sensibility, and evidently considerable gifts for its expression; presently I shall make some demonstration of this point.

2. It gives me no particular pleasure to have to dissent so thoroughly from the strongly held opinion of learned men, some of whom, such as Mr. Fowlie and Mr. Tate, I like personally as well as respect intellectually, and whose views in literary matters it would ordinarily be my impulse to accept.

3. I have no wish to give aid and comfort to those enemies of poetry who, at the sight of anything the least bit extraordinary, run shrieking for their copies of somebody or other's Poetics, and tell you exactly what the poet is and is not allowed to attempt. It should be possible, however, to understand that the poet moves at the will of his genius, and not at his own will, but to disagree all the same with the results which his genius has willed in a particular production; possible, that is, to form and express a judgment of one's own without joining an army.

4. Absurdest of all, but part of the *res gestae* just the same—even the format in which the Bollingen Foundation presents the works of this poet is impressive to the point of being frightening: the size, the handsome type and fine paper, the effect of spacious elegance from so many blank pages—the package itself conveys an impression of such wealth (and of generosity, too, since *Seamarks* is relatively inexpensive) that I feel something already subversive in my failure to admire the contents unreservedly.

5. A last spice is added to my distress by the thought of how little it all matters. There are at this moment in America so many poets by their vociferous factions allowed to be *great*, and this as-

sertion of *greatness* is so often and loudly heard among us, that a critical opinion, whether St.-John Perse may, or may not, be numbered among our great poets, can scarcely be other than trivial. But perhaps on this consideration I may stop telling my troubles, and get on to business.

St.-John Perse takes a lofty, proud, and ancient view of the poetic art. The poet, for him, is again to be bard or prophet, not in the debased sense of "one who foretells the future" but in the older sense: one who lays a spell on the future, so that it shall be as he commands; reciter of the ritual which is to renew the world. In this character, he is the annalist of those vast forces of nature, from which, nevertheless, anhistoric as they are, human motives and institutions arise, and to which these motives and institutions must always be referred again: rain, snow, wind, sea, and so on. But at the same time the poet is a man skilled in the terms and lore of human institutions; and Perse's best passages, in my opinion, are most often those in which he considers curiously, and makes a catalogue of, the oddly detailed, multifarious functions which go to the making of a society:

> . . . he whose inheritance, on land held in mortmain, is the last heronry, with fine volumes on venery and on falconry; he who deals, downtown, in such great books as almagesta, portulans and bestiaries; whose solicitude is for the accidents of phonetics, the alteration of signs and the great erosions of language; who takes part in the great debates on semantics; who is an authority on the lower mathematics and delights in the computation of dates for the calendar of movable feasts (the golden number, the Roman indiction, the epact and the great Dominical letters); he who grades the hierarchies in the great rituals of the language. . . .
>
> —*Exile*, 6, tr. Denis Devlin
> (Bollingen Series XV)

Such places—there are some in *Seamarks*—impress me with the poet's Homeric interest in a real world and its ways, to which his phrasing imparts at once a shrewdness and a legendary distance; with what Miss Chapin in her essay finely calls his "anastrophic voice" and "naked, impudent eye, never impressed by the accepted, the classic view, but . . . with a quick, crude touch of the actual." There is perhaps a resemblance to the sharp-sighted and extremely various interests of Miss Marianne Moore in a letter of Perse to Archibald MacLeish, in which he names some items from his travels which have held his attention:

> . . . in London, at the British Museum, a crystal skull of the Pre-Columbian collection, and at the South Kensington Museum, a child's small boat picked up by Lord Brassey in the middle of the Indian Ocean; at the Kremlin, a woman's bracelet on the raw hock of a stuffed horse, beneath the crude harness of a nomad conqueror; at the Armeria of Madrid an Infante's armor; in Warsaw a letter from a prince on beaten gold; at the Vatican, a similar letter on goatskin; in Bremen a historic collection of unreal pictures for the bottoms of cigarboxes. . . .

But probably the closest modern English comparison is to be found in *The Anathemata* of the Welsh poet and painter David Jones, where you have the same compound of the extremely minute technical and usually archaic detail with the idea of the poem as a vast ritual incantation, though for Jones the ritual is explicitly Roman Catholic.

The same doubleness, equivocating between prophecy and "lore," informs the rhetoric of Perse's poetry, producing its broad phrasing and large lines, its effect of abstraction without generality by means of details very particular and elaborated which yet belong to no identifiable historical context in the poem, though they may out of it: "ranks of beasts saddled with wings along the highways" as e.g., at Delos, but it is not Delos; or "handsome troughs of lapis lazuli in which, dissipating at the touch, a gold-pinned princess made of bone descends the reaches of the centuries, capped in her sisal hair," as in Shub-ad's tomb at Ur, but it is not Ur.

Thus upon hints in artifacts, upon surviving inscriptions of monuments, the poet constructs a sort of hypothetical or generalized dawn-civilization, and, combining with the pathos of ruins his keen intention to speak about present life, recites its eclectic rituals. The ceremonies of his poems have as their purpose the purgation and renewal of the present, the declared surrender of worn-out forms, and rededication to a kind of life which shall be archaic (both as early in time and as superior), aristocratic, and religious at least in its denial of the actualities of a bad history. It is the "myth of eternal return" which Perse designs to sing, and his most passionate rhetoric arises from the deprecation of history and of what has already been, including (especially) literature:

O Rains! wash from the heart of man the most beautiful sayings of man: the most beautiful sentence, the most beautiful sequence; the well-turned phrase, the noble page. Wash, wash, from the hearts of men their taste for roundelays and for elegies; their taste for villanelles and rondeaux; their great felicities of expression; wash Attic salt and euphuist honey; wash, wash, the bedding of dream and the litter of knowledge: from the heart of the man who makes no refusals, from the heart of the man who has no disgusts, wash, wash, O Rains! the most beautiful gifts of man . . . from the hearts of men most gifted for the great works of reason.

—*Rains*, 7, tr. Denis Devlin
(*Exile*, Bollingen Series XV)

This combination of the minute with the very large, of the technical with the rhapsodic and sacramental, is the aesthetic equivalent for the theme of Perse's poetry, the confrontation between human things and their great ground in Nature, in those forces which are at once the possibility and the contradiction of human things. In *Seamarks* this confrontation, which may be named in many particular ways, is most generally between the City and the Sea—"at the hemicycle of the City, where the sea is the stage," "the Sea that came to us on the stone steps of the drama."

Seamarks, as a poem celebrating the sea, includes within itself the recitation of a ritual having the same purpose of celebrating the sea. There are thus three dimensions to take account of, the sea, the rite, the poem.

The sea is as it were the divine ground of this poem, summarizing all possibility, resolving all contradictions, standing to the human world as the Word of God stands to the world it called into being and will destroy; the sea is the home of love and death, also of excrement, menstrual secretions, disease, as of purity and birth. The rite is to insure that human purpose shall be drowned and reborn, submerged in, merged with, emerged from, this sea. The poem which sings this rite is the vehicle for the elucidation of human purpose born of the contemplation of the sea; if this contemplation is sufficiently resolute, the poet's reward will be the creation of a new kind of poetry.

After several readings there remain many things too difficult for me, yet I think it possible to give some account of the poem's plan and such action as it has. The formal divisions are as follows: Invocation; nine Strophes, the crucial ninth amounting in length to about one third of the entire work; a Chorus; and a Dedication.

The central episode of the rite is the consummation of the union between a virgin of the City and "the man from the Sea," "the stranger," "the master"; this union is regarded as standing for all human passion, and as giving a fresh vision of the reconciliation of opposites, meeting of extremes, in the bed which is also the sea, the act of love which is seen as a voyage in a storm, the woman's body which is seen as a ship. The night so passed, subject of the ninth Strophe, stands for the apocalyptic "there shall be no more time" between past and future, the abolition of history and its forms in favor of a new beginning, the purgation of the City, "the custom-ridden land," by the "incorruptible sea judging us," the sea, that "other face of our dreams."

The episodes preluding this marriage consist of the poet's invocation and recitations by various persons: the Master of stars and navigation, the Tragediennes, the Patrician Women, &c. They variously invoke the Sea and its stranger, master, redeemer; or they sacrifice their honors, names, lineage, arts, all achievement, before the unknown future, and in hope of greater blessings to come. Thus the Tragediennes:

> . . . Our veils also we lay down, our frieze cloaks painted with the blood of murders, our silks tainted with wine of the Courts; and our staves also of beggarwomen, and our crooks of suppliants—with the lamp and the spinning wheel of the widows, and the clepsydra of our guards, and the horn lantern of the watch; the oryx's skull rigged as a lute, and our great eagles worked in gold and other trophies of the throne and alcove —with the cup and votive urn, the ewer and copper basin for the guest's ablutions, and the Stranger's refreshment, the flagons and phials of the poison, painted caskets of the Enchantress and the gifts of the Emissary, the golden cases for the message and the papers of the Prince in disguise—with the oar from the shipwreck, the black sail of the portent and the torches of sacrifice; with also the royal insignia, and the tall fans of triumph, and the red leather trumpets of our women Messengers . . . the whole decaying apparatus of drama and fable, we lay down! we lay down! . . .
>
> But we keep, O promised Sea! with our clogs of hard wood, our golden rings in bunches on our wrists of lovers, for the scansion of future works, very great works to come, in their new pulsation and their incitement from elsewhere.

The ninth Strophe, "Narrow are the vessels . . . ," celebrates the mystic-erotic union in language of the night journey by sea:

> Narrow are the vessels, narrow the alliance; and narrower still your measure, O faithful body of the beloved . . . And what is this body itself, save image and form of the ship? nacelle and hull, and votive vessel, even to its median opening; formed in the shape of a hull, and fashioned on its curves, bending the double arch of ivory to the will of sea-born curves . . . The builders of hulls, in all ages, have had this way of binding the keel to the set of frames and planking . . .

The essential imagery is taken as asserting the identity of all history:

> Run your course, transient god. We are your relays! One same wave throughout the world, one same wave since Troy . . . The swell rises and is made woman. The sea with the belly of a loving woman kneads untiringly its prey. And love causes the singing, and the sea the rocking, of the cedar bed on its boards, of the curved hull on its joints. Our bed rich with offerings and with the burden of our works . . .
>
> Virgin nailed to my prow, ah! like her who is immolated, you are the libation of the wine at the cutwater of the bow. . . .

And the moral of all this, or its outcome, is a reconciliation to actualities, particularly the actuality of death, with a reminiscence of Odysseus leaving Calypso:

> . . . "Keep," said the man in the tale, "keep, O non-mortal Nymph, your offer of immortality. Your island is not mine where the tree sheds no leaves; neither does your couch move me, where man does not face his destiny."
>
> Rather the couch of humans, honoured by death! . . . I will exhaust the road of mortal man . . .

On the morning after, when the stranger has gone and life begins again, the Chorus carries its affirmation, "Sea of Baal, Sea of Mammon," through some twenty pages of epithets ("Sea of every age and every name; O Sea of everywhere and of all time") including what I have already quoted: "The incorporeal and very real, imprescriptible," &c.

"The reader has to allow the images to fall into his memory successively without questioning the reasonableness of each at the moment; so that, at the end, a total effect is produced."

—T. S. Eliot

. . . "a symbolism that only to the eye of reason will be forever un-intelligible."

—Katherine Garrison Chapin

. . . "a quality of insight which is not of the provincial rationalism of our time."

—Allen Tate

With the first of these remarks I incline to agree, though the total effect produced in me was not a happy one; the other two, however, set me thinking about the Emperor's new clothes. Little as I like becoming the defender of a provincial rationalism, especially if another kind should be anywhere available, I like still less being forced to accept the somewhat haughty and hieratic suggestions in "forever unintelligible," which, putting the matter beyond argument and demonstration, introduces a somewhat religiose note into the discussion, as though the reader's salvation depended on his unquestioning acceptance of what he would never understand. I like better, in principle, Valéry's saying that there is nothing more powerful or seductive than a god who has no need of mystery.

Yet it is hard not to sympathize with the difficulties of these critics; the eye of reason has indeed its motes and beams, and it is liable to be a narrow eye. It can happen that one admires a poetry without understanding it, or at least a long while before one understands it, and in trying to convince others of the legitimacy of this admiration one may sometimes make impatient and extravagant gestures. But I do not relish, in the literary fashion of the time, this unseemly haste to jettison the works of reason; it smacks of pride. And I am disagreeably impressed with the way in which some admirers of St.-John Perse almost as a matter of course regard their admiration as defining a rare aristocracy of the spirit which may not be questioned; it is like marking an object with a price tag, even if the price tag reads "invaluable": "I believe the poetry of Perse, which has been a powerful influence in the minds of many men who could not remember what it was that so deeply moved them but only that they were moved as a man might be moved by a fragrance he could not remember—that this poetry, like all true poetry, will take its place outside literature and all doctrine, in the desert sunlight where the stone survives" (Archibald MacLeish). "One climbs the slopes of Perse's work painfully, like those Himalayan slopes that lead to the Tibet of the spirit where this poetry was born. It is a poetry of whose existence one can become aware only in solitude or exile, and in a state of grace which demands the talents of the prince and of the conqueror. . . .* One finally reaches this poetry after having suffered . . ." (Alain Bosquet).

Remarks of this sort, in which the authors pay themselves compliments either implicitly or out loud, are painfully affecting; one would like to accept them if it were at all possible, not only in order to become identified as being in a state of grace, &c, but also because not to do so will produce embarrassment. Critically, these statements represent an attempt to write in the style, more or less, of their subject, and consequently read like parodies—Mr. Mac-Leish's success in rising above the demands of reason is as remarkable as his syntax—which have, on inspection, a certain unkind accuracy. In their rather haughty tone, their cultist implications, they provoke the timid reader to hypocrisy, the bolder one to rebellion; neither of them a happy result.

This is perhaps a delicate subject. I do not question the admiration, either its sincerity or its fervor. I regret, however, that the terms in which it is put so rarely leave any margin to the dissenter. And I am glad to make an exception in some part for the interesting essay of Roger Caillois printed in *Exile* (Bollingen Series XV). Since its argument on Perse's behalf depends, however, on the elucidation of etymologies and the metonymic analysis of words now abstract, it does not affect our reception of the poem in an English translation, and I must excuse myself from discussing it.

In giving a scheme for the structure of *Seamarks* I have indicated my opinion that it is not essentially a random, chaotic, or disordered poem at all, but a rather shrewd sort of pageant-narrative instead; and that reason need not abdicate before its larger forms, though I should have a hard time defending the reasonableness of some of its ornaments and metaphors. This scheme, if I have got it even nearly and generally right, provides for the poem a reasonable principle of order, a thematic center to which the most various expressions may be more or less relevantly attached without a loss of essential clarity even where the details are obscure. This element of structure was the more precious to me for having been taught by so many critics that I must by no means look for such a thing but content myself in insoluble mysteries; a view not always discouraged

---

* Not, however, of the critic.

by Perse himself in such phrases, scattered throughout his works, as "A great, delible poem," "the great odes of silence," "one long phrase without pause forever unintelligible," "my poem, O Rains! which will not be written!" in which he seems to declare an ideal of art to which my understanding would be a matter of indifference; or where the Tragediennes in the present poem speak of laying down "the whole decaying apparatus of drama and fable"; or where the poet questions the right of "Sages" to deny him access to "a great poem beyond reason" (*hors de raison*).

But my judgment is to be made on my experience of the poem, not on any rationale which I have discovered in it, or (some will perhaps say) invented for it. And my experience of the poem over several readings—despite a number of brilliant details and a few moving passages—is that I am bored by the poem, and that this boredom grows upon closer acquaintance. The writing—again, I am speaking of the English—seems to me dominantly empty, pretentious, and insolent; much inclined to preen itself and talk about itself; frequently, through the persons of the narrative, promising wonders to come:

> We beg that in sight of the sea promise shall be made to us of new works: of strong and very beautiful works, which are all strength and will and which are all beauty—great seditious works, great licentious works . . .

But the wonders don't come. I sympathize with Perse's impulse to the making of a new art, and to some extent share his impatience with the old, but I do not find that his species of rhapsody is a new art. If you lay down the whole decaying apparatus of drama and fable, and wash from the heart of man the most beautiful sayings of man, I suppose the next question is, What are you going to have instead? And this lofty contempt for the past I find somewhat unbecoming in a writer so bookish and curious, who so largely, and with such exquisite perception, feeds on the past, and of whose poems his most perceptive critic, Roger Caillois, has admiringly said, "Nothing goes into them which does not already contain much art, which has not cost much patience, courage and care, which in short is not entitled to the homage of a devotion." So much we might say also of a museum. (And indeed it is becoming embarrassingly clear that of successive literary fashions which come over the horizon announcing our salvation by novelty each tends to be more derivative, "literary," and, in fact, artsy-crafty, than the last.)

I hope my response does not testify merely to a meanness of spirit in me, a parochialism unable to achieve these heights; but if it does, it will have to stand. Nor can I be certain, once again, how much of my difficulty comes not alone from the translation but also from the necessity of judging this poetry by an imported criticism whose tenets it seems to me I frequently fail to understand, and almost always have to reject. For instance, Mr. Fowlie writes in his handbook on *Contemporary French Literature*: "Almost every critic who has written on Perse has been struck by the opulence of his work, by its solemnity, by the persistent use of *grand* and *grandeur*, of *haut* and *hauteur*, of *vaste*, and other such words which provide the work with cosmic dimensions." I too, certainly, was struck by the use of such terms, especially *grand* and *grandeur*, of which I find seventeen occurrences in a single section of a page and a half, but I was not struck with admiration, and I do not think that English poets provide their work with cosmic dimensions by means of the formula described or anything like it. Earlier in the same essay, Mr. Fowlie writes: "It is impossible to separate the scansion, or the articulation, from the words of the line in Perse's poetry. One supports the other, one authorizes the other, and to such a degree that sound and meaning are dilated far beyond their usual limits." I can sympathize with the essayist's earnest attempt to describe a quality, not easy to isolate even if we agree that it exists, which he sincerely hopes to exhibit as worth our admiration, but I cannot agree that this is criticism; it is, rather, one of those magic gestures with language in which the pen is quicker than the eye: you might separate the scansion from the words in a line by Shakespeare or almost anyone else, but I don't see what you would gain by doing so, or what is admirable in a verse thus detachable or in its opposite; and "dilated" is in particular a deft wave of the wand, a choice just odd enough to steer the mind past its unfortunate synonyms, "distended," "inflated."

I will give an example of the quality which I have called emptiness:

Inonde, ô brise, ma naissance! Et ma faveur s'en aille au cirque de plus vastes pupilles! . . . Les sagaies de Midi vibrent aux portes de la joie. Les tambours du néant cèdent aux fifres de lumière. Et l'Océan, de toutes parts, foulant ses poids de roses mortes,
  Sur nos terrasses de calcium lève sa tête de Tétrarque!

In this brief passage we have the following similarly constructed expressions:

circus of wider pupils
javelins of Noon
gates of joy
drums of nothingness
fifes of light
weight of dead roses
terraces of calcium
head of a Tetrarch

These renderings are all quite literal (except for the uncharacteristically missed opportunity of *sagais* = assagais which gives us "javelins" instead), though the translator might have varied them somewhat by the English expedient of the possessive in place of the construction with "of" to which the French is limited. The expressions themselves are some of them literal and some figurative; taking them singly, we might find some good and others bad, depending on the context, but their combined aim seems to be to bludgeon us into submission by the tasteless filling up of a monotonously repeated form with particulars which, when the relation proposed is a metaphor, may be as trite as "gates of joy" or as arbitrary as "head of a Tetrarch" applied to the Ocean (the translation cannot manage the rime and pun of the original, but where the advantage lies is hard to say). No doubt poetry has always proceeded, and must always proceed, by the metonymic combination of an abstract word with a material one, but I have a feeling that it may be disastrous to advertise the trick so largely:

> . . . the magnetic needle of happiness holds straight on the submerged sands its heavy arrow of massive gold . . .

The extremely commonplace character of "the magnetic needle of happiness"—like the titles of eighteenth century tracts, which someone nicely parodied as "The Tramline of Divinity"—does not altogether obscure the fact that a golden arrow is a fine thing in itself but no use on a compass needle; and I finish by thinking that something like that epigrammatically sums up what is wrong with long stretches of this work, recalling what Socrates had to say about the defect of function in painting everything gold, even the eyes of the statues.

Though the forbidding quality of St.-John Perse's art is supposed to be owing precisely to its novelty, its uniqueness on the present scene, to its possessing pre-eminently those characteristics people intend when they speak admiringly of "the modern" in art, I am very uncertain of its being so new or so unique as all that.

Roger Caillois tells us that Perse has "no perceptible master and seems to discourage imitation . . . at the moment he rises in superb solitude." Other admirers are less certain, and in fact one can assemble from their writings a fair-sized catalogue of authors with whom Perse has affinities, or to whose work his shows a resemblance: Rimbaud, Lautréamont, Claudel, Whitman, Blake ("Prophetic Books"), Nietzsche (*Thus Spake Zarathustra*). The largeness of the gesture, the oppressive ambition of *grandezza*, remind me of Victor Hugo in *La Légende des Siècles*, while the grandiose qualities of the diction not less than the appeal to the primitive and Mediterranean suggest comparison with Leconte de Lisle, though Perse's dawn-civilization is inhabited by Greeks out of Frazer and Jane Harrison instead of Winckelmann Athenians. Among contemporaries writing in English, in addition to David Jones whom I mentioned earlier, Archibald MacLeish has similar ambitions, perhaps, and especially in his long poems a similar manner of presenting them.

These comparisons, mine and the others, uneasily imply that Perse's quality, however high or low you wish to rate it, is a nineteenth century quality, a late-flowering romanticism. Perse, of course, does not consider himself a romantic, and in the letter I quoted from earlier tells the following anecdote from a journey he took into the Gobi desert:

> . . . someone translated to me the beautiful guttural sentence of a migrant lama of the Great Red Sect: "Man is born in the house, but he dies in the desert . . ." For days and days, in the course of long silent rides, I thought over and over that phrase, delectable to the palate of an Occidental who can never be sure of having rinsed his mouth sufficiently of all romantic after-taste . . . until the day when in a lamasery on the border of the desert I was given this trivial explanation: "A dying man must be exposed outside the tent so as not to soil the dwelling-place of the living."
>
> A beautiful snub for the incurable association of ideas of literary culture!

A beautiful snub, and a strangely penetrating anecdote. Here is the poet, religiously rinsing his mouth of all romantic aftertaste—and to do this he goes into a remote desert, on long silent rides, and produces a scene in which a holy hermit speaks cryptic wisdom to him, a scene strikingly like William Wordsworth's dream in the desert of the Bedouin (who was also Don Quixote) who spoke of poetry and geometric truth—and then, by the discovery that the gnomic sentence is susceptible of a practical interpretation, he declares its mystery cancelled out. As if all mystery other than mere antiquity-fakery and Freudian Gothic did not arise in just this way! And it seems to me that the same intransigent either/or governs the split in Perse's poetry, between the splendid and moving perception of objects, and the hollow rambling declamation about mysterious miracles which, poetically speaking, never take place. Wordsworth, according to J. K. Stephens, had the contrary difficulty:

> Two voices are there: one is of the deep;
> It learns the storm cloud's thunderous melody,
> Now roars, now murmurs with the changing sea,
> Now bird-like pipes, now closes soft in sleep:
> And one is of an old half-witted sheep
> Which bleats articulate monotony,
> And indicates that two and one are three,
> That grass is green, lakes damp, and mountains steep:
> And, Wordsworth, both are thine. . . .

So while Perse is "modern," certainly, in his attentive delineation of objects, his imagistic compressions and minute elaborations of detail —"a soft layer of small violet algae, like an otter's fur"—there seems something Wagnerian in the intention of his poetry to be vast, to be excessive, something like program music in its arrangements (the divisions of *Seamarks*, for example, resemble the episodes in a tone poem by Richard Strauss, concerning which clever musicologists are able to tell you what literal action is represented by the notes), and something unabashedly late Romantic in so many of its qualities: its combination of archaism with an appeal to absolute novelty, its promise of great things never dreamed of, the intense Byronism of its exalted picture of the poet as exiled aristocrat confronting the elements. And these two sides, so far as I am able to determine, never connect.

But then, it becomes plainer every year, and with almost every alleged innovation in poetry, as the old pensioners limp home from Missolonghi still talking, that the nineteenth century has never ended, and that the twentieth will either have to be dealt with as a footnote to it ("a brief period of clarity was succeeded by Neo-Archaism and the Biedermeyer Revival") or left out of the chronicle altogether.